ULTIMATE SPECIAL FORCES

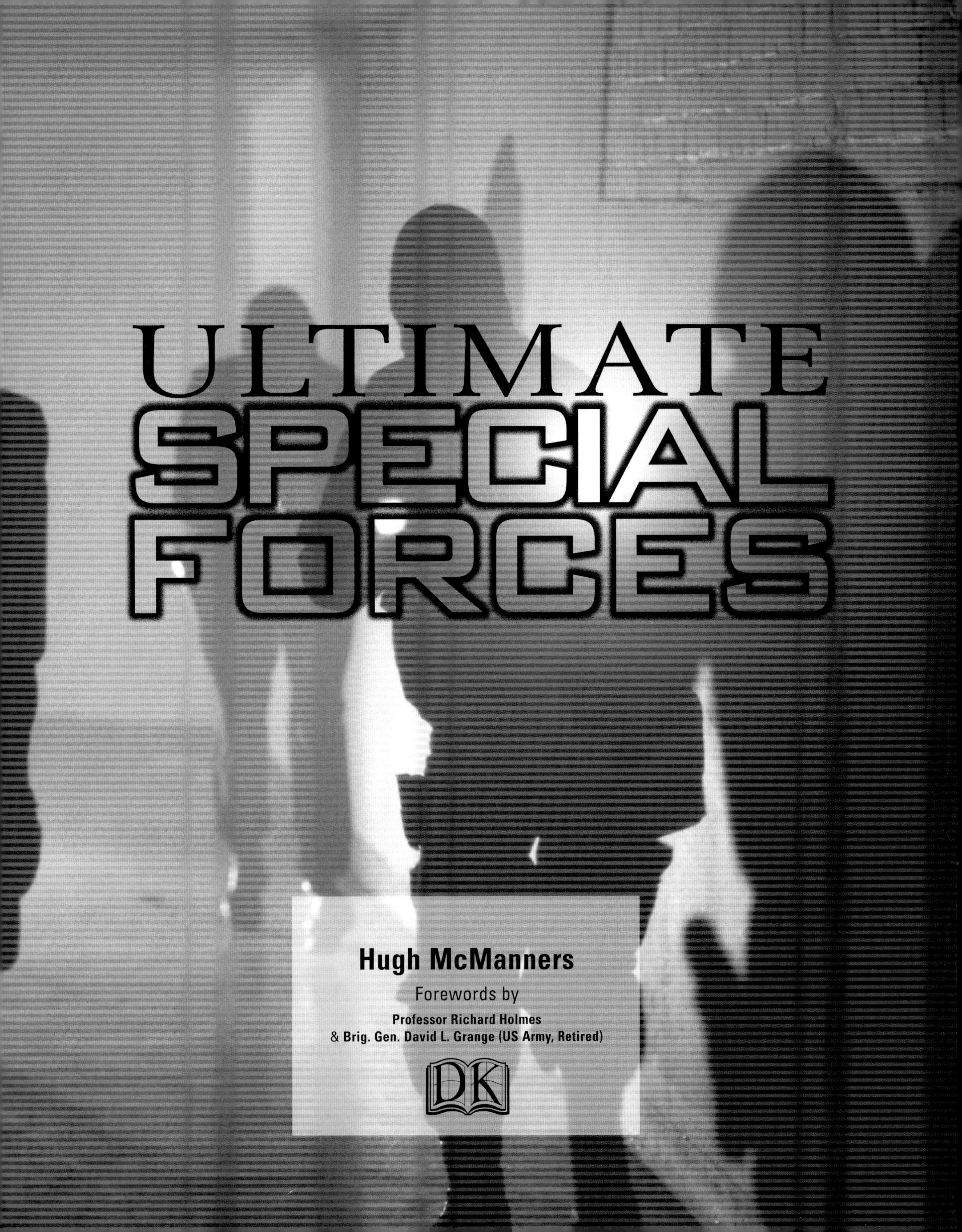

ULTIMATE SPECIAL FORCES

Hugh McManners

Forewords by

Professor Richard Holmes
& Brig. Gen. David L. Grange (US Army, Retired)

DK

LONDON, NEW YORK, MUNICH, MELBOURNE, DELHI

Produced for DK Publishing by

The Brown Reference Group plc, 8 Chapel Place, Rivington Street, London, EC2A 3DQ

Military Editor
Peter Darman

Editors
Dennis Cove, Felicity Crowe
Mark Hawkins-Dady, James Murphy

Senior Designer
Stefan Morris

Designers
Joe Conneally, Thor Fairchild
Dan Newman, Colin Tilleyloughrey

Digital Illustrator
Mark Walker

Editorial Director
Lindsey Lowe

Managing Editor
Tim Cooke

Art Director
Dave Goodman

Production
Matthew Greenfield

Picture Manager
Susannah Jayes

DK PUBLISHING

US Senior Editor
Jennifer Williams

Senior Managing Editor
Martyn Page

Category Publisher
Mary Thompson

Design Assistance
Ian Spick

Managing Art Editor
Marianne Markham

Art Director
Bryn Walls

DTP Designer
Julian Dams

Jacket Designers
Neal Cobourne, Francis Wong

Jacket Editor
Caroline Reed

Production
Louise Daly

First American Edition, 2003

00 01 02 03 04 05 10 9 8 7 6 5 4 3 2 1

Published in the United States by DK Publishing, Inc.
375 Hudson Street, New York, New York 10014

First published in Great Britain in 2003 by Dorling Kindersley, Limited
A Penguin Company, 80 Strand, London, WC2R ORL

A Cataloging-in-Publication record for this book is available from
the Library of Congress
ISBN 0-7894-9973-6

Reproduced by Colourscan, Singapore
Printed and bound by Graphicom, Italy

Discover more at
www.dk.com

Contents

FOREWORDS

Ultimate Special Forces provides an in-depth review of elite fighting forces, primarily those of Britain and the United States of America. Serving for and with elite units from both these countries, as well as elites from France, Germany, and Russia, I can identify with the author's compassion and determination to write this comprehensive book.

Hugh McManners, a veteran Commando of Britain's military profession, lays out a brief history and description of special forces, their weapons and equipment, and the operational tactics of the world's most advanced special forces and other elite units.

The principles of elite units are highlighted throughout the book. Infiltration (entering a zone of operations) by air, sea, and land, anywhere, anytime, comes to life with historical vignettes and descriptions of unit capabilities. British Commandos infiltrating by sea, British and US paratroopers by low-level fixed-wing aircraft, and US Rangers by helicopters flying deep behind enemy lines, illustrate the resourcefulness of elite forces.

The primary types of mission undertaken by the military elite are illustrated through historical examples: Hostage-rescue, raids to seize or destroy enemy personnel and facilities, attacks on high-value objectives in support of larger operations, strategic reconnaissance, and evacuation operations. Although elite forces are only a small part of a nation's armed forces, they are a key component in carrying out the most difficult of missions.

Special operations forces have a unique selection process that ensures the recruitment of people with the "right cut of cloth" to carry out demanding, sometimes seemingly impossible tasks. These forces rely on usable intelligence, reliable means of infiltration and exfiltration, surprise, speed, and violence of action on the objective. The reliability of these prerequisites defines success or failure, and Hugh McManners has captured these capabilities throughout.

Selection procedures vary among the types of special forces, but they all share a knack for finding those with the physical and mental toughness to operate in austere, uncertain environments; the ability to operate alone or in small groups; having the mindset of a meticulous shop worker, and at the same time, the yearning of an adventurer – and someone who knows how to think, not what to think. Selection is critical because, in special operations, the human being is more important than the hardware. Technology supports the operator, not the other way around. The more advanced and specialized the elite unit, the older and higher rank its individual members will be.

Special operations forces are the quiet professionals for the nation they represent. Usually the first to go into harm's way to set the conditions for general purpose forces, they are quite often the last to leave as hostilities wind down. Their mottos are renowned: "Who Dares Wins" (the British Special Air Service), "De Oppresso Libre" ("To Liberate the Oppressed" – the motto of the US 5th Special Forces Group), "Sua Sponte" ("Of one's own accord; voluntarily"– the US 75th Infantry Ranger Regiment), "Devil Dogs" (the US 82nd Airborne Division), and "Rendezvous With Destiny" (the US 101st Airborne Division). In this book, Hugh McManners has captured the essence of the world's ultimate, special, and elite forces.

David L Grange

Brigadier General David L. Grange
(US Army, Retired)

It gives me a double pleasure to write this Foreword. Firstly, because I taught the author, Hugh McManners, when he was at the Royal Military Academy Sandhurst, followed his military career with admiration, and later read his penetrating first-hand account of the Falklands War of 1982 with great interest. Secondly, because I am delighted to see such a complex and often over-dramatized subject addressed with such good sense and breadth. Good sense, because some of what is written about special forces (sometimes even by their ex-members) serves only to reinforce myths which are better dispelled. And breadth, because many of the techniques employed by special forces are used by others too, and it is useful to extend our definition of special forces to consider some other military elites who so frequently enjoy a symbiotic relationship with them. For instance, it is impossible to envisage the British Special Air Service (SAS) without the contribution made to it by the Parachute Regiment, or to think of the British Special Boat Service (SBS) without the Royal Marines.

Of course, the whole issue of special forces has seldom been uncontroversial. On the one hand, conventionally minded officers have sometimes resented their tendency to scoop the brightest and the best. Armed forces in wartime rarely have as many high-quality members as they might wish for, and the demands of special forces have put a severe strain on quality manpower. Combatants in more conventional units sometimes resent the fact that they have had to carry out routine but grueling and costly tasks, while special forces, often enjoying high-level political support, have swept in and stolen the limelight. On the other hand, members of special forces have sometimes talked a little too loudly about their own superiority to "the thundering herd," and have perhaps not appreciated that their ability to strike has often hinged on the preparedness of more conventional troops to fix the enemy to his positions, providing the matador's cloak for the sword of the special forces. The truth, however, is that it has never been a matter of either/or, but of balance and proportion.

The subject remains as controversial as ever at the beginning of the 21st century, as Western armed forces review their military capabilities to meet the demands of a new and often frightening world. Demands for light and more easily deployable forces will inevitably encourage the supporters of special forces, who argue that their utility is increasing. Others, however, will continue to demand a wider capability, and will point to the dangers of two-tier armed forces, with damaging tension between special forces and the heavier forces better suited for a large-scale conventional battlefield. The brief mid-campaign lull in the 2003 war in Iraq saw some of these arguments articulated very publicly.

Although it is too early to hazard a definitive pronouncement on the 2003 Iraq War, it seems that, while light forces were key to the success of the campaign, the shaping of the battlefront was entrusted to forces that would not have looked out of place on the battlefields of earlier desert wars. In short, while proportions may shift, a balance will still have to be struck. However, it is clear that growing technical capabilities must still be matched by those human qualities which have for so long lain at the heart of success in war. It is on these qualities that special forces continue to place such great emphasis.

Professor Richard Holmes

INTRODUCTION

Special forces have a much greater and far more important role to play in the many forms of warfare that face armed forces in the 21st century than they had in the 20th century. Since the two world wars and the consequent Cold War (1945–90), global terrorism has forced significant change. It used to be possible to predict the most likely threats, then equip and train forces to deal with them. But today, military commanders must plan to be totally flexible and able to cope with everything from full-scale armored warfare to sporadic guerrilla operations in urban areas.

Just as there are no obvious threats, there are also no obvious responses. In the 21st century, it will not be possible simply to declare war and start sending in the tanks. An immediate and appropriate response is far more important, with imaginative thinking backed by a wide range of military options – which is precisely what today's hi-tech special forces provide.

However, the general public's perception of special forces has been influenced by a media hungry for heroes and victories. Their operations are often glamorized and inaccurately reported. Special operations are kept secret (for obvious reasons), which upsets many journalists. Any hint that there could have been some kind of failure becomes a big story: Total success is the norm required of military commanders by journalists, who do not understand that every special forces' operation continually lurches from crisis to near disaster until the troops are safely back at base. Special forces troops can be caricatured either as arrogant, swaggering psychopaths, or as gilded heroes achieving miracles of superhuman toughness. Both impressions are wrong.

As special operations become more frequent, which I believe they will, it is vital that the public understands much more of the reality of special forces and their capabilities, stripped of mythology and media hype. This book shows how modern special forces operate, the weapons, skills, and equipment they use, and the methodical way in which they plan and execute their missions. Being masters of their trade, special forces choose the right tools for each particular job, so this book also includes a comprehensive section showing the actual equipment they use. But the most interesting and critical aspect of special forces is the quality of its people. This book therefore shows how they are selected and trained, and how the ideas, bravery, and actions of individual soldiers have created and shaped today's special forces units.

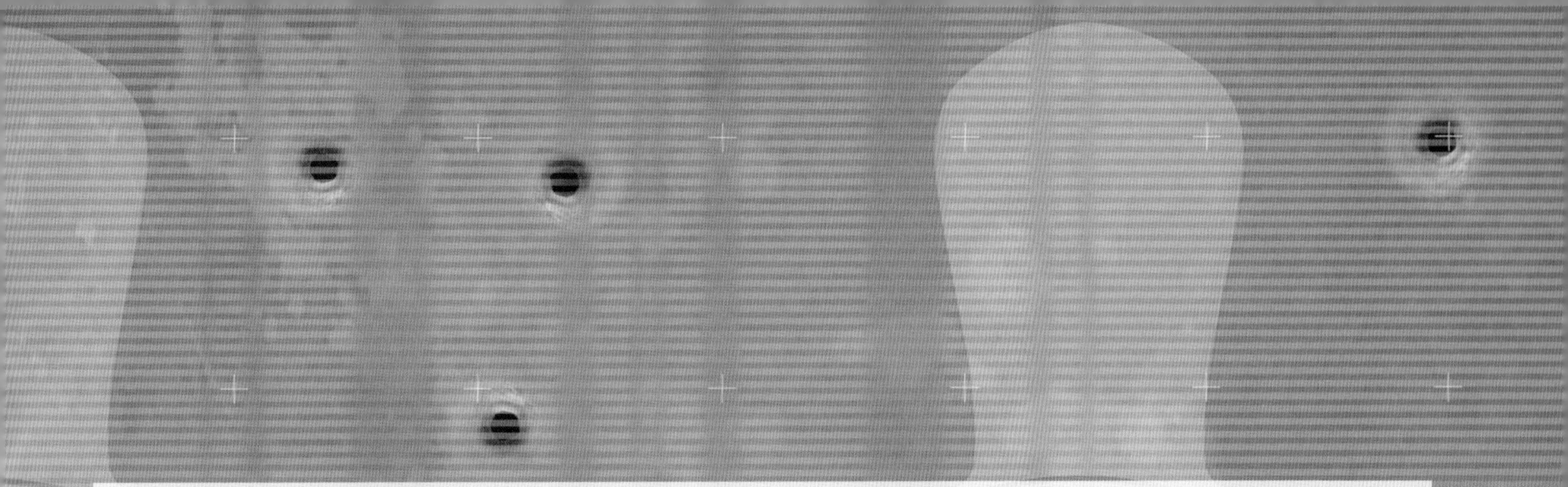

Modern special forces grew in response to the rise of terrorism in the years following World War II (1939–45). Their counter-terrorist role is now more important than ever. The relentless economic drive toward globalization has already stimulated regional opposition in most continents, and increasingly well-organized global terrorism. Future conflicts are certain to be politically complicated, with terrorist tactics and terror groups being used by political organizations and smaller countries to confuse and weaken larger nations. This "asymmetric warfare," in which both the armed forces and political will of larger nations are eroded by a smaller enemy, requires a sophisticated, multi-faceted response, which characterizes modern special force capability.

The Iraq War of 2003 was the beginning of a very new type of "effects-based" warfare, in which computer technology enables military commanders to concentrate firepower and land forces with devastating speed – so-called "network-centric" warfare. For the first time, through the use of this technology, special forces are able to play a major part in conventional operations not just with their characteristic covert intelligence gathering, raiding, and sabotage operations, but by taking over and controlling entire zones of the battlefield, as was seen in 2003 with US Special Forces in northern Iraq. The range and speed of today's missile systems gives unparalleled power to just one man in the right place, with the right training, and the right equipment.

Battles used to be determined by destroying enemy forces, occupying ground, and controlling certain key points or assets. Modern effects-based warfare is radically different and uses military force to achieve a certain predetermined effect – which could be to force a political decision, or to immobilize an army. Creating this effect can be done in many ways; and once it is achieved, the military action switches to creating some other effect.

The potential for special forces in effects-based warfare is enormous. Special forces' operations have always achieved effects far greater than the numbers of troops involved – usually through imaginative, daring, and innovative planning. Fighting is only one way to achieve victory. A British Special Boat Service (SBS) mission in the 1991 Gulf War cut the Iraqi High Command's fiberoptic communications cable at a critical time. The occupation of Baghdad in Iraq in April 2003 was a masterly combination of covert special forces' activity and the careful maneuvering of armored forces. The predicted bloodbath of house-to-house street-fighting never materialized.

Throughout history, special forces have always centered on the individual, making each person feel a member of an elite, with higher standards than other military units and capable of far greater achievements in combat. In many ways, this is a reversal of the usual military training process, which seeks to turn individuals into team members. Individuals are rigorously tested and carefully selected, then kept up to standard with very exacting training exercises on the principle of "train hard, fight easy."

Special forces are totally committed to achieving their mission, either as a group or as individuals. If all else fails, just one man will continue to the target and attempt to execute the operation. Dedication and determination must be combined with a high level of common sense. Sound personal and psychological qualities are more important than fitness or physique, particularly as injuries are a common occupational hazard that must be endured as part of the rigors of an operation.

Special operations are planned using a much greater input than normal from the soldiers taking part. Their personal experience and preferences are utilized to develop plans that stand the greatest chance of success. Special forces are particularly good at evaluating risks, then taking them as sensibly as possible, while knowing that all caution must be abandoned at times in order to achieve surprise.

Special forces have rapidly developing roles in modern warfare, as shown in Afghanistan (2002) and Iraq (2003), as well as in counter-terrorist actions. But, as their role becomes a more accepted part of modern warfare, it is important to remember what they are and where they came from. Special forces were started by individuals with vision – mavericks who were very often opposed by their superiors. As their role becomes increasingly more important, it is vital that special forces continue to evolve – and above all else, avoid becoming conventional in their outlook.

Hugh McManners

Hugh McManners, 2003

WHAT ARE SPECIAL FORCES?

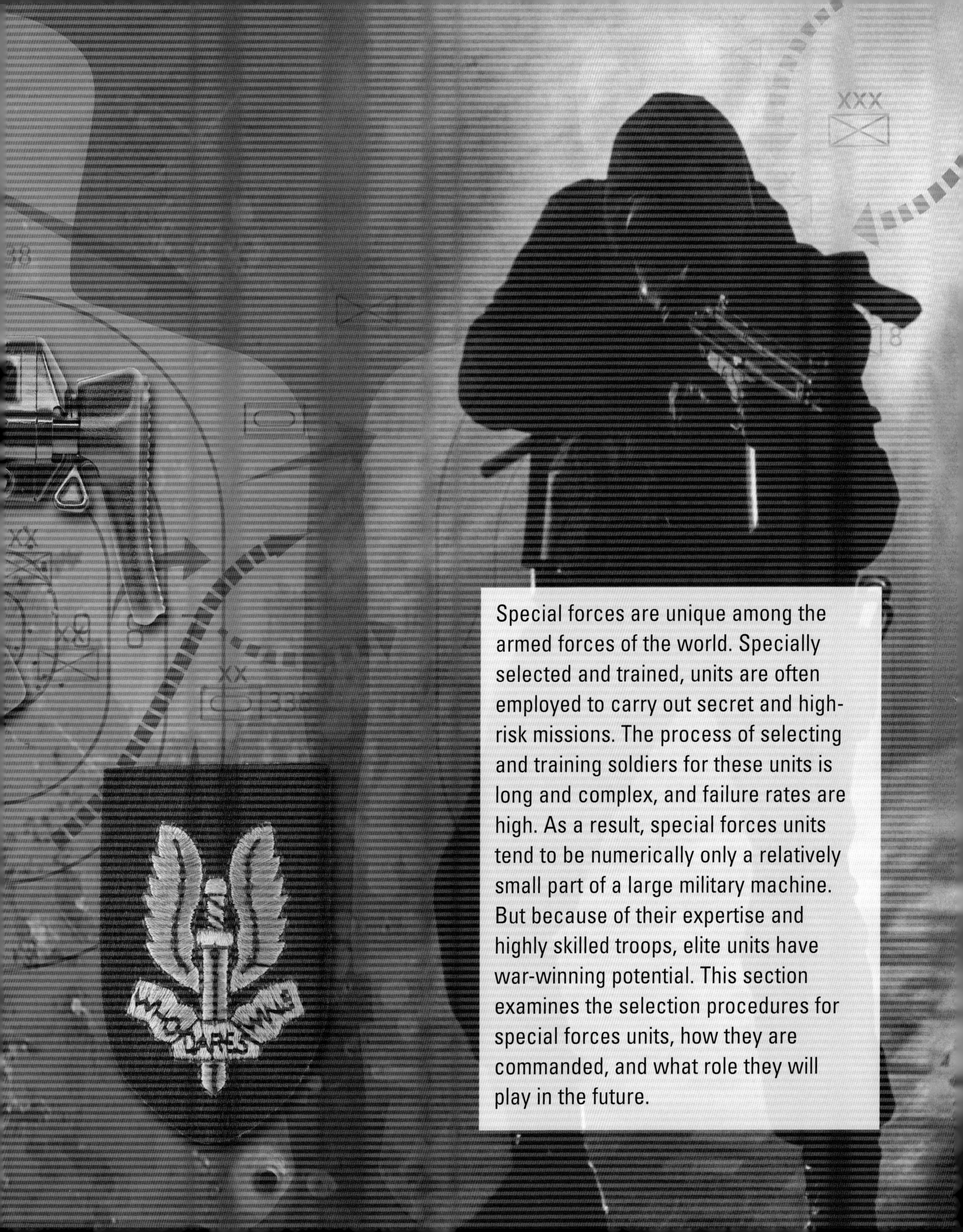

Special forces are unique among the armed forces of the world. Specially selected and trained, units are often employed to carry out secret and high-risk missions. The process of selecting and training soldiers for these units is long and complex, and failure rates are high. As a result, special forces units tend to be numerically only a relatively small part of a large military machine. But because of their expertise and highly skilled troops, elite units have war-winning potential. This section examines the selection procedures for special forces units, how they are commanded, and what role they will play in the future.

Special Forces: Definitions

Special forces are often seen as the glamorous, headline-grabbing elites of the military world, whose real-life exploits are more exciting than those of James Bond. The reality is very different: A life of anonymity, thankless hard work in miserable conditions, morale-sapping danger, and relentless, exhausting training. In wartime, special forces units often operate behind enemy lines for the purposes of reconnaissance and sabotage. Another primary role is in counter-terrorism.

US Green Berets' badge

▲ Guards units
These soldiers are members of Britain's Grenadier Guards Regiment. Although they are highly trained infantry soldiers, and elite troops, the Grenadier Guards are not considered to be special forces because they do not operate behind enemy lines.

At the most basic level, special forces are military units trained for unconventional operations. Although there is a distinct dividing line between conventional and special forces, actual definitions can be difficult. The term "special forces" covers a whole range of units trained for different kinds of operations; since World War II (1939–45), they have played a particularly important role in counter-terrorism, for example. Other "special" tasks or unique operations include acting as bodyguards or, in times of war, penetrating deep behind enemy lines for tasks such as reconnaissance, demolition, and harassment. Countries such as the United States have separate, high-grade special forces in each of their armed services, as well as in their law-enforcement agencies.

Some smaller, less affluent countries have special forces that are not really special – that is, they perform to the same standard as the conventional forces of larger nations. North Korea, for example, has many "special forces," but they are special only in the sense that they have been specifically trained to enter South Korea in the event of war to cause maximum disruption. Sometimes, such spurious forces were created for political reasons, to generate loyalty to the government or to a head of state.

Another important characteristic that distinguishes special units from conventional troops is that their size does not relate to the level at which they are commanded. The British Special Air Service (SAS), for example, is around the size of a tank battalion of the British Army (a total of only 600 men), yet takes its orders from the highest level within a theater of operations during wartime or directly from the British government when dealing with terrorists at home. Similarly, a 12-man US Army Green Beret "A-Team," commanded by a captain, could easily find itself taking its orders from the highest levels within the Pentagon or from the presidential staff at the White House.

▼ SEALs
A US Navy Sea, Air, and Land (SEAL) team aboard a high speed dinghy. SEAL troops are among the best special forces in the world. They can use a wide variety of weapons and assault tactics.

▼ French Foreign Legion
All French Foreign Legionnaires are special forces soldiers. These are Legion infantrymen, part of France's rapid deployment force.

SPECIAL FORCES AND MILITARY ELITES

Most special forces are drawn from a nation's better soldiers, and are trained to a higher standard than conventional units and are given the best equipment. In contrast, military elites are conventional units that enjoy impressive reputations. The British Army's Guards formations, for example, achieved their high standing through being the ruling monarch's bodyguard. Today, the Guards form conventional infantry and armored units, with additional ceremonial duties, and it is the police who guard the British monarch. France's Foreign Legion can be considered a special force within the French armed forces. In addition, it has specialized companies that provide combat swimmers, mountain warfare experts, and other special forces capabilities.

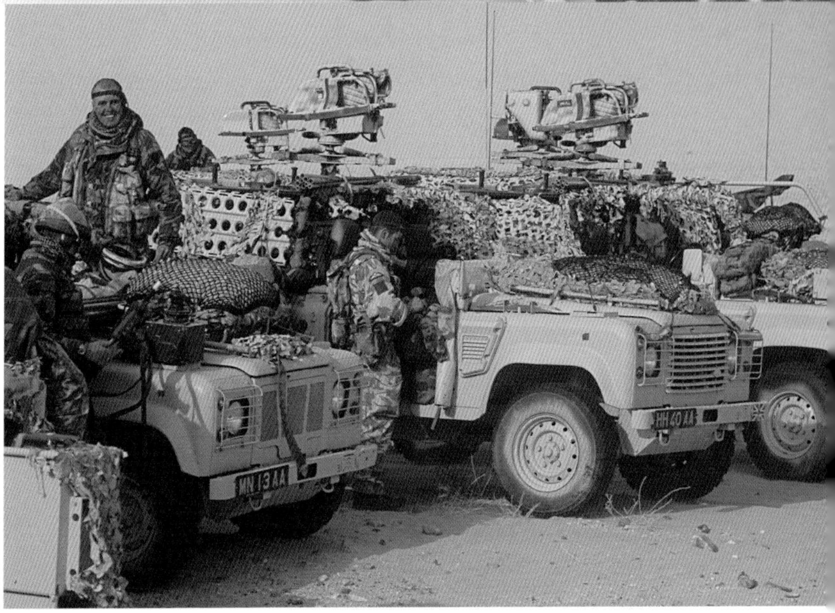

▶ **Paratroopers**
Members of Britain's Parachute Regiment in Iraq in 2003. The regiment is considered a special force because it can fight in small teams after being dropped by parachute into enemy territory. The Parachute Regiment has three battalions, each numbering around 500 troops. In comparison, the US equivalent of the Parachute Regiment, the 82nd Airborne Division, has 14,500 troops.

SPECIAL FORCES AT WAR

In conventional warfare, special forces take on reconnaissance, assault, demolition, and harassment tasks behind enemy lines. The effect of these operations is designed to be very much greater than the numbers of troops involved. Special forces units are capable of taking on every type of land, sea, and air operation, and have a wide choice of vehicles and weapons with which to accomplish their tasks. They can operate on their own, or as part of a larger overall plan involving army, navy, and air force units. There are particular links between special forces and conventional military intelligence-gathering units. The success of special operations requires the best intelligence available, and conversely, special forces teams often provide the only eyes-on-target information available to commanders.

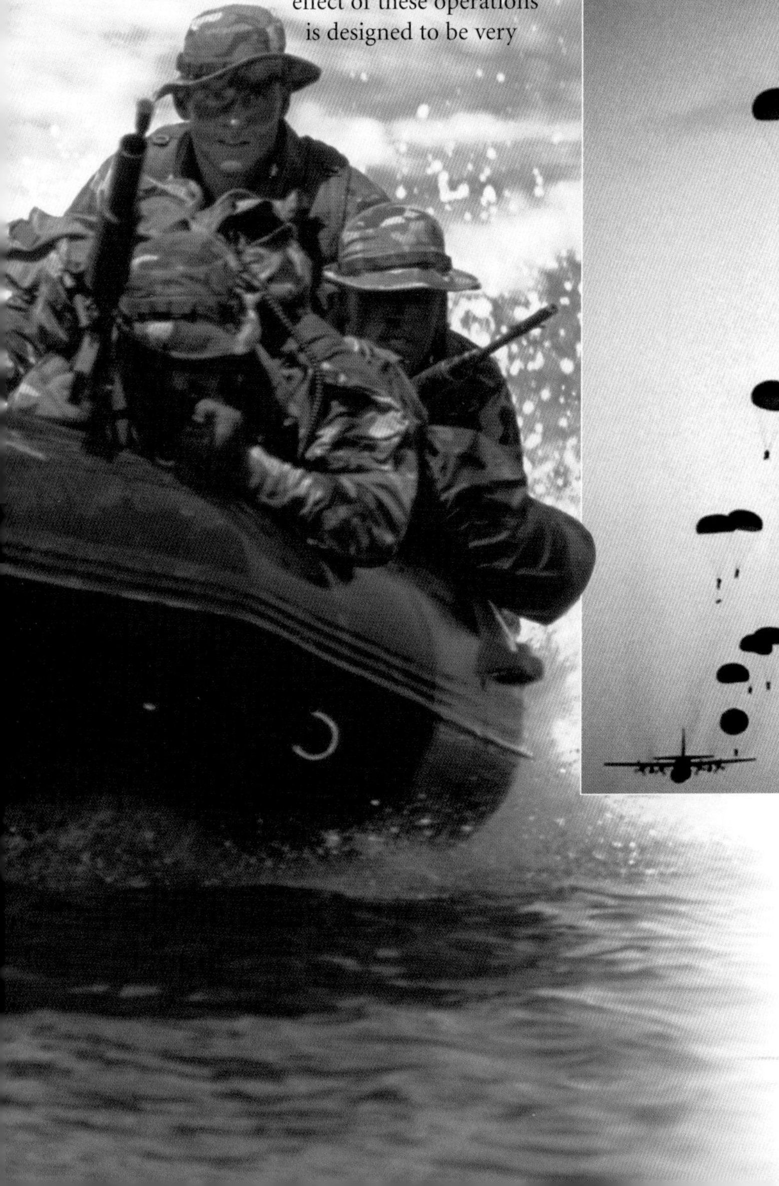

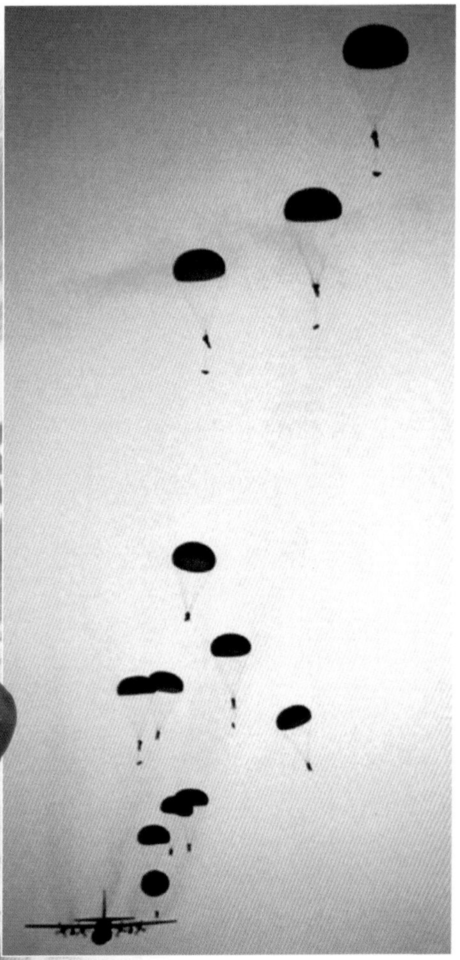

▲ **Israel's elite**
Israeli paratroopers descend from the sky. Israeli paratroop units have traditionally been the best-trained and equipped of all Israel's armed forces.

Training others

An often overlooked role of special forces is to pass on their expertise to others. Their own high level of training makes special forces personnel ideal instructors. The United States, for example, has built alliances by providing equipment and special forces advisers to governments in Central and South American countries.

Military advisers
The soldier on the left, examining the mortar, is a US Green Beret military adviser, in El Salvador in the 1980s.

The idea of special forces acting behind enemy lines is an old one. In 500 BC, when Chinese general Sun Tzu wrote his definitive work, *The Art of War*, he described the need for armies to develop units of what he called "surviving spies" to conduct special operations in enemy territory. Sun Tzu's "surviving spy" still exists today in the idea of what the British SAS call the "grey man" – the special forces expert whom the enemy assumes is too unimportant to bother interrogating.

One particular special forces activity during wartime is the raising of local insurgent groups behind enemy lines – training and equipping men with local knowledge who can win the sympathy of local people so they become "terrorists" to the enemy. British Army officer T. E. Lawrence achieved this in the Middle East during World War I (1914–18), when he encouraged the Arabs to rise up against their Turkish rulers (see p27). His guerrilla force became a thorn in the side of the Turkish Army.

◀ Italian counter-terrorists
Members of Italy's Central Security Unit (CSU) in freefall. A police unit specializing in counter-terrorism, the CSU requires members to undergo years of intense training, including learning parachuting and diving.

COUNTER-TERRORISM

Because of their experience in dealing with terrorist techniques since the end of World War II in 1945, special forces teams are vital in counter-terrorist operations today. The British SAS first encountered terrorism at the hands of communist guerrillas in the jungles of Malaya in the 1950s. US special forces began to develop a counter-terrorist strategy a decade later, as the realization grew that the spread of global terrorism could not be handled by conventional military and police forces alone.

The fight against terrorism

The terrorist attack on the World Trade Center in New York on September 11, 2001, made it clear to governments across the world that international law and order depended upon a coordinated and strategic response. No nation would ever again feel immune to the threat of global terrorism. Special forces will play a determining role in this fight, which some military analysts have described as "World War III."

The Twin Towers
One of the towers of the World Trade Center burns as a second terrorist-piloted plane homes in on its target. The attacks on September 11, 2001, marked a new era in terrorism.

▶ Hostage-rescue drill
Personnel from the Italian Central Security Unit (CSU) demonstrate their rappelling skills during a hostage-rescue exercise. As well as hunting down terrorists, the unit is responsible for VIP protection when high-ranking foreign politicians and diplomats visit Italy.

Counter-terrorism requires special forces to use a wide range of tactics to protect major cities and economic targets such as oil installations. Teams usually work under the command of the police for what are known as "direct action tasks," such as the British SAS storming of the Iranian Embassy in London in 1980 (see pp50–51).

▶ Constant training
A simulated hostage situation during hostage-rescue training for agents of the US Federal Bureau of Investigation (FBI). All special forces units involved with counter-terrorism spend hundreds of hours perfecting rescue drills.

TERRORIST ACTS AND RESPONSES

Terrorists often choose targets that will guarantee them maximum publicity for their views or grievances.

Hijackings of civilian aircraft proliferated in the 1970s, especially in the Middle East where Palestinian groups wanted to draw attention to their fight for an independent Palestinian state.

In the face of this determined terrorist onslaught, special forces units were forced to develop effective responses. Such operations continue to demand constant practice, often with real aircraft, because Middle Eastern terrorism still poses a threat to the citizens and interests of Western Europe and the United States. Similarly, when ships and marine facilities such as oil rigs are attacked, small-boat specialists capable of a surprise assault from the sea are required.

▶ SAS hostage-rescue
British SAS soldiers on the roof of the Iranian Embassy in London, England, in May 1980, during a hostage-rescue operation. Five of the six terrorists were killed.

DEFEATING TERRORISM

In certain circumstances, special forces counter-terrorism units can be deployed outside of their own national boundaries. The Israelis' rescue of their citizens who had been hijacked by Palestinian terrorists and held hostage at Entebbe airport, Uganda, in 1976, was an example of such an operation.

In the future, the defeat of terrorism may at times depend upon special forces using terrorist-type tactics. It will be a challenge to prevent the forces of the law from being seen as indistinguishable from the terrorists they fight.

▲ Helicopter rescue
These RH-53 helicopters were used by the US Delta Force in its failed attempt to rescue Americans being held hostage in Tehran, Iran, in 1980.

Selection procedures

The human factor is the most important part of any special forces operation. The right people can turn disaster into success and have the ability to create their own opportunities. They need to be independent, determined, resourceful, realistic, and tough-minded, but also able to think laterally to arrive at successful yet often unconventional solutions. In conventional military units, such soldiers can become frustrated, and may appear to be ill-disciplined.

▲ **Physical fitness**
A recruit does push-ups as part of the British Parachute Regiment's selection process. A high level of physical fitness is a basic requirement of special forces soldiers.

Although special forces selection courses are very demanding physically, their true purpose is psychological testing. Physical fitness is important only in so far as it enables candidates to take part in the process. By the end of a selection course, most candidates will be suffering from injuries, and will have to get through by looking after themselves and protecting their injury as best they can. Selectors are looking for an individual likely to carry on with a mission regardless of any obstacle or disaster, and even if he is the only person left in a team. This kind of toughness is rare, and emerges only under great pressure. The most unlikely people prove up to the task, whereas those that seem the most impressive at the start sometimes fail to find the inner resources needed to finish the course.

▲ **Night fighting**
US 101st Airborne Division troops on a night exercise. Night-fighting is just one specialized skill that special forces soldiers must master.

TEAMWORK

For some units – such as the US Army Rangers, the US Marine Corps, the British Parachute Regiment and Royal Marine Commandos, and the French Foreign Legion's 2nd Parachute Regiment – selection consists largely of team activity. Soldiers in these forces fight in small teams, so they must be able to work with others under great stress and difficulty. But for other units – such as the US Delta Force, the British Special Air Service (SAS), the US Navy Sea, Air, and Land (SEALs), or the British Special Boat Service (SBS) – while the small team remains the basic grouping, each team-member must be capable of working alone, for long periods, in conditions of great discomfort and danger. These units have selection courses that isolate each person, forcing them to draw on their own resources and self-discipline. Often there is an absence of any sort of urgency, and a deceptively relaxed attitude to the tests. This can lull candidates into a false sense of security.

▶ **Teamwork**
These British Parachute Regiment recruits struggle to carry a steel stretcher. Such exercises reinforce the need for teamwork.

Mental toughness

It is commonly observed that very fit, athletic individuals, used to pushing themselves physically, often cannot cope with the very demanding combination of heavy physical endurance and constant psychological pressure imposed by extreme military selection courses. Physical toughness alone is not enough, as special forces selectors want to find out how each person responds at the limits of his physical endurance. As the saying goes: "When the going gets tough, the tough get going." For the special forces soldier mental toughness must take over when physical reserves have been exhausted. What is needed in a special forces operation is something very different from the macho bravery of popular mythology; rather, a quiet resolve to carry on regardless of the circumstances.

Physical and mental determination
A lone soldier on the selection course for the British Parachute Regiment's Pathfinder Platoon.

◀ **Living off the land**
A British jungle-survival instructor demonstrates how to prepare a chicken for cooking. Living off the land could be a life-saving skill for a special forces soldier.

SPECIAL SKILLS

There are specific selection processes relevant to each unit. For example, SBS and SEAL candidates must be tested as potential divers and for claustrophobia. Most special forces units also undergo training in resistance to interrogation to prepare them for capture. This is vital, because information given away could endanger others and threaten a mission. Such rigorous selection procedures ensure that only the highest caliber soldiers are recruited.

▼ **Realistic training**
These are British Royal Marine recruits on an assault course. Special forces training seeks to replicate actual combat. Often, live ammunition is used.

The multi-skilled soldier

Each member of a small special forces team must be capable of doing more than one job. All have first aid training, and each man trains the others in the basics of his own specialization. In addition, each has a secondary specialization, enabling him to take over that task if the main specialist is killed or wounded. It is each soldier's responsibility to keep physical fitness and basic skills – such as small-arms use, basic radio work, demolitions, parachuting, and navigation – up to standard. Specific operations may also require additional training that might not be military. Team members acquire such skills, for example, civilian construction techniques, on an as-needed basis.

Navigation skills
A soldier of the British Pathfinder Platoon uses a Global Positioning System (GPS) handset.

How special forces are commanded

Special forces carry out special operations – specific missions of an unpredictable and diverse nature. These missions are different from conventional military operations. Properly trained and equipped special forces can succeed only if they are given achievable tasks and commanded in a suitably flexible manner, with the right input from government, military HQ, and other relevant agencies.

▶ **Political control**
The Ministry of Defence (MOD) building in London, England. The MOD sets the policy goals for British special operations units.

The command responsibilities for special forces are complicated and filled with potential for confusion and bureaucracy. In any operation, the actions of the usually small number of special forces troops are directed and supported not only by their military commanders, but also by government agencies and the government itself. In addition, certain types of special forces operations may also require international military and governmental cooperation.

Although the special forces of different countries vary greatly in size and capability, to be effective they must all follow certain basic principles of command.

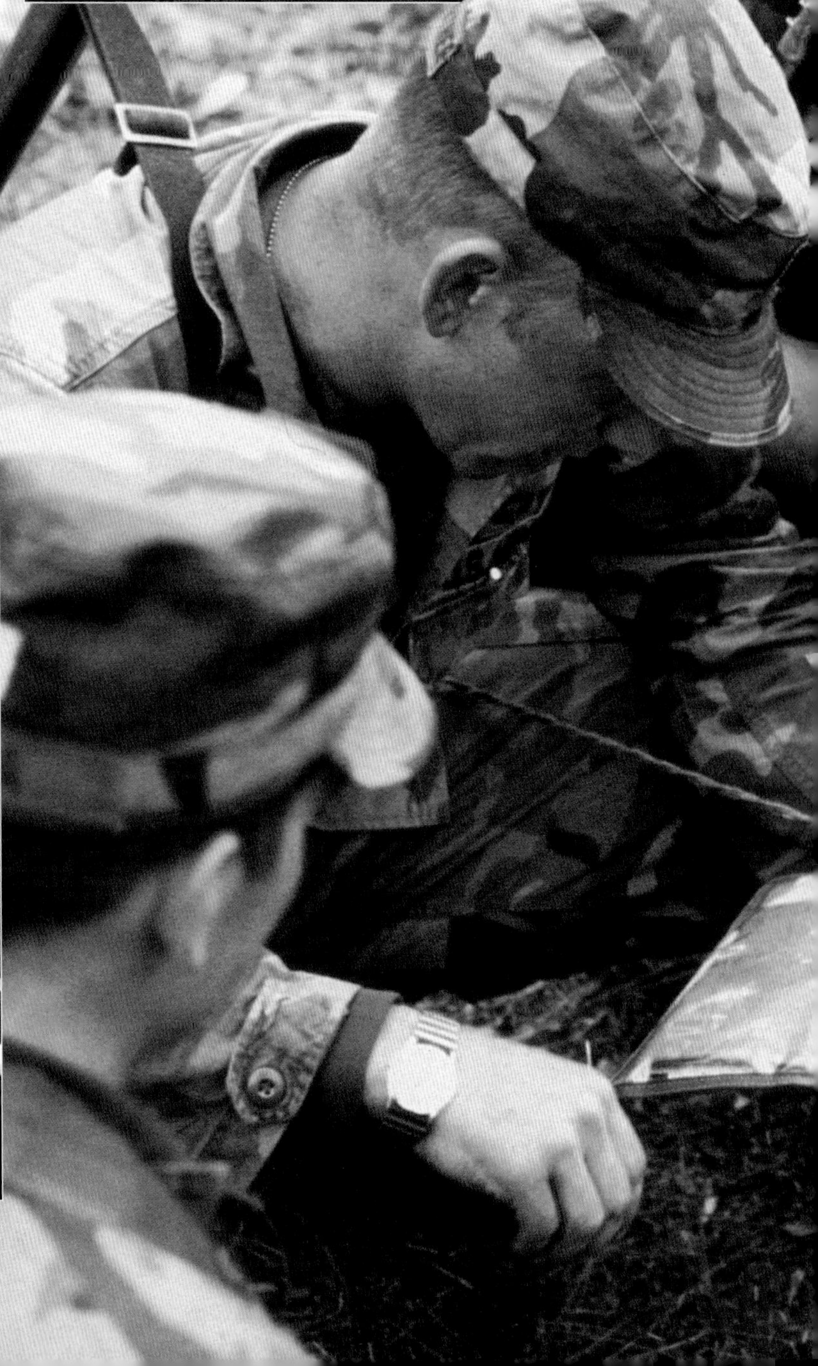

PRINCIPLES OF COMMAND

The first two principles of special forces command seem to contradict one other – that special forces must be given their orders and commanded from the highest levels, but that the operatives on the ground are always right, and should rarely be contradicted or overruled during an operation. Special forces troops on active duty are selected, trained, and trusted to make key decisions at a level that is usually well above their rank or

▶ **Theater of war**
US General Tommy Franks led Coalition forces in Iraq (2003). Special forces teams in the war zone would have reported directly to him.

position in the line of command. When soldiers' lives are at risk during a dangerous mission, only they have the information to weigh up the odds and decide what to do. A decision to abort a mission because the patrol commander suspects it has been detected by the enemy, for example, will only be questioned once the team is safely back at base. Equally, if a patrol commander sees an opportunity to make a strike earlier than planned, he is likely to take it, and explain his reasons after the mission.

At the same time, with enormous military and political implications attached to even their presence on the ground, special forces are often directly controlled at the highest level. Under pressure, there is a strong temptation for higher commanders to attempt to micro-manage special operations – often with disastrous consequences. Thus, special forces commanders at all levels are conditioned to be aware of the implications of their actions. They need to be tough and independently minded in order to make their own decisions, then carry them through in the face of sometimes daunting obstacles.

THE "NEED TO KNOW"

The third principle of command is that of "need to know": Restricting information only to those with a direct need to know it. Before a mission, a special forces unit goes into isolation and is briefed on that one operation alone. If captured and made to talk, soldiers are then unable to reveal details of any other planned or ongoing mission.

◀ **The Pentagon**
High-level US military policy is planned here, in the Pentagon, in Washington, D.C. The "need to know" restriction can cause problems in such large organizations: Agencies are reluctant to give up valuable intelligence without knowing what will be done with it.

◀ **Decision-makers**
"The soldier on the ground is always right" is the usual special forces maxim, particularly on dangerous missions.

The future

Special forces units are constantly looking to the future to determine whether projected developments in technology might improve their performance in the field. The rapid advance of technology creates both advantages and disadvantages: Radically better communications, weapons, and vehicles for the special forces teams, but also many more ways for the enemy to counter their efforts.

▶ **Night operations**
Night vision equipment is always being refined to make special operations possible around the clock.

Special forces are continually evolving – developing and changing their capabilities to stay ahead of new threats. The first modern special forces units were founded during World War II (1939–45) to provide badly needed levels of innovation. Much of what they did was unthinkable to conventional commanders. As the enemy reacted to their tactics, these early units developed new methods of raiding and gathering intelligence, with new weapons, vehicles, and equipment devised specifically for their needs. Today, special forces units continue to operate unconventionally. They are not, for example, limited to the equipment that their military has in store, but are free to buy what is needed, and modify it as required.

A whole commercial industry has developed to help them create the equipment, weapons, and vehicles they require. The industry standards are based on the acknowledgment that being used by a prestigious special forces unit, such as the US Delta Force or the British Special Air Service (SAS), is the highest form of military product endorsement. Radically new types of all-terrain vehicles are being developed, capable of high speeds across rough ground, and with provision for rapid modification in the field to different roles, from covert reconnaissance to battlefield assault. Clothing now exists that

▼ **Virtual reality**
The same technology behind virtual reality training aids such as this simulator will also be used to control pilotless air and ground vehicles, enabling special forces units to mount operations remotely.

Cyberterrorism

Increasingly, terrorists will adopt more sophisticated methods of attacking their perceived enemies. Electronic assaults on a nation's computer networks are increasingly seen as an effective terrorist ploy. Cyberspace is remote, safe, and full of potential targets, a place where "cyberterrorists" can attack the commercial, military, and communications systems of their enemy with fewer risks of being caught. Countering this threat will be a major challenge for special forces in the 21st century.

Future attacks
Air traffic control computer systems could be attacked by cyberterrorists. Special forces units have a role to play in gathering intelligence to prevent such acts.

▲ **Chemical warfare**
This special forces soldier is monitoring levels of toxins using a handheld testing device. Chemical warfare is seen as a major future threat.

keeps the wearer warm even if the material is soaking wet, that dries rapidly, and that allows the body to breathe. Similarly, developments in miniaturization and communications equipment mean special forces soldiers will be able to carry more of everything, particularly ammunition, greatly increasing their capabilities and firepower.

THE 21ST CENTURY

The methods, weapons, and tactics of elite forces commonly spread to conventional military units. The conventional infantry soldiers of today, with their individual radio communications, rapid-fire automatic weapons, and small operational groups, resemble special forces units of the 1990s. Like special forces, conventional combat units are trained to make their own decisions. In particular, the peace-keeping role of modern armies demands far more initiative than conventional war operations of even only 20 years ago. However, the nature of special forces teams means that they remain military innovators because they value and encourage diversity of thought, experience, and expertise far more than conventional units. The special forces soldier of tomorrow is likely to be just as capable of computer hacking as he will be proven in combat, in demolition work, or in intelligence gathering.

The future infantry soldier

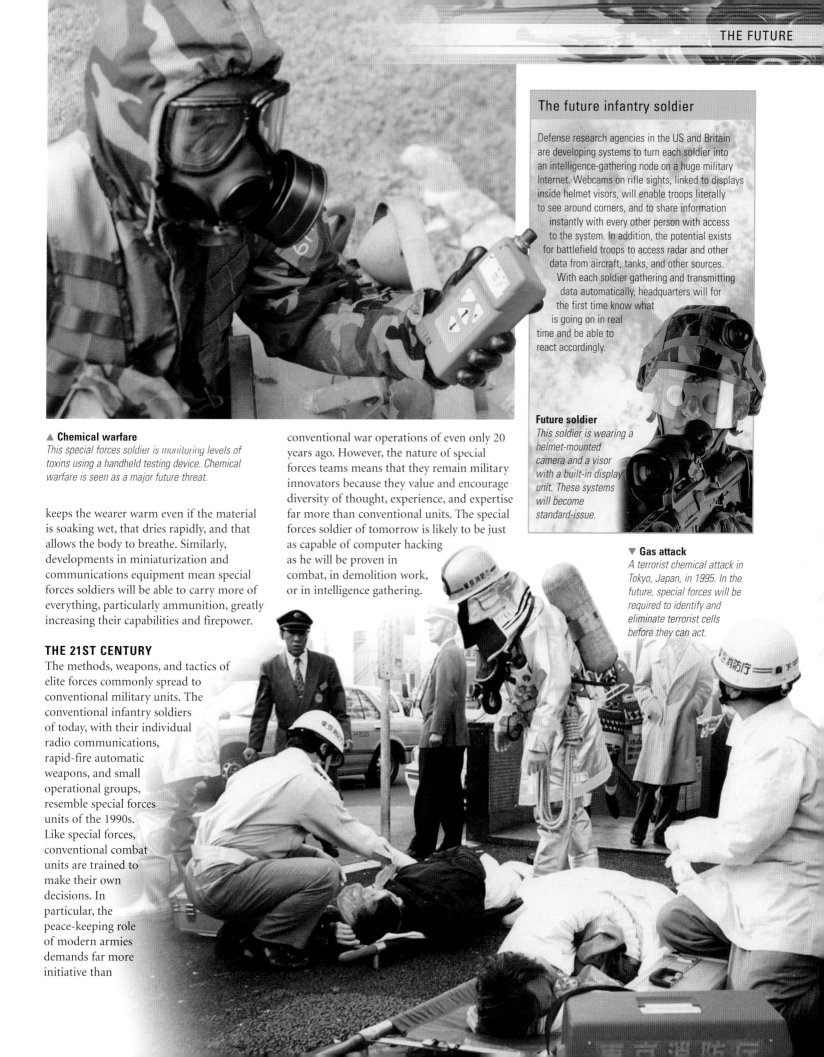

Defense research agencies in the US and Britain are developing systems to turn each soldier into an intelligence-gathering node on a huge military Internet. Webcams on rifle sights, linked to displays inside helmet visors, will enable troops literally to see around corners, and to share information instantly with every other person with access to the system. In addition, the potential exists for battlefield troops to access radar and other data from aircraft, tanks, and other sources. With each soldier gathering and transmitting data automatically, headquarters will for the first time know what is going on in real time and be able to react accordingly.

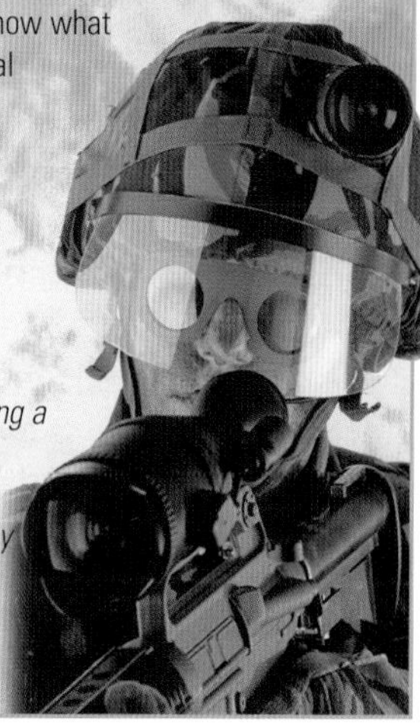

Future soldier
This soldier is wearing a helmet-mounted camera and a visor with a built-in display unit. These systems will become standard-issue.

▼ **Gas attack**
A terrorist chemical attack in Tokyo, Japan, in 1995. In the future, special forces will be required to identify and eliminate terrorist cells before they can act.

HISTORY OF SPECIAL FORCES

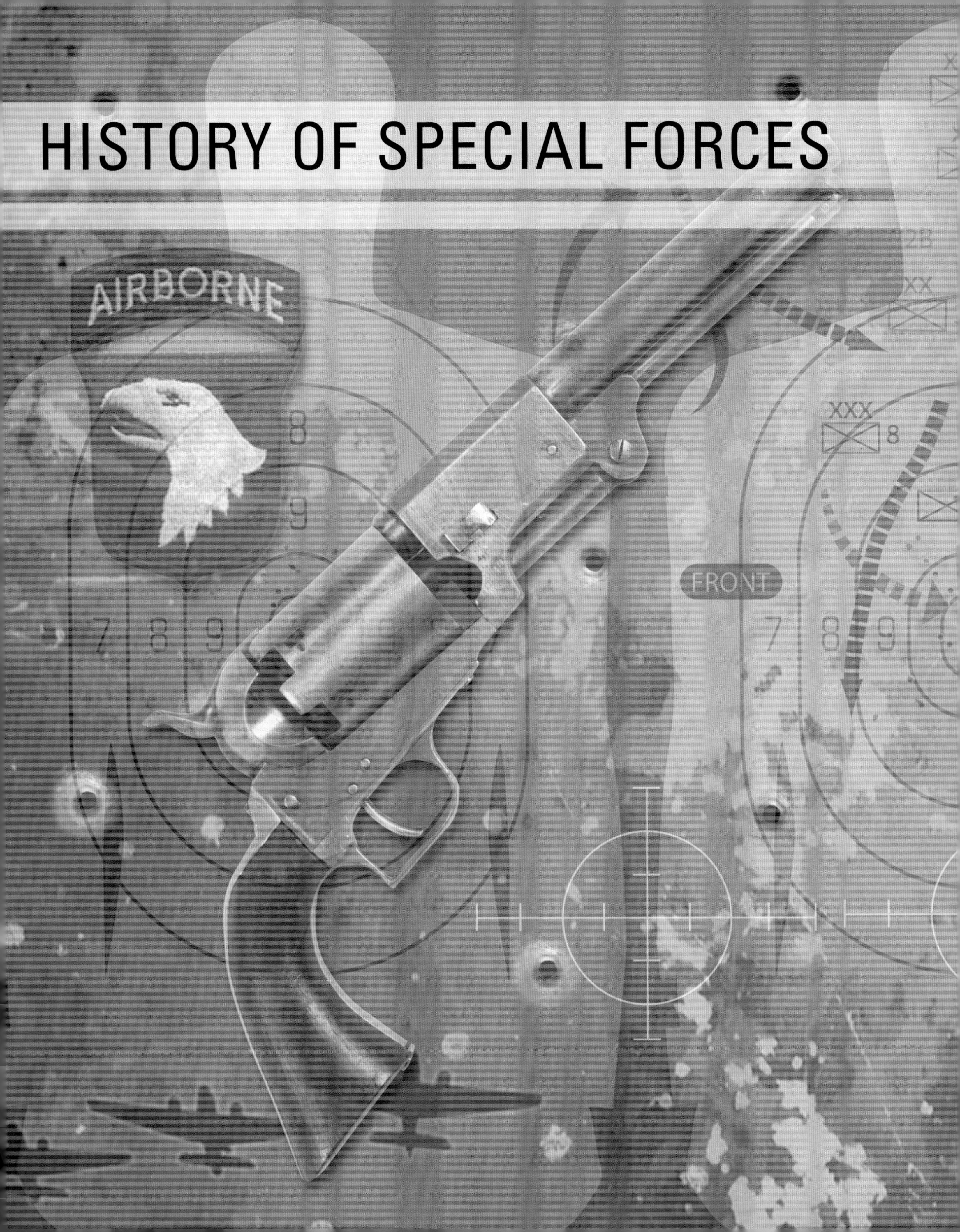

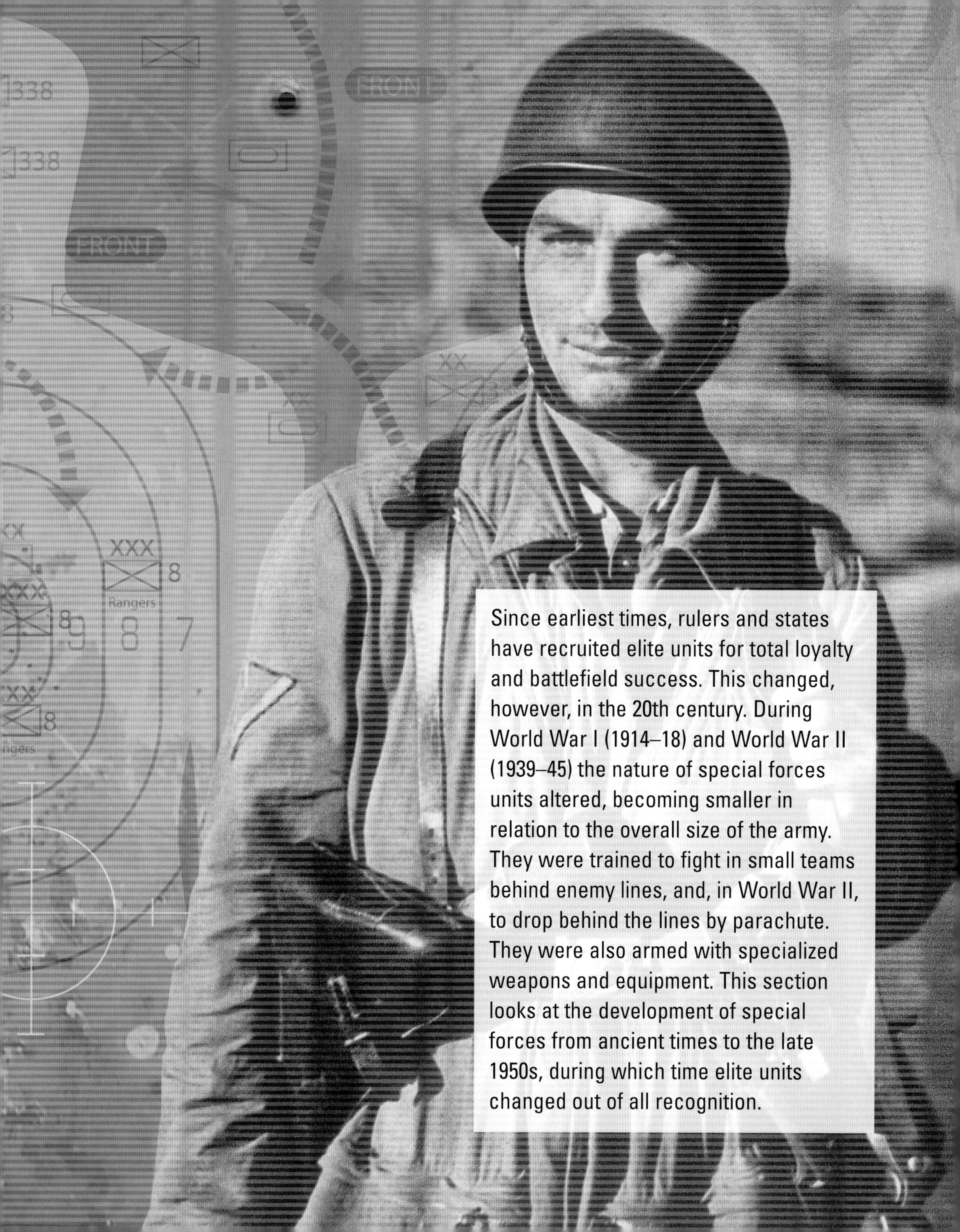

Since earliest times, rulers and states have recruited elite units for total loyalty and battlefield success. This changed, however, in the 20th century. During World War I (1914–18) and World War II (1939–45) the nature of special forces units altered, becoming smaller in relation to the overall size of the army. They were trained to fight in small teams behind enemy lines, and, in World War II, to drop behind the lines by parachute. They were also armed with specialized weapons and equipment. This section looks at the development of special forces from ancient times to the late 1950s, during which time elite units changed out of all recognition.

Early history

From ancient times, rulers have surrounded themselves with soldiers who have been special, either because of their absolute loyalty, or because they were better equipped and trained than the other troops. Originally used as bodyguards, special forces changed over time to become essential, war-winning assets.

The idea of special forces is almost as old as warfare itself. They were special because they had superior training or equipment, or had extensive combat experience. Whether armed with spears, swords, or muskets, elites had one thing in common: They each formed a dependable, battle-winning unit of the army.

In the Persian Empire (550–330 BC), an elite named the Immortals was both the bodyguard of the king, and, in wartime, a key fighting unit. The Immortals got their name because they were kept at a permanent strength of 10,000 men – anyone who died in battle was immediately replaced. In return, the Immortals were totally loyal to the Persian royal family.

In ancient Rome (280 BC–AD 476), the Praetorian Guard, which protected the city, became bodyguards to Rome's emperors. However, the unit went into decline when it became increasingly involved in Roman politics.

The collapse of the Roman Empire in the 5th century AD ushered in the Dark Ages. During this period, although all European rulers had personal guard units, the idea of elite forces was neglected.

THE MEDIEVAL PERIOD

It was only in the 13th and 14th centuries that elite units again began to emerge. In Europe, the Swiss produced infantry units, known as pikemen, who used pikes or spears to lethal effect. In what is now Turkey, the Ottoman Turks formed the Janissaries, an elite body of 12,000 men. First raised in 1326 as the Sultan's

▶ **Union sharpshooters**
Snipers of the Union Army, seen here firing at Confederate soldiers at the Battle of Vicksburg, Mississippi, during the American Civil War (1861–65).

◀ **Turkish Janissary**
This soldier carries a sword and a firearm. The burning cord was used to light the gunpowder to fire the gun.

Ancient elites

Military elites in ancient times tended to be the best-trained and equipped soldiers in the army. The Immortals in ancient Persia were maintained at a permanent strength of 10,000 men, and were the personal bodyguard of the royal family. The Praetorian Guard were the guardians of ancient Rome and its emperors, and numbered 9,000 men.

The Praetorians
A sculpture of the officers and soldiers of the Praetorian Guard of Rome, dating from the 2nd century AD.

The Immortals
Two of the elite troops of ancient Persia, depicted in a carving in the royal palace at Persepolis, Iran.

▲ Colt Army Dragoon pistol (1850)
This pistol was very popular with cavalry raiding units during the American Civil War. Units such as Mosby's Rangers favored firearms over swords when fighting.

Length	13.5 in. (34.3 cm.)
Weight	4 lb. (1.8 kg.)
Rate of fire	12 rpm.
Caliber	.44-in.

◀ Boer commandos
Despised by the British, who considered them an ill-dressed rabble, Boer fighters were, in fact, expert shots, and courageous and hardy soldiers

guard, the Janissaries were Christian prisoners, trained in warfare from childhood. They remained a vital part of the Ottoman army until the Empire collapsed in 1923.

SPECIAL FORCES IN THE 19TH CENTURY

In the 19th century, the Imperial Guard of Napoleon Bonaparte (1769–1821), the French Emperor, was little different from Persia's Immortals. Frequently used in 1813 and 1814 in battles against the Prussians and Russians, the Imperial Guard tipped the scales of victory. However, even this elite unit could not prevent Napoleon's ultimate defeat by the British at Waterloo, Belgium, in 1815.

By the mid-19th century, the nature of special forces had changed: Smaller, less formal formations began to appear. In the American Civil War (1861–65) the Confederates raised raiding forces, such as Mosby's Rangers, to operate behind Union lines and attack railroads and supply depots. Both sides also employed sharpshooters (snipers) to harry the enemy.

Sniper tactics were also employed in the Boer War in South Africa (1899–1902), a conflict that developed between settlers of Dutch extraction and the British who ruled the colony. Boer commandos, who were expert shots and skilled horse riders, inflicted heavy casualties on numerically superior British forces.

The hit-and-run, sniper tactics employed by the Boer commandos would be further refined by German military tacticians, and put to devastating use in World War I.

◀ The Imperial Guard
Napoleon Bonaparte, the French emperor (center), bids farewell to his Imperial Guard as he leaves France for exile on the island of Elba.

PROFILE — Francis Marion

Dates	1732–95
Unit	American Army
Rank	Brigadier-General

Francis Marion was a commander in the American Revolution (1775–83), who waged a very effective guerrilla war against the British. He first saw action against the Cherokee in 1759, and later joined the Revolutionary Army in 1776. A native of South Carolina, when the British overran the state in 1780, Marion raised a militia unit and led it in a series of hit-and-run raids. In classic guerrilla-warfare style, he used the seemingly impassable swamps of the region as a base, earning him the nickname Swamp Fox. After the war he entered politics, serving in the Senate of his home state.

World War I

From the trench deadlock of World War I (1914–18) emerged the first "modern" special forces units: The German stormtroopers. Specially trained and equipped, they operated in small teams, where independent command and individual initiative were of paramount importance in achieving military victory.

▶ **Stormtroop tactics**
German stormtroopers cross no-man's land on the Western Front in France in 1918. Stormtrooper squads were trained to move quickly, bypass any obstacles, and penetrate enemy lines.

By 1917, World War I on the Western Front in northern France and Belgium had reached a stalemate. German troops faced the Allies (primarily the French and British) across a shell-blasted landscape of trench lines, machine-gun posts, artillery positions, and barbed wire. Both sides used enormous quantities of artillery shells and manpower to try to batter their way through the opposing lines. The results were catastrophic. For example, the Third Battle of Ypres, Belgium, began on July 15, 1917, with a massive British artillery bombardment. The British commander, Sir Douglas Haig (1861–1928), hoped to pound the German positions into submission. By the time the battle was halted at the end of October, 400,000 Allied soldiers were dead for little gain. The Germans had lost 270,000 men.

Both sides needed to break the deadlock, but Germany's need was greater because by 1917 the British Royal Navy was depriving Germany of imports of food and raw materials by sinking its cargo ships. German military leaders sought a tactical answer.

The solution seemed to lie in the use of stormtroopers – infantry who could rapidly cross "no-man's land" (the area between opposing trenches) to attack the enemy.

STORMTROOP WARFARE

The new tactics had been tried in September 1917 on the Eastern Front, where the Germans faced the Russians. Devised by German General Oskar von Hutier (see box below), the basis of stormtroop tactics was the use of small battlegroups or squads. Like modern special forces, each squad operated independently, probing for weak spots in the enemy's line and maintaining the momentum of the advance. Behind them, follow-up troops would reinforce any breakthrough.

During the winter months of 1917–18, the Germans created 40 stormtroop battalions. They were initially used in Flanders in northern France in March 1918. At first they achieved spectacular successes, smashing through weak points in the Allied line. However, the Germans were unable to maintain the necessary artillery support and troop reinforcements to capitalize on the breakthrough. By August, the offensive had been defeated and most of the stormtroopers were dead.

"Hutier tactics"

In the late summer of 1917, the German Eighth Army, commanded by General Oskar von Hutier (1857–1934), was besieging the Russian-held town of Riga, capital of Latvia. To take the town, Hutier used specially trained assault infantry – stormtroopers – to break through the enemy's defenses. The attack began on September 1, and Riga fell two days later. "Hutier tactics" were born.

General Oskar von Hutier
In 1917, Hutier (center) was the first military commander to use fast-moving, heavily armed stormtrooper units as a means of overcoming conventional defenses.

▼ **Trench warfare**
A German stormtrooper team fires a heavy machine gun from a trench position on the Western Front in 1918.

◀ **Flamethrowers in combat**
German stormtroopers armed with flamethrowers advance on Allied positions in northern France in March 1918. Flamethrowers were very effective weapons for destroying enemy trenches and gun positions. They also spread panic and fear among enemy soldiers.

The stormtroopers had been defeated by conventional tactics. The Allies had simply retreated, regrouped, and counter-attacked. The German failure meant that the Allies did not develop similar stormtrooper units, although they did have some unorthodox specialized forces in Arabia, such as those led by T. E. Lawrence (see box below).

In World War II (1939–45), German military commanders would again turn to fast-moving frontline troops. The stormtroopers were the forerunners of what the Germans would later call *Blitzkrieg* – Lightning War.

German stormtroopers

German stormtroopers operated in small squads of between 14 and 18 men. Each soldier was heavily armed with a variety of weapons, including machine guns, grenades, flamethrowers, and even small artillery pieces. Their role was to breach enemy lines, allowing the main German infantry force to follow.

German grenades
The stick grenades carried by these stormtroopers could be thrown farther than conventional grenades.

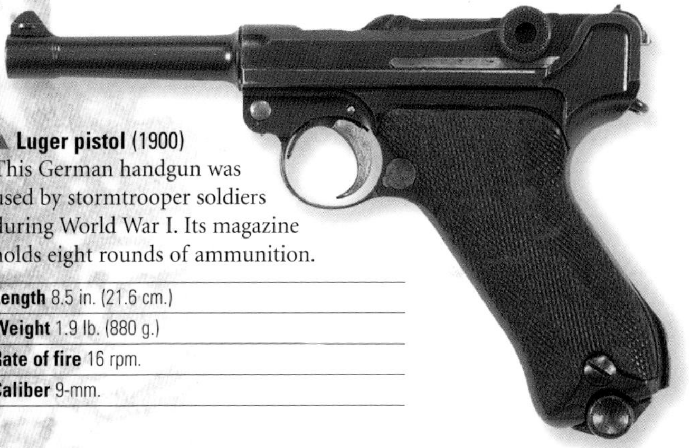

▲ **Luger pistol** (1900)
This German handgun was used by stormtrooper soldiers during World War I. Its magazine holds eight rounds of ammunition.

Length	8.5 in. (21.6 cm.)
Weight	1.9 lb. (880 g.)
Rate of fire	16 rpm.
Caliber	9-mm.

PROFILE: Lawrence of Arabia

Dates 1888–1935
Unit British Army
Rank Colonel

The son of an Anglo-Irish gentleman, Thomas Edward (T. E.) Lawrence became an archaeologist in the Middle East in 1911. When World War I broke out in 1914, he joined British Military Intelligence, and was based in Cairo, Egypt. In 1916 he was sent to Jedda in Arabia to foster an Arab uprising against the ruling Turks, who were allies of Britain's enemy, Germany. Lawrence established good relations with Arab leaders and adopted traditional Arab fighting tactics. He and his Arab allies then embarked on a guerrilla war against Turkish targets. This campaign was a decisive factor in the eventual British conquest of Palestine and Syria. After the war, Lawrence wrote a book about his Arabian experiences: *The Seven Pillars of Wisdom.* He died in a motorcycle accident in 1935.

World War II: British special forces

During World War II (1939–45) British special forces instilled fear and respect in all who crossed their path. Operating deep behind enemy lines, often on highly dangerous missions, the courageous men who volunteered for special forces units such as the Special Air Service (SAS) made a dramatic impact on the war effort. Working in small teams, they would enter hostile territory undetected to strike at the most valuable enemy targets.

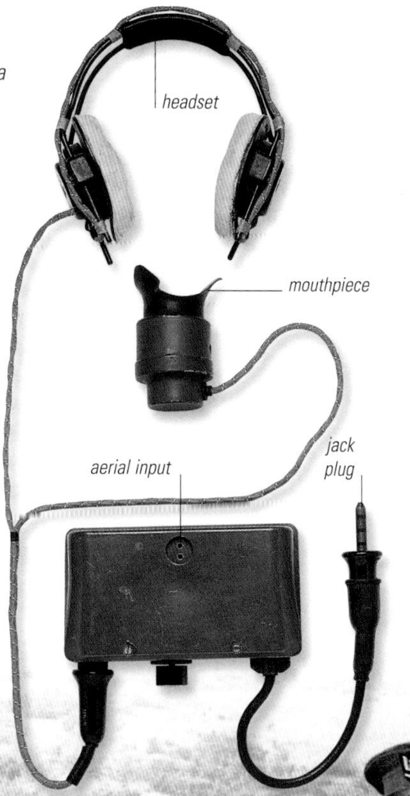

▶ **S-Phone**
This special forces' radio telephone also doubled as a homing beacon for aircraft.

LRDG badge

The story of British special forces is one of the most dramatic aspects of World War II. The creation of these elite fighting units was a powerful example of necessity being the mother of invention. As the British struggled to find a way of hitting back at German and Japanese forces in the early years of the war, special forces units such as the Royal Marine Commandos provided a way of striking at valuable enemy assets, and, in so doing, boosting the morale of an embattled nation. As the war progressed, British special forces

SAS parachute badge

▼ **Stirling's Special Air Service**
SAS troopers pose for a photograph in their desert jeeps. On the far right stands their commanding officer and SAS founder, David Stirling.

◀ **Mine detection**
Commandos use their daggers to search for land mines on a night exercise. Mine clearance was an essential skill for penetrating enemy lines.

▼ **Desert raiders**
LRDG soldiers and their truck behind German lines in North Africa in 1942.

played an ever more central role in the destruction of German and Japanese bridges, railroads, supply depots, weapons research facilities, and other key military installations.

THE BEGINNINGS OF SPECIAL FORCES

British special forces were developed from existing units during the war. The Special Air Service (SAS) was formed in 1941 by a Scottish officer, David Stirling. Serving with a commando unit in North Africa, Stirling saw the potential for special operations behind enemy lines. He felt that a small group of highly trained, highly motivated soldiers could wreak havoc on German supply lines, bases, and morale. He was proved correct. Working with the Long Range Desert Group, (LRDG), who provided transportation and communications, the SAS raided German airfields, destroying numerous planes on the ground. Later, the SAS used jeeps equipped with twin machine guns. These became formidable weapons, ideal for the hit-and-run missions in which the SAS specialized.

Alongside the SAS, another unit was created, known as the Special Boat Squadron (SBS). A branch of the Royal Marines, the SBS specialized in maritime operations, including attacks on enemy shipping and naval bases.

Other special forces formed in World War II included the Parachute Regiment, created as a rival to the German parachute units and modeled along similar lines. In Asia, in the war against the Japanese, the Chindits, under Major-General Orde Wingate (see box, p31), played a vital role in the British campaign for Burma. Other, more specialized units were also created, such as the Australian Coastwatchers, who gathered intelligence on Japanese naval movements (see box below).

NOTABLE ELITE OPERATIONS

Many of the most famous operations of the war were undertaken by special forces. The British Commando raid in 1942 on the German-held port of St. Nazaire, France, was

PROFILE — David Stirling

Dates 1915–90
Unit British SAS
Rank Lt-Colonel

Inspired by personal experience in the North African campaign against the Germans in 1941, British officer David Stirling formed L-Detachment, Special Air Service Brigade, for the purpose of sending small teams of four or five elite troops on daring missions, usually into the desert. The SAS quickly became an integral part of Allied strategic attacks, targeting high-value enemy assets deep behind the lines – installations such as fuel dumps and air bases. Stirling was captured in 1943, and detained in Colditz prison in Germany until 1945. He died in 1990, but his legacy lives on in the traditions of the SAS.

▼ **St. Nazaire Raid**
In March 1942, British Royal Marine Commandos made a daring raid against the dock facilities in St. Nazaire, France. The successful attack prevented the feared German battleship Tirpitz *from using the base. It was a costly victory, however, because 144 men were captured or killed, and 14 small boats were lost. Five Victoria Crosses were awarded.*

The Coastwatchers

The Coastwatchers were brave Australian civilians who sent reports to Allied commanders about Japanese movements in the Pacific. Staying behind on islands captured by the Japanese, they played a vital role in updating Allied intelligence. They also reported on enemy numbers, provided early warning of air attack, and rescued downed Allied pilots.

Coastal spies
A group of Australian coastwatchers pose with their weapons aboard the submarine USS Dace *in 1944.*

▲ **Special Boat Squadron operation**
Two SBS soldiers on their way to a sabotage mission in the Mediterranean Sea during World War II.

a mission to destroy the docks and prevent their use by the German battleship *Tirpitz*. The plan was to ram and destroy the docks by disguising HMS *Campbeltown* as a German vessel and loading it with explosives. The operation was a success: the docks were rendered useless for the remainder of the war and only 64 British commandos lost their lives.

Royal Marine Commandos also took part in a raid on the French port of Bordeaux in December 1942. A group of 10 commandos in two-man canoes paddled 35 miles (56 km.) into the harbor, and, under the noses of the German garrison, planted limpet mines on a number of ships. Five vessels were heavily damaged, two of which later sank. The men who took part became known as the "Cockleshell Heroes," for the Cockle canoes used in the attack.

The Parachute Regiment was engaged in a number of notable operations during World War II. Although the regiment was only formed at the beginning of the war, it grew to become a powerful fighting unit. The Parachute Regiment was involved in an attack on the German radar installation at Bruneval, France, in February 1942. Jumping at night into snow, the unit led by Major John Frost successfully stole top-secret German radar equipment and was evacuated by sea. Three paratroopers were killed and six captured.

British paratroopers also took part in the ill-fated Allied raid on Arnhem in Holland in September 1944. The mission was to capture the vital bridge over the Rhine River to allow Allied tank columns and troops a safe passage into Germany. The Allied force held the bridge for several days in the face of fierce German counterattacks, before being forced to withdraw. Of a total of 10,000 troops, 1,200 were killed and 6,642 taken prisoner.

▲ **Fairbairn Sykes dagger**
The Fairbairn Sykes Commando dagger was standard issue to British special forces units in World War II. Its 7-in. (17.8-cm.) blade was ideal for close-quarters fighting and silent killing.

▶ **Chindits in Burma**
A Chindit patrol plants demolition charges along a stretch of Japanese-held railroad line. The Chindits' missions focused on disrupting Japanese logistics.

▲ **US Ford/Willys Paradroppable Jeep**
This jeep was designed to be dropped by parachute for use by special forces behind enemy lines.

THE IMPORTANCE OF SPECIAL FORCES

Some historians have questioned the importance of the overall contribution made by these relatively small units to the success of the Allied war effort. However, throughout World War II special forces did play a notable role in taking the fight to the enemy. During the bleak early years, when the defeat of Britain seemed inevitable, special forces units not only harassed German, Japanese, and Italian forces, but also did significant strategic damage to their ability to wage war.

Following the Allied invasion of France in Normandy on D-Day, June 6, 1944, British special forces were deployed at the forefront of operations. Their role was to reconnoiter the ground and disrupt enemy supply lines. The visionary officers who created these units left a legacy that is still important today. They foresaw that small, highly trained teams of elite fighters could do great damage to the enemy. As a result, the conduct of military operations has never been the same.

▲ **Airborne force**
Troops from the Parachute Regiment watch for the enemy at the Dutch town of Arnhem in 1944.

PROFILE | **Orde Wingate**

Dates 1903–44
Unit Chindits
Rank Major-General

Major-General Orde Wingate was the eccentric founder of the Chindit force, which operated against the Japanese in Burma during World War II. He was selected for the task by the British War Office, who believed that his experience in guerrilla warfare in Palestine in the 1930s would be valuable in an unconventional war against the Japanese invaders. His long-range assault patrols consisted of 3,000 men. Resupplied from the air, the force wrought havoc by targeting railroad lines and bridges. After Wingate was killed in an air crash in 1944, the long-range operations he pioneered were discontinued.

Chindit badge

World War II: German special forces

The German Army of World War II was one of the greatest fighting formations in history. Integral to its success was a number of elite units that carried out specialized tasks to aid the rapid German style of warfare. These units were commanded by innovative leaders, were highly trained, and were often equipped with the very best weaponry. Their tactics and training were later copied by American and British forces.

▼ **Sturmgewehr 44** (1943)
This assault rifle was very popular with Waffen-SS troops. It possessed greater firepower than bolt-action rifles, and offered greater accuracy. It was first used on the Eastern Front in World War II.

Length	37 in. (94 cm.)
Weight	11.3 lb. (5.1 kg)
Rate of fire	500 rpm.
Caliber	7.92-mm.

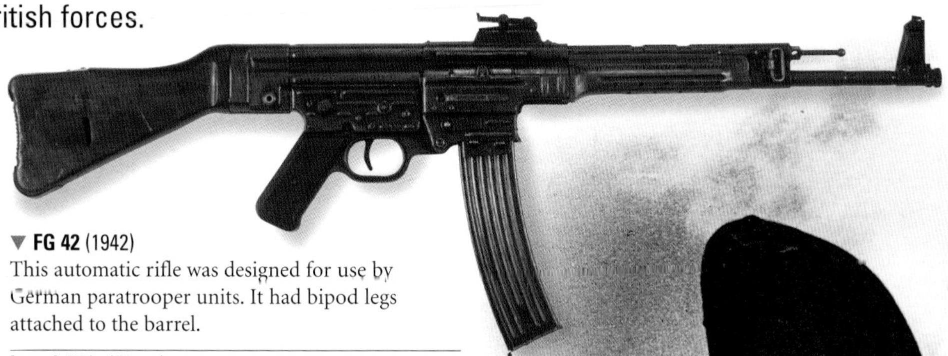

The German *Blitzkrieg* (Lightning War) aimed to win a campaign by decisive and fast offensive action. Combining overwhelming firepower (tanks, artillery, and air support) with rapid forward movement, German forces would first encircle and then destroy enemy units. To do this required high levels of training, coordination of resources on the battlefield, and special forces.

The true predecessors of today's special forces units were the *Brandenburgers*, specially trained German commandos. Operating in small groups, often in civilian clothes, they secretly entered enemy territory to seize key tactical objectives. In May 1940, for example, *Brandenburgers* dressed in Dutch Army uniforms slipped into Holland from Germany and captured a bridge over the Meuse River to enable German tanks to cross and invade.

▼ **FG 42** (1942)
This automatic rifle was designed for use by German paratrooper units. It had bipod legs attached to the barrel.

Length	37 in. (94 cm.)
Weight	9.9 lb. (4.5 kg.)
Rate of fire	120 rpm.
Caliber	7.92-mm.

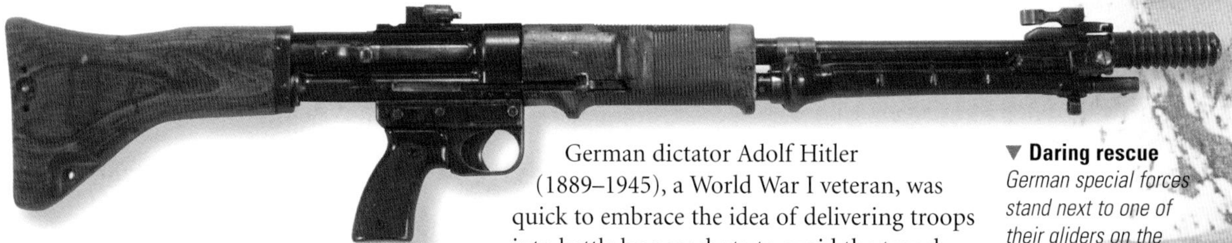

German dictator Adolf Hitler (1889–1945), a World War I veteran, was quick to embrace the idea of delivering troops into battle by parachute to avoid the trench deadlock he had experienced himself. By the outbreak of war in September 1939, therefore, Germany had a fully trained airborne unit, the 7th Parachute Division. Its effectiveness was proved in May 1940 when its troops captured the Belgian fortress of Eben Emael, and key bridges near Rotterdam, Holland.

▼ **Daring rescue**
German special forces stand next to one of their gliders on the mountainside at Gran Sasso, Italy, following their successful rescue of Italian dictator Benito Mussolini in September 1943.

PROFILE — Otto Skorzeny

Dates	1908–75
Unit	German SS
Rank	Lt-Colonel

Skorzeny was one of the most innovative soldiers in the German SS. He formed a special forces unit, *Oranienburg*, in April 1943. In September Hitler ordered him to rescue deposed Italian leader Benito Mussolini, who was being held by Italian partisans. In 1944, Skorzeny kidnapped the son of the Hungarian leader, Admiral Miklos Horthy, thus preventing Hungary's defection to the Allies. During the German counter-offensive on Allied lines in 1944, Skorzeny led a group of English-speaking German troops who, dressed as US soldiers, caused mayhem behind enemy lines. After the war Skorzeny became a businessman.

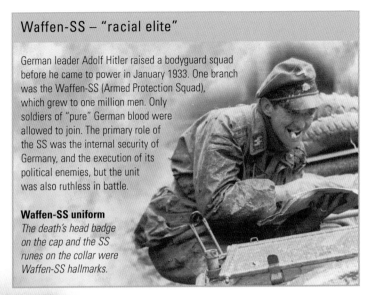

Waffen-SS – "racial elite"

German leader Adolf Hitler raised a bodyguard squad before he came to power in January 1933. One branch was the Waffen-SS (Armed Protection Squad), which grew to one million men. Only soldiers of "pure" German blood were allowed to join. The primary role of the SS was the internal security of Germany, and the execution of its political enemies, but the unit was also ruthless in battle.

Waffen-SS uniform
The death's head badge on the cap and the SS runes on the collar were Waffen-SS hallmarks.

▶ Paratroop drop
German paratroopers drop on the Corinth Canal, Greece, on April 26, 1941. The aircraft are Junkers Ju 52 three-engined transports. Each aircraft could carry up to 16 fully equipped paratroopers.

PARATROOP OPERATIONS

Commanded by General Kurt Student (1890–1978), the paratroopers were tough and disciplined. Student's training regime instilled an aggressive "paratroop spirit," and his men proved tenacious warriors. This was shown in May 1941, when 10,000 German paratroopers captured the Mediterranean island of Crete. Despite heavy casualties, the paratroopers held on until reinforced. The eight-day battle cost the lives of 3,000 paratroopers.

In 1943, paratroopers led by Otto Skorzeny carried out a mission to rescue the Italian dictator, Benito Mussolini (1883–1945), who was being held by Italian partisans at a hotel at Gran Sasso, Italy. Using gliders, the unit landed nearby, burst into the hotel, and freed him.

German paratroop operations continued throughout the war, but after the losses on Crete, there were no more large-scale landings.

▼ Paratrooper equipment
This paratrooper photographed on Crete has a stick grenade tucked into his belt. Its wooden handle increased throwing range. Magazine pouches are mounted on his belt.

▼ Eben Emael
German paratroopers with a Brandenburger *(center) at the Belgian fortress in 1940.*

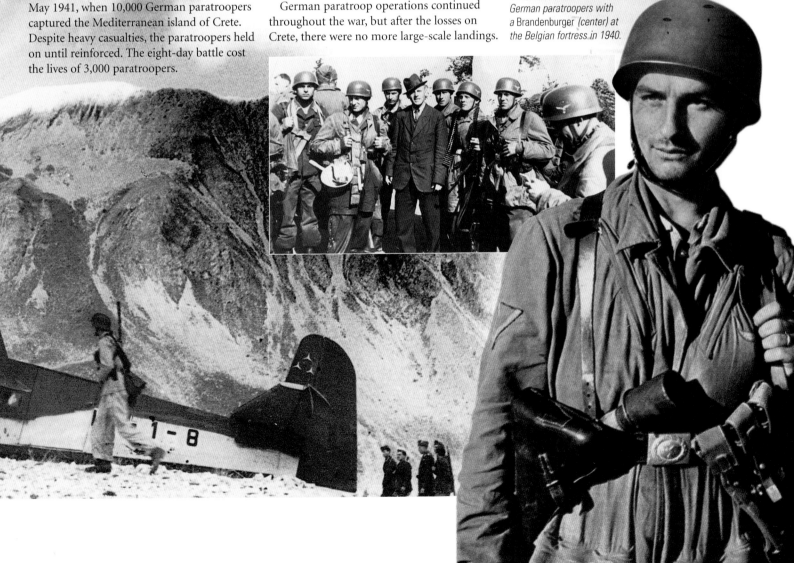

World War II: US special forces

In World War II (1939–45) the importance of behind-the-lines reconnaissance, the numerous high-priority targets, and the many different types of terrain created the need for units with specialized skills. After the United States joined the war in 1941 on the side of Britain and its allies, US special forces units made a major contribution to the final Allied victory.

▲ C-47 (1942)
The US-built C-47 Dakota was the workhorse of the Allies in World War II. It could carry up to 27 paratroopers, and was also used as a glider tug and a gunship.

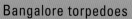

Engine	2 x P&W Wasp radial
Wingspan	95 ft. (29 m.)
Length	64.5 ft. (19.7 m.)
Speed	185 mph. (298 kph.)
Crew	3

In World War II, US special forces were formed to fulfill specific operational roles. The ways in which they were used varied between Pacific and European battlefields.

EUROPEAN ELITES

In Europe, US special forces were deployed in enemy territory ahead of a main advance or amphibious landing in order to disrupt enemy supply lines and to capture or destroy key targets, such as bridges. The US Army Rangers and the US 82nd and 101st Airborne Divisions fulfilled such roles. For example, in 1942 Major William Darby raised a commando-style Rangers force of 520 men. In Italy they used their mountain skills to neutralize German positions, and on D-Day, June 6, 1944, Rangers landed on the Normandy beaches and scaled the vertical cliffs to destroy batteries of German guns.

US airborne forces were the other key European elite. They allowed Allied commanders to land a major force behind the enemy's frontline. Two landmark actions by US paratroops were the drops over France on D-Day, and 101st Airborne Division's

101st Airborne badge

◀ Enemy gun position
US Rangers scale the cliffs on a Normandy beach on D-Day (June 6, 1944) during the Allied invasion of Europe in World War II.

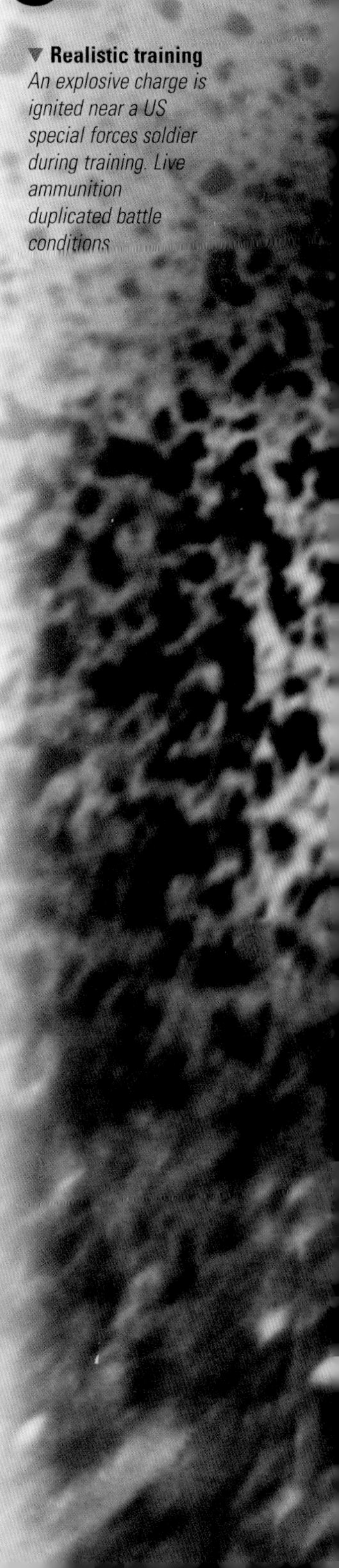

▼ Realistic training
An explosive charge is ignited near a US special forces soldier during training. Live ammunition duplicated battle conditions

Bangalore torpedoes

The Bangalore torpedo was a weapon used by US elite forces to clear pathways through minefields and barbed wire defenses. It consisted of a steel tube 6 ft. (1.8 m) long and 1.5 in. (3.8 cm.) in diameter packed with explosives. It would be pushed into a minefield or under a barbed wire barrier. When detonated, the Bangalore could blast a path 10–20 ft. (3–6 m.) wide. An updated version is in use with the US Army today.

Ranger Bangalores
The Ranger standing on the right is holding a Bangalore.

defense of Bastogne, Belgium, in December 1944. In both cases the paratroops fought heroically against overwhelming odds.

PROFILE — **William Darby**

Dates 1911–45
Unit US Army Rangers
Rank Major

Major William Darby was a former student of the US Military Academy at West Point, Virginia, and the man behind the elite US Army Rangers. In 1942, Darby was charged with creating the US equivalent of the British commandos. He personally selected all of the 520 men who made up the unit, and accompanied them on early operations. The unit distinguished itself in special missions behind enemy lines in North Africa and in Europe. Darby was killed in action on April 30, 1945, just a few days before the war in Europe ended. He was posthumously promoted to the rank of Brigadier-General.

PACIFIC ELITES

In the Pacific, the role of US special forces was to penetrate far behind enemy lines, either to gather intelligence or to attack specific targets. The US Marine Raiders were hand-picked to go ashore along enemy coastlines. They could survive for weeks at a time, raiding Japanese railroads and camps before disappearing back into the jungle. The Marine Raiders distinguished themselves on the Pacific islands of New Guinea and Guadalcanal.

The US Army had its own special forces unit in "Merrill's Marauders," named for its leader, Brigadier-General Frank Merrill (1903–1950). They were a volunteer force of 3,000 soldiers trained for long-range missions against Japanese supply lines and communications in the Burma campaign. The unit traveled great distances on foot through the jungle, inflicting huge losses on the enemy.

With bravery and self-sufficiency, the elite US forces in Europe and the Pacific advanced the final Allied victory.

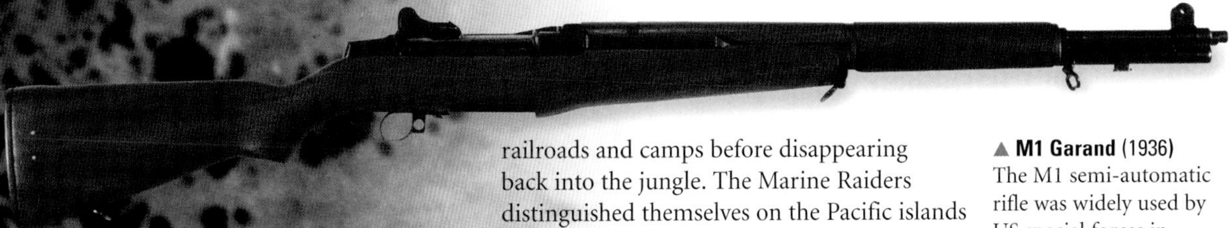

▲ **M1 Garand** (1936)
The M1 semi-automatic rifle was widely used by US special forces in World War II. It offered a great improvement in firepower over the bolt-action M1903 series rifle it replaced.

Length 43.6 in. (110 cm.)
Weight 9.5 lb. (4.37 kg.)
Rate of fire 20 rpm.
Caliber 0.3-in.

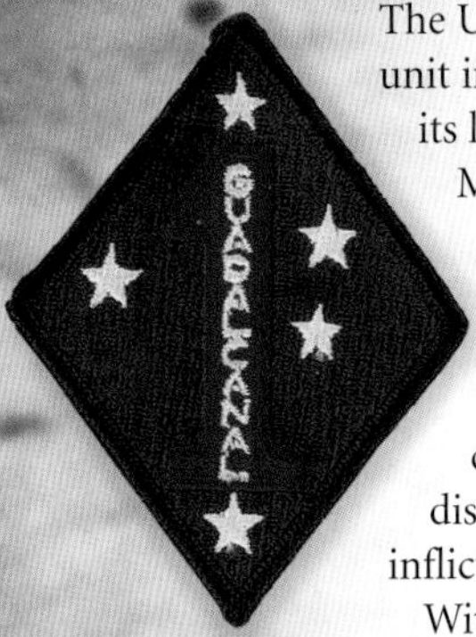

Marine Raider badge

▲ **Mortar crew in Burma**
"Merrill's Marauders" in action in Burma. The unit was organized and trained for long-range penetration behind enemy lines in Japanese-held Burma.

1945–60: British SAS in Malaya

The successful British campaign against communist guerrillas in Malaya between 1950 and 1958 persuaded the Ministry of Defence that the Special Air Service (SAS) had a long-term future. The decisive jungle campaign enabled the regiment to escape any reduction in size, or even possible disbandment, in the army reforms of 1957. The Malayan Emergency established the SAS as experts in jungle operations and in building and benefiting from good relations with local people.

SAS winged dagger badge

Terrorist target
A British truck burns after being attacked by communist insurgents in Malaya. The terror campaign targeted unarmed buses and trucks.

BACKGROUND

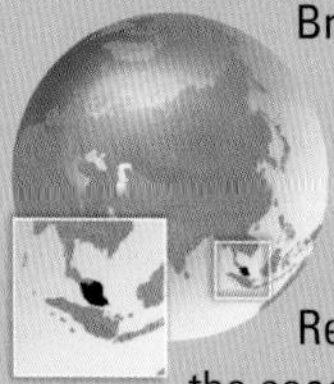

In reorganizing the Malay Peninsula after 1945, the British gave dominance to the largest ethnic group, the Malays. Resentment by the second-largest group, the Chinese, developed into attacks on settlements and plantations by communist guerrillas. A state of emergency was declared, at the height of which, in 1951, 8,000 Chinese guerrillas were supported by 60,000 "Min Yuen," members of the People's Movement. The British relocated Chinese villagers, removing the insurgents' food supply. Forced deep into the jungle, the insurgents appeared safe – until SAS operations began.

In 1950, veteran of World War II (1939–45) and former commander of the SAS Brigade Lieutenant-Colonel Mike Calvert (1913–98) spent a period of six months liaising with the police and army in Malaya and making lone reconnaissance marches. Calvert recommended forming the Malayan Scouts, who would live and move deep in the jungle like the terrorists, and who would win over the indigenous peoples who lived there. The Scouts should work in three- and four-man teams, Calvert said, because the fewer men there were in a team, the more frightened they would be, and therefore the more cautious and silent they would be: They would be more likely to see the enemy before the enemy could see them.

THE MALAYAN SCOUTS

Calvert was given the go-ahead to create the Malayan Scouts in 1950. The unit had an original strength of 100 men. Officers were selected by Calvert himself, and training focused on self-reliance, initiative, and winning over the local native peoples. There was little time for training, three weeks in some cases, before patrols were sent into the jungle.

Calvert devised the unit's operating procedures. A group of up to 14 men would be sent into the jungle to establish a defendable base. From this base small patrols of three or four men would be sent to gather intelligence, spring ambushes, and destroy enemy strongholds. In addition, the Malayan Scouts would wage a "hearts and minds" campaign to gain the trust and cooperation of the indigenous population, who could be useful in aiding the Scouts'

▼ **Owen submachine gun** (1941)
The SAS used the Australian-made Owen submachine gun because of its reliability and rugged construction. The straight, top-mounted magazine carried 33 rounds and was less likely to snag in vegetation. The gun's high rate of fire made it ideal for lead scouts.

Length	32 in. (80.6 cm.)
Weight	9.5 lb. (4.2 kg.)
Rate of fire	700 rpm.
Caliber	9-mm.

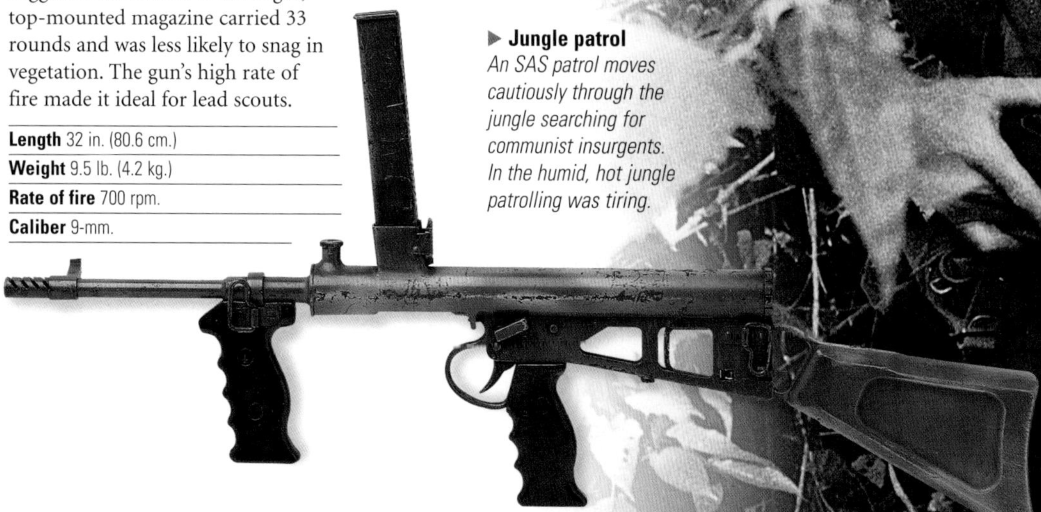

▶ **Jungle patrol**
An SAS patrol moves cautiously through the jungle searching for communist insurgents. In the humid, hot jungle patrolling was tiring.

Poster campaign
The British used posters to encourage the local population to inform on the communist guerrillas.

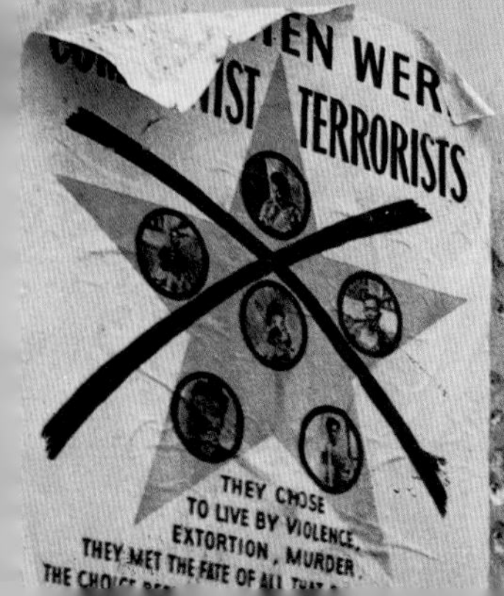

◀ Searching for the enemy
SAS soldiers check a village hut for communist guerrillas in the 1950s. The British moved many villagers into specially built settlements. This had the effect of depriving the guerrillas of food and support. They had to move farther into jungle areas, where they could be attacked by SAS patrols.

patrols. By 1952 Calvert had been sent home to Britain, but his ideas and the unit he had founded had been so successful that the Malayan Scouts were reorganized, becoming 22 SAS Regiment.

MALAYAN OPERATIONS

The SAS long-range patrols were arduous: Weeks of living in semi-darkness beneath the jungle canopy, filthy and soaking wet. As well as booby traps and enemy ambush, the soldiers endured hostile wildlife, from elephants, snakes, and tigers to leeches and mosquitoes. They avoided established tracks, which could be easily ambushed by the communist terrorists, and were taught to move very slowly, often through dense vegetation. Although Iban trackers had been brought in from Borneo, many SAS men developed equally effective tracking skills. For example, Sergeant Turnbull once tracked a group of terrorists for 14 weeks.

After many successful 13- and 14-week operations, in 1958, D Squadron parachuted into the swamps of Telok Anson, on the west coast of Malaya. After 10 days the SAS located the camp of Ah Hoi or "Baby Killer," a communist terrorist leader. The squadron split into two units and carefully surrounded the camp. They forced a total of eight guerrillas, Ah Hoi among them, to surrender.

This was the last major SAS operation of the war. It had made a significant contribution to the British victory, and had assured its own future.

Hearts and minds

The Malayan campaign set the tactics for future counter-insurgency operations by British and other special forces. Field Marshal Sir Gerald Templar had set in place a combined military, propaganda, welfare, and humanitarian aid programme. Its aim was to win the "hearts and minds" of the people on whom the communist guerrillas depended for food and shelter, by separating those people from the guerrillas and protecting them in encampments.

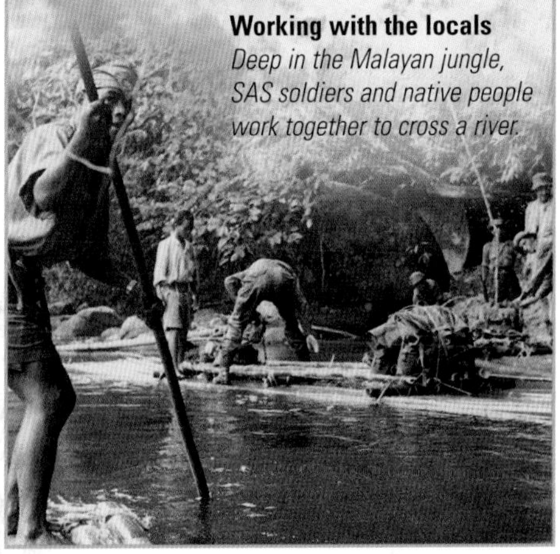

Working with the locals
Deep in the Malayan jungle, SAS soldiers and native people work together to cross a river.

The Malayan Scouts

The Malayan Scouts were formed by Mike Calvert in 1950. The unit's role was to live in the jungle for long periods, win the confidence of the local people, and force the guerrillas into the open, where the regular army could defeat them. Calvert sent small patrols into the jungle, which began to win over the trust of the aboriginal tribes by establishing medical clinics. The Scouts were redesignated 22 SAS Regiment in 1952.

Realistic jungle training
A Malayan Scout on exercise. He uses an air rifle to shoot at his "opponents," and wears a fencing mask to protect him from return fire.

1945–60: US special forces in Korea

At the start of the Korean War (1950–53), small-unit elites were almost non-existent in United Nations' armies. However, the need for highly trained soldiers to perform missions such as reconnaissance and amphibious demolitions soon became apparent. As a result, by late 1950 increasing numbers of special operations forces were being commissioned.

Flamethrower tank
An American flamethrower tank opens fire against communist North Korean and Chinese forces during the opening phase of the Korean War (1950–53).

World War II (1939–45) ended with Korea divided at the 38th parallel. North Korea was a Soviet communist satellite state under Kim Il-Sung, while the southern Republic of Korea (ROK) was run by a right-wing, pro-Western government with Syngman Rhee as president. United Nations (UN) efforts to reunify Korea had failed, and military aggression steadily increased between the two nations. On June 25, 1950, the forces of the North invaded the South and sent the ROK army into retreat. In response, the UN dispatched a US-led coalition force to stop the communist expansion. China backed North Korea from October 1950. The three-year war that followed was inconclusive. Both sides were drained financially, and Korea remained divided.

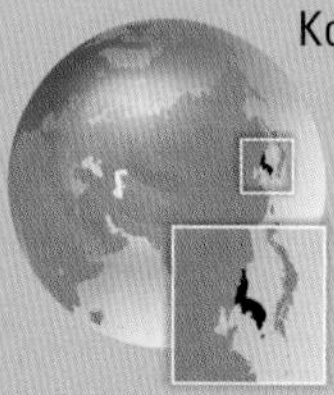

Two main factors drove the development of special forces units in the Korean War (1950–53). First, the Korean coastline stretches for over 1,000 miles (1,600 km), and coastal reconnaissance could only be conducted by specialized amphibious units. Second, partisans behind enemy lines required elite operatives to coordinate their efforts with United Nations (UN) actions.

AMPHIBIOUS OPERATIONS

US Navy Underwater Demolitions Teams (UDTs) were specialists in covert amphibious infiltration and removing underwater obstacles. Only 11 UDT personnel were active in 1950, but the number soon increased to 300. As well as blowing up coastal roads, tunnels, and bridges, they also performed a major hydrographical survey at Inchon – the site for the huge US amphibious landing in September 1950 – under the noses of enemy positions.

The UDTs were not the only US amphibious elites operating in Korea. On July 5, 1950, the GHQ 1st Raider Company was created. Its missions included sabotage, reconnaissance, and raids behind enemy lines. Its first action was on September 12, 1950, at Kunsan Bay. Raiders made an amphibious landing, intending to draw enemy attention away from the Inchon landing planned for September 15. A firefight resulted in the deaths of three Raiders, but the company still took part in the Inchon landings three days later, assisting an assault against an enemy airfield.

The North Korean People's Army

The North Korean People's Army began the Korean War with an army of 135,000 men. It was an efficient and combat-hardened military force of 10 infantry divisions and an armored brigade. Modern weapons were supplied by the Soviet Union. They included T34 tanks and 76-mm. self-propelled guns. More importantly, the North's army was well trained and commanded.

Expert soldiers
The officers of the North Korean People's Army received extensive training in how to fight modern war

▼ Heavy firepower
US Army Sherman tanks prepare to meet an attack by the North Korean Army in 1951. During the war special forces units assisted conventional forces in holding back communist forces.

PARTISAN AND CONVENTIONAL ELITES

Another important special forces unit was the 40-strong Special Mission Group (SMG) under the auspices of the CIA's Joint Advisory Commission, Korea (JACK). It was a mix of US troops and Korean partisan fighters. As well as coastal demolitions and sabotage, SMG also conducted prisoner snatches, assassinations, and guerrilla warfare, and could deploy by any means, from parachute to sub-aqua gear.

The US relied on its larger infantry, airborne, and marine elites to perform some specialized roles. US Marines handled major amphibious landings, such as that at Inchon. In the US Army, Ranger Infantry Companies (Airborne) were created specifically for the Korean War, passing recruits through a four-week cold-weather course at Camp Carson, Colorado. At the town of Munsan-ni, north of Seoul, in March 1951, Rangers made a parachute drop in an attempt to cut off retreating Korean forces. Heavily outnumbered, the Rangers nonetheless captured the town and fought off enemy attacks, despite 50 percent casualties.

Another airborne action was conducted by the 187th Airborne Regiment. On October 22, 1950, 1,470 paratroopers were dropped near Pyongyang, the North Korean capital. Their mission was to stop a freight train carrying hundreds of US prisoners, and take as many as possible back to US lines. The train failed to arrive due to bad weather. Yet such was the skill of the paratroopers that they wiped out the enemy's 239th Infantry Regiment.

As a result of their success in the Korean War, the size and capability of US special forces were expanded through the 1950s.

▶ **Inchon landings**
US Marines storm ashore at Inchon in September 1950. The 1st Marines Division's amphibious assault at Inchon was behind North Korean lines. Although very risky, the landing forced the North Koreans to retreat.

▲ **Browning Automatic Rifle** (1918)
This was used by special forces in Korea as a light machine gun. Its magazine held 20 rounds and it had an effective range of 1,800 ft. (550 m.). It could fire single shots or bursts.

Length 47 in. (120 cm.)
Weight 20 lb. (8.8 kg.)
Rate of fire 650 rpm.
Caliber 7.62-mm.

▲ **US Rangers**
US Rangers open fire behind enemy lines with a Bofors anti-aircraft gun.

UN forces

US forces were by far the largest contingent of the United Nations (UN) army in Korea, with 300,000 US servicemen in total. Twenty other countries contributed a total of 44,000 soldiers. The countries included Belgium, Colombia, Luxembourg, and Thailand, with British and Commonwealth countries accounting for 50 percent of the non-US forces. The smallest contributions came from Denmark, India, Italy, Norway, and Sweden, who provided medical personnel only.

Canadians
Canadian infantry during the Korean War (1950–53).

1945–60: Israeli special forces

First created in the 1920s to defend Jews in Palestine from Arab attacks, the forerunners of today's Israeli special forces were outnumbered by their enemies. However, throughout the 1940s and 1950s the Israelis raised a number of specialized military units to protect Israel's territorial integrity. The learning experience was often painful, but eventually Israel created elite units to fight larger Arab formations.

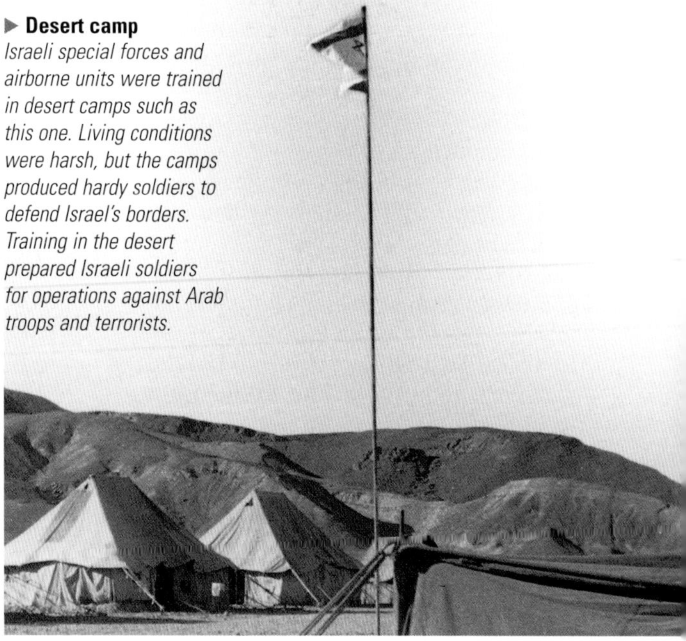

▶ **Desert camp**
Israeli special forces and airborne units were trained in desert camps such as this one. Living conditions were harsh, but the camps produced hardy soldiers to defend Israel's borders. Training in the desert prepared Israeli soldiers for operations against Arab troops and terrorists.

◀ **Early special forces**
An Israeli elite reconnaissance unit, photographed in the late 1940s. The soldiers of such Israeli units were highly trained and well-motivated.

Between 1920 and 1945, Palestine was under a British mandate. The citizens included Jews and Arabs and they frequently fought each other. The British mostly sided with the Arabs, and while the Arabs were allowed to carry weapons, the Jews were not. As a result, in the 1920s the Jewish population formed underground resistance movements to resist Arab terrorist attacks and eventually to force the British out of Palestine.

The largest and most powerful of those underground movements was the "Defense" (*Hagana* in Hebrew). In 1941, the *Hagana* formed the Smash Companies (PALMACH), which were early special forces groups. Among the PALMACH were the undercover Mistaravim teams. These special teams dressed as Arabs and were used to secretly move weapons and equipment. While the PALMACH handled land-based assignments, the *Hagana* also needed a maritime unit. So, in 1943, the *Hagana* formed the Sea Companies (*Plugot Hayam* – PALYAM – in Hebrew), which were underwater demolition and maritime activity units.

REORGANIZATION

In 1948, when the Israel Defense Force (IDF) was formed, all the resistance movements were joined together. The PALYAM became *Shayetet* 13. One of the *Hagana* outfits, the Golany unit, was turned into the IDF Golany Infantry Brigade.

When reassigned under the IDF command, the Golany Infantry Brigade formed the Special Reconnaissance Platoon. This platoon acted as a pathfinder for the infantry brigade.

Unlike the other reconnaissance platoons that existed in each of the Golany brigade's battalions, however, the Special Reconnaissance Platoon was also in charge of destroying key enemy strongholds, and missions such as demolition and intelligence gathering. Because the state of Israel was officially proclaimed in 1948, the Special Reconnaissance Platoon was the first official Israeli special forces unit.

OPERATIONS

In the early 1950s, Israel's Arab neighbors launched thousands of assaults against its borders, aimed mainly at civilians. The IDF retaliated, but the conventional infantry units were simply not equal to the task. So, in 1951, the IDF formed Unit 30 to carry out

PROFILE | **Ariel Sharon**

Dates b. 1928
Unit Parachute Corps
Rank General

A controversial soldier and, since 1973, politician, Ariel Sharon is one of the founding fathers of Israel's special forces tradition. In the 1950s he created a highly successful specialized commando force, Unit 101, and then the fledgling Parachute Corps. He commanded an armored division in the Arab–Israeli war of 1967. His independent-minded leadership brought him close to court martial and disgrace in the Yom Kippur War of 1973, when he was accused of disobeying orders. Nevertheless, he went on to become leader of Israel's Likud Party and was elected prime minister in 2001.

▶ **Israelis in the desert**
The members of this Israeli special forces unit of the early 1950s are resting following a retaliatory raid against an Arab guerrilla camp.

retaliation missions in small and well-trained teams. In August 1953, the IDF formed Unit 101, composed of between 20 and 25 men. It was integrated with the paratroopers after only five months. As in other successful special forces, constant training under simulated battle conditions produced troops who fought well in actual combat.

This was proved true in the 1956 Arab–Israeli War, when, on October 29, 1956, 395 Israeli paratroopers in 16 aircraft landed in the Mitla Pass in the Sinai Desert and held it in the face of heavy Arab attacks.

By 1960 Israel's special forces had been turned into a battle-winning force, capable of defending Israel's frontiers.

The Mitla Pass

The main road in the Sinai Desert runs east from the Suez Canal through the Mitla Pass, then splits to go north and south. Whoever controls the Mitla Pass controls road traffic through the Sinai. During the 1956 Arab–Israeli War, 395 Israeli paratroopers dropped from aircraft and landed in the pass. The Egyptians had troops entrenched in the pass, but the Israeli paratroopers attacked them during a night assault and defeated them. This helped to win the war for Israel.

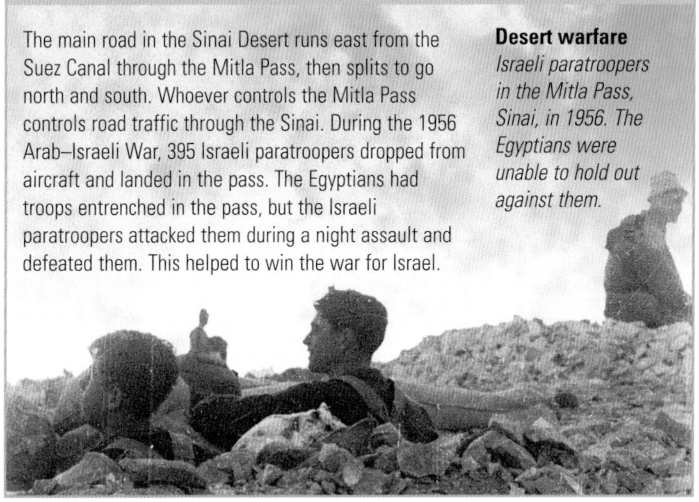

Desert warfare
Israeli paratroopers in the Mitla Pass, Sinai, in 1956. The Egyptians were unable to hold out against them.

▼ **Sten Gun** (1941)
Popular with Israeli soldiers during the 1940s and 1950s, the Sten had few working parts. This made it easy to strip down for cleaning. Its magazine held 32 rounds, and the gun had an effective range of 130 ft. (40 m.).

Length	30 in. (76.2 cm.)
Weight	6.6 lb. (3 kg.)
Rate of fire	550 rpm.
Caliber	9-mm.

▼ **M1A1 Carbine** (1942)
The M1A1 held 15 rounds and had a range of 886 ft. (270 m.). The folding buttstock made it suitable for use by Israeli paratroopers.

Length	35.6 in. (90.5 cm.)
Weight	5.5 lb. (2.5 kg.)
Rate of fire	650 rpm.
Caliber	0.3-in.

1945–60: Brushfire wars

The years after World War II (1939–45) saw numerous conflicts break out within the empires of the European nations. Fanned by communist and nationalist ideology, these "brushfire wars" – named for the way that wild fires can spring up and spread rapidly in dry scrub land – required new military tactics and strategies. Special forces units, created by the Europeans in World War II, were adapted to fight a new type of war: Counter-insurgency.

▲ **Revolutionary leader**
Mao Zedong (1893–1976) was a Chinese communist theorist, soldier, and statesman whose ideas on revolution inspired the developing world.

The main international battlegrounds during the 1950s and 1960s were Southeast Asia and Africa, as European powers such as Britain and France prepared to restore their colonial territories to the indigenous inhabitants. Local national liberation groups within the colonies often turned to violence to hasten or shape political independence. The British, for example, experienced significant trouble in Cyprus, Oman, and Aden (now Yemen). Between 1952 and 1960, British troops in Kenya fought a campaign against guerrilla insurgents. Some 600 British Army and police personnel were killed, in contrast to 11,500 rebels dead and 2,500 captured.

The conflict in French Algeria was bloodier still. The war of independence (1954–62) left 20,000 French and approximately one million Algerian Muslims dead, the highest casualties of any independence war of the 20th century. During the 1950s France was also battling to retain its Indochina colony in Southeast Asia.

SOUTHEAST ASIA

As in Africa, Southeast Asia's insurgents were principally motivated by communism (such as the ideology of Mao Zedong (1893–1976), the Chinese communist leader) or nationalism. The Dutch were ejected from the Dutch East Indies by the Indonesian People's Army by

Colonial units

Algerian paratroopers
A unit of locally raised paratroopers marches through the streets of Algiers in the late 1950s.

Both the British and the French made extensive use of local expertise and soldiers during their colonial conflicts. In Malaya, British special forces used the hunting and tracking skills of the aboriginal Senoi Pra'ak people, who killed hundreds of insurgents using blowpipes. In Algeria in the 1950s, the French recruited many local people to quell the rebellion instigated by the FLN. By 1960, for example, of the 500,000 troops of the French Army in Algeria, 170,000 were Muslim Algerians.

1949. The French were defeated in Indochina by the guerrillas of Ho Chi Minh (1890–1969) after nine years of war (1946–54). The conflict evolved into another 10 years of war (1965–75) between South Vietnam (with direct US aid) and communist North Vietnam. It became apparent to Western governments that special units using new tactics, specifically counter-insurgency skills, were needed to fight these native insurgents.

COUNTER-INSURGENCY

Counter-insurgency warfare demanded unconventional skills. Covert intelligence, long-range surveillance, ambush, and civilian liaison missions (including first aid clinics) were more effective tools against insurgents than standard infantry tactics. Specialized units were created and trained to fulfill these roles.

In Malaya, for example, the British reactivated the Special Air Service (SAS) of World War II. Four-man patrols infiltrated deep into enemy territory, mapping enemy activity, ambushing terrorist patrols, and capturing enemy leaders. The SAS also operated in a "hearts and minds" role. This involved liaising with local people to build up anti-communist resistance at a local level. They performed a similar role in Borneo from 1963, and were joined by SAS troops from Australia and New Zealand. In the Aden conflict (1964–67) the SAS also showed how useful they were as forward observers for artillery and airstrikes, a primary role of modern special forces.

Holland, France, and Portugal relied heavily on elite units of paratroopers for their counter-insurgency. In the Dutch East Indies, the Dutch military used three special forces companies to track, ambush, and kill key enemy leaders. In Indochina and Algeria, French paratroopers pioneered the tactics of rapid airborne assault. French Foreign Legion troops in Algeria attacked the bases of Algerian rebels by means of large-scale parachute landings, and French developments in helicopter assaults laid the foundations for future airborne tactics.

The colonial wars of independence that followed World War II clarified the role of modern special forces, and confirmed that small elite units could achieve results out of all proportion to their size.

Foreign Legion badge

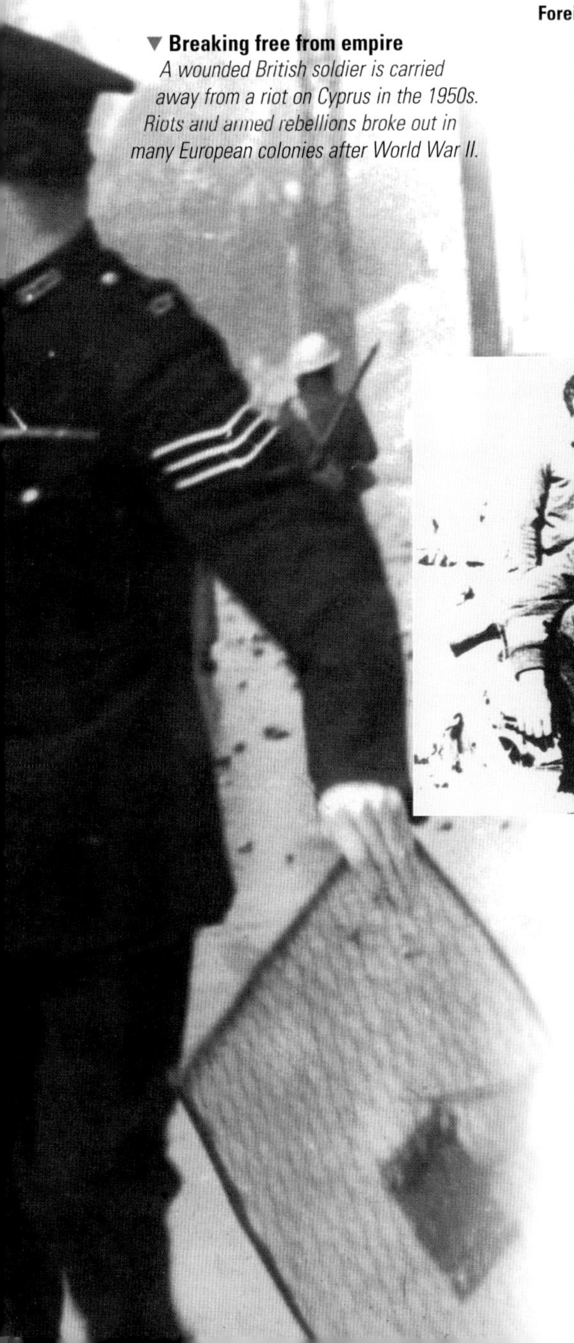

▼ Breaking free from empire
A wounded British soldier is carried away from a riot on Cyprus in the 1950s. Riots and armed rebellions broke out in many European colonies after World War II.

The FLN

Algerian insurgents
FLN recruits at a guerrilla camp in the south of Algeria. The FLN was ruthless, but was inferior to the French troops it fought against.

The *Front de Libération Nationale* (National Liberation Front or FLN) was the nationalist guerrilla force in Algeria between 1954 and 1962. Although inspired by Ho Chin Minh's communist insurgency, the FLN was firmly nationalist and Islamic in outlook. The excesses of French rule meant that the FLN was always able to enlist new members until Algeria achieved independence in 1962.

▲ Mountain troops
British SAS troops in northern Oman in 1959. SAS patrols were lightly armed to allow them to travel fast.

▶ Hostile terrain
This is the Jebel Akhdar in Oman. SAS soldiers climbed it to defeat Omani separatists in 1959.

MODERN SPECIAL FORCES

This section gives in-depth accounts of the role, training, and actions of the greatest special forces units from around the world. The elites featured include the US Army Rangers, Delta Force, the Green Berets, the US Marine Corps, and the US Navy SEALs. European special forces include the British SAS and Parachute Regiment, the French Foreign Legion 2nd REP, the German GSG-9, and the Russian *Spetsnaz*. In addition, there are detailed descriptions of landmark operations carried out by these units, including the US Marine battle at Hue (1968), the British SAS storming of the Iranian Embassy (1980), and the US Army Rangers in Iraq (2003).

British SAS

The soldiers of the British Special Air Service (SAS) are versatile troops who possess a variety of skills, including operating behind enemy lines, intelligence gathering, counter-terrorism, and hostage-rescue. With an illustrious history and the best troops in the British Army, the SAS is one of the foremost elite units in the world, especially in terms of the number of roles it fulfills.

The British Special Air Service (SAS) has gained a reputation that is second to none in the world of professional soldiering. High-profile operations, such as the rescue of hostages from the Iranian Embassy in London in 1980 (see pp50–51), have propelled the SAS into the public's imagination. But hostage-rescue is only one role of the British SAS.

First formed in 1941, during World War II (1939–45), the SAS comprised soldiers trained to operate in small, self-contained teams behind enemy lines. Once behind the lines, units would carry out sabotage and gather intelligence. During the 1950s and 1960s, the SAS also developed counter-insurgency skills (see box on p47). In addition, during the British government's fight against the terrorists of the Irish Republican Army (IRA) in Northern Ireland, the SAS conducted anti-terrorist operations against the IRA. SAS counter-terrorist training and tactics were further refined in the 1970s, when hostage-rescue became part of the SAS mission.

Winged dagger

Since the siege of the Iranian embassy in London (1980) was ended by a dramatic SAS assault, the regiment has acquired a legendary status. Its now famous insignia – a dagger on a pair of wings – has entered the popular imagination, as has the motto that is displayed beneath the dagger, "Who Dares Wins," summing up the SAS determination to rise to any challenge. The colors of the wings, Oxford and Cambridge blue, are credited to the respective university rowing teams of "Jock" Lewes and Lieutenant Langton, two of the original members of the SAS in World War II (1939–45).

Winged dagger belt-buckle
The SAS badge was designed in North Africa in 1941, during desert operations in World War II.

ORGANIZATION

The so-called Sabre fighting squadrons – A, B, D, and G – form the core of the SAS Regiment. Each Sabre squadron is divided into four 16-man troops: Mountain Troop, Boat Troop, Mobility Troop, and Air Troop. Within each troop the basic operational unit is a four-man patrol, typically made up of specialists in medicine, signals, demolitions, and languages.

The SAS selection process is rigorous (see pp48–49), and even after membership of the unit is achieved, the ongoing training program is just as intense. For example, close-quarter battle (CQB) and hostage-rescue are practiced at the SAS base's

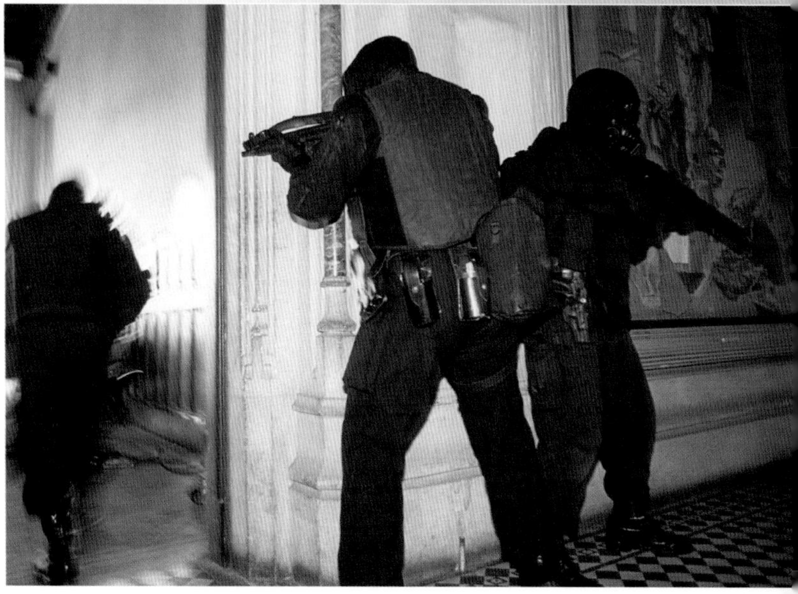

▶ **Hostage rescue**
Rescuing hostages is an important counter-terrorist skill. The SAS trains in specially designed buildings, as here, learning how to move fast and identify friend from foe in confined spaces.

▼ Air Troop soldier
Each SAS Sabre Squadron has a 16-man Air Troop. Members of the troop are trained in all aspects of parachuting. This SAS soldier is making a high altitude, low opening (HALO) descent.

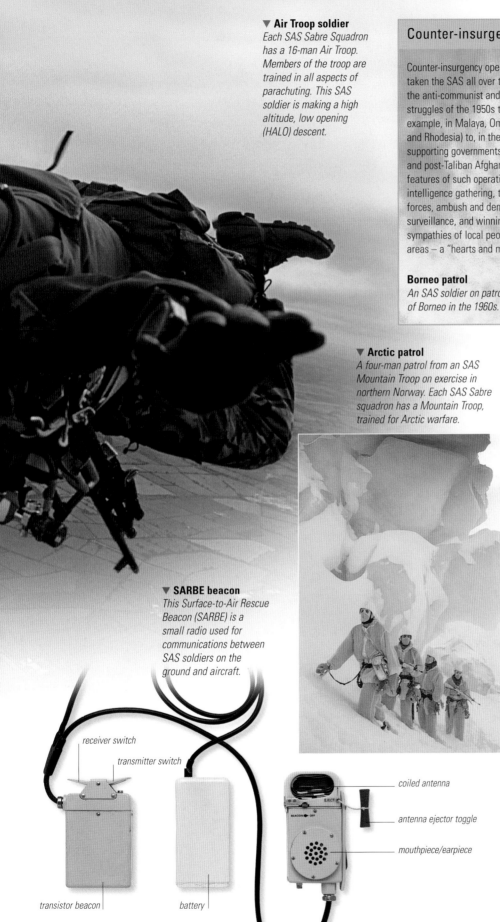

Counter-insurgency

Counter-insurgency operations have taken the SAS all over the world, from the anti-communist and anti-guerrilla struggles of the 1950s to the 1970s (for example, in Malaya, Oman, Borneo, and Rhodesia) to, in the 21st century, supporting governments in Sierra Leone and post-Taliban Afghanistan. Essential features of such operations include intelligence gathering, training local forces, ambush and demolitions, surveillance, and winning over the sympathies of local people in disputed areas – a "hearts and minds" policy.

Borneo patrol
An SAS soldier on patrol in the jungle of Borneo in the 1960s.

▼ Arctic patrol
A four-man patrol from an SAS Mountain Troop on exercise in northern Norway. Each SAS Sabre squadron has a Mountain Troop, trained for Arctic warfare.

"Killing House," an urban-conflict environment in which room clearances can be simulated using live rounds.

CONTINUOUS TRAINING

Admission to the SAS means more specialized training. In Air Troop, for example, the hazardous high altitude, low opening (HALO) form of parachuting must be mastered. Boat Troops are experts in diving, amphibious landing techniques, and ship assaults. In this way the SAS is equipped to meet every kind of challenge, from conventional warfare to combating crime.

▼ Small boats
SAS Boat Troops specialize in the operation of small boats, such as this Rigid Raider speeding through the Brunei jungle.

▼ SARBE beacon
This Surface-to-Air Rescue Beacon (SARBE) is a small radio used for communications between SAS soldiers on the ground and aircraft.

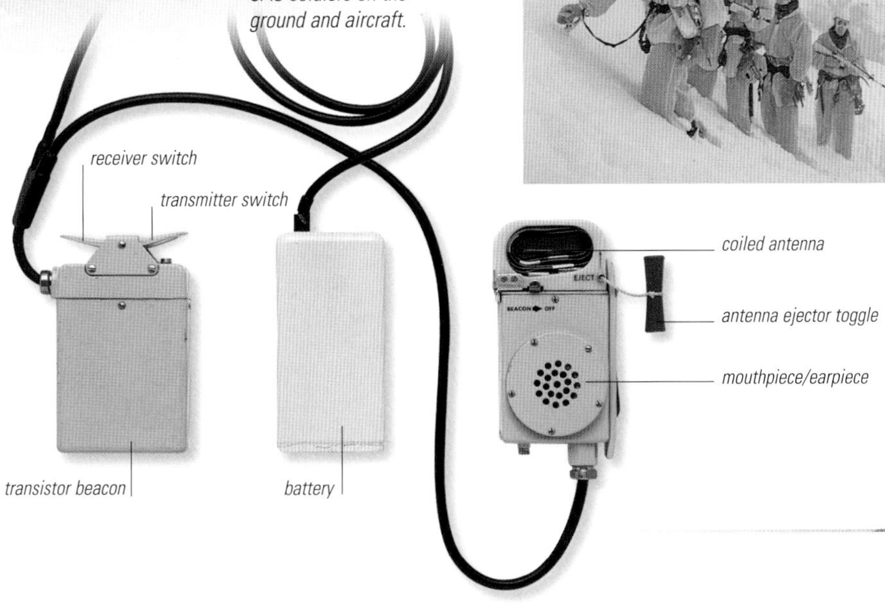

British SAS: Selection

The selection and training regime for the British Special Air Service (SAS) is one of the most grueling in the world. Only those who are mentally and physically tough enough succeed. Selection tests take place in very inhospitable environments, including mountains and jungles. Those who pass will have earned the right to join one of the world's most famous special forces units.

▶ Fully equipped
This recruit carries a 55 lb. (25 kg.) bergen (backpack) plus weapon, safety equipment, food, and water.

The British SAS draws potential recruits mainly from the Parachute and other infantry regiments, although a large number of tank operators, engineers, and artillerymen also attempt to pass the selection process. The process – from beginning to final acceptance into the SAS – takes almost two years. Applicants prepare by building up their physical fitness, but it is often mental stamina and sheer willpower that will make the difference between success and failure.

SELECTION AND CONTINUATION

After three days of introductory lectures and physical training, the selection process itself begins at SAS Headquarters at RAF Credenhill, near Hereford, England. Three weeks of road runs and cross-country marches force many recruits to drop out or be returned to their unit. Test Week concludes Phase One. It consists of several 19–25-mile (30–40-km.) forced marches and the notorious "Fan Dance", an arduous 37.5-mile (60-km.) march. Of every 125 recruits who begin Selection, only 10 pass.

▼ Selection
Recruits like this one barely get a chance to rest during Selection. Minimal sleep and long days drain energy and undermine morale.

Test Week

The "Long Drag" is the final hurdle at the end of Selection's Test Week. It is an arduous 40-mile (60-km.) solo march across the toughest terrain in the Brecon Beacons in Wales. Each recruit carries over 55 lb. (25 kg.) in his bergen (backpack) Conducted over Pen-y-fan, the highest point in the Brecon Beacons, the Long Drag encompasses some of the highest peaks in the area, and must be completed in 20 hours. It is unforgiving, with the area's frequent and harsh weather changes sapping recruits' strength and willpower. Men have died on the challenge, but it remains an SAS benchmark.

Solo run
The Fan Dance is deliberately designed as a solo exercise, because without support from team members, a recruit must rely on his own sheer willpower and strength of character to get him through.

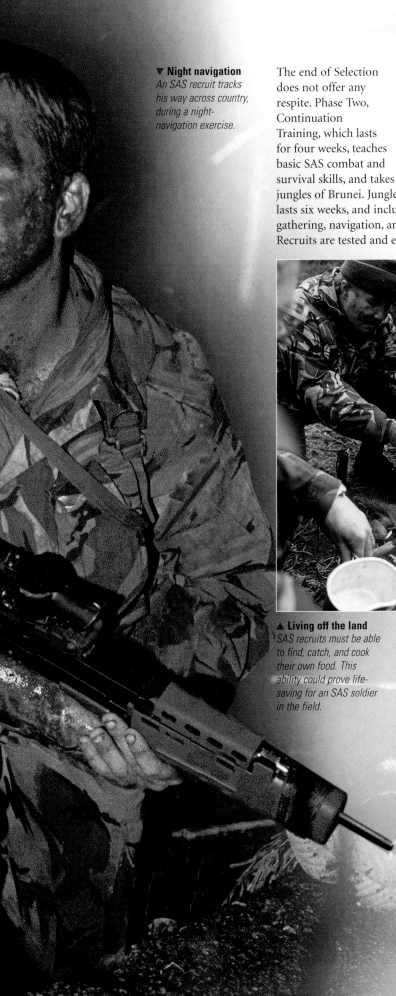

▼ **Night navigation**
An SAS recruit tracks his way across country, during a night-navigation exercise.

The end of Selection does not offer any respite. Phase Two, Continuation Training, which lasts for four weeks, teaches basic SAS combat and survival skills, and takes recruits to the harsh jungles of Brunei. Jungle-survival training lasts six weeks, and includes first-aid, food gathering, navigation, and military tactics. Recruits are tested and evaluated throughout.

▶ **Survival skills**
Recruits are trained in making shelters and protecting themselves from the elements, using the minimum of materials.

▲ **Living off the land**
SAS recruits must be able to find, catch, and cook their own food. This ability could prove life-saving for an SAS soldier in the field.

Navigation exercises – through dense vegetation in searing heat – sap recruits' energy, and many candidates fail. A promising candidate who gets injured might be invited to try again another time.

Candidates also receive intensive instruction in basic combat tactics, field medicine, signaling, and basic demolition. Failure to meet exacting standards results in recruits being returned to their unit. Combat survival ends in an escape-and-evasion exercise and a resistance-to-interrogation test.

Those recruits remaining do parachute training. Most pass, and can claim the coveted beige beret. The selection ordeal over, they can finally join the SAS on a year's probation.

First aid training

One of the most important skills learned by SAS recruits is field medicine. Operating deep behind enemy lines, with little prospect of rescue, places an enormous emphasis on the ability to treat wounded team members effectively. In a four-man team, one man will be a highly qualified field medic. He learns not only how to stabilize a wide range of injuries, but also how to perform emergency surgery and administer life-saving drugs. To gain first-hand experience of the types of injuries suffered in battle – typically burns and gunshot wounds – SAS members spend time in hospital Emergency Rooms. Learning from medical professionals who deal with trauma injuries teaches the SAS medics the crucial skills needed to save lives.

Emergency treatment
The skill of a team medic, like this one, can save a man's life, even in the most dire circumstances.

Terrorist siege
One of the Iranian terrorists stares out from the embassy building during the siege. He and his comrades were members of the Democratic Revolutionary Front for the Liberation of Arabistan.

British SAS: Iranian Embassy siege, 1980

In 1980, the British public knew little of the Special Air Service (SAS). However, television footage of violent explosions and black-hooded figures rappelling down the façade of the Iranian Embassy in London changed that. This was a very new type of response to terrorism.

BACKGROUND

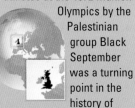

The massacre of 11 Israeli athletes at the 1972 Munich Olympics by the Palestinian group Black September was a turning point in the history of Western counter-terrorism (see German GSG-9 p116). This act prompted European nations to substantially upgrade their counter-terrorist/hostage-rescue capabilities. The Munich massacre emphasized that local police forces, no matter how well trained, did not possess the expertise or experience to deal with a dedicated terrorist attack. In Britain, this realization resulted in the refinement of Special Air Service (SAS) counter-terrorist training and tactics. By 1980 the SAS was prepared to meet any terrorist threat, and the success of Operation Nimrod in that year – the ending of the siege at the Iranian Embassy in London – sent a clear message of deterrence to all international terrorists.

On April 30, 1980, six armed terrorists from the Iraqi-backed Democratic Revolutionary Front for the Liberation of Arabistan took over the Iranian Embassy in London's Princes Gate. The lives of 26 hostages were at stake, including a Metropolitan police officer, PC Trevor Lock. From the start, the terrorists claimed they had wired the embassy with high explosives, which would kill everybody as well as destroy the building. Their demands included the release of 91 Arab prisoners who were being held in Iran. The terrorists were Iranian themselves, from the oil-rich southern region of Khuzestan, but were opponents of the religious Ayatollah Khomeni regime that governed Iran. The terrorists' demands were flatly refused by the Iranians.

▲ **Forced entry**
At the rear of the embassy, an SAS team roped down to the second-story balcony and blew out the windows to gain entry.

By early afternoon, the so-called Special Projects Team (members of B Squadron, 22 SAS, including troop commander Dick Arthur, see below) was on its way to London. They drove to a barracks in Regents Park, while two other SAS men went to the Iranian Embassy to begin planning a hostage-rescue.

ASSAULT PLAN

As police negotiators talked to the terrorist leader, Oan, the SAS prepared an assault plan using a model of the building. The electricity supply to the embassy was cut off, and all but one permanently open phone line. On day five of the siege (May 5) at 1:45 pm. there were shots from inside the embassy, and at 7:00 p.m. the body of

PROFILE — Dick Arthur

Dates 1951–96
Unit 22 SAS
Rank Captain

Captain Dick Arthur was a troop commander in B Squadron, and on Operation Nimrod he was in one of the rooftop rappel teams. Originally an officer in the Royal Marines, Arthur was decorated by the Sultan of Oman during the Dhofar War in the 1970s (Dhofar is a province of Oman). He then joined the Parachute Regiment in order to enter the SAS. After Operation Nimrod, he attended the Army's Staff College at Camberley, Surrey, worked on Special Forces deployments in the Ministry of Defence, and on SAS operations in various parts of the world. Rising to the rank of colonel, his life and career were cut short by cancer.

▶ **SAS assault**
Once the SAS team had entered the building, flames began to emerge from the windows, and a hostage made his way to safety across the balcony.

the Iranian press attaché was pushed out of the front door, with the threat that one hostage would be killed every 30 minutes thereafter until the terrorists' demands were met in full. For the assault teams, the waiting was finally over.

THE ASSAULT

At 7:23 p.m. eight SAS men rappelled down from the roof to the second-story balcony at the rear of the building. Frame charges were quickly fitted to the second-story front windows and blown. The team threw in stun grenades and CS gas canisters, and then went inside. The SAS soldiers on the balcony at the rear were unable to detonate their frame charge because one man had become entangled in his rope. They were forced to use sledgehammers to gain entry. Stun grenades were thrown into the building, and then the SAS team went in, hunting for the terrorists before they could begin to kill the hostages.

The terrorist leader, Oan, was killed on the second-story landing as the SAS soldiers made their way to the third-floor telex room where the hostages were being held. The three terrorists guarding them killed one of their captives and wounded two others, before all the gunmen were shot by the SAS. Two terrorists died immediately and another was wounded. Meanwhile, a terrorist was killed in the hallway near the front door, and another had been killed in an office in the back of the building. The one remaining terrorist was quickly captured. During the assault one hostage was killed and two were wounded, but the rest were unharmed.

Operation Nimrod was regarded as a success and became a textbook assault that has been studied ever since by special forces teams across the world.

▲ **Frame charges**
The SAS hostage-rescue team entered the embassy by detonating explosive charges set around the window frames.

Roof assaults

Two pairs of black-clad SAS troopers rappelled from the embassy roof, and a third pair from the front balcony of the building next door (No. 15 Princes Gate), ready to blow out the windows with high-explosive frame charges. But then, one SAS man became caught up when his rope twisted, highlighting the dangers inherent in assaults that rely on such rappelling techniques.

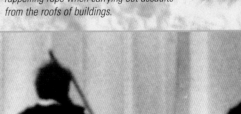

Rappelling equipment
SAS soldiers use strengthened synthetic rappelling rope when carrying out assaults from the roofs of buildings.

Patron of terror
Osama bin Laden (b. 1957), whose al Qaeda terror network was behind the attacks on the United States on September 11, 2001, and other terrorist acts.

BACKGROUND

On September 11, 2001, four US airliners were hijacked and used as flying bombs, destroying New York's World Trade Center, and severely damaging the headquarters of US military planning, the Pentagon. One airliner also crashed near Pittsburgh, Pennsylvania, pushing the total death toll to nearly 3,000. In response, President George W. Bush (b. 1946) ordered US military and security forces into a general "war on terror." The evidence suggested that the attacks were linked to Osama bin Laden's al Qaeda terrorist network, based in Afghanistan, and protected by that country's ruling Taliban regime. By early October 2001, US and British special forces were already working with the Afghan Northern Alliance fighters against the Taliban and al Qaeda. Despite the quick collapse of the regime, fighting continued in the Afghan mountains into 2002.

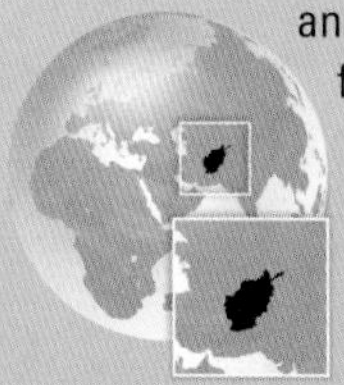

British SAS: Afghanistan, 2002

British special forces have been at the forefront of the current "war on terror." Within three weeks of the attacks of September 11, 2001, elements of the Special Air Service (SAS) had deployed to Afghanistan. Their mission was to strike at the al Qaeda terrorist cells operating from bases in the country and help remove Afghanistan's ruling Taliban regime, a major supporter of al Qaeda's campaign against the West.

It was a natural move to deploy the British Special Air Service (SAS) to Afghanistan after the September 11, 2001, attacks. During the Soviet occupation of the country (1979–89), SAS units had infiltrated to assist the Mujahedeen ("holy warriors") in their insurgency war against Soviet and Afghan communist forces. During this time, the SAS had built up a deep understanding of the Afghan terrain and people. They also possessed skills relevant to Afghan operations: The Mountain Troops within the SAS Sabre Squadrons had the advanced mountaineering ability to cope with Afghanistan's terrain, and many soldiers had acquired some knowledge of the local Pashto and Dari languages.

DEPLOYMENT AND FIRST ACTIONS

SAS units were operating inside the country less than three weeks after the attacks on September 11. The first clash between Taliban forces and SAS units took place in late September in the hills surrounding the Afghan capital, Kabul. This was a probing reconnaissance mission to test out Taliban responses. SAS troops inflicted casualties and then withdrew.

The SAS units in Afghan territory cooperated closely with US special forces. The primary objective was to launch or coordinate strikes against al Qaeda training camps and military bases, and also to hunt for al Qaeda's elusive leader, Osama bin Laden. Six major training camps were identified. Using Laser Target Designators, the SAS soldiers guided air-launched bombs directly into the enemy camps, which they obliterated. When airstrikes were not possible, soldiers made rapid airborne assaults using helicopters.

As part of the SAS's brief to assist the Afghan Northern Alliance troops in their war against the Taliban, they arranged airstrikes against Taliban positions, trained Northern Alliance soldiers in the use of advanced weaponry, and sometimes assisted Alliance soldiers in battle.

MAJOR ENGAGEMENTS

During November 25 to 27, in an isolated 19th-century fortress north of Mazar i Sharif, 600

▼ **Friendly invaders**
As part of the "hearts and minds" campaign, thousands of leaflets were dropped to assure ordinary Afghans that troops came in peace.

◀ **Night-time entry**
SAS soldiers arrive in Afghanistan. Their role was to help the Northern Alliance advance south and capture Kabul from the Taliban.

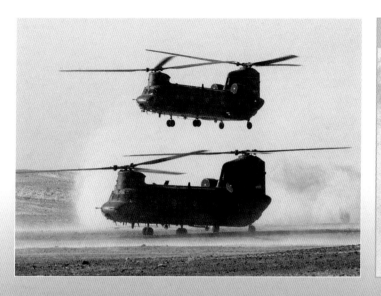

The Taliban

The Taliban (meaning "Students") were the ruling force in Afghanistan from 1996 to 2001. Their leadership was economically and socially disastrous for the war-ravaged nation. The regime's extreme fundamentalist form of Sunni Islam imposed on the country the most oppressive religious laws in the Islamic world. The Taliban attracted Western wrath after September 11, 2001, because of their protection of Osama bin Laden (leader of the al Qaeda terrorist network) since his expulsion from the Sudan in 1996.

Fundamentalist fighters
Taliban soldiers being driven to the front in December 2001 to fight the Northern Alliance.

▲ CH-47 Chinooks
Two CH-47 Chinook helicopters land in northern Afghanistan, carrying US and British special forces.

Taliban prisoners held there rioted after killing an American interrogator. They raided an armory full of Russian-made assault rifles and rocket launchers, and a fierce battle followed. SAS units and US special forces guided massive airstrikes onto the prisoners' positions, but some bombs were misguided, injuring SAS soldiers and killing a number of Afghan allies. The SAS became involved in heavy firefights with the prisoners, who were killed or wounded until the last 50 surrendered.

The largest SAS action, however, occurred during Operation Anaconda (March 2002). SAS units aided the massive push by US forces to clear Taliban and al Qaeda strongholds in the Shah-i-Kot mountains of eastern Afghanistan.

The war in Afghanistan ended in mid-2002 with the toppling of the Taliban regime. Undoubtedly, the British SAS did much to secure victory.

▼ The mission over
British troops, including SAS soldiers, board a C-130 Hercules transporter following the end of hostilities in Afghanistan in 2002.

US Army Green Berets

The United States Army's Green Berets (so-called because of their distinctive caps) form the largest special forces organization in the world. They proved themselves with successful and largely secret missions during the Vietnam War (1965–75), often crossing national borders in pursuit of the enemy. With more than 8,000 troops and their own aircraft, plus a large civilian affairs' force ready to administer occupied territory, the Green Berets can operate as an independent unit.

▲ **C-130 Hercules transport aircraft**
The workhorse of the Green Berets. The nose arms are for picking up soldiers from the ground. A helium balloon is attached to a soldier with a rope, which is scooped up by the nose arms while the aircraft is in flight.

Green Berets' cap badge

The Green Berets are ready for all types of unconventional and clandestine warfare, anywhere in the world. Known as United States Army Special Operations Command (USASOC), the Green Berets trace their beginnings to October 1961. In the early years of the Green Berets, regular Army commanders were suspicious of the elite nature of the unit. However, President John F. Kennedy (1917–63) saw the need for such a force, and his support led to its expansion.

The role of the Green Berets is largely intelligence gathering and raiding behind enemy lines. They are also concerned with training insurgent forces within enemy territory, as well as with counter-terrorist and unconventional warfare missions. Their size and the breadth of their skills gives the President a wide range of options when a situation requires a military response.

▲ **Learning to teach**
Green Beret troops are trained to teach local inhabitants the basics of warfare.

DELIVERY METHODS

Green Berets are able to get into and out of an area of operations by sea, land, or air. By sea, they use small boats and canoes; they can also go ashore by swimming, or by using special underwater breathing equipment that does not produce tell-tale bubbles. On land, the unit uses all types of transport, from motorcycles and quad bikes to four-wheel-drive all-terrain vehicles. For deployment by air, each soldier is a fully trained parachutist, and many are also skilled in the use of steerable parachutes, ideal for missions that require precision landings.

The A-Team

The Green Berets' basic unit is the 12-man "A-Team," which can operate on its own or in conjunction with others. Each man is multilingual, and trained as an expert in more than one special forces skill. The team can carry out its own intelligence-gathering operations, as well as carry out demolition missions, operate sophisticated communications equipment, repair its own weapons, and administer medical treatment.

The specialists
Each member of a Green Beret A-Team specializes in at least two roles.

▶ **Physical fitness**
Long marches carrying heavy equipment are part of Green Beret training and operations. Very high levels of strength, fitness, and endurance are required.

ORGANIZATION AND TRAINING

There are seven Green Beret groups, each around 1,200 strong, based at Fort Bragg in North Carolina. In addition, the 75th Ranger Regiment can be called upon to provide a reinforcing strike force. The Green Berets also have three Psychological Operations groups ("Psyop units"), which employ a variety of techniques, including television and radio broadcasts, to influence the emotions, morale, and behavior of enemy troops and civilian populations.

Alongside the military force, the USASOC's Civil Affairs battalion is on standby to handle the administration of occupied territories, deal with refugees and humanitarian aid, and liaise with other governments.

Training for the Green Berets includes a grueling 23-day Assessment and Selection course that tests each soldier's fitness, psychological stability, determination, and leadership skills – all under extremely punishing conditions. The course includes the US forces' solo navigation exercise, which has to be completed while carrying a heavy load and rifle. At 11 miles (18 km.) it is the forces' longest solo land navigation course.

One aspect of training is the emphasis placed on language skills. Being able to communicate with local people in an area of operations is vital. Around 2,000 officers and soldiers from all branches of the US Army start Green Beret training each year, but only half qualify.

▶ Local forces
In a war, each Green Beret soldier can become the equivalent of a general. By training local people, he can create a pro-American army.

Instructors

Weapons training
A US Green Beret adviser teaches a newly recruited Vietnamese man basic weapons skills during the Vietnam War (1965–75).

One of the Green Berets' primary roles during a war is to organize and train, behind enemy lines, fighting forces made up of local people. Their work with various mountain peoples during the Vietnam War was particularly effective. Winning over skeptical local inhabitants and helping them to achieve combat success against their oppressors requires good language skills and organizational abilities.

▲ Fighting Saddam Hussein
A Green Beret in action in Iraq in March 2003. The Green Berets were heavily involved in the war against the dictator Saddam Hussein and his regime.

US Army Green Berets: Nam Dong, 1964

The battle of Nam Dong (1964) is one of the most famous actions of the entire period of American involvement in Vietnam. Against massive odds, 12 United States Green Berets and a group of South Vietnamese fighters held off 900 communist troops who subjected them to a ferocious onslaught for more than five hours. The courage shown at Nam Dong was an inspiration to US troops throughout Vietnam.

Local combatants
US special forces troops were used to train South Vietnamese fighters like these at Nam Dong.

BACKGROUND

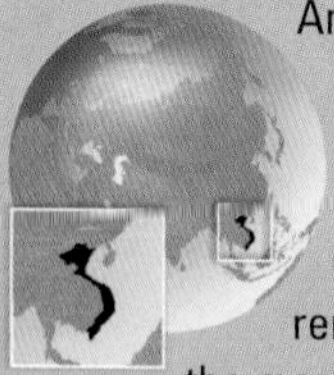

The actions of US special forces, before full-scale American involvement in the Vietnam War (1965–75), remain one of the most compelling aspects of the conflict. They were vital in the battle for hearts and minds in the dense jungles of South Vietnam, and in training local villagers to hunt down the South Vietnamese communist rebels, the Viet Cong (VC). US personnel were also involved in a controversial program of resettlement and counter-insurgency.

In military operations, special forces teams undertook reconnaissance missions, and larger forces went on search-and-destroy operations behind enemy lines, calling in airstrikes or artillery. By 1964 the entire 5th Special Forces Group was deployed, controlling all special operations. An example of growing US involvement in the conflict came at Nam Dong in July 1964, when a dozen US special forces soldiers led a group of local fighters into combat.

Camp Nam Dong was a small US military base near the Vietnamese border with Laos. Surrounded by barbed wire and booby-trapped pits, it was designed to impede the Viet Cong (VC) from entering Vietnam via the Ho Chi Minh trail, which ran along the border between Vietnam and Laos. In July 1964, 160 local fighters, led by a dozen American troops from Special Forces Detachment A-726, were all that stood against 900 soldiers of the VC and North Vietnamese Army (NVA).

THE BATTLE OF NAM DONG

Leading up to the night of July 5–6, 1964, the troops of Team A-726 sensed trouble brewing close by the Nam Dong camp. Captain Roger Donlon, the commanding officer, told his men to prepare for an attack from the VC, despite the lack of concrete intelligence. Donlon's gut instincts were to prove correct.

Shortly after 2:00 a.m., the compound erupted in a huge explosion. NVA and VC troops opened up on the US outpost with mortars and machine guns, sending the 12 Green Berets and their South Vietnamese allies running for cover. A barrage of mortar fire pounded the base, and Donlon was hit twice by shell fragments. The first shell tossed him into the air, leaving him dazed. A second mortar exploded near him, seriously wounding him as shrapnel pierced his arm and stomach. Nonetheless, Donlon galvanized the efforts of the troops under his command as he rushed from position to position, indicating targets and boosting morale.

Through a combination of training, experience, determination, and sheer courage, Donlon and the soldiers under his command drove back wave after wave of enemy attacks. For five hours the communist forces attempted to breach the compound's perimeter. Under constant and accurate fire, several US soldiers and dozens of South Vietnamese troops were felled by mortar shells and machine-gun fire. Enemy

▼ **Wounded hero**
Captain Roger Donlon, the commanding officer of the US base at Nam Dong, surveys the devastation the morning after the battle.

PROFILE

Roger Donlon

Dates b. 1934
Unit Special Forces Group, Team A-726
Rank Captain

Captain Roger Donlon was one of the heroes of the conflict in Vietnam. He was commander Special Forces Team A-726, which was deployed to train Montagnards (people from Vietnam's Central Highlands) in warfare. During one night in July 1964, he inspired his men to fight off an assault on their camp at Nam Dong by 900 enemy soldiers. He sustained several injuries, but continued to direct his troops. For his courage and leadership he received the Congressional Medal of Honor, and later retired as a full colonel. He now works to foster US–Vietnamese reconciliation.

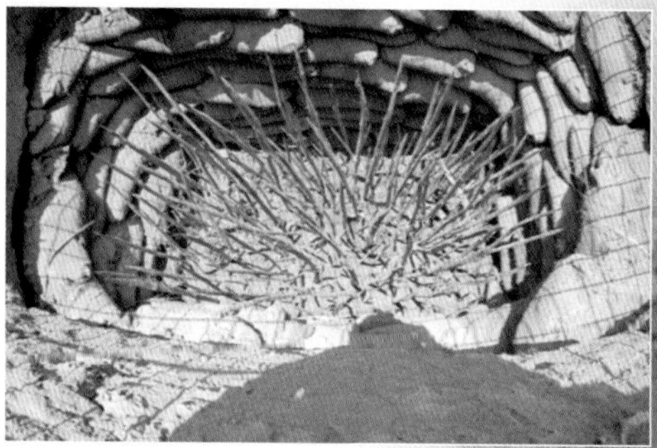

▲ **Booby traps**
Concealed pits of sharpened bamboo stakes were used to protect US camps like the one at Nam Dong. In Vietnam, booby traps were built by both sides.

munitions experts tried to blast their way in, but they were driven back by the defenders. Acts of heroism were frequent throughout the battle. Donlon, though hampered by his injuries, rushed to each casualty, tearing strips off his uniform to make bandages. Other members of his team did likewise, and saved the lives of many of their comrades.

As the night slowly turned to dawn, the communists' attacks became more sporadic, and it became increasingly clear that the weakened group of US and South Vietnamese soldiers had succeeded in holding off an enemy force five times its strength.

At 7:00 a.m. on July 6, US reinforcements arrived and the North Vietnamese force withdrew. The victory was not won without losses, however: 55 of the Nam Dong defenders had died, including three members of Team A-726, and 65 others were wounded.

Donlon and the US special forces team, along with their South Vietnamese allies, had shown great bravery in the face of overwhelming odds. This fact was later recognized by the US government, when Captain Donlon was awarded the Congressional Medal of Honor, and two others in his team were awarded the Distinguished Service Cross posthumously. Four more received the Silver Star, and five others the Bronze Star, decorated with a "V" for valor.

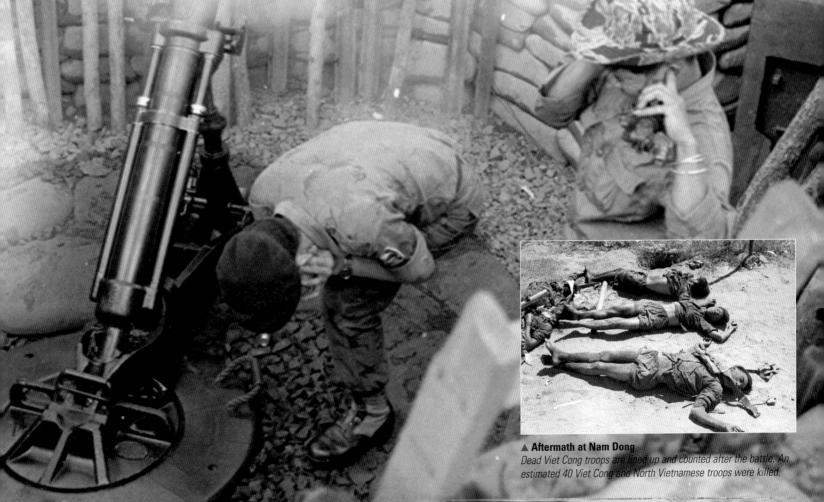

Montagnards

The word "Montagnards" originates from the French for "Mountain dwellers," and was the generic term used to describe an ancient people who lived in the central highlands of Vietnam. Long before the United States had become involved in the region, the Montagnards had struggled for independence from the Vietnamese, and were even courted as potential allies by the communist revolutionary leader Ho Chi Minh during the French-Indochina War (1946–54). However, when the Viet Cong began to threaten their way of life, the Montagnards took the side of the South Vietnamese and their American allies. In this alliance, the Montagnards were given military training by US special forces teams, receiving lessons in both guerrilla warfare and conventional combat tactics. The Montagnards, with their local knowledge, were regarded as ideal for flushing out Viet Cong fighters from the depths of the dense Vietnamese jungle.

Medical aid
One of the ways in which special forces won local support for US war aims in Vietnam was by offering medical help.

▼ Mortar fire
A Green Beret soldier covers his ears as he fires a mortar during the battle of Nam Dong. Each Green Beret camp had mortar and machine-gun positions to defend against Viet Cong attack.

▲ Aftermath at Nam Dong
Dead Viet Cong troops are lined up and counted after the battle. An estimated 40 Viet Cong and North Vietnamese troops were killed.

Combat assistance
In addition to training, Green Berets sometimes took part in actual combat against guerrilla forces.

BACKGROUND

Despite the United States' traditional influence in the Central American region, the Soviet Union became increasingly convinced that Central America was an ideal breeding ground for communist insurrection following Fidel Castro's 1959 revolution in Cuba. For the next 30 years, Soviet agents aided left-wing guerrilla movements in many nations across the region, including Nicaragua and Guatemala, El Salvador's neighbor. In response, the United States began sending special forces teams to the region, including the famous Green Berets, in order to train and educate the local armed forces in the tactics needed to defeat insurgents. El Salvador erupted into bloody civil war in 1979, and the left-wing *Farabundo Marti National Liberation Front* (FMLN) guerrillas gained strength over the next four years. Green Beret Mobile Training Teams were rushed to the country to train and assist the El Salvadoran Army to defeat this threat.

US Army Green Berets: El Salvador, 1981–85

In 1981 US President Reagan dispatched 55 US special forces military advisers to aid the El Salvadoran government in its fight against a leftist guerrilla movement, the FMLN. The Green Berets successfully set up a new training regime for the El Salvadoran Army and several counter-insurgency battalions.

The introduction of US military advisers into politically unstable countries had become a tool of foreign policy for successive American administrations leading up to the crisis in El Salvador during the 1970s and 1980s. The Green Berets had been providing military training to pro-US regimes ever since the Vietnam War (1965–75). With the Cold War still being waged with the USSR, the spread of left-wing revolutionary groups across Central America alarmed the US. On becoming President in 1981, Ronald Reagan (b. 1911) declared his intention to "roll back communism" in Central America, starting with El Salvador.

Shortly after taking office, President Reagan dispatched a Mobile Training Team comprising 55 Green Beret advisers to El Salvador. Their job was to teach the El Salvadoran Army better techniques for defeating a resilient band of Marxist-led guerrillas, known as the *Farabundo Marti National Liberation Front* (FMLN). The shadow of the Vietnam War, where the costly US involvement began with sending military advisers, still loomed over US foreign policy. Reagan thus ordered the Green Berets to avoid combat zones. Their responsibility was training only.

▼ **Military skills**
A US Green Beret military adviser teaches map-reading skills in El Salvador in the 1980s. Lessons in such skills were a key part of the training for the El Salvadoran counter-insurgency units.

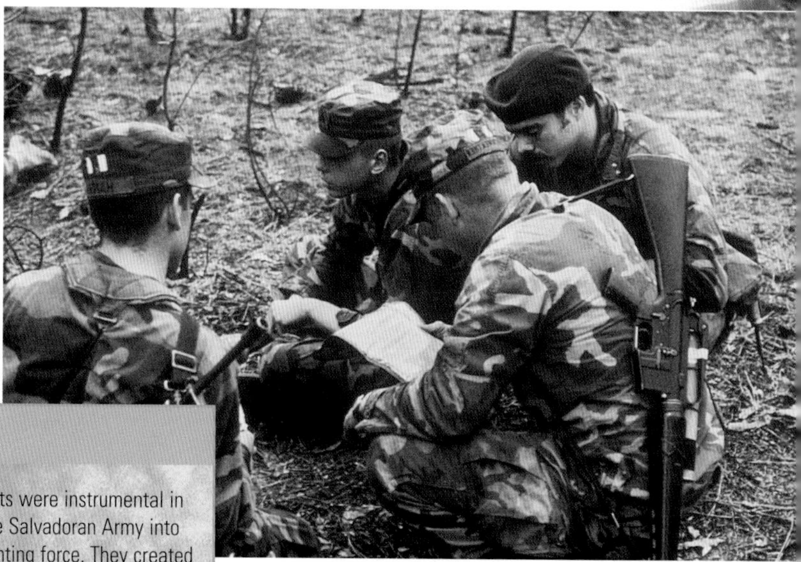

REBUILDING THE ARMY

Upon arrival, the Green Berets set about transforming the El Salvadoran Army into an effective fighting unit, capable of taking on the guerrillas and winning. Several elite counter-insurgency battalions were also created, with the specific role of fighting the guerrillas in a more professional and effective manner than had previously been tried. The El Salvadoran Army had gained a reputation for brutality and summary justice, as death squads roamed the streets rounding up suspected guerrillas and sympathizers and executing them. Conspiracy theorists suggest that the Green Berets colluded with the death squads, but there is little evidence to support the claim.

The training regime set up by the Green Beret advisers was comprehensive and impressive. US special forces are trained to be able to teach anything from firing a rifle to flying a helicopter, and in El Salvador they

The El Salvadoran Army

The Green Berets were instrumental in reorganizing the Salvadoran Army into an effective fighting force. They created and trained several counter-insurgency battalions, which became the benchmark standard within the Salvadoran Army (30,000 men). These elite battalions were a vital tool in the suppression of the communist guerrilla movement, and the reform of the hitherto disorganized Salvadoran Army also made a significant contribution to the fight.

Counter-insurgency soldier
The counter-insurgency battalions trained by the Green Berets were equipped with American weapons, such as the M16 assault rifle.

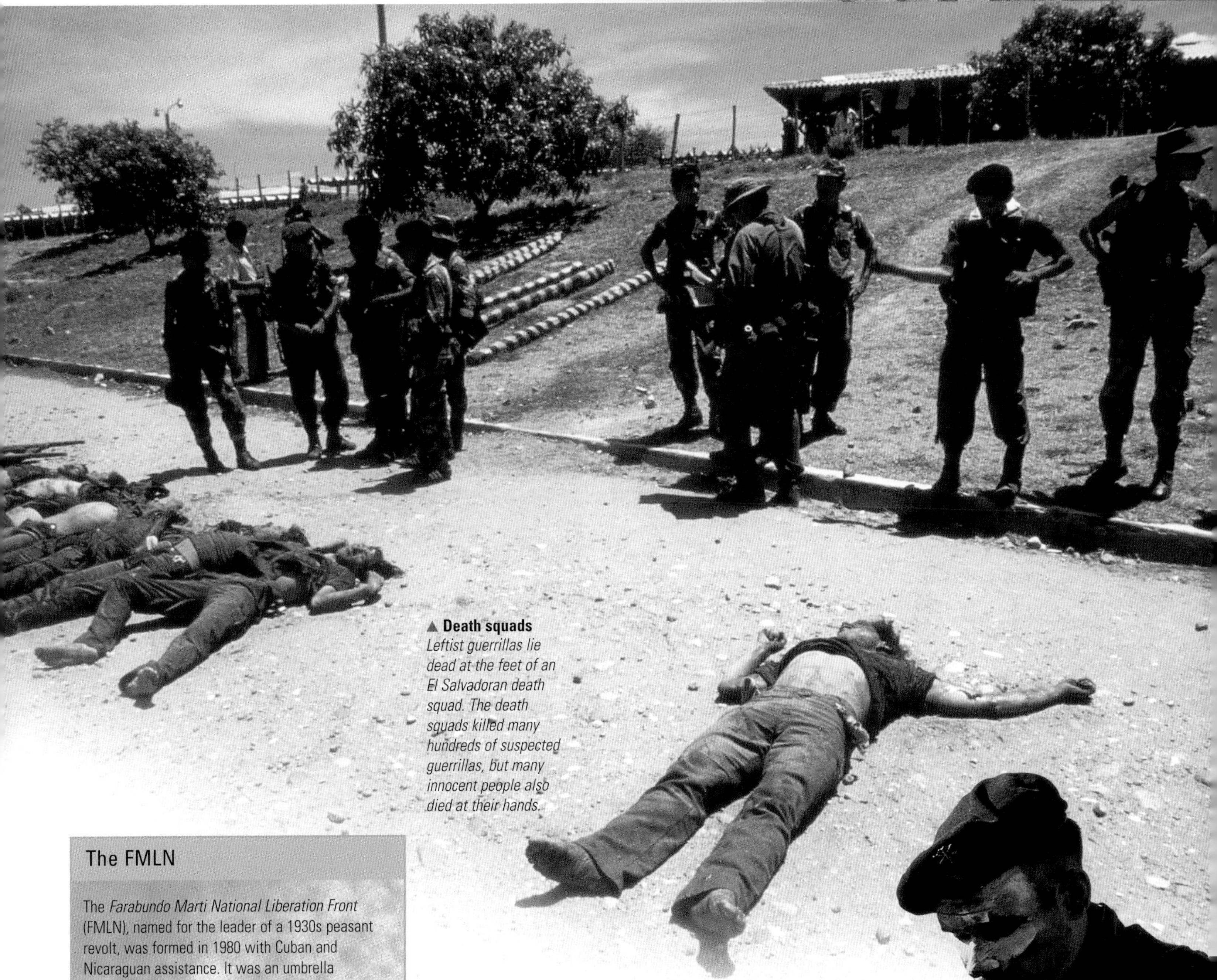

▲ **Death squads**
Leftist guerrillas lie dead at the feet of an El Salvadoran death squad. The death squads killed many hundreds of suspected guerrillas, but many innocent people also died at their hands.

The FMLN

The *Farabundo Marti National Liberation Front* (FMLN), named for the leader of a 1930s peasant revolt, was formed in 1980 with Cuban and Nicaraguan assistance. It was an umbrella organization composed of five leftist groups wishing to overthrow the El Salvadoran government. It was the main protagonist in the conflict in El Salvador.

Determined resistance
Though relatively lightly armed, the fighters of the FMLN were tenacious and determined foes.

put all their experience and expertise to good use. They instructed the new counter-insurgency battalions in the use of a range of weapons including assault rifles, grenade-launchers, and pistols.

The new battalions, under Green Beret guidance, began to thwart the insurgents to the stage where, in 1985, the FMLN realized it could not continue to fight the El Salvadoran Army in a conventional fashion. Although fighting continued for another six years, the FMLN was unable to topple the El Salvadoran government. The Green Berets had succeeded in their mission.

▶ **US adviser**
Green Beret advisers were sent to El Salvador to help stabilize the country's government.

US Army Delta Force

The "war on terrorism" announced by President George W. Bush following the attacks of September 11, 2001, on the New York World Trade Center and the Pentagon in Washington, D.C., put the spotlight on the United States special forces. Chief among these is the elite Special Forces Operational Detachment–Delta (SFOD–D), better known as Delta Force. It is the US Army unit specifically charged with combating terrorism.

The creation of Delta Force in 1977 was the result of a long campaign by its eventual founder, Colonel Charles Beckwith (see box below), who was influenced by his experiences on an exchange tour with the British Special Air Service (SAS). It is not surprising, therefore, that the formal organization and tactics of Delta Force reflect those of the SAS.

▶ **Hostage-rescue**
A Delta Force soldier in full hostage-rescue gear. Hostage-rescue and counter-terrorism are two of Delta Force's primary duties.

ORGANIZATION AND OPERATION

Delta Force, based in the US Army's large military base at Fort Bragg, North Carolina, is reputed to number approximately 360 personnel and is divided into A, B, and C Squadrons and then into troops. Within these troops, further specialization occurs, although much of the detail is closely guarded.

Delta Force excels at freefall parachuting and amphibious landing techniques. Its skill at fast-moving land operations was highlighted in the 1991 Gulf War, where the unit worked with the British SAS to call in airstrikes that eliminated Iraqi mobile Scud missile launchers operating in western Iraq.

Supporting the three active Delta Force squadrons are a helicopter platoon and units dealing with training, logistics, signals, and medical treatment. Delta Force maintains close links with the 160th Special Operations Aviation Regiment (160 SOAR, see pp86–89), which provides full helicopter support.

◀ **Parachute skills**
Delta Force soldiers prepare for a high altitude, low opening (HALO) jump. The HALO technique allows a parachutist to accurately drop onto a chosen landing site. Also, because parachutes can show up on enemy radar, the method decreases the chance of detection.

▼ **Heavy fire-support**
Hummer multi-purpose vehicles equipped with .50-caliber M2 Browning machine guns provide effective mobile support units for Delta Force's ground operations.

PROFILE — Charles Beckwith

Dates 1929–94
Unit Delta Force
Rank Colonel

As a result of the rise in global terrorism in the early 1970s, the US government decided that a specialized counter-terrorist unit was required. US Army Colonel Charles Beckwith, a veteran of the Vietnam War (1965–75), had spent a year-long exchange tour with the British Special Air Service (SAS) in the early 1960s, and he was charged with the task. In 1977 Beckwith created the US Delta Force, and it was he who led the ill-fated rescue attempt of the 52 US hostages being held in the US embassy in Tehran, Iran (1980). Beckwith retired in 1981 and wrote *Delta Force*, a history of the unit he had founded.

▲ **VIP protection**
Delta Force provides bodyguards for senior military personnel. Here they are accompanying US General Norman Schwarzkopf during the 1991 Gulf War.

Delta Force at Fort Bragg

Fort Bragg in North Carolina is a large US Army military base of which Delta Force occupies just one part. Great secrecy surrounds the unit's training, but the facilities are supposedly the most sophisticated in the world, and are said to include shooting ranges, swimming and diving pools, and simulated conditions for all types of counter-terrorism, from subway trains to a section of an airliner. Urban-assault and hostage-release scenarios are known to take place in the graphically named "House of Horrors."

Delta Force HQ
Hidden from prying eyes, Delta Force trains its soldiers in anti-terrorist operations among the buildings of Fort Bragg.

RECRUITMENT AND TRAINING

Recruits to Delta Force come primarily from the United States Army Special Operations Command (USASOC), commonly known as the Green Berets (see pp54–59), and the US Army Rangers (see pp68–73). However, Delta Force recruits are taken from any branch of the US Army when there is a need for highly specialized skills, such as fluency in foreign languages.

◀ **Fast escape**
Delta Force soldiers' are rapidly extracted from danger on a rope beneath a helicopter.

With a focus on fighting terrorism and hostage-rescue missions, marksmanship and intensive close-quarters battle (CQB) skills feature prominently in Delta Force training. In addition, reconnaissance and target spotting in support of airstrikes and laser-guided missiles have become major functions for US special forces, as was demonstrated in the Gulf War of 1991, in Afghanistan in 2002, and in Iraq in 2003. As a means of improving their skills, Delta Force engages in frequent personnel exchanges with the British SAS (see pp48–53) and with the special forces teams of other US allies.

The "House of Horrors"

The "House of Horrors" is the primary training facility for Delta Force soldiers. It is a set of rooms where various terrorist scenarios can be played out. In order to become expert in hostage-release and close-quarter combat situations, it is vital that trainees learn surprise assault tactics, and also to quickly distinguish the enemy from friend or hostage. Intensive weapons training is also essential to effective operations. The training includes the "double tap" method of shooting, where every target is shot twice to ensure a kill: A wounded terrorist could return fire or kill a hostage.

Training to tackle terror
The "House of Horrors" is based on the British SAS "Killing House." Live ammunition is used to create authenticity.

US Delta Force: Gulf War, 1991

As US-led Coalition forces prepared to drive Iraqi troops from Kuwait in 1991, Iraqi leader Saddam Hussein ordered the firing of Scud ballistic missiles into Israel. He hoped to suck Israel into the war, and thereby put pressure on neighboring Arab states to enter the war on his side. Acting swiftly, the Coalition sent the US Delta Force and other nations' special forces into Iraq to track down and destroy the mobile Scud launchers.

Iraqi Scud attack
Damage caused by a Scud attack on the US Army base at Dhahran, Saudi Arabia, in 1991, in which 27 US troops were killed.

BACKGROUND

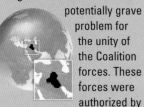

Iraq's Scud missile attacks against Israel were a potentially grave problem for the unity of the Coalition forces. These forces were authorized by the United Nations to liberate Kuwait after the Iraqi invasion in 1991. Iraq's leader, Saddam Hussein (b. 1937), intended to inflame the mutual hostility between Israel and its Arab neighbors. Many of those Arab countries were now supporters of the Coalition. By firing Scuds into Israel, Saddam hoped that Israel would be forced to enter the war – and that this, in turn, would impel Arab states to support Iraq. If some Arab governments refused active support of Iraq, there was a chance that popular Arab feeling could bring about the overthrow of these regimes. However, the Israeli government, led by Prime Minister Yitzhak Shamir (b. 1915), resisted the temptation to respond to Iraq militarily, despite Scud missiles hitting the Israeli capital, Tel Aviv. This policy allowed the Coalition to prosecute a focused war, without wider political complications in the region.

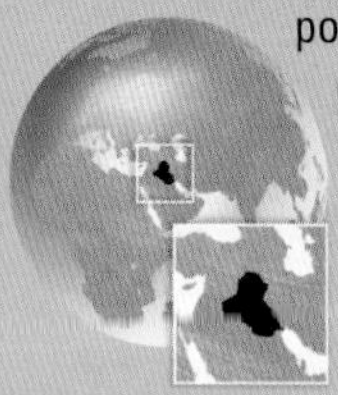

Delta Force operatives were deployed to Saudi Arabia as part of the Joint Special Operations Task Force (JSOTF) in early February 1991. Their principal aim was to locate targets within Iraq, particularly Scud missile-launchers, and provide target guidance for Coalition ground-attack aircraft.

DESERT STEALTH

The Delta Force teams were deployed at night by aircraft of the 160th Special Operations Aviation Regiment (160th SOAR). From MH-60 Black Hawk and MH-47E Chinook helicopters, the Delta operatives were dropped into isolated desert locations in western Iraq. They then took up positions around Al Qaim on the Syrian border: It was ideal firing territory for Iraqi Scud missiles, with central Israel within range.

The Delta Force units moved only at night. During the day they stayed hidden in camouflaged positions, to avoid detection and

▶ **Helicopter back-up**
A CH-53 Stallion transport helicopter ferries supplies from forward operating bases to the Delta Force units deep behind Iraqi lines.

▶ **F-15 strike force**
Delta Force teams on the ground called in F-15 fighter-bombers to attack the Scud-missile launch sites they had discovered in the Iraqi desert.

Iraq 2003

Delta Force was heavily involved during the US-led war against Iraq in 2003. An estimated 10,000 US troops – about 10 percent of the total US force in action – were special forces, with Delta Force forming a small but significant unit within that elite. Details of actual operations remain largely confidential, but verified roles included target-designation for airstrikes; hunting and assassinating key figures in Saddam Hussein's Ba'ath Party and Republican Guard; sabotaging infrastructure, such as electrical plants; and intercepting Iraqi communications. Delta Force also worked with US Marines, Rangers, and US Navy Sea, Air, and Land (SEAL) operatives in the rescue on April 1, 2003, of US Army Private Jessica Lynch, who had been taken prisoner by Iraqi troops while on convoy duty.

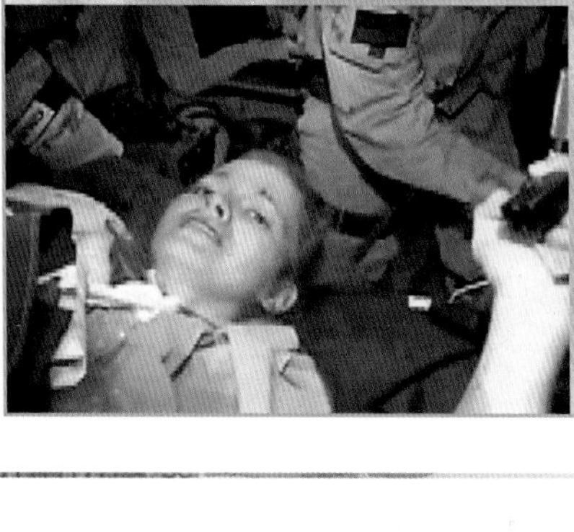

Jessica Lynch
The television images of soldier Private Jessica Lynch, rescued from an Iraqi hospital by US special forces, were a morale boost for the US public.

the danger of dehydration. Tracking down the mobile Scuds was difficult. Sometimes only the visible flames of a night launch betrayed a position. When found, a launcher's coordinates were transmitted to the Coalition's central command, and an attack aircraft allocated to make a strike. Delta Force then acted as forward observers, giving references for an accurate attack, or, more usually, "illuminating" the target with Laser Target Designators (LTDs). Laser-guided missiles dropped from the aircraft followed the LTD signal to hit the launcher. As well as Scud launchers, Delta Force also helped destroy other key targets, including radar sites, bunkers, and supply depots.

DIRECT ACTION

Occasionally, Delta soldiers neutralized Scuds themselves. Their M136 AT4 Light Anti-Armor Weapons could destroy a Scud launcher up to 984 ft. (300 m.) away. At distances up to, and over, 1 mile (1.6 km.), Delta snipers employed .5in.-caliber Barrett M82A1 rifles to disable Scud transporter engines, leaving the launchers as stationary targets for Coalition strike aircraft. Sometimes, Delta soldiers also killed Scud crews with small-arms fire.

VEHICLE ASSAULTS

The most dramatic Delta operations employed Chenworth Fast Attack Vehicles (FAVs). These are heavily armed dune buggies, capable of transporting three soldiers, supplies, and various armaments, including anti-tank missiles, grenade launchers, and 30-mm. cannon. With a top speed of 55 mph. (90 kph.), and a range of 320 miles (515 km.), the buggies either made rapid cross-border reconnaissance or attack incursions into Iraq, or were deployed by Chinook helicopter to hunt Scuds. With night-vision goggles enabling travel after dark, Delta teams could track the Scud launchers during transit and destroy them in high-speed assaults.

These efforts by Delta Force and other units paid off. By mid-February only isolated Scud firings were taking place. By the end of the month (when the Coalition's land offensive began) all Scud attacks on Israel had ceased.

The Scud missile

The Scud surface-to-surface missile was first deployed by the Soviet Union in the mid-1960s. It was originally designed to carry a 100-kiloton nuclear warhead or a 2,000-lb. (900-kg.) conventional warhead, with a range of around 100–180 miles (160–290 km.). Its principal threat in 1991 was its potential to hold chemical or biological agents in its warhead. Iraqi forces modified Scuds for a greater range, largely by reducing warhead weight and enlarging their fuel tanks. This meant that they could hit Israeli cities from western Iraq.

Iraqi Scud
A Scud missile being towed through the streets of Baghdad during a military ceremony. In the Gulf War Scuds took off from mobile launchers.

▶ **Search team**
Delta Force soldiers searched isolated installations deep in the Iraqi western desert, looking for potential weapons of mass destruction.

◀ **Desert mobility**
The heavily-armed Fast Attack Vehicles (FAVs), or dune buggies, used by Delta Force were invaluable in the terrain of the Iraqi desert.

Australian SAS

Australia's Special Air Service (SAS) is the country's primary special forces unit. Since its formation in 1957, during the communist rebellion in colonial British Malaya, it has seen action across the globe, including in Afghanistan (2002) and Iraq (2003). Today, it has six squadrons, and contains the specialized counter-terrorist Tactical Assault Group (TAG) and the Offshore Assault Team (OAT).

▶ **Black Hawks**
The Australian SAS uses UH-60 Black Hawk helicopters for military and counter-terrorist missions.

Faced with a rise in demand for anti-guerrilla (counter-insurgency) operations after World War II (1939–45), the Australian Army formed the 1st Special Air Service Company on July 25, 1957. Its inspiration was the British Special Air Service (SAS). Originally only 180-men strong, the Australian unit was soon overstretched, and its manpower was increased. On August 24, 1964, the SAS Company became the Special Air Service Regiment, with three Sabre combat squadrons, an HQ squadron, and a Training squadron. It was deployed to Brunei and Borneo in 1965 in support of British counter-insurgency operations there. Subsequent deployments included the Australian involvement (1966–72) in the Vietnam War, numerous peace-keeping and humanitarian operations, the 1991 Gulf War, and the post-September 11, 2001, "regime change" wars in Afghanistan (2002) and Iraq (2003).

ORGANIZATION

Today, the SAS has six squadrons: three Sabre squadrons (combat units), the 152nd Signals Squadron (with a troop of signalers attached to the HQ element of each Sabre squadron), a Base Squadron (supplies, equipment, and administration), and a Training Squadron. One Sabre squadron is always on counter-terrorist standby. The remaining two perform traditional special forces roles, such as infiltration, demolitions, assassinations, reconnaissance, and tactical assaults. Like the British SAS, the squadrons are divided into four troops, for HQ, airborne, amphibious, and vehicle-mounted roles.

The counter-terrorist Sabre squadron also contains the Tactical Assault Group (TAG) and Offshore Assault Team (OAT). TAG is an elite force specializing in hostage-rescue and counter-terrorist assaults in urban and transportation situations. It is formed from soldiers who already have two years' service in the SAS. The OAT has similar areas of expertise but specializes in maritime counter-terrorism, such as assaults on oil rigs, ships,

Australian counter-terrorism

Hilton Hotel terrorist attack
The aftermath of the Hilton Hotel bombing, 1978, which led to the SAS's counter-terrorist role.

At 0:40 a.m. on February 13, 1978, the Hilton Hotel in central Sydney, venue for an international political conference, was devastated by a terrorist bomb, which killed two people and injured six more. The incident was the first major terrorist attack on Australian soil, and the government responded by giving counter-terrorist responsibility to 1st Squadron SAS. In addition, it approved the creation of a dedicated counter-terrorist unit, the Tactical Assault Group, in August 1978, building it a state-of-the-art barracks and training center.

◀ **Offshore capability**
Members of the Offshore Assault Team check a pier for terrorist explosives.

▼ **Tactical mobility**
SAS soldiers in Afghanistan (2002). The larger vehicle is a Long Range Patrol Vehicle; the smaller is an all-terrain logistics (supplies) vehicle.

and coastal installations. TAG and OAT operatives are qualified in high altitude, low opening (HALO) and high altitude, high opening (HAHO) parachuting techniques.

SELECTION AND TRAINING

Any serving member of the Australian Defence Force, including air and naval personnel, can volunteer for SAS selection.

A six-week endurance course is conducted in the Australian outback at Polkobon Ranges. Candidates prove their worth with tests such as daily 25-mile (40-km.) runs carrying 88-lb. (40-kg.) loads, and five-day survival exercises on one day's worth of rations. Only about 20 percent of candidates pass, but those who do go on to 12 months' continuation training to learn fundamental SAS skills. These include parachuting, escape and evasion, patrolling, demolitions, counter-terrorist assaults, weapons handling, and communications. A candidate failing any section may be Returned to Unit. If successful, he joins an SAS squadron.

▶ **War in Iraq, 2003**
SAS soldiers were part of the Australian commitment to the war in Iraq launched in 2003. This soldier is armed with a US 5.56-mm. carbine.

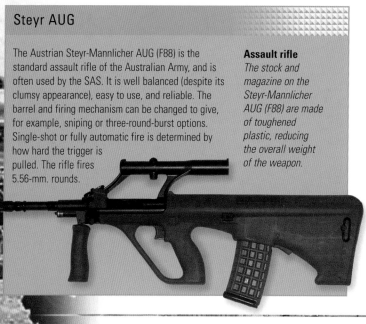

Steyr AUG

The Austrian Steyr-Mannlicher AUG (F88) is the standard assault rifle of the Australian Army, and is often used by the SAS. It is well balanced (despite its clumsy appearance), easy to use, and reliable. The barrel and firing mechanism can be changed to give, for example, sniping or three-round-burst options. Single-shot or fully automatic fire is determined by how hard the trigger is pulled. The rifle fires 5.56-mm. rounds.

Assault rifle
The stock and magazine on the Steyr-Mannlicher AUG (F88) are made of toughened plastic, reducing the overall weight of the weapon.

▲ **Artillery support**
An Australian 105-mm. artillery gun during the Vietnam War. Artillery was often used to support SAS units in the jungle.

BACKGROUND

Anti-communist feeling ran high in Australia after World War II (1939–45). When war broke out in Vietnam (1965), it was seen as a direct challenge to Australia's territorial integrity. On April 29, 1965, the Australian prime minister, Sir Robert Menzies (1894–1978), stated his view that a communist "takeover of South Vietnam would be a direct military threat to Australia and all the countries of South and Southeast Asia." By that time, Australian military advisers were already in Vietnam, so when the United States asked for further involvement, the Australian government accepted, and began a buildup of combat troops. The deployment of Australian armed forces ran from 1965 to 1972. Despite success in the field, and despite the skill of Australia's special forces in hunting down enemy guerrillas, the conflict would prove as difficult and damaging for Australia as it was for the United States.

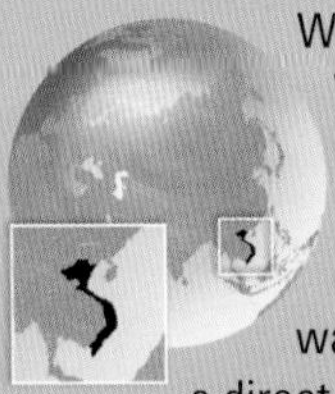

Australian SAS: Vietnam, 1966–72

In 1966, the 1st Squadron Australian Special Air Service (SAS) was deployed in the Vietnam War (1965–75). Its area of operations was Phuoc Tuy province, 43 miles (70 km.) southeast of Saigon (now Ho Chi Minh City). The SAS was to provide support for the conventional infantry of the 1st Australian Task Force, gathering vital intelligence through covert reconnaissance operations, while also attacking Viet Cong communist guerrillas with ambushes and search-and-destroy missions.

▶ **On patrol**
SAS soldiers pause for a rest in a village during a jungle patrol. They are carrying a mixture of M16 and SLR assault rifles.

The Australian military high command believed that its SAS soldiers were best employed in Vietnam in covert intelligence gathering. Four- or five-man SAS patrols probed deep into Viet Cong (VC) guerrilla territory, staking out jungle trails or observing VC bases, or living among Vietnamese villagers for long periods. In this latter "hearts and minds" role, they instructed civilians in everything from village defense to veterinary procedures, and were invaluable for gaining the confidence of the villagers. They became known to Australian commanders as "the eyes and ears of the 1st Australian Task Force."

SPECIAL OPERATIONS

The SAS soldiers also combined intelligence gathering with combat by ambushing VC units and seizing documents or surviving personnel before disappearing back into the jungle. Such was their elusiveness and effectiveness that the VC labeled them "ma rung" ("jungle ghosts") and offered $5,000 to any VC who killed or captured one of them.

More specialized operations were often conducted with US special forces. In the operation code-named "Bright Light," SAS and US Navy Sea, Air, and Land (SEAL) teams worked together across the Vietnamese border in Laos in secret missions to locate and rescue American prisoners of war.

Australian SAS in Borneo

The Australian SAS refined tactics that would prove useful in Vietnam when the 1st Squadron SAS was deployed in Borneo (1964–66) to assist British forces battling communist insurgents operating from neighboring Indonesia. Both the British and the Australian SAS had vital roles in building up grass-roots resistance to the communists, training local units of tribesmen (called Border Scouts), and providing medical aid to jungle communities. They also made covert crossings into Indonesia, identifying communist staging posts, then directing British artillery strikes.

Australian ally
An Australian SAS soldier in the Borneo jungle during an operation with British SAS troops.

▶ Huey helicopter (1963)
This US helicopter was used by the Australian SAS to transport patrols into and out of the jungle in Vietnam. It could carry up to 12 troops.

Engine	P&W T400-CP-400
Rotor span	48 ft. (14.6 m.)
Length	57 ft. (17.5 m.)
Cruising speed	140 mph. (224 kph.)
Crew	2

▼ In the jungle
An SAS jungle patrol. With such poor visibility in the dense foliage, SAS and VC forces could literally bump into one other. The quick reactions of the SAS soldiers generally gave them the edge.

COMBAT TACTICS

Inevitably, SAS teams became involved in large-scale actions. After major engagements between VC and Australian infantry, such as that at Long Tan rubber plantation on August 18, 1966, the SAS hunted down fleeing survivors using their first-rate tracking skills. At other times they were ordered to destroy entire enemy camps. The breadth of operations meant using innovative tactics. Along with the 9th Squadron Royal Australian Air Force (RAAF), the SAS pioneered rapid helicopter troop deployments using rappelling techniques. They also devised a new emergency evacuation procedure, whereby three soldiers at a time were hooked onto a rope dangling from an airborne helicopter before being flown out of an area.

If SAS teams were ambushed, they would return massive small-arms fire and grenades, while either pulling back to establish defensive positions or pushing forward to attack. SAS soldiers chose their own weapons: The US M16A1 and the FN FAL were the assault rifles of choice, with M60 machine guns and grenades providing heavier support.

The SAS was a tiny fraction of the Australian forces in Vietnam but had a major battlefield effect. In five years of fighting, the SAS killed 500 VC fighters, losing only one man in combat.

The SAS in Vietnam

A report from the Australian Army Operational Research Group (1967) explained that, while SAS soldiers made only one quarter of the Australian contacts with the enemy, they accounted for around half the total of VC killed by Australian troops. One senior commander even claimed: "If for every 100 combat infantry the allies could kill 80 enemy a year as the SAS do, then there would be no worthwhile enemy left alive after a year."

VC dead
Viet Cong guerrilla fighters lie dead after a firefight with the Australian SAS.

US Army Rangers

The US Army Rangers are a three-battalion-strong elite force used in both conventional and specialized infantry combat roles. With origins dating from the 17th century, today they are one of the US Army's most flexible units, with one battalion always ready to deploy anywhere in the world at very short notice.

▶ **Hard training**
A recruit to the Rangers struggles to complete the assault course during Ranger School.

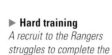

The US Army Rangers are defined by unconventional warfare. "Ranger" frontier troops fought Native Americans in the late 17th century. In 1756 Major Robert Rogers (1731–95) formed nine companies of Rangers, employing guerrilla tactics during the French and Indian War (1754–63), as the North American theater of the Seven Years' War is known. Rangers also participated in the American Revolution (1775–83) and the Civil War (1861–65). But it was World War II (1939–45) that gave birth to the modern Rangers. In 1942 General George Marshal (1880–1959) authorized the creation of a US equivalent of the British commandos – the 1st US Army Ranger Battalion. Six Ranger battalions were formed, serving with distinction in the Italian campaigns.

Following the Korean War (1950–53) the Rangers were officially disbanded, although their training program remained to provide elite leadership training. Ranger units, however, were revived during the Vietnam War (1961–75) in 13 companies of the 75th Infantry Regiment. In 1974, the Rangers were formally reactivated as the 1st and 2nd Battalions 75th Infantry (Ranger) Regiment. The 3rd Battalion was added in the 1980s, and total regimental strength grew to around 2,500 personnel. The Rangers have been involved in almost all major US campaigns since the mid-1970s, including post-September 11, 2001, actions in Afghanistan in 2002 and in Iraq in 2003.

Ranger scroll

RANGER OPERATIONS

The 75th Ranger Regiment falls under the umbrella of the US Joint Special Operations Command. Its remit is special operations, either in support of regular US/allied forces or as a unilateral strike group. Typical missions include airborne assault, demolitions, covert reconnaissance, and recovery operations. There is a deep-reconnaissance platoon for missions behind enemy lines, and specially trained combat swimmers and high-altitude parachutists.

The US Army Rangers emphasize continual readiness. One Ranger battalion each month – known as the Ranger Ready Force (RRF) – is configured to make operational deployment possible within 18 hours of orders. High mobility means that the Rangers are relatively lightly armed. Support weapons

▶ **Urban combat**
Rangers are trained to fight in different environments. These Rangers are learning how to fight in urban areas, which entails searching rooms and buildings for the enemy.

Ranger ideology

The US Army Rangers, like many other US special forces units, has a distinct ideology or philosophy. The psychology behind these creeds is to foster a unique *esprit de corps* among the men of the unit and to provide a sense of identity. In addition, they serve as a moral code in both wartime and peacetime to which all members of the regiment adhere and aspire. It is compulsory for all successful recruits into the regiment to memorize the Ranger Creed. The first letter of each phrase in the creed corresponds to the letters that make up the word "Ranger," and it espouses qualities such as honor, gallantry, dedication, and fortitude.

Combat elite
US Army Rangers know their creed and live up to its spirit, especially in combat.

The airborne brotherhood

The US Army Airborne School at Fort Benning, Georgia, is the US Army's centralized parachute-training center. Any US soldier can volunteer for parachute training, but for many elite US forces the "parachute qualified" badge is a compulsory requirement. The course lasts for three weeks. The first week consists of ground training, learning the basic techniques and principles of jumping and landing. Week two involves practice jumps and landings from a 34-ft. (10.4-m.) tower and using a Swing Landing Trainer. Finally, week three sees the soldiers make five parachute jumps of increasing complexity, including one at night. Those who complete the jumps are designated as "parachute qualified."

Parachute training *Rangers board a C-130 Hercules transport aircraft prior to making a jump. All Rangers are trained parachutists, and are capable of making night descents.*

include 60-mm., 81-mm., and 120-mm. mortars, Javelin anti-tank missiles, and the Stinger air-defense system, which are all portable on foot.

RANGER TRAINING PROGRAMS

The 75th Ranger Regiment is based at Fort Benning, Georgia. It has a Ranger Training Brigade to implement leadership and long-range reconnaissance training. Rangers are recruited only from airborne-qualified US Army soldiers. Officers attend the Ranger Orientation Program (ROP) and enlisted soldiers follow the Ranger Indoctrination Program (RIP), where the physical and mental stamina of the applicants is assessed. Once through ROP or RIP, a soldier is assigned to a Ranger battalion as an operational Ranger and learns the basics of Ranger-style combat. Ranger School is a punishing two-month leadership course, usually attended about 9 to 12 months after joining the battalion. It includes training in mountain and tropical warfare and is open to personnel outside the Ranger Regiment. Few ROP and RIP graduates fail, but those who do are returned to their original units. Those who pass receive the prestigious Ranger tab, signifying "Ranger Qualified" status.

▼ Unarmed combat *Ranger School teaches recruits the techniques of unarmed combat so that they can defend themselves and kill with their bare hands.*

▼ Arctic Ranger *Rangers can be deployed to any location in the world. This Ranger is dressed in Arctic clothing and is armed with a lighter, shorter variant of the SAW machine gun.*

US Army Rangers: Panama, 1989

Operation Just Cause, the United States' invasion of Panama in 1989, saw the combat deployment of the whole US 75th Infantry Regiment, the Rangers. The operation was the Rangers' third since the regiment's reactivation in 1974. It was claimed as a welcome success following the failure of the Tehran Embassy hostage-release attempt (1980) and the inter-service failures surrounding the invasion of the Caribbean island of Grenada (1983).

Popular liberators
Panamanian civilians during the invasion. In general, US troops were welcomed by the majority of Panamanians, who wished to be rid of Noriega.

BACKGROUND

The roots of the Panama crisis lay in the fact that an area of vital economic and strategic significance to the United States was being run by a corrupt military strongman, General Manuel Noriega. Indicted in the United States on drug racketeering charges in 1988, Noriega responded to Panama's President Eric Delvalle's attempt to remove him from his post by encouraging a coup. Despite the imposition of US sanctions, a 1989 presidential election (the result of which Noriega overruled), and an attempted counter-coup, Noriega's grip on power in in the country, backed up by his paramilitary Dignity Battalions, tightened. Following the Panamanian National Assembly's declaration in 1989 that a state of war existed with the United States, the drugs charges against Noriega, and the killing in December 1989 of an American marine by Panamanian soldiers, President George Bush (b. 1924) declared war and ordered the invasion of Panama by conventional US troops and special forces.

Operation Just Cause was the largest deployment of the recently enlarged Rangers Regiment, which then numbered three battalions. The Rangers formed the bulk of the operation's "Task Force Red" special forces group.

NIGHT-TIME ASSAULT

Parachuting into Panama at low level at 1:00 a.m. on December 20, the first 500 Rangers were ordered to secure the Torrijos-Tocumen International Airport, headquarters of the Panamanian Air Force. A further 500 Rangers were ordered to occupy Rio Hato airfield. These objectives were achieved within two hours, with the aid of support from AH-6 helicopters and an AC-130 Spectre gunship, against relatively limited opposition from elements of the Panamanian Defense Force (PDF). However, a group of 150 Rangers encountered strong opposition from PDF units defending the terminal building. This situation was complicated by the presence in the terminal of 400 civilians (including US citizens), recently arrived on an international flight. Some PDF soldiers attempted to use the civilians as hostages, but gave up in the face of overwhelming odds.

The early successes allowed for the safe deployment of conventional forces. With the initial airfield objectives achieved, the 1st Battalion came under the control of the 82nd Airborne Division. It was ordered, later that

▲ **Spectre gunship**
This is an AC-130 Spectre gunship. Spectres provided US forces with support fire during the invasion.

▼ **Ranger patrol**
A Ranger searches for the enemy. One of the problems Rangers encountered in Panama was that the opposition wore US-made uniforms, which made identification difficult.

◀ **Mopping up**
A group of Rangers trades fire with enemy forces on the outskirts of Panama City. In general, opposition to the US invasion was patchy and uncoordinated, but pockets of resistance still had to be cleared.

PROFILE

Manuel Noriega

Dates b. 1934
Unit Panamanian Army
Rank General

Manuel Noriega was part of the military coup that removed President Arnulfo Arias from power in 1968. He was appointed chief of military intelligence by coup leader Omar Torrijos (1929–81), and acquired a reputation for ruthlessness. After Torrijos's death in 1981, Noriega was promoted to chief of staff by Dario Paredes, whom he succeeded to the position of General in 1983. Noriega incited conflict with the United States through his increasingly blatant political fraud, violence, and drug racketeering. Operation Just Cause ended his regime in a matter of days and he was arrested. In 1992 he was sentenced to 40 years in a Florida prison.

morning, to subdue the Panamanian special forces, known as the Mountain Troops, in their compound outside Panama City. After breaking through the perimeter defenses of the compound, the Rangers met with little resistance. In the afternoon, Company C of the 3rd Battalion of the Ranger Regiment (approximately 150 men) was sent to clear the PDF's headquarters (called the Comandancia) in Panama City. The building had already been softened up by other US forces as the opening move of Operation Just Cause.

A SUCCESSFUL CONCLUSION

In subsequent days the Rangers' duties were more varied, from mopping up final resistance from General Noriega's paramilitary units, the so-called "Dignity Battalions," to guarding buildings – including the Vatican Embassy, to which Noriega had fled. With military actions over in the last days of December, the Rangers returned to their base at Fort Benning, Georgia, having achieved their objectives and proved their worth. Five Rangers died, and nearly 50 were wounded, but Just Cause was considered an undeniable success.

◄ **Street arrest**
A Ranger arrests a member of Noriega's Dignity Battalions in Panama City. The Dignity Battalions were paramilitary units entirely loyal to the Panamanian dictator. They were good at terrorizing the local population, but were no match for well-trained troops such as the Rangers.

▼ **Hummer backup**
A Ranger Hummer vehicle patrols Panama City following the US invasion.

Stealth fighter

Stealth deployment
The US F-117A Stealth fighter being refueled during a mission. In Panama it easily penetrated air defenses to drop its bombs.

The F-117A Nighthawk, popularly known as the Stealth fighter, became an icon of US military sophistication in the 1990s, by virtue of its futuristic design and "stealth" technology, which made it invisible to radar. Operationally capable by 1983, it was first used in combat in Operation Just Cause. With the increased reliance on precision, laser-guided attack from the air in US military strategy since then, the F-117s has enjoyed an increasing prominence in conflicts from Yugoslavia to Iraq. Its armaments include the Paveway range of precision laser-guided bombs and unguided, freefall bombs.

Saddam Hussein
The US-led war in Iraq in 2003 aimed to remove the brutal and internationally isolated regime of dictator Saddam Hussein.

BACKGROUND

The regime of Saddam Hussein (b. 1937), which lasted from 1979 until 2003, turned Iraq into an oppressive one-party state. The country was characterized by violence against individuals, groups, and even whole ethnic populations, such as the Kurds, who were the target of a murderous gas attack in 1988. Saddam's aggressive foreign policy also led to disastrous wars. An attempt to capture the Shatt al-Arab waterway from neighboring Iran in 1980 evolved into an eight-year struggle, costing an estimated one million Iraqi lives. Saddam's invasion of the oil-rich state of Kuwait on Iraq's southern border in 1990 resulted in defeat by a US-led coalition, routing his army. Finally, determined to put an end to Saddam's regime and its suspected weapons program, US and British forces invaded Iraq in March 2003.

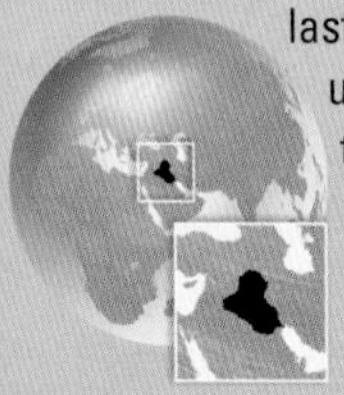

US Army Rangers: Iraq, 2003

In March 2003, US military planners were faced with a problem. The war against Iraq was developing well in the south, but Turkey's refusal to allow US forces to use its territory for a northern land invasion was creating an operational vacuum north of the capital, Baghdad. The answer lay in airborne deployment, and especially in the skills of the US Army 75th Ranger Regiment.

Securing the northern region was vital to the US-led invasion of Iraq for several reasons. First, the oilfields around the cities of Mosul and Kirkuk could be seized and protected from possible destruction by Saddam's desperate forces. Second, a new front in the war would be opened, thereby trapping Iraqi forces around Baghdad in a massive north–south pincer action. Third, Coalition forces could mobilize the support of anti-Saddam Kurdish fighters in the region, and also be in a position to prevent Turkey, which was worried about Kurdish intentions, from making its own military claims on the area.

The key to all these objectives was securing several strategic airfields in the northern region for use as forward supply bases in subsequent operations. With a land advance being impossible, the US Army turned to its airborne forces, including the elite 75th Ranger Regiment.

CAPTURING H1

"H1" was an important Iraqi airfield situated near the Syrian border. Not only would its 33,000-ft. (10,000-m.) runway permit the landing of large transport aircraft, but it also sat astride an old oil pipeline that featured in US development plans. On the night of March 25–26, 1,000 US troops of the 173rd Airborne Brigade and 75th US Rangers, plus units of Green Berets, secured the airfield in a dramatic night-time parachute drop.

The night-time deployment provided an element of surprise and would give the Rangers – who train hard in night-fighting and the use of night-vision devices – a tactical advantage were the landing to be opposed. C-17 Globemasters provided air transport, each capable of carrying 102 paratroopers and related equipment. With such aircraft, the

Night drops

Night-time parachute drops present many challenges, and all candidates must make at least one to qualify as a Ranger. Potential hazards include troops getting lost and disoriented, injuries on landing (it is hard to judge the distance to the ground), and difficulties retrieving equipment. To overcome these, each Ranger wears night-vision goggles to give a clear view of the landing zone, while Global Positioning Satellite (GPS) devices enable precise orientation once landed. Homing beacons on equipment allow easier retrieval.

Night exit
Paratroopers exiting a C-130 Hercules aircraft during a night-time parachute drop.

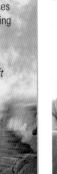

▲ Green Berets
The Rangers that were dropped into northern Iraq quickly linked up with US Green Berets (shown here), who were working with the Kurdish forces opposed to Saddam Hussein's regime.

▼ Vigilance
A Ranger looks for Iraqi troops through the sights on his M16 assault rifle. He is wearing a desert camouflage uniform.

Iraqi Army

The Iraqi Army in early 2003 was still a large force. Western intelligence estimated that it possessed about 2,200 main battle tanks, around 2,400 armored personnel carriers, 900 other fighting vehicles, and about 100 attack helicopters. Total army manpower was 375,000 troops. These seemingly impressive figures, however, masked major underlying weaknesses. Poor leadership and training, badly maintained or obsolete equipment, and very poor morale reduced the army's effective strength by around 50 percent. Saddam's best troops remained the 26,000 Republican Guards.

Conscript force
The bulk of the Iraqi Army were conscripted infantry, such as these infantrymen. Iraqi troops generally had low morale and were poorly led by their officer corps.

▲ Night assault
US Army Rangers in a defensive position, following their parachute drop into northern Iraq.

Rangers were also able to deploy their Ranger Special Operations Vehicles – modified and armed Land Rovers used for airfield seizures.

US special forces and Kurdish soldiers had already sealed off the approach roads to the airfield, so the troops parachuted in without meeting resistance. Special "whisper" microphones allowed them to communicate in almost complete silence. Once on the ground they quickly set up a defensive perimeter and secured the area for landings by further US transporters. It was a textbook example of airborne deployment, providing a crucial base for operations in northern Iraq.

▶ Spoils of war
A Ranger sits in the turret of a captured Iraqi T-72 main battle tank. Many Iraqi units simply disappeared in the face of US forces.

OTHER MISSIONS IN IRAQ

During the conflict, US Rangers operated in a special forces capacity throughout Iraq. They were guard elements in the rescue of Private Jessica Lynch from an Iraqi hospital, and they destroyed air-defense batteries around important cities. Overall, the US Rangers played a major part in the US–British victory over Saddam that came in mid-2003.

Israeli paratroopers

Israel's parachute units have been at the forefront of Israeli operations since the nation was founded in 1948, proving vital in the successful outcomes of the Six Day War (1967) and the Yom Kippur War (1973). Today, the Israeli Defense Forces (IDF) contain the elite Parachute Brigade, which is part of the Infantry Corps. Its training standards are among the highest of any airborne unit, and its personnel regularly go into action in Israel's disputed territories.

Israeli parachute forces originate from 1948 and Israel's War of Independence against neighboring Arab states. By 1953 Israel had formed the small, elite parachute Unit 101 to combat Arab terrorist infiltration. Under the military leader Moshe Dayan (1915–81), this unit was soon merged with other paratroop units, greatly increasing in size to become a brigade during the mid-1950s. The Parachute Brigade quickly showed its combat prowess. It fought with distinction during the Six Day War (1967) against Egypt, Syria, and Jordan, breaking through front-line Egyptian positions and capturing east Jerusalem.

Counter-terrorism has also provided a constant role for Israel's airborne soldiers. In 1972, for example, paratroopers disguised as flight technicians freed hostages from a hijacked airliner at Israel's Lod Airport. More famously, in 1976, paratroopers with elite infantry rescued passengers and crew from a hijacked Air France airliner at Entebbe, Uganda. More recent actions include assaults against the headquarters and units of radical Islamic/pro-Palestinian terror groups, such as HAMAS (see box above).

HAMAS

A principal target of Israeli paratroopers is the terror group HAMAS (the Arabic abbreviation for Islamic Resistance Movement, and also a word for "courage"). Formed in 1987, HAMAS aims to replace Israel with an Islamic Palestinian state through a campaign of bombings and suicide bombings in Israeli cities, gun attacks on Israeli settlements, and ambushes of Israeli military patrols. Despite its heavy losses at the hands of Israeli special forces, it is constantly bolstered by foreign funds and new recruits.

Terrorist cells
HAMAS members train for suicide attacks against Israeli civilians.

The first parachute units

In 1948, Israeli Prime Minister David Ben-Gurion (1886–1973) ordered Yoel Palgi, a Jewish resistance fighter in World War II (1939–45), to form a shock paratroop unit. Palgi improvised with 4,000 second-hand parachutes and a mixture of foreign aircraft and equipment, but was able to recruit a high percentage of war veterans. The unit's skill and bravery in action against Arab terrorist cells during the 1950s ensured its future in the IDF.

Parachute landing
An Israeli paratrooper in 1956 after a successful desert drop.

STRUCTURE AND TRAINING

The Parachute Brigade is one of four brigades that make up the Infantry Corps. In addition to the Parachute Brigade's standard infantry battalions, it contains specialized anti-tank, anti-aircraft defense, engineering, signals, and

▶ **Helicopter landings**
As well as being able to jump from aircraft, Israeli paratroopers are trained to make a fast exit from helicopters.

▼ **Training**
Training for the Israeli paratroopers pushes recruits to their limits, with full days and little rest.

▲ C-130 Hercules
An Israeli C-130 transport aircraft. The high-mounted engines allow desert landings: Sand does not get sucked into them.

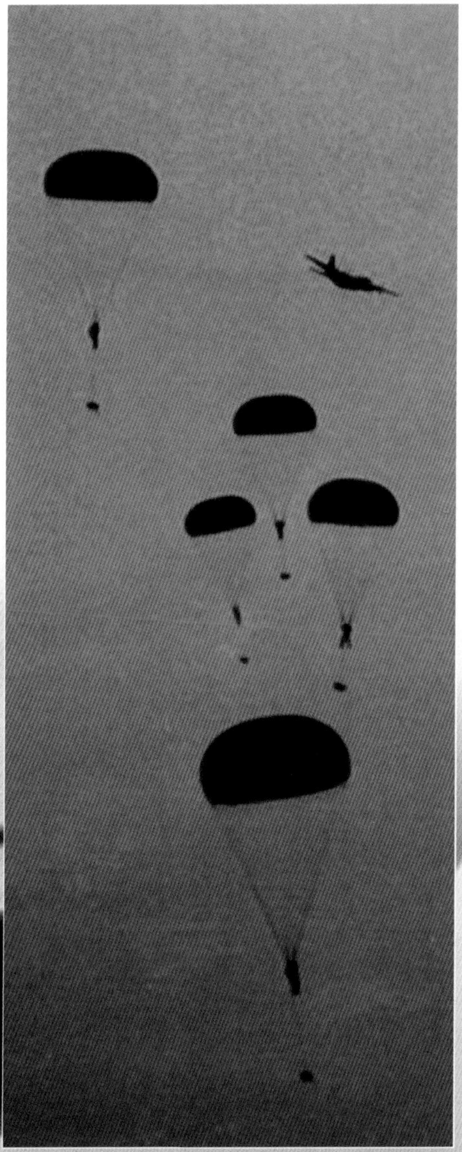

▶ Slow descent
Israeli paratroopers regularly dropped to intercept terrorist groups who were trying to enter Israel. These troops are using the "static line" technique. In static line jumps, parachutes open automatically on exiting the aircraft, enabling a large force to be dropped at low altitude onto the same landing zone.

reconnaissance companies. Other paratroop-trained elites (not part of the Parachute Brigade) are the secret *Sayeret* (Reconnaissance) anti-terrorist units.

Only around half the candidates pass the tough paratrooper training program. The training begins with instruction in basic infantry skills and punishing physical exercises. To earn the paratrooper's wings, a candidate must succeed in the IDF Jump School, learning parachute techniques and making five jumps. If successful, a candidate enters the Parachute Brigade, but must also take either Non-Commissioned Officer or Officer training. These extremely high training standards produce paratroopers who are ranked as being among the best in the world.

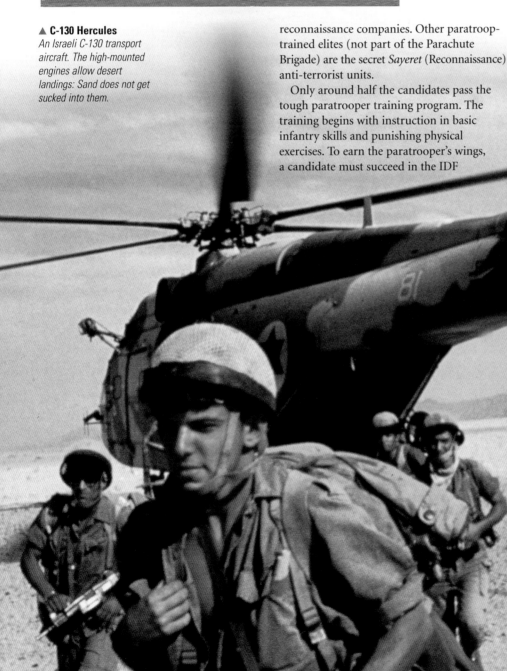

Israeli paratroopers: Entebbe, 1976

Idi Amin
The Ugandan dictator gave his full support to the hijackers, yet he had close ties with Israel and took great pride in wearing Israeli insignia on his uniform.

BACKGROUND

The hijacking of Air France Flight 139 in June 1976 came during a particularly intense and bloody period in Israel's turbulent history. Just three years before, in 1973, Israel had fought the Yom Kippur War against Egypt and Syria, and, in the intervening period, had suffered a series of terrorist attacks on civilians, military personnel, and political leaders, heightening Israeli tension. So, in 1976, when four terrorists took control of a flight leaving Tel Aviv with dozens of Jewish passengers on board, and flew the plane to Entebbe, Uganda, the Israeli government acted decisively. The elite Israeli *Sayeret Mat'Kal* special forces team was ordered into action and they planned a daring operation to free the hostages.

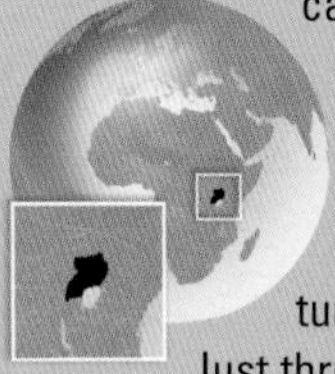

On June 27, 1976, four hijackers took over an Air France flight leaving Israel and ordered it to fly to Entebbe, Uganda, with 246 passengers on board. Israeli special forces, the *Sayeret Mat'Kal*, launched a daring raid, covering 2,200 miles (3,520 km.), to rescue the hostages. Their skill and guile achieved one of the most spectacular rescues in modern history.

At 12:30 p.m. on June 27, 1976, four terrorists armed with guns and grenades boarded Air France Flight 139 at Tel Aviv, Israel. The group consisted of two terrorists from the German Baader-Meinhof gang and two members of the Popular Front for the Liberation of Palestine (PFLP). They took control of the Boeing 707 airliner and ordered the pilot to fly to Entebbe airport in Uganda, Africa, where they landed. On June 30, the hijackers demanded the release of 53 prisoners held in jails across the world. A deadline of July 1 was given, after which the hostages would be executed.

Israel's long reach

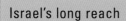

Train hard, fight easy
Israeli special forces showed themselves to be among the best trained and led soldiers in the world during the daring Entebbe rescue.

The logistical planning for the Entebbe hostage-rescue was a remarkable feat, and the raid itself remains one of the most daring of its kind in history. Uganda is 2,200 miles (3,520 km.) from Israel, and yet in only a matter of days, Israeli special forces were able to formulate a plan that flew them from Lod Airport in Israel straight onto the runway at Entebbe, where they killed the terrorists and rescued the hostages. This ability to reach across the globe to carry out such a mission is an option available only to the most professional and elite special forces. The successful conclusion to the Entebbe raid showed Israel's special forces to be among the very best in the world.

▼ The black Mercedes
The plan to fool the hijackers by approaching in a replica of Idi Amin's Mercedes was ingenious, and became one of the most famous aspects of the rescue.

PLANNING THE RAID

The elite Israeli hostage-rescue unit, *Sayeret Mat'Kal*, received orders to prepare a plan to rescue the hostages being held in the airport terminal. On July 1, the 100 non-Jewish passengers on the flight were released, leaving only the Jewish contingent and the crew. Despite initial concerns and reluctance, Israeli Prime Minister Yitzhak Rabin (1922–95) gave permission to attempt a rescue. The rescuers spent hours preparing the assault and practicing each phase in a specially constructed mock-up of the old terminal building at Entebbe where the hostages were being held. Under the command of Lieutenant-Colonel Jonathan Netanyahu, the unit planned to land on Entebbe's runway, and then proceed to the old terminal building disguised as representatives of Idi Amin, traveling in a copy of Amin's trademark black Mercedes. The success of the mission depended on the element of surprise.

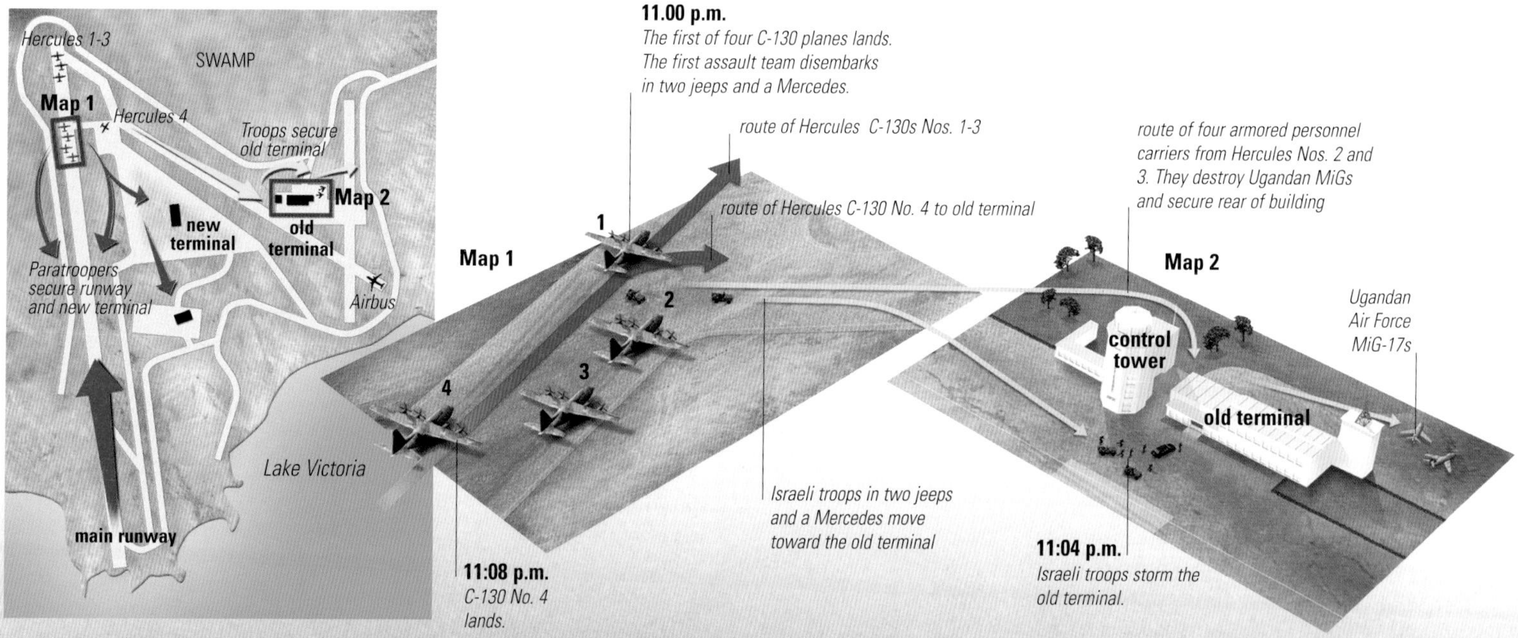

▲ The plan of attack
The Israeli convoy had some distance to cover from the runway to the old terminal building. The element of surprise was key to the success of the mission.

THE OPERATION

On July 23, four C-130 Hercules transport planes set off from Israel for Uganda. At 11:00 p.m. the lead aircraft touched down at Entebbe. Immediately, two jeeps and the Mercedes were unloaded and began to move in convoy toward the old terminal building. The Israeli troops, disguised as Ugandans, opened fire on two guards outside the terminal, spreading confusion among the terrorists. The Israelis began to clear the terminal building. As they progressed, the troops had difficulty in determining the terrorists from the hostages, and some passengers were accidentally fired on.

As the assault continued, the next two C-130s landed, unloading four armored personnel carriers, which went about destroying eight Ugandan Air Force MiG fighters stationed at the base. Within only 15 minutes of the first C-130 landing, the airport had been secured and the hostages rescued. Israeli losses were limited to Jonathan Netanyahu, who was killed, while two hostages died. The Israelis had shown the world that terror could be tackled and defeated by the clinical application of controlled force.

▶ Israeli jubilation
The hostages received a heroes' welcome in Israel. The Entebbe incident had captured the imagination of the Israeli population, and when the hostages returned, crowds celebrated their rescue.

▼ C-130 Hercules
When the first plane landed, Israeli troops leapt out to place beacons for the other aircraft, and then secured the airport.

Rioting in Freetown
Despite the presence of 2,000 United Nations troops, widespread violence broke out in Sierra Leone in 1999. Here, a UN vehicle chases away looters.

BACKGROUND

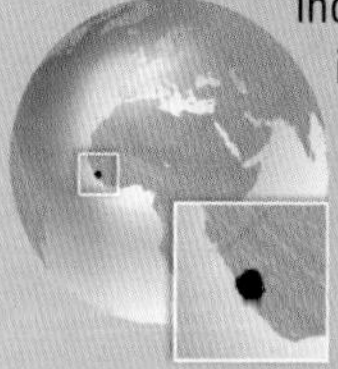

Sierra Leone is a former British colony that gained independence in 1961. The government was elected by the people until 1967, when a military dictatorship took over. The following years were a time of political turbulence and violence.

In 1991, a civil war between government forces and rebel groups broke out across Sierra Leone. The war was bitter and bloody, and lasted for eight years. The main rebel group, the Revolutionary United Front (RUF) headed by Foday Sankoh, signed a ceasefire with President Ahmad Tejan Kabbah in May 1999. Yet violence continued, and on April 29, 2000, United Nations (UN) troops were deployed in a peace-keeping capacity. By early May the ceasefire agreement was canceled. Sankoh's RUF took 500 UN soldiers prisoner and began an assault on the capital, Freetown. British troops assisted the Sierra Leonean military in repelling the attack and controlling the city. Sankoh was eventually captured, and in 2002 another ceasefire agreement was signed.

British Parachute Regiment: Sierra Leone, 2000

On Sunday May 7, 2000, 800 soldiers of the 1st Battalion Parachute Regiment began to deploy in Sierra Leone in Africa to bolster a beleaguered United Nations (UN) peace-keeping force. Although its original task was to evacuate foreign civilians, the Regiment was also involved in combat, particularly during a high-risk hostage-rescue mission, Operation Barras.

The Parachute Regiment's first task in Sierra Leone was to secure the country's main international airport at Lunghi, to the north of the capital, Freetown. It was accomplished without incident, but the situation remained volatile. Over the next four days British paratroopers established defensive positions around the airport, keeping it open in order to continue the evacuation of overseas civilians. On May 18, men of the Pathfinder Platoon killed four rebels in a Freetown gun battle, following the capture of Foday Sankoh, the leader of Sierra Leone's main rebel group, the Revolutionary United Front (RUF).

HOSTAGE SITUATION

Over the next few months the paratroopers preserved an uneasy stability. Then, on August 25, 2000, units of the militia gang known as the West Side Boys took hostage 11 soldiers of the British Army's Royal Irish Regiment. Five men were released shortly afterward in exchange for a satellite telephone. The freed men returned with accounts of torture, mock executions, and food and water deprivation.

▲ **Mortar support**
A British soldier guards a mortar position during Operation Barras, the mission to rescue the hostages.

▼ **Patrol team**
A British Parachute Regiment team on patrol in a heavily armed Land Rover in Sierra Leone in 2000.

The British government realized that it had to act quickly to save the remaining hostages. The rescue mission, codenamed Operation Barras, was set for September 10, 2000.

OPERATION BARRAS

A unit of Special Air Service (SAS) soldiers and 150 paratroopers took off from Freetown in three Chinook helicopters, with two Lynx helicopters providing fire support. Their destination was the West Side Boys' camp, 50 miles (80 km.) east of Freetown: Three villages on the Rokel Creek River – Geri Bana, Magbeni, and Forodogu. The hostages were in Geri Bana.

The attack began at 6:40 a.m., when the helicopter gunships poured fire onto rebel positions. A single Chinook helicopter carrying the SAS soldiers and a unit of paratroopers swooped into Geri Bana. The other two Chinooks landed paratroopers on the opposite bank of the river. The hostages were quickly liberated and Foday Kallay, the rebel leader, was captured. Firefights broke out, which the British troops dominated through accurate fire from their assault rifles, machine-guns, and grenade launchers. The hostages and Kallay were airlifted out of the combat zone, but the battle continued until 4:00 p.m. When the shooting stopped, one SAS noncommissioned officer was dead and another wounded, but all of the hostages were safe. The rebels, by contrast, had lost their leader, plus 25 dead and 18 captured.

The West Side Boys

The 400-strong West Side Boys were just one of many rebel gangs flourishing in Sierra Leone's lawless state. Copious supplies of alcohol and drugs made the West Side Boys unpredictable and extremely violent. The group was commanded by "Brigadier" Foday Kallay, who encouraged gratuitous torture and rape. The "Boys" included many brutalized child and women "soldiers." Despite their lack of military professionalism and discipline, a mixture of drug-induced fearlessness and long experience of guerrilla fighting in the region made them dangerous opponents for United Nations troops.

Child soldiers
The West Side Boys contained many child soldiers. They had been brutalized by years of warfare. Here, a group surrounds the remains of a UN soldier.

◄ **Paratrooper patrol**
British paratroopers on patrol in Sierra Leone in 2000. The soldier at the front of the column is armed with a machine gun variant of the SA80 assault rifle.

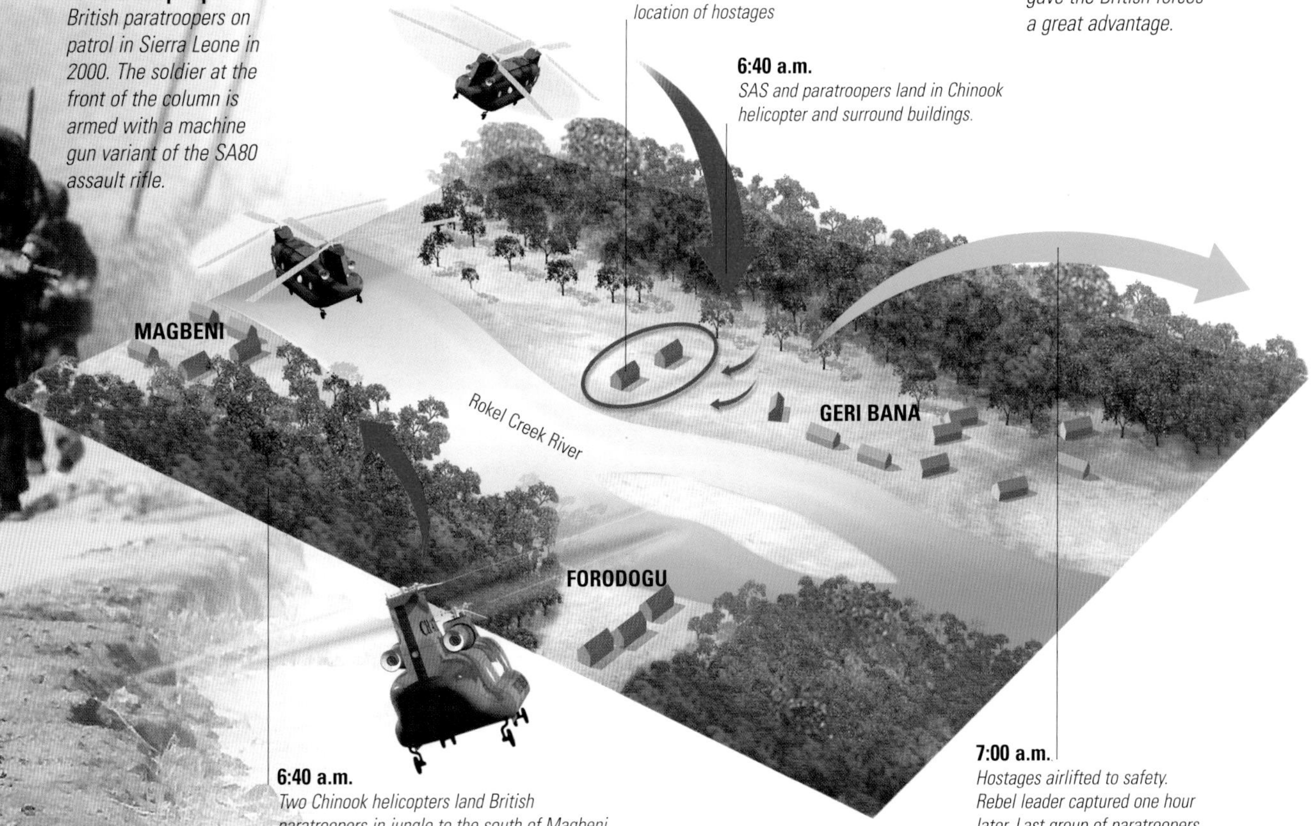
location of hostages
6:40 a.m.
SAS and paratroopers land in Chinook helicopter and surround buildings.
MAGBENI
Rokel Creek River
GERI BANA
FORODOGU
6:40 a.m.
Two Chinook helicopters land British paratroopers in jungle to the south of Magbeni to cut off reinforcements to Geri Bana.
7:00 a.m.
Hostages airlifted to safety. Rebel leader captured one hour later. Last group of paratroopers airlifted out of Geri Bana at 4:00 p.m.

▼ **Helicopter rescue**
The combined Parachute Regiment and SAS force approached the enemy position in helicopters. The element of surprise gave the British forces a great advantage.

Russian Spetsnaz

Spetsnaz is short for "Voiska Spetsialnoye Nasranie," a Russian term meaning "troops of special purpose." Formed in 1945, the unit was refined during the Cold War (1945–90) for roles ranging from assaults and demolitions to spying and assassination. Since the collapse of the Soviet Union in 1991, a number of successful missions have proved *Spetsnaz* to be an elite counter-terrorist force.

The term *Spetsnaz* refers to a collection of Russian elite forces that fulfill a broad range of specialized military roles, from hostage-rescue to intelligence-gathering. There are *Spetsnaz* units within the Russian Army and Navy, and also within the Federal Security Bureau. *Spetsnaz* troops are hand-picked from all branches of the Russian military, and training in the many required disciplines lasts up to five years.

Russian partisans

In the struggle against the German invaders during World War II (1939–45), special groups of Russian soldiers were trained to conduct long-range assault and demolition operations behind enemy lines. Russian civilian resistance fighters, or partisans, were vital to their success, acting as guides for military teams. In return, the partisans were trained in the techniques of sabotage. These combined units effectively became Soviet special forces groups and were the seeds of the modern *Spetsnaz*.

Partisan fighter
A Russian partisan in World War II. Partisans became part of Russian special forces units.

ORGANIZATION

Before the break-up of the Soviet Union in 1991, there were about 30,000 *Spetsnaz* troops. Each Soviet Army contained a brigade of *Spetsnaz*, numbering 1,300 troops divided up into 10-man teams. There were also four *Spetsnaz* naval brigades – one in each Soviet fleet – plus other groups stationed throughout the Soviet Union according to need.

▲ **Urban combat**
Spetsnaz *recruits learn city fighting techniques on a Moscow range. Urban combat is one of the most dangerous aspects of special forces work.*

▶ ***Spetsnaz* soldier**
A Spetsnaz *soldier with his machine gun, seen in the war against the Chechen rebels. This picture was taken in winter. The gloves are to prevent his fingers sticking to gun metal.*

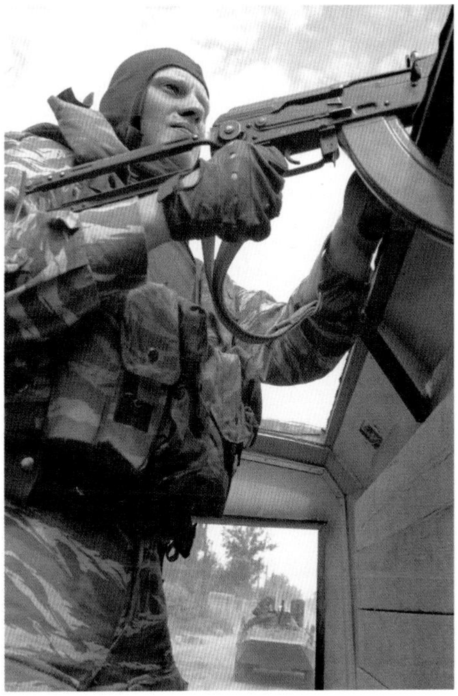

▲ **Invisible troops**
Spetsnaz *troops, such as this one, often wear ordinary Russian military uniforms. This allows them to work unnoticed among regular units.*

Today, there are four major *Spetsnaz* groupings. *Spetsnaz* FSB consists of two teams controlled by the Federal Security Bureau. Alpha Team is primarily responsible for counter-terrorism. In 2002, 200 of its troops were involved in rescuing 700 civilians who were being held hostage in a Moscow theater by 50 Chechen terrorists. The second unit, Vega Team, looks after security around sensitive installations, such as nuclear power plants. The *Spetsnaz* MVD unit consists of elite combat troops comparable to the US Army Rangers (see pp68–73). In contrast, the *Spetsnaz* GRU group is comparable to the British Special Air Service (see pp46–53), and specializes in cross-border reconnaissance and assassinations. The Russian Navy also has its own *Spetsnaz* force, involved in the protection of shipping and in coastal reconnaissance missions.

TRAINING

Recruits to *Spetsnaz* units undergo an initial training program that lasts six months. Part of this time is spent in the forests of Siberia in northern Russia, learning wilderness survival techniques. In addition to instruction in elite-standard infantry skills, other courses include parachuting, lock-picking, foreign languages, and rappelling. Hand-to-hand combat, assassination techniques, and knife fighting are also taught. *Spetsnaz* training is severe, and its live-firing exercises replicate the dangers of real combat. Fatalities are common, and the men who emerge at the end of the program are among the most formidable soldiers in the military world.

Helicopter gunships

Spetsnaz units rely heavily on the firepower of helicopter gunships in assault operations. The main gunship is the Mi-24 Hind. This large helicopter is armed with a 12.7-mm., four-barreled Gatling gun that has a 4,000 rpm. fire rate. It also carries anti-tank rockets and missiles. The Hind can deliver considerable firepower, but its performance is dated. Hinds are being replaced by more versatile craft.

Mi-24 Hind
This Hind helicopter is armed with rockets and missiles for battlefield anti-tank missions.

▶ ***Spetsnaz* recruits**
Russian paratroopers on parade. Many Spetsnaz *soldiers are recruited from among paratrooper units.*

President Amin
Hafizullah Amin was president of Afghanistan when Soviet forces invaded. He was assassinated by the Spetsnaz.

BACKGROUND

In April 1978, Mohammad Daoud, president of Afghanistan, was killed in a violent coup. He had tried to keep Afghanistan neutral between the US and Soviet power blocs, while drawing aid from both. The new president, Mohammad Taraki, was firmly pro-Soviet. He attempted a Soviet-style reform of Afghanistan's traditionalist society. This prompted armed rebellion throughout the Muslim population, and the situation was further inflamed by the anti-Islamic policies of Prime Minister Hafizullah Amin (from March 1979). Hearing of a Soviet plot to remove him, Amin responded by having Taraki killed in his palace (September 14, 1979). Amin then declared himself president. With rebel groups controlling much of Afghanistan, and, fearing that defeat of the Afghan regime could incite revolt in the Soviet Union's own Muslim states, Soviet forces invaded to begin a 10-year occupation.

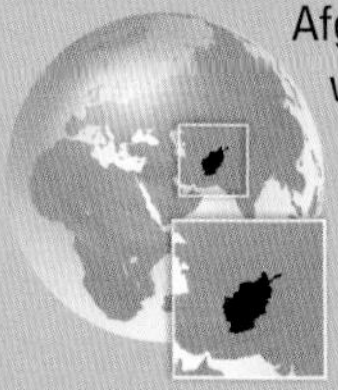

Russian Spetsnaz: Afghanistan, 1980s

The *Spetsnaz* played a key part in the Soviet Union's invasion and occupation of Afghanistan between 1979 and 1989. Although 10 years of Afghan guerrilla resistance eventually forced a Soviet withdrawal, *Spetsnaz* operations were the most successful element of the invaders' military efforts, taking the war into the guerrillas' heartlands.

Spetsnaz involvement in Afghanistan began with a deployment on December 10, 1979, to Bagram, a strategically vital town just to the north of the Afghan capital, Kabul. These soldiers, and units from the Soviet 105th Guards Airborne Division, seized Bagram over the following two weeks, while also moving southward to capture and occupy Kabul International Airport by December 24.

That date signaled the beginning of the Soviet invasion proper. *Spetsnaz* troops made lightning seizures of key installations, such as the strategic air bases at Shind and Kandahar, in advance of the main land invasions. The ruthlessness of the *Spetsnaz* units was demonstrated on December 25 by the assassination of Afghan president Hafizullah Amin, who was executed, along with his family and staff.

▶ **Hind gunships**
A pair of Mi-24 Hind helicopters sweep over a valley in Afghanistan. Spetsnaz *troops often used Hinds to move around the country, striking at enemy guerrilla bases.*

▼ **Soviet armor**
A Soviet armored column moves through an Afghan village in the 1980s. In the background are the mountains where the Mujahedeen located their bases.

GUERRILLA WARFARE

By mid-January 1980, the Soviets had, in effect, taken over Afghanistan. Yet a tenacious guerrilla war continued, waged by Afghan and pro-Islamic Mujahedeen factions. These groups favored hitting Soviet columns and bases with ambushes, then disappearing back into the Afghan mountains before Soviet forces could respond. As US forces had experienced in the Vietnam War (1965–75), the death tolls from such actions could be individually small but significant overall. Conventional military tactics were unsuccessful in overcoming the Afghan guerrillas, so in 1983 *Spetsnaz* troops were given the task of developing a more innovative form of warfare.

▶ **Ambush**
This Afghan Army column en route to Kabul has just been ambushed by the Mujahedeen. The guerrillas were so effective that the Spetsnaz *were given the task of attempting to destroy them.*

▲ **AKS-74** (1974)
This assault rifle was used by *Spetsnaz* troops during the war in Afghanistan. Its curved magazine held 30 rounds, and its metal stock could be folded, making it useful in confined spaces.

Length	36.5 in. (92.8 cm.)
Weight	8.6 lb. (3.9 kg.)
Rate of fire	100 rpm.
Caliber	5.45-mm.

SOVIET BATTLE TACTICS

The *Spetsnaz*'s primary roles were to destroy the Mujahedeen's mountain strongholds and bases, to interrupt their supply columns, and to conduct covert reconnaissance.

The first role required competent mountaineering skills, something initially lacking because *Spetsnaz* training produced soldiers to fight in flat European terrain. Yet *Spetsnaz* troops became increasingly effective in this respect. Helicopters would make several landings 2–3 miles (3–5 km.) from the objective, setting down troops during only one of the landings to confuse the enemy. *Spetsnaz* units then advanced under cover of darkness to wipe out entire villages. Helicopter gunships often assisted with rocket fire. But *Spetsnaz* casualties were heavy, and torture, mutilation, and execution awaited those captured alive by the Afghan fighters.

Assaults on guerrilla supply columns used helicopters, ambushes, mine-laying, or even all three. Ambushes were dangerous, not least because of the threat of massive detonations of guerrilla explosives when hit by Soviet fire.

Only those *Spetsnaz* troops with excellent mountaineering skills conducted covert reconnaissance. Soldiers set up hidden observation posts in the mountains. From there they sent encoded messages to their home bases to organize ambushes, airstrikes, or mine-laying operations.

As the war progressed, *Spetsnaz* troops were frequently used as forward units in major infantry maneuvers. By the late 1980s, the availability to the Mujahedeen of US Stinger surface-to-air missiles made helicopter deployment increasingly perilous.

By 1989 *Spetsnaz* units were fighting a losing battle against a well-motivated enemy, and in that year the Soviet Union withdrew from its unpopular war.

The Mujahedeen

Holy warriors
Mujahedeen fighters in Afghanistan believed Allah was on their side against Soviet forces. Their guerrilla tactics eventually secured victory.

"Mujahedeen" means "holy warriors," and refers to Islamic guerrilla fighters. In Afghanistan, they were a group of diverse factions, each with different territorial claims. Fighting between factions was as common as opposition to the Soviet forces. When the communist regime in Afghanistan collapsed in 1992, the Mujahedeen conflicts turned into civil war. During the Soviet occupation, however, they were transformed from poorly armed tribesmen into a powerful insurgent group, supplied by the USA.

US 160th SOAR

The 160th Special Operations Aviation Regiment (SOAR) is the aviation wing of US Army Special Operations Command. Flying state-of-the-art helicopters, the regiment handles the airborne deployment and mission support of US special forces units, often involving high-risk night-time infiltration (delivering troops and supplies) and exfiltration (evacuations).

The 160th Special Operations Aviation Regiment (Airborne) was formed on May 16, 1980. Following an aborted attempt to rescue hostages from the US embassy in Iran in 1980, US military planners recognized the need for a purpose-trained aviation wing to support special forces operations. A small team was created using personnel from various US Army airborne units, including the 101st and 159th Aviation Battalions. The new unit became known as Task Force 160. In October 1981 it achieved battalion status, becoming the 160th Aviation Battalion. The battalion first served in Operation Urgent Fury, the US invasion of Grenada in 1983. Such was the demand for the unit's skills that it achieved regimental status in 1990. Today, SOAR has 1,800 personnel and consists of three main operational battalions, with plans for a fourth to meet increased demand for special-operations aviation capability.

▶ **MH-47**
The MH-47 helicopter has a probe at the front for refueling from a tanker plane in flight.

160th SOAR badge

TACTICS AND EQUIPMENT

The 160th SOAR functions within the US Army Special Operations Command (USASOC). Typical tactical roles include covert infiltration and exfiltration of special forces units, medical evacuation, close-air support for ground assaults, resupply missions, and rescue operations. Because many of the 160th's activities take place at night, the regiment has acquired the nickname "Night Stalkers."

The regiment fulfills such demanding roles through its extremely high standard of equipment and pilots. Helicopters are its primary vehicles. They include the OH-6A Cayuse, the AH-6 "Little Bird" attack helicopter, the MH-60 Black Hawk, and the MH-47E Chinook. Together, these aircraft provide the full range of airborne attack, deployment, and resupply capabilities. All are fitted with cutting-edge technology, including night-vision devices, laser-targeting

Night-vision goggles

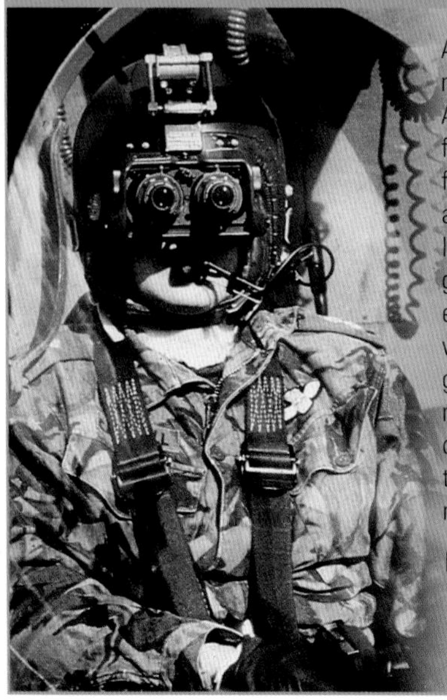

Aircrew of the 160th SOAR wear night-vision goggles, such as the ANVIS AN/AVS-6 system, when flying night operations. The goggles fit on the pilot's helmet visor-guard and provide vision in all starlight and lowlight conditions. Because the goggles have a separate lens for each eye, the pilot has full-depth vision, while the close fit of the goggles gives peripheral view. The newer AN/AVS-7 system also displays instrument information to the eyepieces to give aircrew even more sophisticated control at night.

Night-vision goggles
Night-vision goggles like these allow the pilots of the 160th SOAR to fly their helicopters in the dark.

▼ **Expert fliers**
Pilots of the 160th SOAR train for hundreds of hours to become expert fliers.

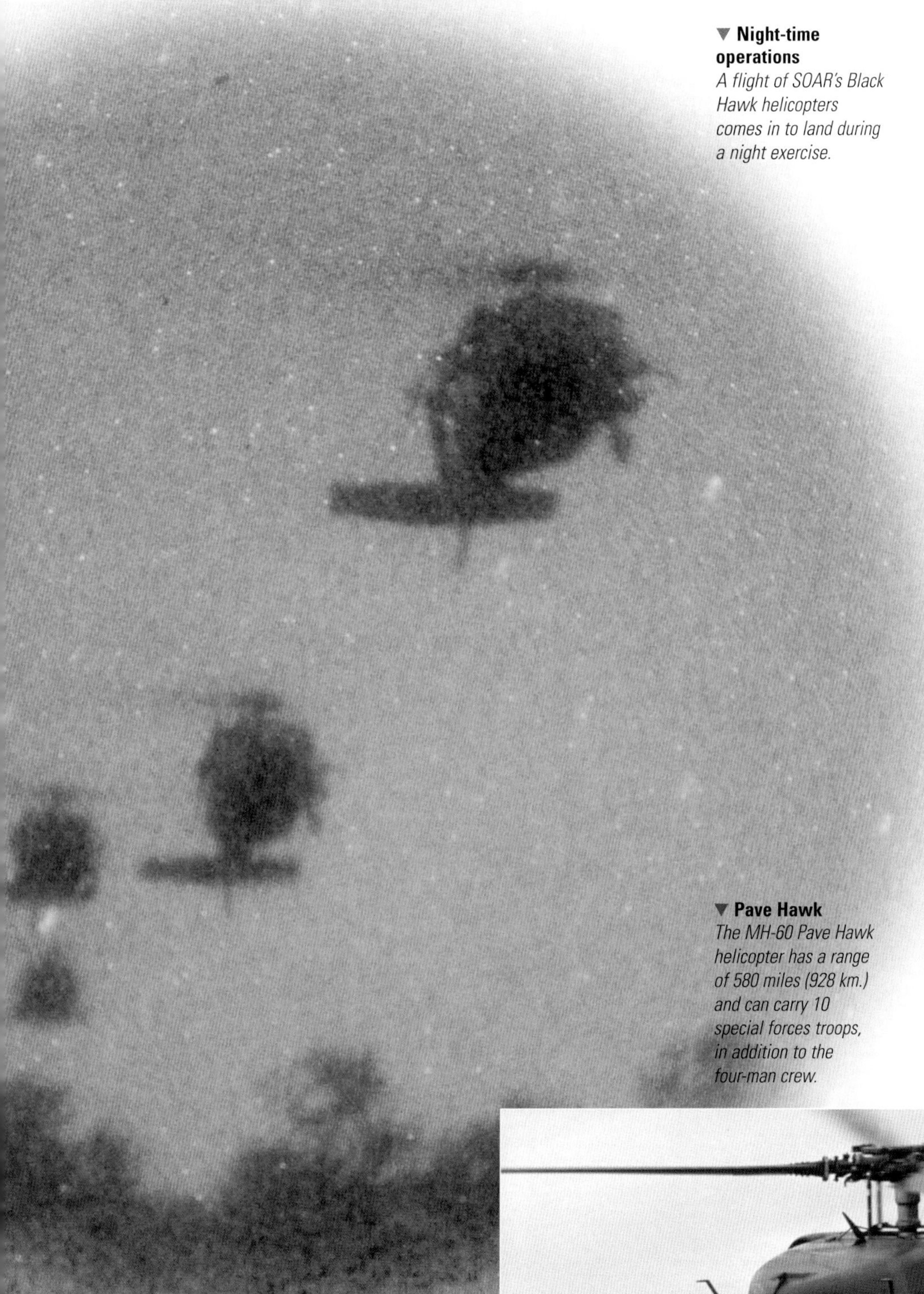

▼ Night-time operations
A flight of SOAR's Black Hawk helicopters comes in to land during a night exercise.

The "Little Bird"

The "Little Birds" are a series of helicopters operated by the 160th SOAR based on the OH-6A Cayuse. The basic OH-6A is a light tactical helicopter with high maneuverability and a top speed of 150 mph. (240 kph.). It is used in deployment, observation, attack, and medical-evacuation roles. The regiment also employs two variants: the MH-6 transport/utility model to carry up to nine fully armed troops; and the AH-6 attack version, with armament options of 2.75-in. rockets, a 7.62-mm. minigun, Hellfire missiles, a 30-mm. cannon, and a .50-caliber machine-gun.

OH-6A "Little Bird"
The "Little Bird" is a highly versatile light helicopter used by the 160th SOAR.

designators, and fast-rope rappelling systems for lowering personnel to the ground. In addition, the helicopters are equipped with infrared suppressive exhausts (to reduce the aircraft's visibility to enemy night-vision devices and surface-to-air missile systems).

TRAINING

A dedicated Training Company handles candidates, who must be experienced Army pilots, preferably with 1,000 flight hours' experience (including 100 hours using night-vision technology). A seven-day psychological and physical assessment at Fort Campbell, Kentucky, is followed by eight months of rigorous training. This emphasizes low-level flying, tactical flying over different terrains, and adverse-weather flying. Pilots also learn how to use night-vision goggles and bomb-targeting devices, and are taught special forces escape, evasion, and survival skills. Now numbering 1,800 personnel, and flying the world's most sophisticated helicopters, SOAR pilots are some of the best-trained in military aviation.

▼ Pave Hawk
The MH-60 Pave Hawk helicopter has a range of 580 miles (928 km.) and can carry 10 special forces troops, in addition to the four-man crew.

US 160th SOAR: Mogadishu, 1993

On October 3, 1993, a flight of Black Hawk helicopters from the US 160th Special Operations Aviation Regiment (SOAR) delivered 140 soldiers of the elite Delta Force and Army Rangers into Mogadishu, capital city of the African state of Somalia. However, their mission – to capture supporters of a prominent warlord – went wrong. Two helicopters were shot down, and 19 US soldiers were killed and almost 100 wounded. It was one of the worst days in recent US military history, but also the occasion of desperate acts of heroism and bravery.

Ranger patrol
A US Army Ranger on duty in Mogadishu, Somalia, in 1993. The role of US special forces units was to protect the United Nations food convoys.

BACKGROUND

US involvement in Somalia began in 1991 when the country's civilian government collapsed under civil war. As clan and factional warlords fought for control, the population began to starve. The United Nations (UN) began a large-scale humanitarian effort, Operation Provide Relief, to supply food aid. This was generally successful, but the precarious situation in Mogadishu, the Somali capital, prompted the launching of Operation Restore Hope, a limited military action intended to bring some measure of peace to the streets. One warlord in particular threatened UN operations: Muhammed Farrah Aidid. His militiamen were well armed with modern rifles, rocket launchers, and even a few tanks. After frequent attacks by his supporters on UN personnel, the capture of Aidid became a top priority. US special forces Delta Force and the Army Rangers were called in.

The United States was in Somalia as part of the United Nations (UN) peace-keeping operation. In the face of increasing aggression toward UN forces, a plan was drawn up to strike at the heart of the problem – warlord "General" Farrah Aidid and his supporters. Intelligence from agents on the ground suggested that two of Aidid's key lieutenants would be meeting in the heart of Mogadishu, the sprawling Somali capital. It was decided to seize them in a "snatch" operation.

▶ **Urban operation**
In October 1993, US special forces soldiers, facing enormous odds, were pinned down in Mogadishu's streets.

THE ASSAULT

Operation Task Force Ranger (TFR), as the mission was named, was launched during the midafternoon. MH-60 Black Hawk helicopters from the 160th Special Operations Aviation Regiment (SOAR) flew the special forces soldiers into the operational area and provided aerial support. As the aircraft approached they received no fire from the ground. Delta Force and US Army Rangers then descended from the helicopters by rope. The Rangers cordoned off the target house and the Delta members stormed the building. At this point, everything started to go wrong.

Incoming small-arms fire from Aidid supporters increased on the US forces. Vehicles from a US convoy sent out to collect the targeted local militiamen were hit by mortar fire, and a rocket-propelled grenade (RPG) succeeded in bringing down an MH-60 Black Hawk, which crashed in the street below. Other US helicopters flew to the crash scene to rescue the injured crew. Special forces teams rappelled onto the site from hovering MH-60s, but three of these helicopters were also hit, one crashing into the ground after an RPG hit on its tail rotor.

Throughout the night the US troops on the ground held off thousands of armed Somalis in a series of intense firefights. Rescue finally came early the next morning, with the arrival of the hastily assembled Quick Reaction Force, made up of locally based UN troops.

PROFILE

Muhammed Farrah Aidid

Dates 1930–96
Unit not applicable
Rank "General"

Muhammed Farrah Aidid, a self-styled "general" of the large Hawiye clan, was a major figure in the overthrow of Somali president Siad Barre (1919–95), having served him for many years. Aidid was heavily involved in the subsequent civil war. His forces were well armed and vicious, and were a constant thorn in the side of the United Nations' troops. Evading capture, he declared himself president of Somalia after forcing UN forces to abandon the country in 1995. His dominance was short-lived, however: He was shot dead during factional fighting in 1996.

▼ **UH-60 Black Hawk**
US 160th SOAR helicopters, including Black Hawks like these, are painted black for use at night. Highly maneuverable and heavily armed, they are an effective way to get special forces troops to the area of operations.

▼ Confronting hostile crowds
The situation on the ground in Mogadishu was confused and frightening. Hostile crowds like these hindered US troops in carrying out their tasks.

THE AFTERMATH

The US soldiers and pilots showed immense bravery against terrible odds. In strict military terms the operation was a success because 24 prisoners had been taken, but the human cost was high: 19 US servicemen dead, 84 injured, and 500 Somalis killed. The confidence and international credibility of US special forces were severely shaken by the experience.

The Technical

The "Technical" is a four-wheel-drive truck with some form of heavy weapon: a heavy machine-gun or an anti-tank rocket. It is a regular sight in many developing countries, being widely adopted by guerrilla groups and urban militias. It is also used as a personnel carrier, with troops and militiamen clinging to any available space. While no match for purpose-built military vehicles, it operates well in harsh conditions, and is popular with those who cannot acquire modern equipment.

Mobile firepower
This "Technical" acts as both a mobile heavy weapon platform and a personnel carrier.

▼ Anti-terrorist operations
US special forces soldiers place a Somali detainee in the back of their vehicle.

French Foreign Legion 2nd REP

The *Deuxième Régiment Étranger de Parachutistes* (2nd REP – 2nd Foreign Parachute Regiment) is the airborne unit of the French Foreign Legion. Although one of the youngest Legion formations, it is also among the most battle-tested. Today, the 2nd REP is France's airborne spearhead. The 1,500 paratroopers who make up the regiment are multi-skilled soldiers, capable of deployment anywhere at short notice.

2nd REP cap badge

The 2nd REP had a troubled early history. Between July 1948 and November 1949, three parachute battalions were created to provide shock troops for the bloody French colonial war in Indochina (see pp42–43). They suffered disproportionately. The 1st Battalion *Étranger de Parachutistes* (1st BEP), for example, was entirely wiped out and then reformed in 1950. Then both the 1st and 2nd BEPs were lost at the battle of Dien Bien Phu in Indochina in 1954 (see box on p91).

After the war in Indochina, the 1st and 2nd BEPs were reformed, increased to regimental size, and renamed 1st and 2nd Regiments (REPs). They were deployed to fight in French Algeria in 1955. In April 1961, following the French government's decision to withdraw from Algeria, the 1st REP was involved in a mutiny, which was put down. The 1st REP was then disbanded.

AIRBORNE FORCES

The 2nd REP, however, was reformed in late 1961 and placed under the leadership of Lieutenant-Colonel Caillard, under the overall command of the French 11th Parachute Division. The 2nd REP subsequently became an elite airborne commando force capable of operations ranging from conventional infantry warfare to hostage-rescue missions. Notable actions during its history include anti-guerrilla warfare in Chad (1970s); helping to free 28 French children from a hijacked bus on the Djibouti/Somali border (1976); a paratroop rescue of 2,000 European civilians from separatist rebels in the Congo (1978); and peace-keeping operations throughout the world.

▼ Rifle training
A paratrooper in training, using the 5.56-mm. FAMAS assault rifle. This weapon is favored by Foreign Legion paratroopers.

▲ Freefall jumping
Many members of the regiment are trained in high altitude, low opening (HALO) techniques.

The kepi

The kepi is the traditional ceremonial headgear of the French Foreign Legion. Its origins are in the Legion's first base camp at Sidi-bel-Abbès, Algeria, where the white-colored high crown and wide brim protected against the scorching North African sun. Private-rank soldiers wear a white kepi (actually a dark hat with a white cover), while noncommissioned officers and officers wear a black kepi, with the cover removed.

A Legion parade
The soldiers in this French Foreign Legion parade in Algeria are wearing the unit's traditional white kepi.

TRAINING

In 2003 the regiment numbered about 1,500 personnel, and was based in Calvi, Corsica. All men pass through Legion basic training before going on to parachute school with the 2nd REP. Parachute training lasts five weeks. During this time each recruit must make six jumps of increasing difficulty, the final one being with a full pack and weapons at night. Once the jumps are successfully completed, the paratrooper qualifies to join the 2nd REP. The soldier can go on to take advanced high-altitude parachute training during a three-week commando course in combat and reconnaissance skills.

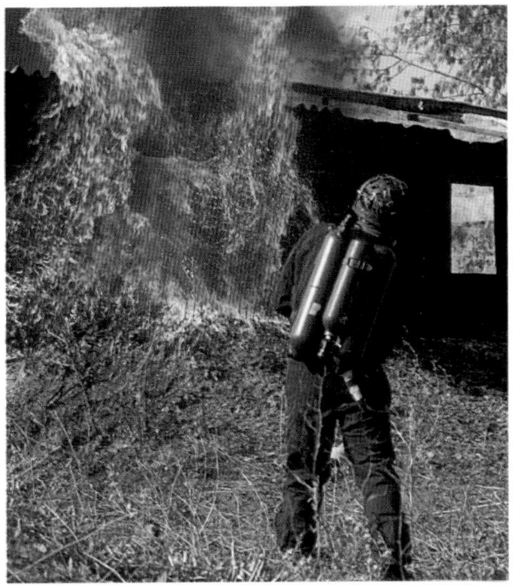

▶ Flamethrower
The paratroopers of the French Foreign Legion use a wide variety of weapons, including flamethrowers.

Dien Bien Phu

The battle of Dien Bien Phu in Indochina represented the French attempt to defeat the nationalist-communist Indochinese forces ("Vietminh") in a pitched battle and so provide leverage in ongoing peace negotiations. French paratroopers occupied the valley (in present-day northern Vietnam) by airdrop on November 20, 1953, and began turning it into a fortress. Of the 15,000 French soldiers, 1,500 were Legion paratroopers. Suffering terrible losses from an onslaught of over 50,000 Vietminh troops and artillery, the French surrendered on May 7, 1954. French control in Indochina collapsed.

Dropping into Dien Bien Phu
A Legion paratrooper watches as his comrades drop into the fortified valley of Dien Bien Phu in 1953.

ORGANIZATION

The 2nd REP has four combat companies; an Equipment and Repair Company; a Regimental Command and Services Company; and a Reconnaissance and Support Company. This last unit also contains an elite airborne long-distance reconnaissance platoon, which can be used to carry out target-finding or secret operations missions.

The combat companies have different tactical specialties. Urban combat, night fighting, and anti-tank warfare are the responsibility of 1 Company. Mountain and arctic warfare is the preserve of 2 Company; 3 Company specializes in amphibious warfare; and demolitions, sabotage, and sniping are the tasks of 4 Company. The Reconnaissance and Support Company provides artillery support, including fire from 120-mm. mortars and vehicle-mounted anti-tank missiles. This support means that, in wartime, the landing zones chosen by the 2nd REP can be protected from enemy assault.

All elements of the 2nd REP are fully trained to operate from both helicopters and fixed-wing aircraft.

▲ Jump training
Foreign Legion paratroopers board a Transall transport aircraft at their base in Corsica, heavily laden with parachutes and bergen backpacks.

Mining town
The town of Kolwezi is at the center of a mining area. Rebels seized it in the hope of using the area and its European residents as bargaining chips.

BACKGROUND

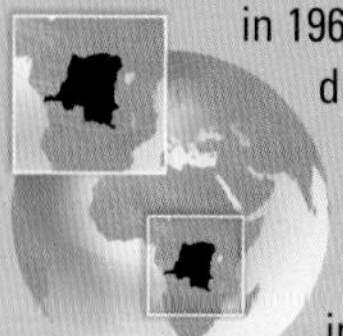

The independent Democratic Republic of Congo was born in 1960, after decades of Belgian rule. Immediately, rebel forces in Katanga province – a region containing much of the country's rich mineral and metal reserves – attempted to form their own breakaway state. The initial rebel offensive was quashed with UN support, but the province remained turbulent. In 1971 Congo became Zaire, but the new name did not stop the Katanga separatists, now operating from bases in neighboring Angola. In 1978, a large group of rebel Katanga Tigers made a bold cross-border incursion into Zaire, attacking the town of Kolwezi. The Kolwezi area is a mining region with large deposits of coal, zinc, silver, gold, and platinum. The rebels hoped to capture this valuable zone and use the Europeans working in the area as hostages in subsequent negotiations. When this tactic failed, they began killing the hostages. Since most of the captives were French, the French government felt bound to act to save them. The 2nd REP was thus mobilized.

French Foreign Legion 2nd REP: Kolwezi, 1978

In May 1978, separatist rebels seized the town of Kolwezi in Katanga province, southern Zaire, taking hostage some 2,300 European (mostly French) citizens. The French government initiated Operation Leopard, a two-day airborne action using the 2nd French Foreign Legion Parachute Regiment (2nd REP) to rescue the hostages.

▶ Parachute assault
The threat of imminent death to the hostages at Kolwezi left no option but the danger of a mass parachute assault.

The catalyst for Operation Leopard was reports that the European hostages in Kolwezi were being killed by the Katanga Tigers. Southern Zaire's extensive metal-mining industries attracted many nationalities, but a large part of its European community was French. When an airdrop of Zairian Army paratroops on May 16 failed to rescue the captives, the French government ordered the 2nd REP under Colonel Philippe Erulin to carry out a hostage-rescue mission.

OPERATION LEOPARD

Erulin put together Operation Leopard in less than 24 hours. On the night of May 17, the entire regiment began the long flight down from Camp Raffali, Corsica, to the Zairian capital, Kinshasa, aboard DC-8 aircraft. Once at Kinshasa, 2nd REP had to rely on Zaire's air force to take it to Kolwezi. Just four C-130s were available, insufficient to take the whole regiment at once. The situation in Kolwezi was deteriorating rapidly, so there was no option but to make a two-wave jump. The first wave consisted of the 1st, 2nd, and 3rd Companies (about 500 men), packed aboard the aircraft. The 4th and Support Companies would drop in the second wave.

On May 19, 2nd REP began its drop over the outskirts of Kolwezi Old Town. The landing was virtually uncontested by the rebels, who were busy looting and killing in the town itself. The paratroopers went straight onto the offensive, using urban-warfare tactics and heavy firepower. In contrast, the Tigers were disorganized, without proper defensive lines

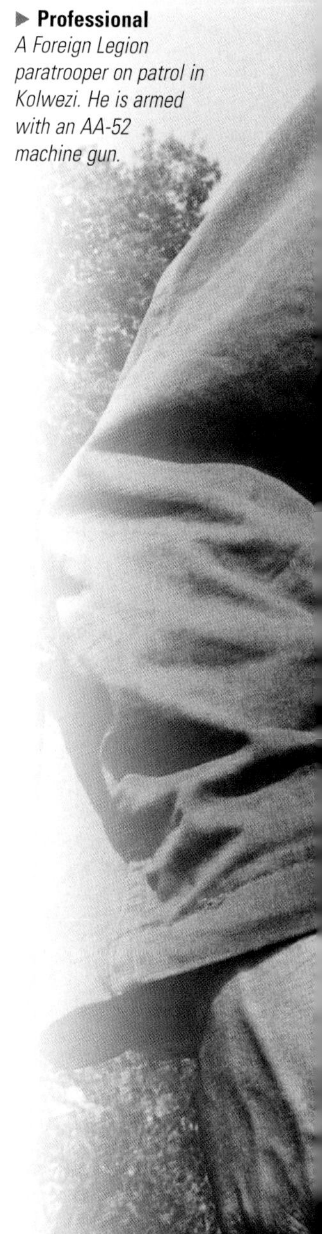

▶ Professional
A Foreign Legion paratrooper on patrol in Kolwezi. He is armed with an AA-52 machine gun.

▲ Clearing Kolwezi
A 2nd REP soldier kicks in the door of a house in Kolwezi in search of rebel soldiers. Individual Tigers tried to hide in houses hoping they would remain undiscovered. However, the paratroopers searched the town thoroughly. No one escaped.

PROFILE: Colonel Philippe Erulin

Dates 1937–79
Unit 2nd REP
Rank Colonel

Colonel Philippe Erulin was the ideal commander for the Kolwezi mission. He was a veteran of France's war in Algeria, and had a deep understanding of counter-insurgency operations. Erulin had taken charge of 2nd REP on July 9, 1976, and demonstrated daring leadership. In Kolwezi, he had no advance information about the drop zone, the location of the hostages, or the nature of the opposition, but his confidence in the Legion saw him literally jump into the unknown with his men. His after-action report stated that the mission took "important but calculated risks." Erulin died of a heart attack in 1979 while still a serving officer.

or coherent tactics. They did, however, respond with heavy small-arms fire and some tenacious acts of individual resistance. Although the town had to be cleared house by house, by sunset on May 19 much of Kolwezi was in French hands and many European citizens were finally safe.

FRENCH VICTORY

The second wave of paratroopers landed on May 20 near Lubumbashi, just east of Kolwezi. As they advanced from the drop zone, French troops fought a heavy engagement with the Tigers on the approaches to Kolwezi, killing 80 rebels for few French casualties. They helped to secure the New Town area and then went on to rout rebel troops in Metal Shaba. Over the next five days the two groups of 2nd REP forced the survivors back across the border into neighboring Angola.

Five soldiers died and 20 were wounded in the liberation of Kolwezi. Hostage losses were much heavier – around 300 dead. However, 2,000 were liberated.

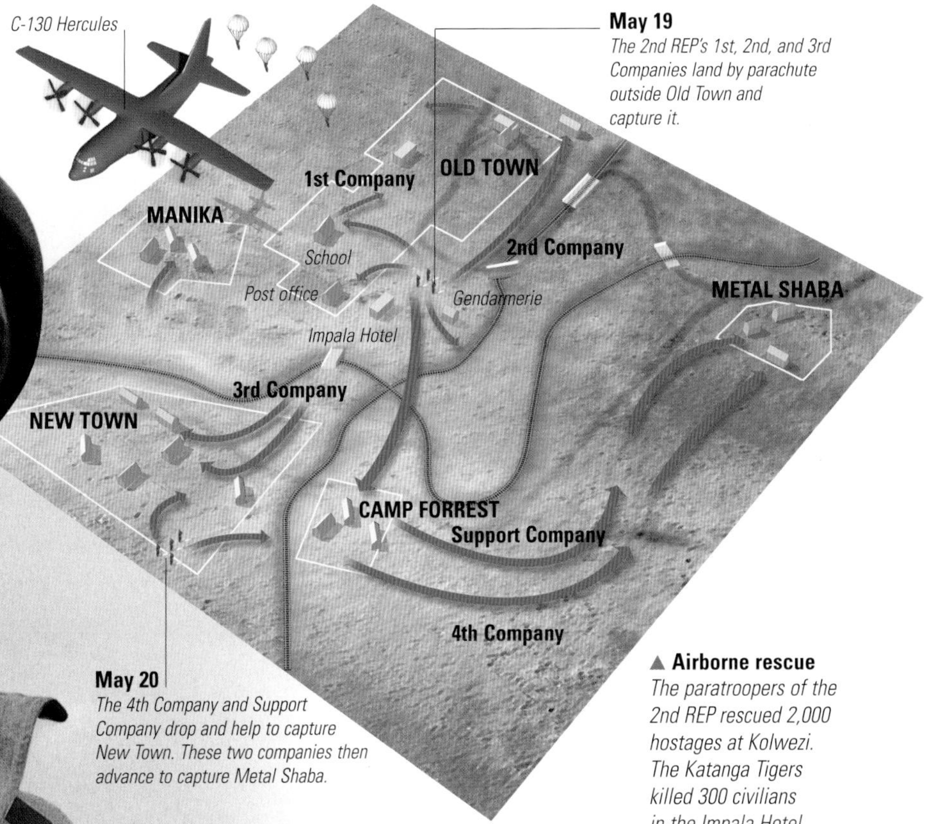
C-130 Hercules
May 19
The 2nd REP's 1st, 2nd, and 3rd Companies land by parachute outside Old Town and capture it.
1st Company
OLD TOWN
MANIKA
School
2nd Company
Post office
Gendarmerie
METAL SHABA
Impala Hotel
3rd Company
NEW TOWN
CAMP FORREST
Support Company
4th Company
May 20
The 4th Company and Support Company drop and help to capture New Town. These two companies then advance to capture Metal Shaba.

▲ Airborne rescue
The paratroopers of the 2nd REP rescued 2,000 hostages at Kolwezi. The Katanga Tigers killed 300 civilians in the Impala Hotel.

The Tigers

The Katanga Tigers have been a force in Congolese/Zairian politics since 1960. They have troubled most of the country's regimes and switch political philosophies with ease. During the 1970s, they were about 4,000 strong and led by Major Mufu, fighting mainly from bases in Angola, with the aim of establishing an independent province in the south of the country. They are still active today.

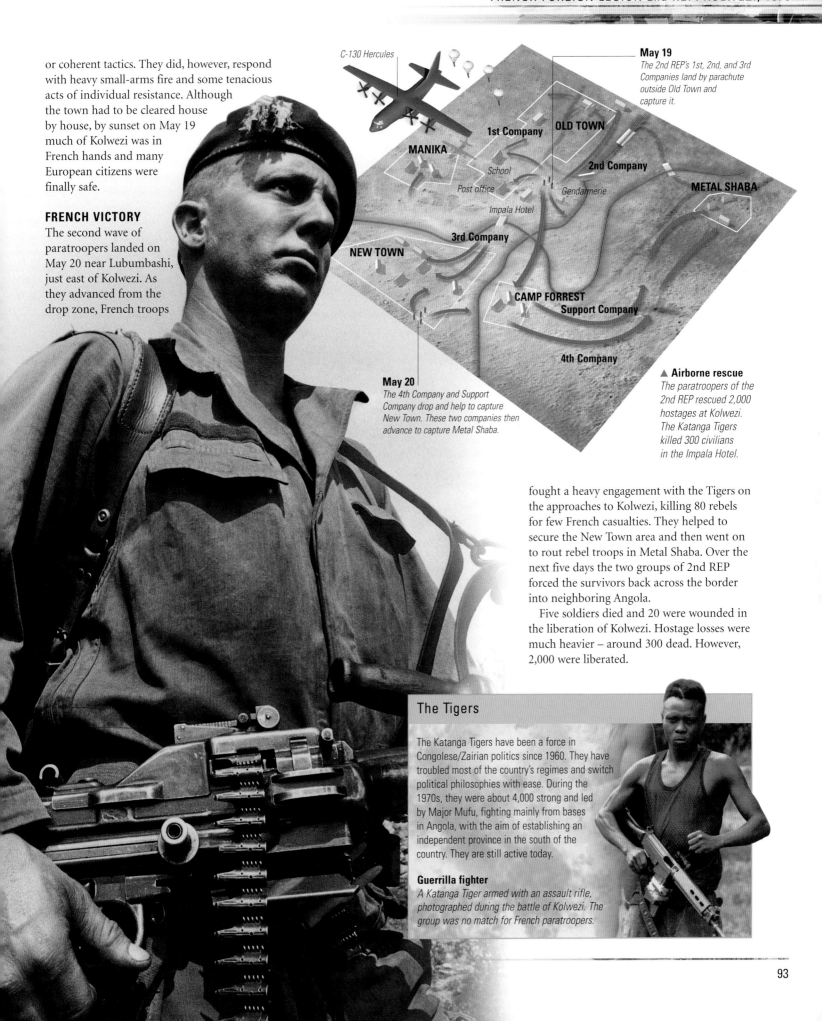

Guerrilla fighter
A Katanga Tiger armed with an assault rifle, photographed during the battle of Kolwezi. The group was no match for French paratroopers.

US airborne forces

The US Army's airborne divisions are the largest and best-equipped parachute force in the world, with more combat power than the armies of most countries. In 2003, the US 82nd Airborne Division's actions in Iraq re-established parachute drops as a viable operation of war. Powerful and mobile, with the latest weapons, helicopters, and vehicles, US airborne divisions are innovators of fast-moving, global military force.

▲ **Operation Urgent Fury**
The 82nd Airborne saw extensive action against the People's Revolutionary Army of Grenada in 1983, when US forces invaded the Caribbean island to overthrow the government.

The airborne forces of the United States Army are among the most decorated and respected units in American service. The origins of the two most famous – the 82nd and 101st Airborne Divisions – lie in World War I (1914–18), when both were infantry units. The units were reborn as parachute divisions during World War II (1939–45), when the term "Airborne" was attached to their names.

82nd Airborne Division badge

AIRBORNE OPERATIONS

Both the 82nd and the 101st Airborne Divisions saw action in World War II (1939–45), taking part in operations in Italy and North Africa, and playing crucial roles in the Allied invasion of France in June 1944 and the Arnhem Offensive in Holland later the same year. The 101st fought a famous action at the Belgian town of Bastogne during the Ardennes Offensive in December 1944, where they held off German forces for several days against all the odds.

The fame of US airborne forces was further enhanced during the Vietnam War (1965–75). This conflict, between American-backed South Vietnam and communist North Vietnam, saw the introduction of a new fighting technique: Large formations of US troops were deployed to the battlefield by helicopter. The 101st Airborne Division was at the forefront of this pioneering move. Swooping down behind enemy lines and taking the fight to the opposition remains the principal fighting strategy of the "Screaming Eagles," as the 101st are known.

The 82nd Airborne Division saw action in Grenada, in the Caribbean Ocean, in 1983; Panama in

▼ **Air mobility**
UH-60 Black Hawk helicopters can transport vehicles and 105-mm. artillery pieces via a cargo hook on the fuselage.

The Sheridan

The M551 Sheridan is an armored reconnaissance airborne assault vehicle in use with the 82nd Airborne Division. The Sheridan first entered service in 1968 and is armed with a 152-mm. gun/missile launcher, a 7.62-mm. machine gun, and a 12.7-mm. anti-aircraft gun. It was used in Vietnam and the Gulf War of 1991. It is operated by a crew of four.

One of a kind
The Sheridan remains the only US tank capable of being dropped by parachute.

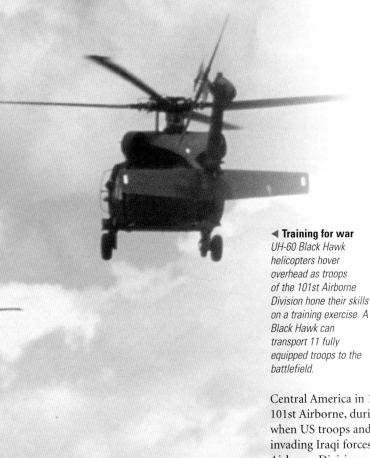

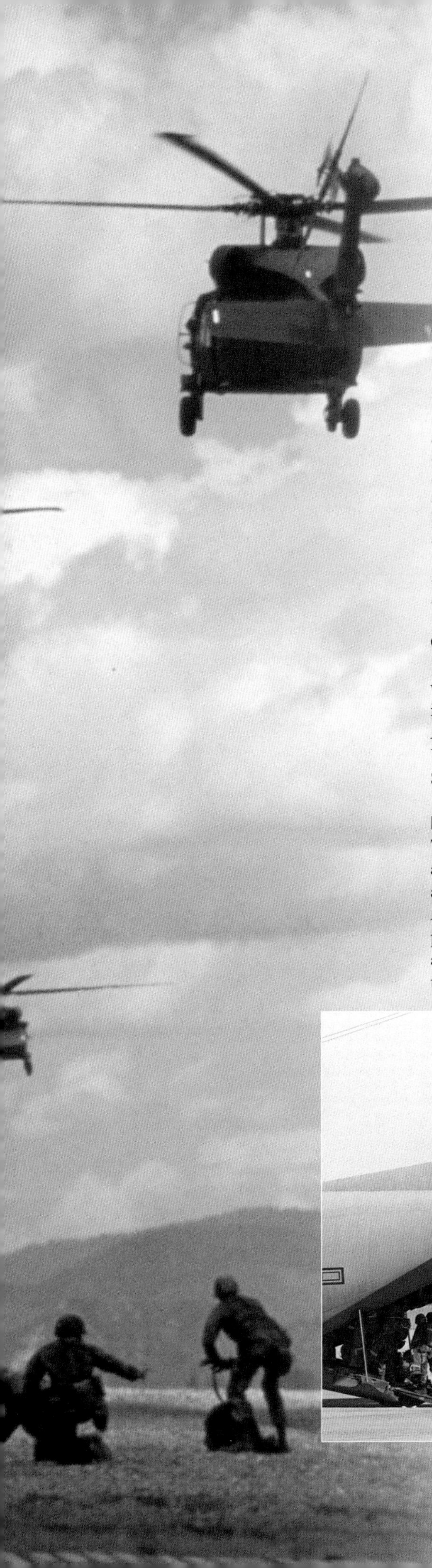

◀ **Training for war**
UH-60 Black Hawk helicopters hover overhead as troops of the 101st Airborne Division hone their skills on a training exercise. A Black Hawk can transport 11 fully equipped troops to the battlefield.

Helicopter strike force

The US airborne divisions are equipped with hundreds of UH-60 Black Hawk transport helicopters that transport troops to and from the battlefield. In addition, the AH-64 Apache is a formidable fighting machine that is used to clear landing areas and provide fire support for ground operations. The CH-47 Chinook provides the heavy-lift capability to bring in vehicles and artillery pieces.

Apache armaments
Armed with anti-tank missiles, rockets, and a 30-mm. automatic cannon, an Apache can be called by ground units to bring devastating firepower onto enemy positions.

Central America in 1989; and, along with the 101st Airborne, during the 1991 Gulf War, when US troops and their allies drove the invading Iraqi forces out of Kuwait. The 101st Airborne Division was also involved in the US–British action to overthrow Iraqi dictator Saddam Hussein and his regime in 2003.

DEPLOYMENT TACTICS

The principal difference between the two US airborne units is the manner in which they are deployed. The 14,500-strong 82nd Airborne Division reaches the battlefield by parachute. Jumping from a variety of large aircraft, including the C-130 Hercules transport plane, thousands of men can be set down behind enemy lines, equipped with all the necessary supplies and vehicles. In contrast, the 16,000-strong 101st Airborne Division is transported to the field of operations by helicopter. The 101st Division's vast helicopter fleet consists of more than 275 aircraft, including UH-60 Black Hawks and AH-64 Apache gunships.

SELECTION AND TRAINING

All new recruits to the US airborne forces undergo nine weeks of basic training, followed by a three-week Basic Airborne Training course, which includes parachute descents from a 250-ft. (77-m.) tower and a series of jumps from aircraft. Completing the program earns the recruit the right to join one of the US airborne regiments.

Highly trained personnel, combined with the latest weapons, helicopters, and vehicles, gives the United States a global-capable airborne strike force.

◀ **Troop transport**
Members of the 82nd Airborne Division paratroopers board a C-130 Hercules transport plane. The aircraft carries 64 fully equipped paratroopers.

Mourning the dead
US soldiers honor their fallen comrades. Casualties such as the 56 men killed on "Hamburger Hill" made the Vietnam War very unpopular in the United States.

BACKGROUND

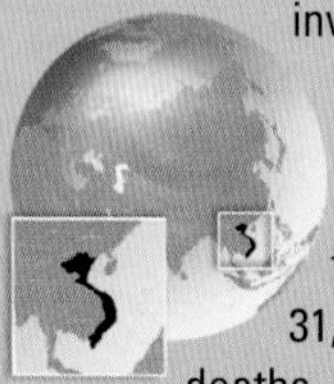

A turning point in the Vietnam War (1965–75) and the US involvement in it came in 1969. After four years of fighting, and 31,000 US combat deaths, opposition to the war was increasing both in the US and internationally. Under new president Richard Nixon (1913–94), a policy of "Vietnamization" involved the steady withdrawal of US troops and the scaling-back of US military actions, with a parallel build-up of the resources and expertise of South Vietnamese forces. US soldiers still fought the communist North Vietnamese Army (NVA) and their Viet Cong guerrilla allies, but on a reduced scale. The communist forces preferred small-unit actions, and from 1969 more US troops were lost to booby traps and mines than to enemy fire. Thus, in May 1969, US soldiers were unprepared for an 11-day battle for the peak of Ap Bia Mountain in the A Shau Valley of northern Vietnam.

US Airborne Forces: Hamburger Hill, 1969

During the Vietnam War (1965–75) Ap Bia Mountain became known as "Hamburger Hill" to US troops. A US search-and-destroy mission near the Vietnam–Laos border met fierce resistance by North Vietnamese forces. The fight for the mountain, officially designated "Hill 937," involved thousands of opposing troops in one of the most ferocious battles of the entire war.

In early May 1969, US military-intelligence reports indicated that the strategic A Shau Valley, in Vietnam's central highlands, was the center of a build-up of the 29th Regiment of the North Vietnamese Army (NVA), perhaps even threatening the nearby city of Hue. Eight US battalions, including three from the 101st Airborne Division, and forces of the South Vietnamese Army (ARVN) were sent to the area to engage the enemy.

US and ARVN forces were deployed on May 10, 1969. Combat began when B and D companies of the US 3rd Battalion, 187th Regiment, ascended the 3,000-ft. (915-m.) Ap Bia Mountain, known as Hill 937. Ferocious fighting broke out between US troops and the NVA, and the US soldiers were soon struggling for dominance. The steep slopes and dense undergrowth made Hill 937 extremely difficult to assault, especially as the NVA had established solid defensive positions.

On May 11, Lieutenant-Colonel Weldon Honeycutt, commander of the 3rd Battalion, upgraded the assault to a battalion-size operation. Company B pushed hard up the northwest slope, but was stopped by intense small-arms fire, mortar rounds, and rocket-propelled grenades. Company C was sent in to assist, while Company D made its own assault from the northeast. Even with the support of US artillery and airstrikes using napalm, the hill remained in NVA control.

THE BATTLE OF HILL 937

Further attacks by the three US companies over the next two days made little progress. The entrenched NVA showed remarkable resilience to the constant assault, which included lethal AC-47 gunship fire. US casualties increased, requiring more high-risk helicopter landings to airlift the casualties to

▼ **Deployment**
Bell UH-1 transport helicopters bring in US soldiers for the attack on "Hamburger Hill" in May 1969.

Helicopters

Between 1965 and 1975, US helicopters flew over 36 million sorties (missions) over Vietnam, for purposes of attack (as gunships), transportation, or medical evacuation ("medevac"). The Bell UH-1 helicopter worked across all these categories: It was the workhorse of the entire war. Bell 209/AH-1G Cobras were devastating gunships, and Sikorsky CH-54 Tarhe Skycranes did heavy lifting and troop transportation.

Airborne workhorse
A flight of Bell UH-1 helicopters during the Vietnam War. Each one could carry up to 12 combat troops.

▲ **Medical evacuation**
A soldier of the US 101st Airborne Division on "Hamburger Hill" uses colored smoke to direct an incoming medical-evacuation ("medevac") helicopter.

safety. In addition, the mountain slopes proved to be a major hazard, with the incessant rain turning them to mud.

On May 14, the US 1st Battalion, 506th Regiment, was also sent in. It made a major push from the southwest, intending to cut off NVA reinforcement routes from Laos. From May 15 to 18, the 1st and 3rd Battalions worked their way slowly up the hill and a massive combined push on May 18 yielded significant gains but not a decisive victory.

By this stage, Hill 937 was occupying the full attention of the US civilian and military command and a worldwide public. Major-General Melvin Zais, the 101st's commander, decided to employ overwhelming strength to complete the mission.

On May 20, all the available US forces made a concerted drive for the summit of Hill 937. The force was overwhelming, although remaining NVA soldiers still managed to produce tenacious resistance from their bunkers. However, once the fighting had ceased, occupation of the summit revealed that many of the NVA fighters had simply disappeared back into the cover of the jungle; many of their bunkers were standing empty.

◀ **Hillside firefight**
Soldiers of the US 101st Airborne Division fight NVA troops on the slopes of "Hamburger Hill."

▼ **US casualty**
A wounded soldier of the US 101st Airborne Division waits to be taken to hospital. Images such as these had a serious effect on US public opinion.

Machine guns

Machine-gun firepower
A US soldier uses a machine gun to shoot at North Vietnamese troops during the Vietnam War.

A general-purpose machine gun functions as either a light automatic weapon (that is, a light machine gun), when mounted on a bipod and fired from the shoulder, or as a sustained-fire, long-range weapon (that is, a heavy machine gun) when mounted on a tripod or light vehicle and when provided with an optical sight. In Vietnam, US troops made great use of machine guns against the enemy. Because of their high rate of fire and long range, machine guns are essential infantry weapons.

AFTER THE BATTLE

US casualties on what became known, a few days later, as "Hamburger Hill" were 56 dead and 420 wounded. Over 700 NVA soldiers died, representing a significant defeat for the communist forces. Yet, in the strange tactical climate of Vietnam, Hill 937 was abandoned only two days after capture and subsequently reoccupied by the NVA. The action seemed to the US public to be another pointless slaughter. The battle was to be one of the last major US search-and-destroy missions of the war.

US Marine Corps

The United States Marine Corps (USMC) is a completely self-contained force, with its own armor, strike aircraft, and helicopters. It is larger than the entire armed forces of many of the United States' allies. Able to deploy anywhere in the world at very short notice, Marine units can remain at sea indefinitely, and do not need land bases from which to operate. Nicknamed the "Leathernecks," the USMC is famed for the toughness of its troops.

US Marine Corps badge

The United States Marine Corps (USMC) can trace its origins back to the beginning of the American Revolution (1775–83), when American colonists fought against British rule. Modeled on the British Royal Marines, the USMC was founded as a seaborne landing force for the fledgling US Navy. Since those early days, the USMC has been at the forefront of every military action that the United States has undertaken, and has performed over 300 amphibious landings on foreign shores. It is not surprising, therefore, that the Marine Corps is associated with some of the most famous battles in modern history, such as the capture of the island of Iwo Jima from the Japanese in 1945, and the defense of the American base at Khe Sanh in the Vietnam War (1965–75).

Today, the Marines (who number about 172,000 men) are still leading US forces into battle. An example of this took place in March 2003, when the 45,000 men of the 1st Marine Expeditionary Force (MEF) took the lead in the war to topple Iraqi dictator Saddam Hussein.

ORGANIZATION

The Marine Corps, part of the US Department of the Navy, is essentially a rapid-reaction force, tailored to deploy to anywhere in the world at short notice. The structure of the USMC is such that it can also be considered an army in itself, containing all the necessary elements to operate independently for any period under any conditions. The Corps boasts a powerful array of military hardware, including tanks, attack helicopters, and fighter aircraft, as well as landing craft and assault ships. In addition, the Corps is supported by a full complement of logistical and maintenance units, capable of keeping the Marines operational in the field.

Traditionally, a typical USMC operation involves a large-scale amphibious assault on an enemy-held coastline by an MEF of around 40,000 soldiers. This is followed by a drive inland to secure a beachhead. A typical MEF would consist of a command element and reconnaissance units, a Marine division of 18,000 soldiers organized into three infantry regiments, one artillery regiment, one tank battalion, one anti-aircraft battalion, one combat engineering battalion, and one light-armored battalion. In addition, the MEF would include a Marine Aircraft Wing with 15,000 Marines and 300 aircraft, and a Service Support Group of 9,000 Marines to provide maintenance, transportation, and health care. In modern warfare, amphibious assaults are relatively rare, but the USMC retains the ability to carry out such assaults.

Such is the fearsome reputation of the United States Marine Corps that its

▲ **V-22 Osprey**
The Osprey is a tiltrotor, multi-mission aircraft. It can carry up to 24 Marines. (See Transport aircraft, p181.)

The few, the proud

The Marine Corps takes great pride in the unique spirit, or *esprit de corps*, it engenders. The USMC brotherhood, whose motto is "The few, the proud," fosters a fierce bond among the troops, which often continues long after a Marine leaves the Corps.

Marine discipline
A Marine Corps drill sergeant berates a squad of new recruits.

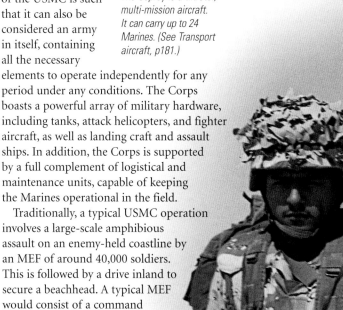

involvement can have a powerful impact on the enemy, psychologically as well as militarily. Perhaps this is why the Marine Corps still spearheads US forces into battle, and is often given the toughest missions against the most determined enemy.

MARINE RECRUITS

The inhospitable environments in which the USMC often operates require a special type of character on the part of those who make up the force. For this reason, the selection and training procedure is geared toward finding the exceptional men and women who will be up to the job. For recruits, a grueling 12-week Boot Camp at the Marine Corps Recruit Depot in San Diego, California, is where basic soldiering skills are learned. This is followed by further training at the nearby School of Infantry at Camp Pendleton, California, before the new Marines head off for active duty. For officers, Quantico, in Virginia, is the training ground where the USMC's future leaders are developed.

Particular emphasis is placed on weapons skills and maintenance. The Marine Corps prides itself on the caliber and personal qualities of its troops, and recruits only those most able to meet its stringent demands. This ensures that it is staffed by tough and highly trained soldiers who can be deployed anywhere in the world.

▼ **USMC boats**
The USMC is equipped with a number of powerful boats that are suitable both for patrolling inland waterways and for ferrying supplies from warships to the shore.

USMC hardware

The USMC is an exceptionally well-equipped force, with the latest military hardware and the most powerful weapons systems. Armaments include around 400 M1A1 Abrams tanks, 600 amphibious assault vehicles, 70 155-mm. howitzers, and many different types of missiles, mortars, and auxiliary vehicles. The powerful firepower the Marines can muster is augmented by a fearsome array of aircraft and helicopters. These vehicles include 200 F-18 Hornet fighter-bombers and 130 AV-8B Harrier ground-attack planes. Helicopter assets include 240 CH-46E Sea Knights and around 150 AH-1W Super Cobra gunships.

Abrams tank
The M1A1 Abrams main battle tank (MBT) has a 120-mm. gun and three 7.62-mm. machine guns.

▶ **The LAV**
The Marine Corps has hundreds of these Light Armored Vehicles (LAVs). They are used in a variety of roles, including air-defense, reconnaissance, and on the battlefield in support of ground troops. The chains on the wheels provide a better grip in icy conditions.

◀ **Armored mobility**
Marines aboard an armored personnel carrier. The weapon is a 5.56-mm. Squad Automatic Weapon.

US Marine Corps: Hue City, 1968

Attacking an urban area is among the most daunting, difficult, and dangerous of military operations. The battle to retake Hue City in central Vietnam in 1968 showed how US Marine draftees with no experience of urban fighting could defeat a determined and well-organized enemy. Without artillery and air support, the Marines were on their own – yet still succeeded.

Embassy battle
Like Hue, the US embassy in Saigon was a VC target during the Tet Offensive in 1968.

BACKGROUND

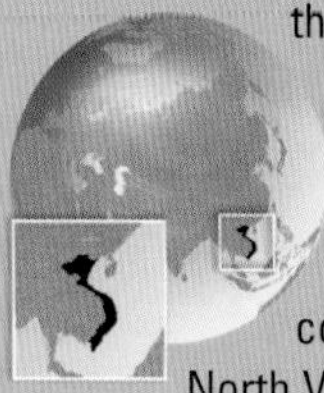

By July 1967, fighting between US forces and their allies, the South Vietnamese Army (ARVN), and the communist North Vietnamese Army (NVA) and Viet Cong (VC) had reached a stalemate. There were disagreements between the NVA, who wanted to consolidate their forces as part of a change of strategy, and the Viet Cong, who wanted to continue their guerrilla war to overthrow the South Vietnamese government.

After discussions in Hanoi, North Vietnamese President Ho Chi Min and his military commander, General Vo Nguyen Giap, decided to mount a joint campaign in January 1968. The NVA would attack the northern provinces, while the Viet Cong struck in the south. The campaign would start during the Lunar New Year celebrations (Tet), when many troops in the South Vietnamese Army would be away on leave.

On January 31, more than 84,000 NVA and VC troops attacked provincial capitals, district capitals, and villages. The old imperial city of Hue in central Vietnam was a key objective.

The North Vietnamese Army (NVA) began their ground attack on the city of Hue in central Vietnam under cover of darkness on the night of January 31, 1968, supported by rocket and mortar fire. The city was split in two by the wide – inappropriately named – Perfume River. To the north lay the walled Old City, characterized by closely packed buildings and a grid of narrow streets. To the south lay the more open ground of the New City. A small South Vietnamese force of 100 men resisted the NVA offensive, but by dawn had been pushed back to its command post in the north-west of the Old City.

RETAKING HUE

Amid reports of the chaos caused by other attacks across Vietnam as the NVA launched the Tet Offensive, two US Marine companies, plus engineers and three tanks, advanced to protect the city. They were ambushed by Viet Cong (VC) forces but survived and reached Hue. Without heavy fire support, however, they could not enter the Old City.

On February 4, two US Marine Corps battalions were ordered into the New City, which was soon the scene of serious street fighting. The communists had turned every building into a mini-fortress. Snipers occupied the upper stories, with machine-gun nests lower down. Enemy mortar fire covered all US approach routes, and entrances to buildings were booby-trapped. Individual infantrymen with supplies of extra ammunition for their AK-47 assault rifles lurked in well concealed "spider holes," ready to engage the newly arrived US Marines.

There was no front line in this desperate house-by-house, street-by-street fight. Each day, the Marines, who were conscripts used to fighting in open countryside, advanced using heavy covering fire from their own small arms, M48 tanks, and lightly armored Ontos rifle weapon carriers. They cleared every house one by one, often more than once.

▼ **The ruins of Hue**
The devastation in the Old City of Hue caused by the Tet Offensive and by the US Marines' operation to retake it.

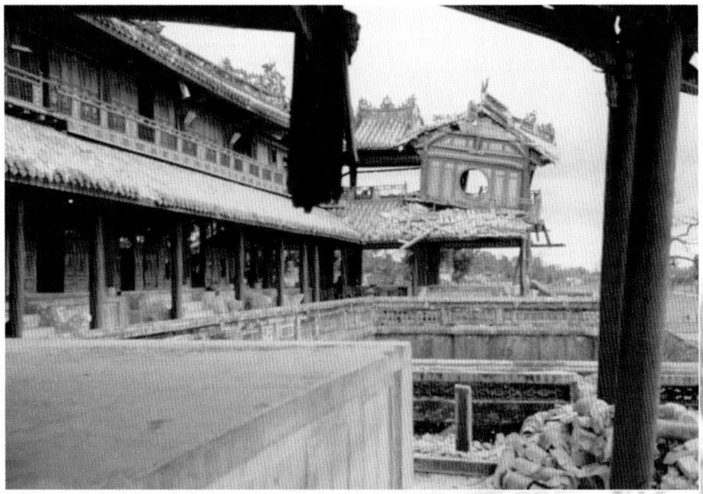

Although they used artillery, it created large amounts of debris and made progress more difficult. The monsoon storms restricted close air support. The M16 rifle, which many US soldiers had previously regarded as a lightweight plastic toy, proved its worth in Hue. Bursts of automatic fire kept defenders' heads down while attackers sprinted forward.

VC saboteurs blew up bridges, so all resupply and casualty evacuation was by boat or helicopter. Each night, the VC and NVA tried to recapture buildings, and set fresh booby traps.

By February 9, the south of the city was retaken, and 12 days later the Old City was also under US control. On

Khe Sanh

As an initial part of General Giap's Tet Offensive, the NVA besieged the US combat base of Khe Sanh, 50 miles (80 km.) from Hue, on January 21, 1968. The scale and intensity of the attack took the Americans by surprise. The desperate situation at Khe Sanh, and the urgent need to relieve the base and its defenders, diverted US attention in northern Vietnam from the defense of key urban areas at a critical time. Only 10 days after the Khe Sanh siege started, the main Tet Offensive began.

Siege at Khe Sanh
The US outpost at Khe Sanh comes under fire during a North Vietnamese attack. The siege lasted 77 days and left 51 Marines dead.

February 22, a gap opened in the monsoon cloud cover. The Americans launched a massive air raid, dropping a variety of munitions, including bombs and napalm canisters. Under cover of the raid, a new series of US ground attacks finally completed the recapture of Hue. Thanks to the Marines, the vital city was back in US hands.

▲ **Sniper search**
US Marines in Hue City scan the area in search of the enemy.

Napalm

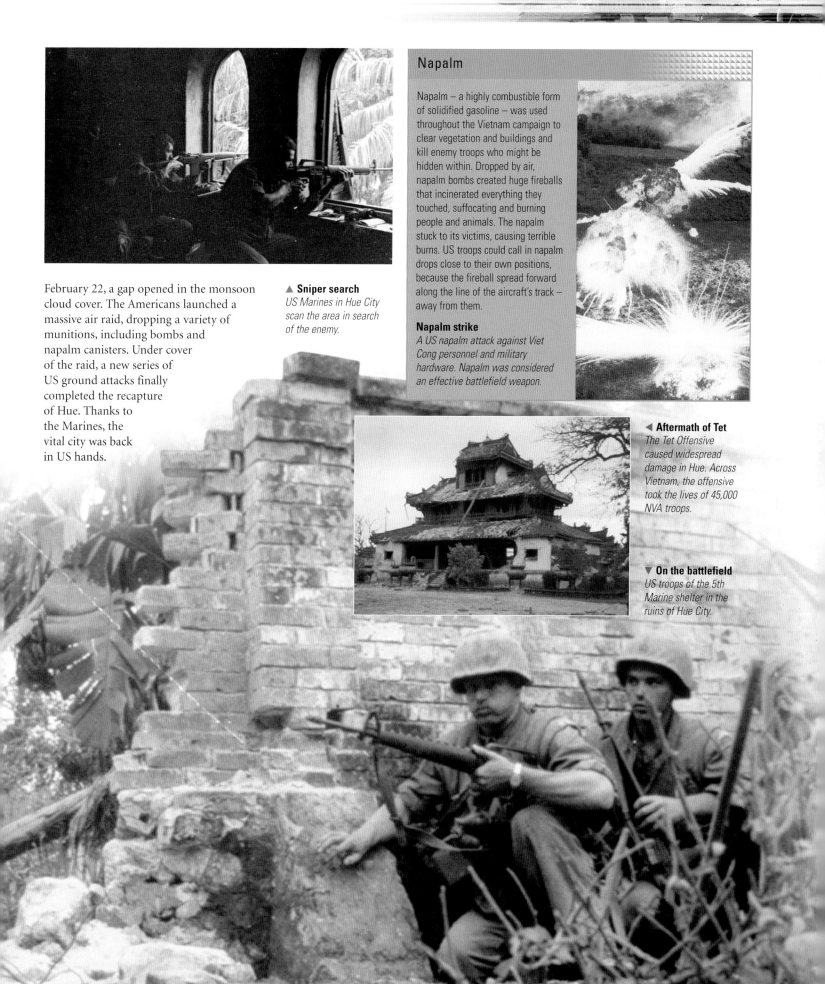

Napalm – a highly combustible form of solidified gasoline – was used throughout the Vietnam campaign to clear vegetation and buildings and kill enemy troops who might be hidden within. Dropped by air, napalm bombs created huge fireballs that incinerated everything they touched, suffocating and burning people and animals. The napalm stuck to its victims, causing terrible burns. US troops could call in napalm drops close to their own positions, because the fireball spread forward along the line of the aircraft's track – away from them.

Napalm strike
A US napalm attack against Viet Cong personnel and military hardware. Napalm was considered an effective battlefield weapon.

◀ **Aftermath of Tet**
The Tet Offensive caused widespread damage in Hue. Across Vietnam, the offensive took the lives of 45,000 NVA troops.

▼ **On the battlefield**
US troops of the 5th Marine shelter in the ruins of Hue City.

US Marine Corps: Baghdad, 2003

The US Marines were at the forefront of battle from the moment American and British forces entered Iraq on March 20, 2003. The long advance from Kuwait north toward the capital city, Baghdad, was punctuated by heavy clashes with Iraqi forces. In Baghdad itself the Marines faced two divisions of the Iraqi Republican Guard, but superior Marine technology and tactics cut through the defenses.

UN inspections
United Nations weapons inspector Mohamed Elbarasei outlines Iraq's nuclear capability at the UN in New York.

BACKGROUND

Following the terrorist attacks on New York on September 11, 2001, the US government became increasingly concerned about Iraq's possible development and stockpiling of weapons of mass destruction (WMDs). Iraqi dictator Saddam Hussein had used such weapons before – against Kurdish peoples in northern Iraq in 1988 and against Iranian forces in the Iran–Iraq War (1980–88). Intelligence suggested that Saddam was continuing to produce chemical and biological agents, was attempting to produce nuclear weapons, and possessed 20 ballistic missiles with a 400-mile (650-km.) range.

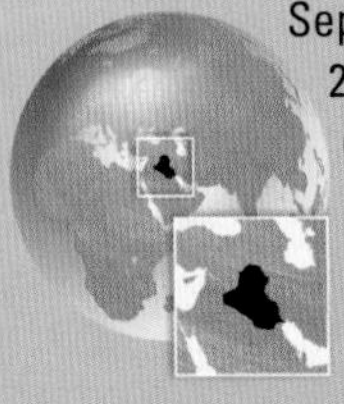

The United States and its allies judged such developments to be a threat to international interests and a breach of United Nations resolutions. On this basis, President George W. Bush (b. 1946) authorized the invasion of Iraq to overthrow Saddam's regime.

By April 1, 2003, elements of the US Marine Corps were about 19 miles (30 km.) from the outskirts of Baghdad. Their advance up the southeastern side of Iraq had been hard. On March 21, for example, the 1st Marine Division had clashed with the Iraqi 51st Mechanized Division on the approaches to Basra, Iraq's second city. The US Marines, along with the British 7th Armoured Brigade, were involved in a massive artillery duel with the enemy. However, precision 155-mm. howitzer fire and airstrikes by Marine Apache attack helicopters smashed the Iraqi defenses and the 51st Division surrendered. About 8,000 Iraqi soldiers were taken prisoner.

The Republican Guard

The Republican Guard were the elite of Saddam Hussein's army. Formed in 1979 as a personal guard for Saddam's regime, by the mid-1980s the unit had grown to 60,000 men. The Republican Guard received better training and equipment than the regular army. The 1990–91 Gulf War inflicted huge losses on them, and their strength dropped to 40,000 troops.

Iraqi elite troops
The Republican Guard was equipped with tanks, but by the end of the 2003 war, much of its armor had been destroyed.

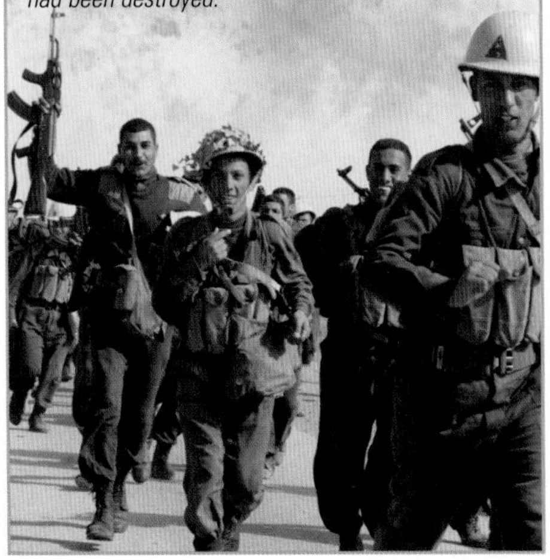

The Marines continued their northward advance. Their next big challenge was Nasiriyah, a heavily defended town 186 miles (300 km.) southeast of the Iraqi capital. There, the Marines were involved in determined urban combat, and were subjected to constant small-arms fire and rocket-propelled grenade attacks. The Marines, in cooperation with assaults by US Cobra helicopters and Abrams tanks, had to flush out each pocket of Iraqi resistance.

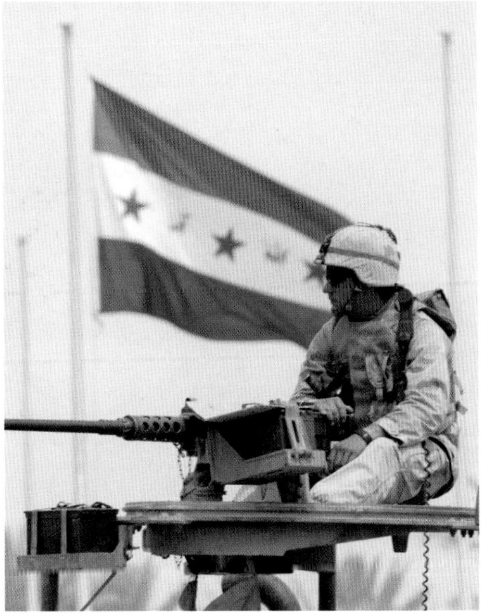

▲ Eve of victory
A US Marine mans a 12.7-mm. Browning machine gun as he keeps watch in the Iraqi capital city, Baghdad. The Iraqi national flag flutters in the background.

THE BATTLE FOR BAGHDAD

Fighting in Nasiriyah continued for days, but by March 25 the Marines had crossed the Euphrates River and advanced to the city of al-Kut, 100 miles (160 km.) from Baghdad. Al-Kut was secured with a bloody fight, and a vital bridge across the Tigris River was taken. Baghdad was now in Allied sights. In the Marines' sector, two elite units of the Iraqi Republican Guard defended the approaches to Baghdad. These forces had been already been seriously weakened by Allied airstrikes, and Marine artillery and anti-tank weapons added to the destruction. Under this

▼ US Marine Corps
Marines of the 4th Regiment take up position on the banks of the Tigris River in April 2003.

Urban fighting

Urban terrain is the most dangerous of all combat environments. Attacks can come from any angle and direction. Ambushes are common, tactical movement is difficult, and it takes a large amount of manpower to clear streets and buildings. In Iraqi cities in March and April 2003, heavy US firepower proved decisive. Iraqi troops were attacked with machine-guns, tank fire, and grenades. Shoulder-launched rockets also proved useful in clearing Iraqi soldiers from buildings.

Sniper danger
US Marines in Baghdad run for cover, having come under fire from a concealed Iraqi sniper.

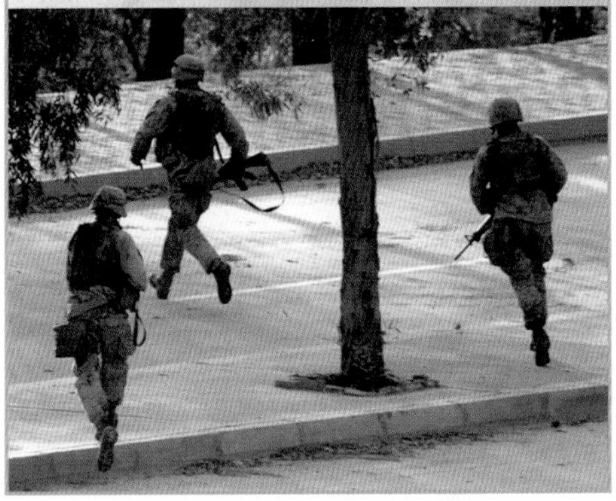

relentless firepower the two Iraqi divisions finally collapsed, and by April 3 the US Marines and 3rd Infantry Division reached the imposing Baghdad International Airport, only 15 miles (24 km.) from downtown Baghdad.

By April 5, Marines were probing the southeastern suburbs of the city itself, encountering resistance from members of the Republican Guard and Saddam Hussein's Ba'ath Party militia. Pushing on street by street, the Marines captured Rashid military air base on April 7. On the same day, several thousand Marines made an amphibious crossing of the Diyala River to move into the eastern side of the capital. They also seized two bridges across the river to allow US reinforcements to enter Baghdad. By April 9, the Iraqi regime had evidently collapsed.

Although the Marines and all Allied forces still faced weeks of sporadic firefights, the major military objectives had been met. President George W. Bush formally declared the end of the military offensive in May 2003.

▶ **Keeping the peace**
Troops of the 4th Marine Regiment in their Hummer vehicles patrol the newly won streets of Baghdad on April 9, 2003.

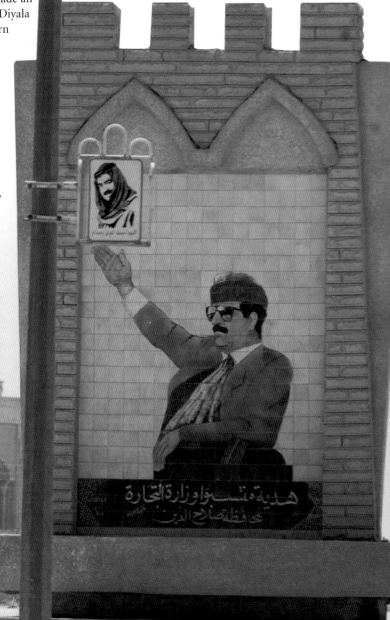

▼ **Baghdad patrol**
A Light Armored Vehicle (LAV) from the Marine Corps moves down a deserted Baghdad street. The wall poster (right) shows the deposed Iraqi dictator, Saddam Hussein.

US Navy SEALs

In 1962, President John F. Kennedy (1917–63) commissioned the first two US Navy Sea, Air, and Land (SEAL) teams for operations against communist guerrillas in Vietnam. Their successes in gathering intelligence, marine landings, and other activities proved their value. Today, eight SEAL teams cover the spectrum of special operations.

US Navy SEAL insignia

The name SEAL stands for Sea, Air, and Land: Although SEAL teams operate in the full range of tactical environments, their defining role is amphibious special operations, in particular covert deployments along enemy-controlled coastlines or river systems. Mission objectives can be extremely broad, but SEAL responsibilities include hydrographic surveys (surveys of seas and rivers) at landing zones, amphibious reconnaissance, assaulting enemy coastal installations, and underwater mine clearance. SEALs are also trained in assaults on maritime vessels, and have received extensive operational experience in this role during board-and-search missions in the Persian Gulf in the 1990s.

SEAL teams are trained, however, to operate in any special-operations capacity, and in all types of environment – temperate, desert, arctic, jungle, or urban. More recent operations have been as diverse as conducting false amphibious landings to divert Iraqi forces in the 1991 Gulf War; urban combat in the streets of Mogadishu, Somalia, in 1993 (see pp88–89); and hunting the fighters of the Taliban regime and the al Qaeda terrorist network in the mountains of Afghanistan in 2002.

▲ **Dune buggy**
The SEAL Desert Patrol Vehicle is a three-man dune buggy, designed to operate in hostile terrain. It has a 2,000-cc. engine.

▲ **SEAL Delivery Vehicle (SDV)**
The SDV delivers SEAL teams underwater to their target area. It is an all electric vehicle, powered by rechargeable batteries.

ORGANIZATION

The US Navy SEALs consist of 2,000 personnel. They are organized into eight teams, each of about 200 men and 50 officers. Generally, each team has a dedicated geographical area of operation. For example, Teams 1, 3, and 5, based on the West Coast of the United States, are responsible for Asia, the Middle East, and South Korea respectively. The East Coast units – Teams 2, 4, and 8 – have Europe, South America (and the Caribbean), and Africa as their regions of focus. Other SEAL teams have tactical priorities, such as domestic counter-terrorism. However, since the terrorist attacks on the United States on September 11, 2001, and the country's declared "war on terror," it has been common for one SEAL team to operate in the geographical zone or tactical area of another.

Amphibious delivery methods

For covert missions, SEALs are commonly deployed by submarine, and then swim ashore using special breathing apparatus that releases no bubbles. Alternatively, the SEAL Delivery Vehicle (SDV) can carry six SEALs in flooded compartments. Bigger, and with a greater range, the Advanced SEAL Delivery System (ASDS), a mini-sub with two crew, can carry 16 SEALs in a dry environment. On the surface, SEALs use canoes and inflatable boats for coastal landings and fast patrol craft for interception.

Mark V craft
The Mark V craft is used to carry special-operations forces, primarily SEAL combat swimmers, into and out of the area of operation. It has a top speed of around 50 mph. (80 kph.).

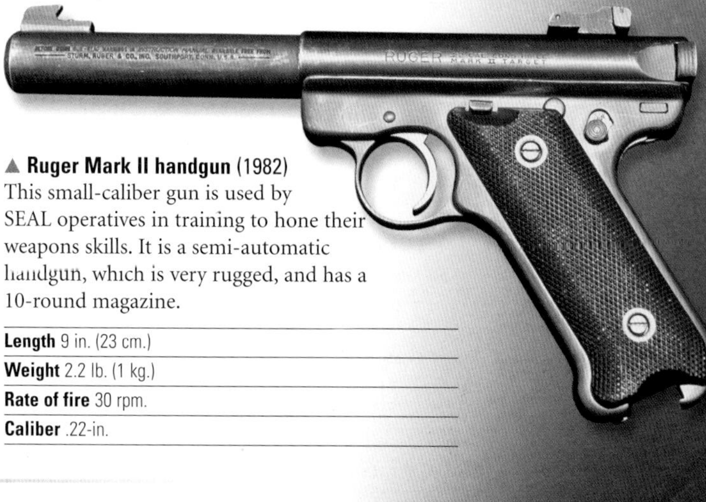

▲ **Ruger Mark II handgun** (1982)
This small-caliber gun is used by SEAL operatives in training to hone their weapons skills. It is a semi-automatic handgun, which is very rugged, and has a 10-round magazine.

Length	9 in. (23 cm.)
Weight	2.2 lb. (1 kg.)
Rate of fire	30 rpm.
Caliber	.22-in.

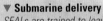

◀ **Diver training**
The US Naval Special Warfare Center offers intensive training. This SEAL operative is on a diving course.

NAVAL SPECIAL WARFARE GROUPS

SEAL teams are part of the four Naval Special Warfare Groups (NSWGs), under Naval Special Warfare Command. SEAL Teams 1, 3, 5, and 7 belong to NSWG-1, while Teams 2, 4, 8, and 10 are part of NSWG-2. They are given operational support by Naval Special Warfare Units. In addition, NSWG-3 and NSWG-4 contain SEAL Delivery Vehicle Teams (SDVTs) 1 and 2 respectively, which handle the clandestine delivery and evacuation of SEAL teams into and out of the zone of operations, using vehicles ranging from submarines to assault boats.

Highly trained, well equipped, and with the capability of operating anywhere, the SEALs are one of the most effective and flexible special forces units in the world.

The SEAL teams

All SEAL teams have a standard operating capability – reconnaissance, intelligence-gathering, hostage-rescue, and amphibious-landing skills – taught during basic training. In addition, some teams possess specific operational abilities. SEAL Team 2, for example, has an Arctic-warfare capability, while SEAL Team 4 has Spanish-language speakers as standard because it is oriented toward operations in South America.

Weapons skills
SEALs on a desert exercise. Troops spend hours refining their tactics to become experts in close-quarter battle techniques.

▼ **Submarine delivery**
SEALs are trained to leave and enter a submarine while the vessel is traveling underwater, as shown here.

US Navy SEALs: Selection

The US Navy Sea, Air, and Land (SEAL) special forces have one of the toughest selection programs of any military unit in the world. The Basic Underwater Demolition/SEAL (BUD/S) course lasts over four months, and only about 30 percent of applicants complete it. If a recruit passes, he still faces 18 weeks of stress completing his airborne and SEAL Qualification Training.

▶ Underwater training
In this part of SEAL selection candidates perform tasks in a swimming pool, with their wrists bound.

SEAL training begins with a five-week Indoctrination period. The candidate is assessed physically and psychologically, and the conditions of SEAL service are explained to him. He will also have to pass the SEAL Physical Screening Test (PST). The PST determines whether the applicant has the physical requirements to begin SEAL training. It includes a 1,500-ft. (457-m.) swim to be completed in under 12 minutes 30 seconds, using breaststroke or sidestroke; 42 push-ups in under 2 minutes; 50 sit-ups in the same amount of time; and a 1.5-mile (2.4-km.) run, wearing boots, in under 11 minutes 30 seconds. Even greater challenges face those who pass the rigors of PST.

◀ Basic training
SEAL recruits in the water during the eight-week Basic Conditioning course. The course tests each candidate's mental and physical toughness.

"Hell Week"

Endurance test
These "Hell Week" recruits are freezing and wet. They must draw on massive willpower to keep going.

"Hell Week," held in the fourth week of BUD/S, is aptly named. In teams of 5 to 7 people, candidates undergo five days of physical exercises at the limits of endurance. Often candidates are soaking wet, freezing, and on the edge of hypothermia. They will have only four hours sleep in the whole week. They must crawl through waist-deep mud and carry a small boat for several miles. "Hell Week" is designed to show up those who perform badly under pressure and look after themselves rather than their teams.

BASIC CONDITIONING

The six-month Basic Underwater Demolition/SEAL (BUD/S) course takes place at the Naval Special Warfare center in California. It is punishing in the extreme.

The first phase, Basic Conditioning, lasts eight weeks, with a continual program of running, swimming, and physical-fitness exercises. Some elements of combat swimming and seamanship are learned, but the first four weeks test mainly the applicant's motivation, physical toughness, and team working. During "Underwater Acclimation" (popularly known as "drown proofing"), recruits are thrown into a swimming-pool with their wrists and ankles bound. They must stay afloat for 20 minutes and perform numerous tasks, such as retrieving facemasks from the bottom of the pool.

"Hell Week" is arguably the most arduous individual test in all special forces training. After this, there is some respite, with four weeks on hydrography (study of the seas).

DIVING AND LAND WARFARE TRAINING

The diving phase of BUD/S instructs the recruit in the basics of combat swimming, and lasts eight weeks. The recruit learns mainly scuba techniques for combat infiltration by training in open-circuit (using compressed air) and closed-circuit (using 100 per cent oxygen) methods.

The nine-week Land Warfare course teaches the SEAL candidates advanced infantry combat tactics and procedures. These include training with weapons, demolitions, rock climbing, navigation, marksmanship, covertly entering and exiting an operational zone, and small-unit tactics. Strenuous runs and swims are incorporated

▲ Entry requirements
To be considered for SEAL selection, candidates must first pass the Physical Screening Test.

▲ **Non-stop training**
Even after qualification, training continues. These SEALs are learning the skill of "fast-roping" from a helicopter.

▲ **Assault-course training**
Routines on the assault course build up physical stamina for work in the water.

into the exercises, usually conducted to tight deadlines. The last three-and-a-half weeks of the course take place at San Clemente Island, California, where candidates undergo an extended exercise to demonstrate all they have learned during BUD/S.

BECOMING A SEAL

On completion of BUD/S, the candidate attends the three-week parachute-qualification course at the Army Airborne School in Fort Benning, Georgia. After this, he returns to the Naval Special Warfare Center for SEAL Qualification Training (SQT). This is a 15-week course teaching advanced SEAL skills, which include communications, small-boat handling, close-quarter fighting, sniping, and tactical parachuting. The SQT takes the candidate to operational standard. If he passes SQT he is awarded a Naval Special Warfare insignia, the Trident, and receives a SEAL Naval Enlisted Classification (NEC) code. Before being assigned to his first operational unit, the SEAL soldier goes on a three-week Basic Cold Weather Maritime Training course in Kodiak, Alaska.

Training does not stop once a soldier becomes a member of a SEAL team. Ongoing on-the-job programs can teach every conceivable relevant skill, from foreign languages to 30-week medical courses.

Ready for anything

US Navy SEAL training is designed to produce soldiers capable of fighting in any environment, even though SEALs are most commonly associated with amphibious warfare. Under the orders of the Naval Special Warfare Command, SEALs can be called on for missions ranging from hostage rescue to anti-armor patrols, and can be deployed to any area in the world. Once in-theater, SEALs need only minimal acclimatization. During the 2001 war in Afghanistan, for example, SEAL teams operated high in mountainous terrain.

Instant deployment
SEALs are trained to be prepared for any eventuality. This can mean being deployed anywhere in the world at short notice. This SEAL soldier is fighting in Afghanistan (2001).

Helicopter war
SEAL units were deployed by helicopter in the Vietnam conflict – the first war where this method was used.

BACKGROUND

With the signing of the Geneva Peace Accords in May 1954, Vietnam was divided in half. The United States replaced the French as guarantor of a democratic Republic of Vietnam – South Vietnam – while the Soviet Union and the People's Republic of China performed a similar role with the northern zone, called the Democratic Republic of Vietnam. By the early 1960s, South Vietnam was facing an invasion from the combined forces of the Viet Cong (VC) and the North Vietnamese Army (NVA). In addition, the South was plagued by political instability and corruption, which weakened its military efforts against external enemies. Meanwhile, the VC guerrillas continued to gain in strength, outmatching Southern forces in commitment, popular support, and fighting skills. It seemed only a matter of time before the South fell. In response, the United States offered the South military and political support in a war that would last until 1975.

US Navy SEALs: Vietnam, 1963–72

In the special forces community, the US Navy Sea, Air, and Land (SEAL) teams are generally accepted to have been the toughest and most effective special forces units operating in Vietnam. Although US forces did not become fully engaged in Vietnam until 1965, the first SEAL teams were sent there in 1963, with the tasks of long-range reconnaissance, ambush, sabotage, and assault missions, particularly in the Mekong Delta in southern Vietnam, where the Viet Cong (VC) were inflicting heavy losses on South Vietnamese troops.

In 1966, there were 80,000 VC troops based in the Mekong Delta, mounting savage attacks from the safety of their swamp and rice paddies, using the 4,000 miles (6,500 km.) of largely uncharted waterways to reach out into the rest of South Vietnam. From 1963, SEAL Teams One and Two (200 men each) were committed to the war in the region. Initially, 20 separate SEAL reconnaissance teams of varying strengths were inserted into the delta along its tracks, trails, and waterways, to act as observation units, mapping the area and determining VC supply routes. Great care, skill, and stealth were required to avoid detection. Resupply was impossible, so food, ammunition, and explosives for a week or more had to be carried in backpacks. It was vital that the VC did not know that they were being observed, so no trace of the teams could remain once their mission was over. Only when the SEALs were certain they knew what was going on in their area did they bring in fresh teams to mount operations.

SEAL TACTICS

Because the SEALs were using accurate intelligence, success rates were very high, both in terms of dead VC (around 900 confirmed killed), and also of the disruption and fear they created in the minds of the enemy.

▲ **Hitting VC strongpoints**
Two SEALs watch as naval artillery fire destroys a VC position in the Mekong Delta in 1966.

The Viet Cong

The "Viet Nam Cong San" (Viet Cong) originated in the 1950s, and by the 1960s had become the military wing of both the communist Provisional Revolutionary Government and its political party, the National Liberation Front. With the active support of the North Vietnamese Army (NVA), the Viet Cong (VC) aimed to overthrow the South Vietnamese government, reunifying North and South. The VC practiced systematic terror and coercion, using North Vietnamese soldiers living undercover in the south to recruit, train, and equip their cadres. Before 1968, most VC were from the south, but after the VC losses in the 1968 Tet Offensive, large numbers of NVA soldiers were brought in.

Soldiers of the Viet Cong
Viet Cong personnel were usually lightly armed with rifles and hand-held rocket launchers. This allowed them to infiltrate areas quickly.

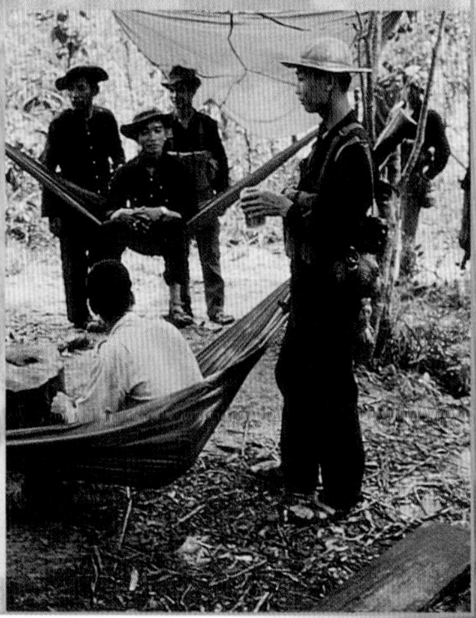

The SEALs rapidly became experts in the use of booby traps – which are particularly effective in jungle warfare – lacing VC trails with Claymore anti-personnel mines and loops of high-explosive cord. They conducted operations in complete silence by means of hand signals, and developed high levels of intuitive understanding. They were also experts in unarmed combat and in silent methods of fighting. There were several occasions when SEAL teams were captured on missions inside North Vietnam, only to kill their captors and escape.

▲ **Storming ashore**
A SEAL team comes ashore from speedboats in the Mekong Delta during an operation against the VC.

▲ **Camouflaged uniforms**
The camouflaged uniform of the SEALs blended in perfectly with the landscape of the Mekong Delta.

SEAL OPERATIONS

Missions would often start with the careful insertion of several three-man teams by means of heavily armed boats. In one operation in 1968, they captured documents that revealed a network of VC water wells and bunkers, which were then bombed. Alternatively, fiberglass attack boats with powerful outboard engines and shallow drafts enabled SEALs to get into narrow waterways and make rapid getaways.

SEAL operations were mounted by hunter-killer teams of between three and seven men. Larger teams were inserted from fast patrol boats, which also provided fire support. When going into dense swamps where boats could not be used, naval helicopters were used to enable troops to rappel or jump directly into the combat zone.

Between 1968 and 1970, the SEALs were operating against the VC along the entire South Vietnamese coastline. They were also used to rescue downed aircrew, for the clearing of underwater obstacles, laying demolitions to allow US ships to move up-river, and in cross-border missions inside North Vietnam. SEAL teams sabotaged many North Vietnamese harbors and bridges – although this has never been officially acknowledged. In operations against VC political figures, SEALs carried out snatch, ambush, and assassination operations.

The last SEAL units left South Vietnam in 1972. In nine years of fighting they had lost only 49 soldiers.

◀ **River patrol**
US armored troop carriers on patrol in the Mekong Delta in 1968.

The Mobile Riverine Force

The Mobile Riverine Force (MRF), or Task Force 117, was formed in 1967 to prevent Viet Cong domination of South Vietnam's myriad waterways. Drawn from infantrymen of the US 2nd Brigade, 9th Infantry Division, the troops lived in barrack-ships, which were protected by howitzers and mortars mounted on pontoons. "Monitor" fire-support boats, operating from bases in the swamps and rice paddies of South Vietnam, also worked closely with the SEAL teams.

On patrol
A heavily armed US "Monitor" moves through one of the waterways of the Mekong Delta. The lush vegetation on the banks provided many potential hiding places for the Viet Cong.

British Royal Marines

The Royal Marines are part of the Royal Navy, and form the commando infantry of 3 Commando Brigade, which is Britain's fast-moving amphibious force. Operating from the sea, Royal Marine commandos are landed on an enemy shore as a complete fighting formation, with an artillery battery, an engineer troop, and other supporting units. In order to become a Royal Marine, recruits must undergo one of the toughest training regimes in the British military.

▲ **Gulf War, 2003**
Royal Marines in action in southern Iraq in March 2003. The soldier closest to the camera has a dust cover over his rifle.

The Royal Marines were formed in 1664 during the reign of King Charles II (1630–85), when they were known as the "sea soldiers" because they fought on board ships, repelling enemy boarding parties, and providing snipers to kill enemy sailors. For the next three centuries, the role of the Royal Marines remained unchanged: To fight from ships. However, their role changed in World War II (1939–45) when, for the first time, they landed from the sea to attack German coastal positions.

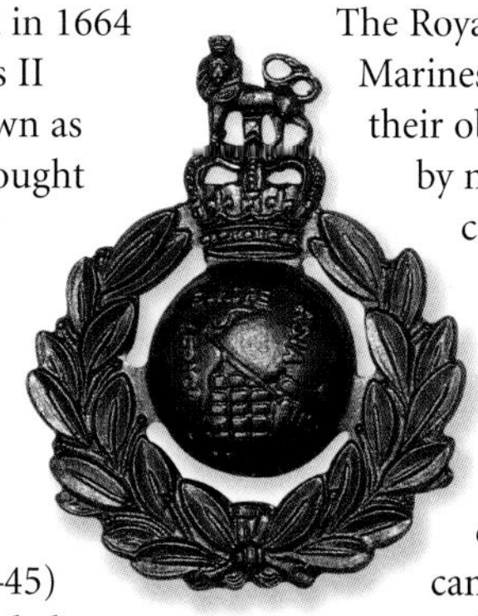

Royal Marines badge

The Royal Marines reach their objective by means of craft such as HMS *Albion* and *Bulwark*, vessels that are equipped with docking facilities for smaller boats. In addition, Royal Marines can be launched by helicopter from the aircraft carrier HMS *Ocean*. This ship can carry up to 500 Royal Marines and up to 18 medium-sized helicopters, each of which can carry up to 15 troops. In the years since 1945, the Marines have conducted amphibious assaults in many conflicts, including the Falklands War of 1982, the Persian Gulf War of 1991, and the Iraq War of 2003.

ORGANIZATION AND STRUCTURE

The Royal Marines are organized into three Commando groups, each numbering about 600 men. The groups are part of 3 Commando Brigade, which also has artillery units, reconnaissance experts, and naval gunfire controllers. In addition, 3 Commando Brigade has its own air defense battery and a specialized logistics regiment that takes care of supplies. The brigade has its own squad of engineers, and two air squadrons that provide troop-carrying Sea King helicopters. Scimitar and Striker light armored vehicles (LAV) from the Household Cavalry Regiment form a mobile support unit when the Royal Marines go into battle. The men of 539 Assault Squadron are in control of the landing craft.

Mountain and Arctic Warfare Cadre

3 Commando Brigade endeavors to train as often as possible in arctic conditions. It is necessary to be able to make amphibious landings under all climatic conditions, and specifically to maintain expertise in mountain and extreme cold weather operations. Unique skills, knowledge, and experience are required for operations in extreme cold weather, where the environment is just as hostile as the enemy. Members of the Brigade Patrol Troop are also Mountain and Arctic Warfare Cadre instructors, and are ready to train others for operations in arctic regions.

Cold weather soldier
A member of the Mountain and Arctic Warfare Cadre demonstrates climbing techniques using ice picks and crampons.

COMMANDO TRAINING

Becoming a Royal Marine commando is tough. Commando training is as much a psychological test as it is a physical one, with an emphasis on mental alertness and attention to duty even when physically exhausted.

There are four tests, which must be completed within set time limits. However, before the tests are attempted, candidates must first complete an arduous 10-day Royal Marine commando exercise. This takes place over inhospitable and remote terrain on Dartmoor in southwest England. It is designed to test survival skills as well as endurance levels. The recruits get very little sleep and walk about 70 miles (110 km.) across an unforgiving landscape. The exercise starts with a landing from the sea and incorporates commando skills such as climbing, rappelling, and assault tactics.

▶ **Commando training**
Recruits tackle the rope crawl section of the assault course at the Royal Marine training facility at Lympstone Camp, England.

▼ **Sea assault**
Royal Marine Commandos storm ashore from a hovercraft during an exercise in the Gulf of Oman.

The final Commando tests take place on consecutive days. The Endurance Course is first: A 1.5-mile (2.4-km.) cross-country run through many obstacles, followed by a 4-mile (6.4-km.) run back to camp. Immediately on arrival recruits must fire their weapon and score 6 hits out of 10 on a small target. Pass time is 77 minutes, or 70 minutes for officers.

The next day recruits carry out the Tarzan and Assault Course test, which includes rope climbs high in the air. The Nine Mile Speed March is completed as a unit, running and marching wearing full fighting equipment. Finally, the candidates must complete the Thirty Mile Load Carry. The time limit is eight hours, or seven for officers.

▼ **Rigid Raider attack**
A line of Rigid Raider assault craft on exercise in Scotland. Each small boat can carry eight Marines and has a top speed of 30 knots.

539 Assault Squadron

Formed in 1984, 539 Assault Squadron is the Royal Marines' own small-scale "navy," and is based at Turnchapel in Plymouth, England. The squadron carries men and equipment on raiding missions, as well as special forces and communications team insertions, using whichever craft is best suited for the job and conditions. The squadron operate four Landing Craft Vehicle Personnel (LCVP), four hovercraft, 16 Rigid Raider assault, craft, and 21 Medium Inflatable Boats.

Airlift capacity
The Rigid Raiders of 539 Assault Squadron can be airlifted by helicopter, as shown here.

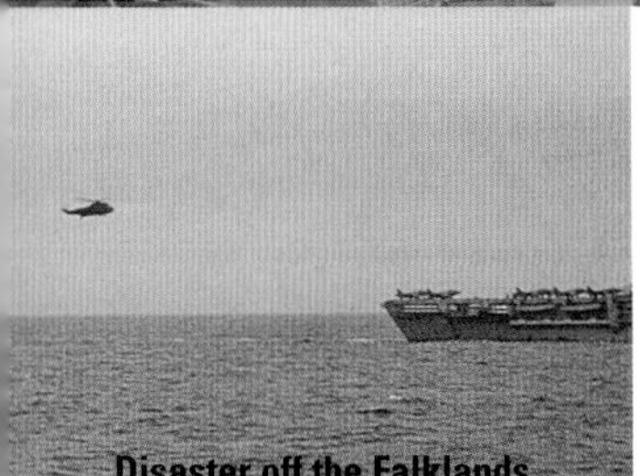

Disaster off the Falklands
A Sea King helicopter is transferring SAS troops from the carrier HMS Invincible *during the Falklands War. Shortly after this photograph was taken it crashed into the sea, killing 14 SAS soldiers.*

BACKGROUND

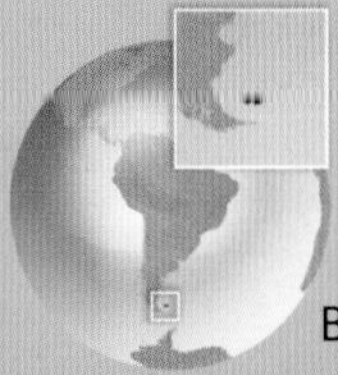

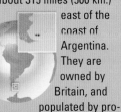

The Falkland Islands lie about 315 miles (500 km.) east of the coast of Argentina. They are owned by Britain, and populated by pro-British English-speakers. However, Argentinians have long claimed sovereignty over the islands, which they call the Malvinas. The two national governments discussed British sovereignty in the 1970s but reached no agreement. The Argentinian invasion of the islands on April 2, 1982, with well-equipped marine forces, broke international law. The United Nations (UN) demanded Argentina's withdrawal, but to no avail. Despite the enormous supply problems posed by a long sea transit, and with no ports en route, British prime minister Margaret Thatcher (b. 1925) authorized the dispatch of a task force to recapture the Falklands. Despite UN opposition, but with US intelligence assistance, Britain succeeded in landing military forces on the islands, and its special forces played a vital role in defeating the enemy and restoring British sovereignty over the Falklands.

British Royal Marines: Falklands, 1982

British special forces went ashore in the Falkland Islands weeks before the main British force arrived, concealing themselves in windswept tussock grass by day, and moving at night. With British warships still far away, they were on their own, relying on fieldcraft and camouflage to escape detection, while determining the location and strength of enemy units.

The British Falkland Islands are situated in the South Atlantic and consist of two main islands – West and East Falkland – and over 100 smaller ones. Farther south lies the remote island of South Georgia, another British dependency. Argentinians invaded South Georgia on March 19, 1982, and occupied the Falklands on April 2.

The battle for South Georgia, in late April, was a purely special forces operation. However, it nearly turned into a disaster when members of the Special Air Service (SAS) attempted to land on the island by helicopter on a blizzard-swept glacier, and by using Gemini assault boats. Two of the helicopters were lost, and one of the boats was almost swept away. On April 25, an improvised force of the Royal Marines' Special Boat Service (SBS), the SAS, and 3 Commando Brigade's Reconnaissance Troop captured South Georgia's main port of Grytviken. They were supported by naval gunfire guided in by two teams from 148 Commando Forward Observation Unit (148 FOU), Royal Marines.

ON THE FALKLANDS

SBS teams landed on the Falkland Islands in early May, and for several weeks sent back intelligence to Royal Marines' commander

Argentine Army

The Argentine Army was a mixture of ill-trained conscripts and tough, well-trained professionals. They brought with them a large quantity of weapons, ammunition, and high-quality equipment, but found the Falklands weather daunting. Some units were poorly led by officers with little concern for their men. But others fought strongly, and had to be driven, soldier-by-soldier, from well-fortified positions under cover of darkness, using heavy-artillery support and careful infantry tactics.

Prisoners of war
Royal Marines Captain Rod Bell, a Uruguayan-born Spanish-speaker, interrogates enemy prisoners captured by the SBS at Fanning Head, just before the main landings on May 21.

▲ **SAS deployment**
Members of D Squadron, 22 SAS, at the end of the war. They are guiding in a helicopter from Beagle Ridge, north of Port Stanley, using a colored smoke-flare. The crates hold MILAN anti-tank missiles.

▼ **Falklands warrior**
The author, Hugh McManners, in the Falklands. His weapon is a 5.56-mm. assault rifle. His backpack holds food, ammunition, and spare clothing.

◄ **Falklands climate**
An SAS and 148 FOU forward base at the end of the war. The severe Falklands winter had begun, and these cold and tired soldiers had to wait several days after hostilities had ceased before a helicopter could fly them back to their base on HMS Intrepid.

Brigadier Julian Thompson, who was deciding where to make his landing. Once the landing area was decided upon, at San Carlos, East Falkland, SBS teams and a naval gunfire team from 148 FOU were infiltrated there. The night before the main landings (May 20), a combined SBS and 148 FOU team used thermal-imaging equipment to locate an Argentine heavy weapons company already in the area. They attacked it with the aid of naval gunfire from HMS *Antrim*. As the main force landed at San Carlos, the SBS mounted night raids and collaborated with 148 FOU teams, which directed naval fire against enemy positions.

▲ **Comrades in arms**
A combined SBS/148 FOU team break for a photograph. They are at a makeshift range at San Carlos, adjusting the sights of their weapons before a night-raiding operation.

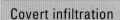

WINNING THE WAR

As the SAS moved into the barren center of East Falkland, and onto the key feature of Mount Kent, SBS teams moved covertly around the difficult waterways of the island's northern inlets. Forward observation teams sent back intelligence on enemy positions. These teams included a 148 FOU position that overlooked Port Stanley, the capital. In the last two weeks of the war it directed naval gunfire on enemy radar and artillery positions in and around the town.

This gunfire demoralized the Argentinian garrison, contributing to the enemy's surrender on June 14. The men of 148 FOU had played a key part in the British victory.

Covert infiltration

Low-flying helicopters, equipped with night-vision equipment, or Gemini assault boats were used to land special forces teams on the coastlines of the Falklands for long, arduous reconnaissance missions. Extreme weather conditions made insertions hazardous and meant that eventual pickups could not be guaranteed. So these teams had to be prepared for long walks and an unpredictable survival phase at the conclusion of each operation. Only minimal rations could be carried, and reconnaissance operations tended to last about 12 days, so the teams invariably ran out of food.

Sea King
Sea King helicopters were the workhorses of the special forces in the Falklands, lifting teams from their ships, and flying them at low level, by night, across enemy territory to their drop-off points.

British Royal Marines: Basra, 2003

The British part of the 2003 war on Iraq was code-named Operation Telic. In the vanguard were the Royal Marines. Their initial objective was to secure Umm Qasr, but their ultimate goal was to take Basra. The British forces reached the outskirts of Basra by March 23, 2003, but the city not did fall until April 7.

Operation Telic began on March 20, 2003, with the Royal Marines thrusting into the Al Faw peninsula in the southeastern corner of Iraq. There, the soldiers of HQ 3 Commando Brigade and 40 and 42 Commando Royal Marines helped seize several vital oil terminals and the port of Umm Qasr, 30 miles (48 km.) south of Basra.

ASSAULT ON BASRA

After Umm Qasr, the Marines continued the northward drive to Basra. Intelligence suggested that the city was defended by one Iraqi army brigade of about 2,000 men and around 1,000 paramilitary soldiers loyal to the regime. Although the Iraqi high command had withdrawn its best divisions north to defend the capital, Baghdad, those left behind were well-armed and entrenched. Resistance toughened as the Marines neared the city's outskirts. On April 23, British and US forces became engaged in a major tank and artillery battle outside Basra. Their overwhelming firepower defeated the Iraqi force, and by March 25 the Royal Marines were pushing into Basra's perimeter and engaging in urban combat.

▶ **Into Basra**
Royal Marines on Basra's outskirts. Iraq's regime had pulled its best units back to Baghdad, leaving mostly inferior garrison units to defend Basra.

The Marines adopted two basic roles. First, they assisted other British forces by cutting off the Iraqi troops in Basra, preventing them from interfering with the US advance to Baghdad. Second, they began combat raids into the city to crush continuing resistance.

THE FINAL OFFENSIVE

One major action was Operation James, named for James Bond, on March 30. Three rifle companies of Marines, supported by Challenger tanks, attacked the Basra suburb of Abu al Khasib. Another company landed by helicopter on the opposite side of the suburb to prevent enemy escape. This classic "hammer and anvil" action resulted in 30 Iraqi troops killed, command bunkers captured, and several Iraqi tanks destroyed, and was typical of subsequent operations. In this way, the Royal Marines steadily chipped away at Iraqi opposition in the city.

The increasing severity of the humanitarian problems in Basra

▼ **Sea King delivery**
A Sea King helicopter prepares to take off near the port of Umm Qasr, having landed some Royal Marines (top left of picture).

◀ **Desert soldiers**
Royal Marines in camouflage uniforms are flown into Basra by helicopter during Operation James.

Iraqi-sponsored terrorism
A member of Islamic Jihad, one of the terrorist groups given money and weapons by the regime of Saddam Hussein.

BACKGROUND

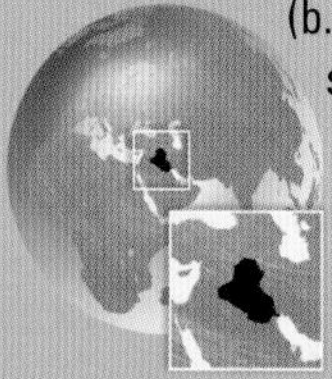

In 2002 the Iraqi regime of dictator Saddam Hussein (b. 1937) was suspected of continuing to develop its chemical, biological, and nuclear weapons of mass destruction. After much debate, the United Nations (UN) Security Council passed Resolution 1441 (December 2002), ordering weapons inspectors into Iraq and demanding full Iraqi compliance. The United States, Britain, and Spain felt that Iraq did not comply fully, but these three nations were unable to win UN backing for military action against Saddam. In spite of this, in March 2003 US and British forces invaded Iraq to topple the Iraqi leader. British troops tackled the country's southeast region, a Shia Muslim area traditionally hostile to Saddam.

SBS in Iraq

The elite members of the Royal Navy's Special Boat Service (SBS) played a significant role in the Al Faw peninsula during the initial land invasion of Iraq. SBS operatives made amphibious reconnaissance of the Iraqi coastline, identified underwater obstacles, designated targets for airstrikes, and captured two offshore oil-tanker moorings. They also made amphibious landings and engaged Iraqi units, in order to test enemy defenses prior to the main advance.

Diving elite
SBS divers used their special skills in Iraq in 2003 to reconnoiter docks and landing sites for possible later use by British and US forces.

◀ **Sea assault**
A soldier from 539 Assault Squadron reports to HQ. During the 2003 invasion of Iraq, the small boats of this squadron landed Royal Marine teams on the beaches of the Al Faw peninsula.

meant it was essential to liberate the city rapidly. The final push to clear Basra came on April 6. After shelling enemy positions, Marines and other British units pushed into the heart of the city. The Marines were met by sporadic but intense machine-gun and sniper fire, but their superior capabilities, aided by night-vision technology, eventually overcame the resistance.

By April 7, Basra was in British hands, with only one Marine having been killed in the battle. It is a testimony to the Marines professionalism that they instantly switched from combat to peace-keeping roles, and gained the general respect of Basra's people.

▲ **Advancing inland**
After landing on the Al Faw peninsula, Royal Marines advance inland toward Basra.

German GSG-9

Grenzschutzgruppe-9 (GSG-9 or Border Guard Group 9) is Germany's primary police counter-terrorist unit. Created in response to the massacre of 11 Israeli athletes at the Munich Olympics in West Germany in 1972, GSG-9 has since conducted some of the most successful hostage-rescue missions of any elite force. Today, GSG-9's three specialized units can handle a full range of land, maritime, and airborne operations.

▶ **Special weapons**
Hostage-rescue operations require special equipment. This GSG-9 officer has a variant of the Heckler & Koch MP5 submachine gun, fitted with a silencer.

During the 1972 Munich Olympics, eight Palestinian terrorists seized 14 members of the Israeli Olympic team, demanding the release of 200 jailed Arab guerrillas from an Israeli prison, in addition to their own safe exit from Munich. Two hostages were immediately shot. Allowing the terrorists to move the remaining hostages to a nearby airport, Bavarian police mounted a rescue operation. During the mission, another nine Israeli hostages were killed by the Palestinians before they were overcome, with five killed and the remaining three captured. Overall, the deaths of 11 of the 14 hostages meant the operation could only be seen as a complete failure. As a result of the incident, shown live on worldwide television, West Germany laid plans for the creation of its own elite counter-terrorist force.

GSG-9 insignia

CREATING GSG-9

Grenzschutzgruppe-9 (GSG-9) was created to meet this need. Ulrich Wegener, a counter-terrorist expert within the West German Federal Border Guard, had practical control over the new unit. Assisted by foreign counter-terrorist agencies, he built the force in less than a year from applicants chosen through a rigorous selection process. GSG-9 became operational with two combat-ready units on April 17, 1973.

The elite credentials of GSG-9 were finally proved on October 18, 1977. A GSG-9 team stormed a German Lufthansa jet which had been hijacked by four Arab terrorists and flown to Mogadishu airport, Somalia. In a high-risk action three of the terrorists, but no

Anti-terrorist units

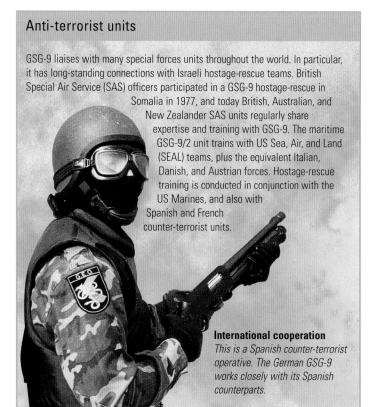

GSG-9 liaises with many special forces units throughout the world. In particular, it has long-standing connections with Israeli hostage-rescue teams. British Special Air Service (SAS) officers participated in a GSG-9 hostage-rescue in Somalia in 1977, and today British, Australian, and New Zealander SAS units regularly share expertise and training with GSG-9. The maritime GSG-9/2 unit trains with US Sea, Air, and Land (SEAL) teams, plus the equivalent Italian, Danish, and Austrian forces. Hostage-rescue training is conducted in conjunction with the US Marines, and also with Spanish and French counter-terrorist units.

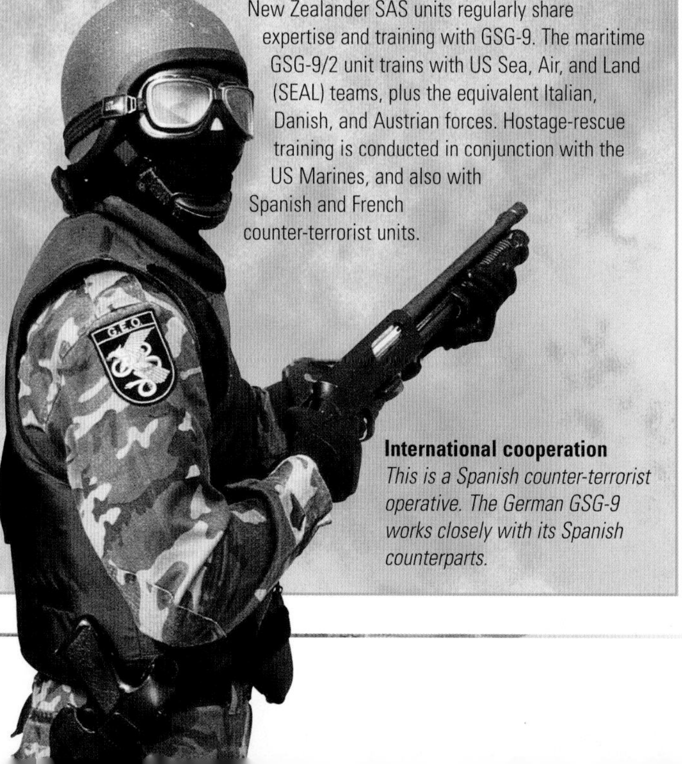

International cooperation
This is a Spanish counter-terrorist operative. The German GSG-9 works closely with its Spanish counterparts.

◀ **Rappelling**
A GSG-9 team rappels from a hovering helicopter. This highly dangerous tactic is used to get teams quickly onto the roofs of buildings.

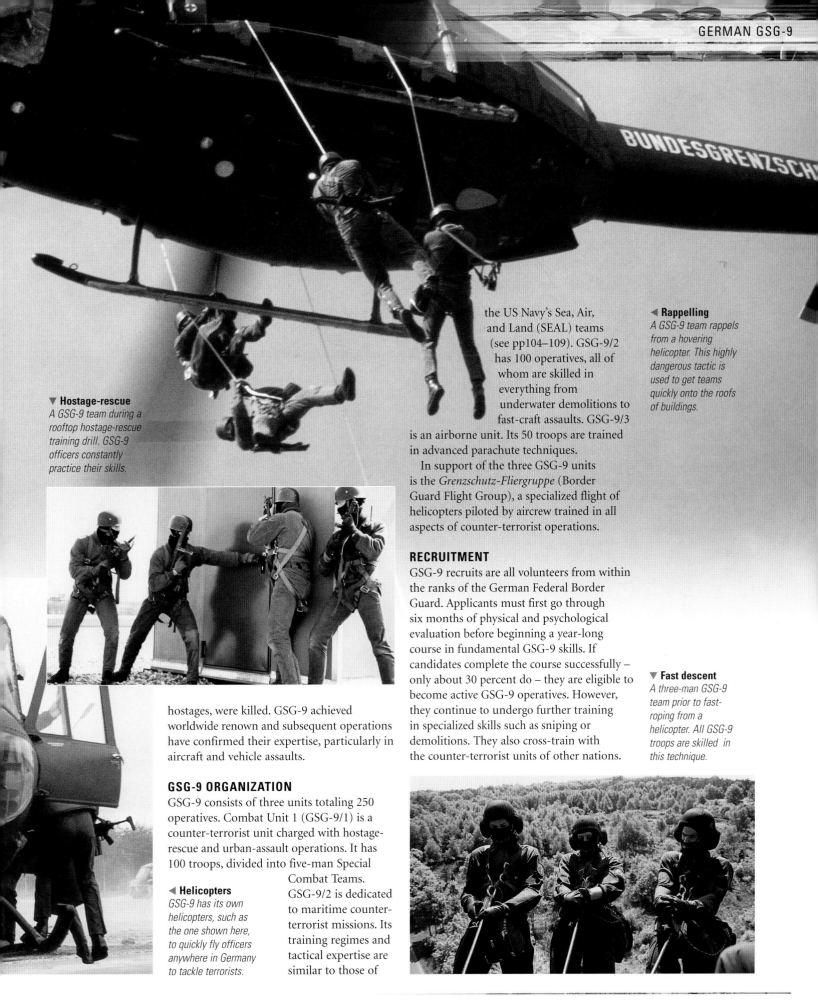

▼ **Hostage-rescue**
A GSG-9 team during a rooftop hostage-rescue training drill. GSG-9 officers constantly practice their skills.

◀ **Helicopters**
GSG-9 has its own helicopters, such as the one shown here, to quickly fly officers anywhere in Germany to tackle terrorists.

hostages, were killed. GSG-9 achieved worldwide renown and subsequent operations have confirmed their expertise, particularly in aircraft and vehicle assaults.

GSG-9 ORGANIZATION

GSG-9 consists of three units totaling 250 operatives. Combat Unit 1 (GSG-9/1) is a counter-terrorist unit charged with hostage-rescue and urban-assault operations. It has 100 troops, divided into five-man Special Combat Teams. GSG-9/2 is dedicated to maritime counter-terrorist missions. Its training regimes and tactical expertise are similar to those of the US Navy's Sea, Air, and Land (SEAL) teams (see pp104–109). GSG-9/2 has 100 operatives, all of whom are skilled in everything from underwater demolitions to fast-craft assaults. GSG-9/3 is an airborne unit. Its 50 troops are trained in advanced parachute techniques.

In support of the three GSG-9 units is the *Grenzschutz-Fliergruppe* (Border Guard Flight Group), a specialized flight of helicopters piloted by aircrew trained in all aspects of counter-terrorist operations.

RECRUITMENT

GSG-9 recruits are all volunteers from within the ranks of the German Federal Border Guard. Applicants must first go through six months of physical and psychological evaluation before beginning a year-long course in fundamental GSG-9 skills. If candidates complete the course successfully – only about 30 percent do – they are eligible to become active GSG-9 operatives. However, they continue to undergo further training in specialized skills such as sniping or demolitions. They also cross-train with the counter-terrorist units of other nations.

▼ **Fast descent**
A three-man GSG-9 team prior to fast-roping from a helicopter. All GSG-9 troops are skilled in this technique.

Scourge of freedom
A member of the Popular Front for the Liberation of Palestine on trial at a Brussels court in the 1970s.

BACKGROUND

Following Israel's crushing defeat of its hostile Arab neighbors in the Six Day War (1967), Palestinian independence movements turned to terrorism as a means of resistance to Israeli rule. Several groups emerged, including the Popular Front for the Liberation of Palestine (PFLP). Simultaneously, in the 1970s, West European countries were also becoming the focus for terrorist actions by groups opposed to their capitalist economies, particularly from Marxist or anarchist groups. One such group was the Baader–Meinhof Gang in Germany, which later became known as the Red Army Faction (RAF). During the 1970s, German and Palestinian terror groups began to cooperate in training and information. When PFLP terrorists hijacked a German airliner in 1977, demanding the release of RAF prisoners (the RAF leaders had been captured in 1975), the West German government faced a serious crisis. It was an obvious challenge for the recently formed GSG-9 anti-terrorist squad.

German GSG-9: Mogadishu, 1977

This 1977 operation by *Grenzschutzgruppe-9* (GSG-9 or Border Guard Group 9) remains a textbook example of a hostage-rescue assault against a hijacked aircraft. In a well-planned, lightning action, using stun grenades and submachine guns, a GSG-9 team entered a Lufthansa jet and neutralized the four terrorists before they could harm the crew and 86 passengers. The operation won GSG-9 international fame.

▶ **Freedom**
The freed hostages return to Germany following their rescue by GSG-9. The operation had been a complete success.

On October 13, 1977, four terrorists of the Popular Front for the Liberation of Palestine (PFLP) group hijacked a Lufthansa Boeing 737 flying between Majorca and the German Federal Republic (West Germany). The four hijackers (two men, two women) were led by a determined but unstable terrorist who called himself "Captain Mahmoud," but whose real name was Zohair Youssef Akache. They demanded the release of 11 Red Army Faction terrorists from German prisons. For four days the aircraft shuttled around the Middle East, often denied permission to land, but sometimes landing anyway to refuel. At Aden, in the Yemen, the hijackers killed the pilot after hearing he had fed information to the authorities. On October 17 the co-pilot was forced to fly to Mogadishu, the capital of Somalia. It was here that GSG-9 would act.

PREPARATIONS

GSG-9 began its preparations only a few hours after the airliner was hijacked. Teams pursued the Lufthansa jet across the Middle East. At 5:30 p.m. on October 17, a 30-strong hostage-rescue force landed at Mogadishu's airport. It was commanded by Colonel Ulrich Wegener, founder of GSG-9, with two British Special Air Service (SAS) officers as observers. The GSG-9 equipment included rubber-coated lightweight assault ladders, for silent placement against the aircraft and climbing, and stun grenades, capable of producing an ear-splitting bang and blinding flash.

Akache was informed that his demand for the prisoner release was being met. He set a deadline of 2:45 a.m. on October 18 for the prisoners to arrive at Mogadishu, and for a ransom of 10 million US dollars to be paid. Wegener

◀ **Surveillance**
Somali guards keep a close watch on the hijacked Boeing 737 at Mogadishu. The GSG-9 assault force crept up on it from the rear.

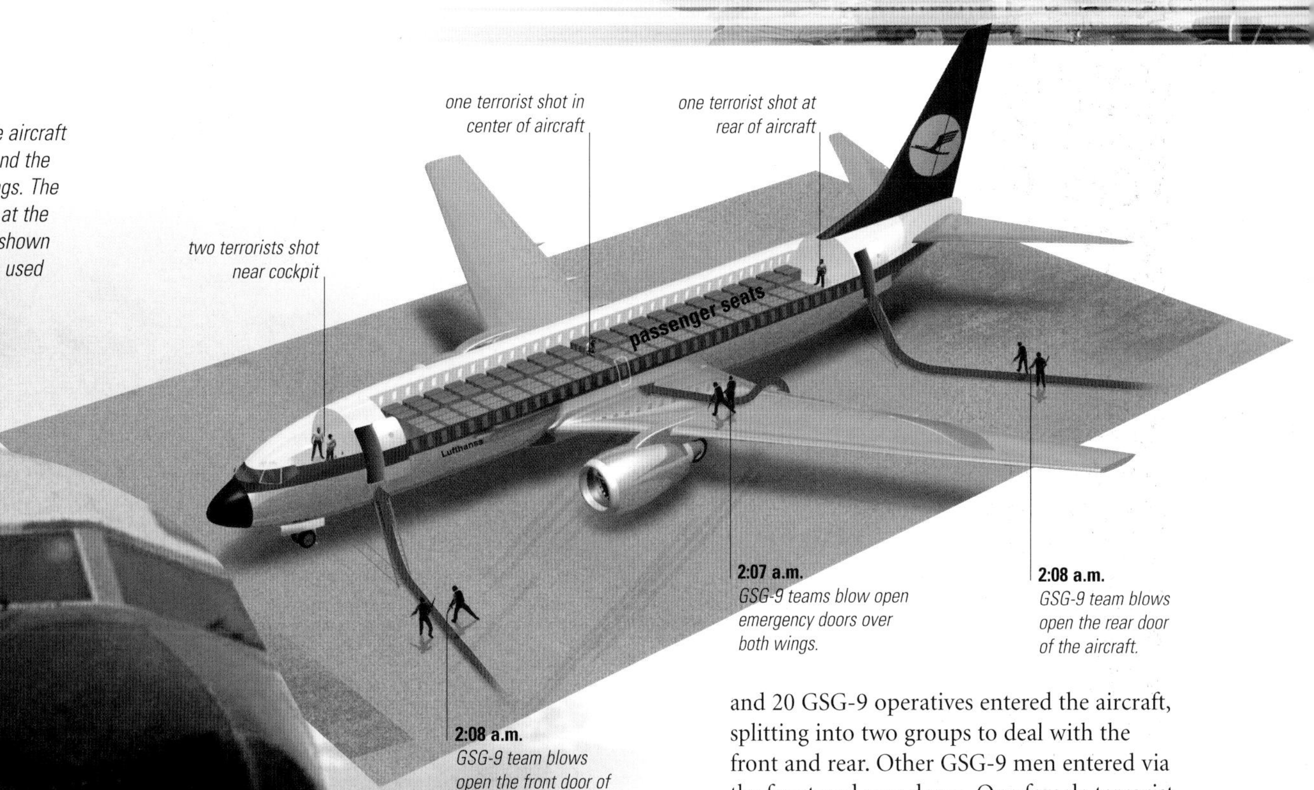
one terrorist shot in center of aircraft
one terrorist shot at rear of aircraft
two terrorists shot near cockpit
passenger seats
2:07 a.m.
GSG-9 teams blow open emergency doors over both wings.
2:08 a.m.
GSG-9 team blows open the rear door of the aircraft.
2:08 a.m.
GSG-9 team blows open the front door of the aircraft.

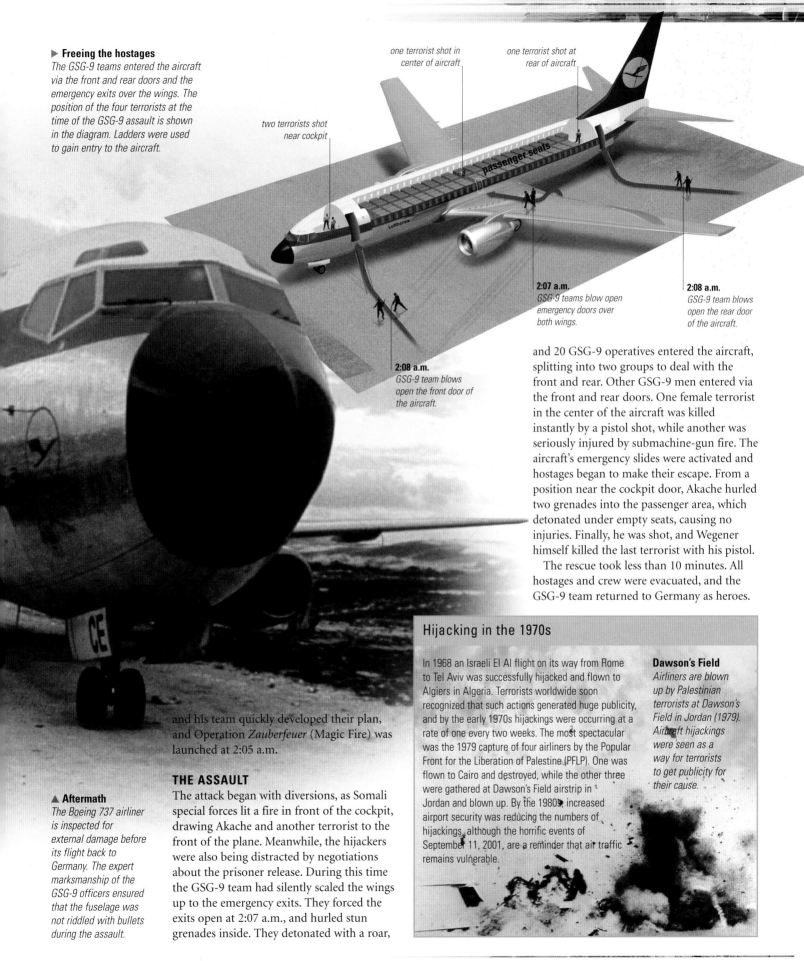

▶ **Freeing the hostages**
The GSG-9 teams entered the aircraft via the front and rear doors and the emergency exits over the wings. The position of the four terrorists at the time of the GSG-9 assault is shown in the diagram. Ladders were used to gain entry to the aircraft.

▲ **Aftermath**
The Boeing 737 airliner is inspected for external damage before its flight back to Germany. The expert marksmanship of the GSG-9 officers ensured that the fuselage was not riddled with bullets during the assault.

and his team quickly developed their plan, and Operation *Zauberfeuer* (Magic Fire) was launched at 2:05 a.m.

THE ASSAULT

The attack began with diversions, as Somali special forces lit a fire in front of the cockpit, drawing Akache and another terrorist to the front of the plane. Meanwhile, the hijackers were also being distracted by negotiations about the prisoner release. During this time the GSG-9 team had silently scaled the wings up to the emergency exits. They forced the exits open at 2:07 a.m., and hurled stun grenades inside. They detonated with a roar, and 20 GSG-9 operatives entered the aircraft, splitting into two groups to deal with the front and rear. Other GSG-9 men entered via the front and rear doors. One female terrorist in the center of the aircraft was killed instantly by a pistol shot, while another was seriously injured by submachine-gun fire. The aircraft's emergency slides were activated and hostages began to make their escape. From a position near the cockpit door, Akache hurled two grenades into the passenger area, which detonated under empty seats, causing no injuries. Finally, he was shot, and Wegener himself killed the last terrorist with his pistol.

The rescue took less than 10 minutes. All hostages and crew were evacuated, and the GSG-9 team returned to Germany as heroes.

Hijacking in the 1970s

In 1968 an Israeli El Al flight on its way from Rome to Tel Aviv was successfully hijacked and flown to Algiers in Algeria. Terrorists worldwide soon recognized that such actions generated huge publicity, and by the early 1970s hijackings were occurring at a rate of one every two weeks. The most spectacular was the 1979 capture of four airliners by the Popular Front for the Liberation of Palestine (PFLP). One was flown to Cairo and destroyed, while the other three were gathered at Dawson's Field airstrip in Jordan and blown up. By the 1980s, increased airport security was reducing the numbers of hijackings, although the horrific events of September 11, 2001, are a reminder that air traffic remains vulnerable.

Dawson's Field
Airliners are blown up by Palestinian terrorists at Dawson's Field in Jordan (1979). Aircraft hijackings were seen as a way for terrorists to get publicity for their cause.

French GIGN

The *Groupe d'Intervention Gendarmerie Nationale* (GIGN), or the National Gendarmerie Intervention Group, is the French national counter-terrorist group. Although small, with fewer than 90 full-time members, it is considered to be one of the best anti-terrorist units in the world. It has achieved some notable successes since its formation in 1974, and cross-trains with other European and American counter-terrorist groups.

▲ **GIGN sniper**
Snipers are an important part of GIGN's capability. Marksmanship is given a high priority within the unit. Hundreds of hours are spent on rifle ranges.

GIGN was created in 1974 from volunteers drawn from the *Gendarmerie Nationale*, France's paramilitary police force, responsible for law enforcement outside the country's major urban centers. Initially 15 policemen were selected and trained for the new group.

Within months the new force was enduring a baptism of fire, making a series of armed interventions inside French prisons to put down rioting – at Loos-les-Lille, Eysses, Caen, Mulhouse, Colmar, and Dijon.

GIGN badge

On February 3, 1976, during unrest in the former French colony of Djibouti, East Africa, a school bus was stormed by an armed Somali terrorist group. A GIGN team was immediately sent to bring the hijack to an end. Once at the site, the unit employed ingenuity in an effort to minimize casualties. Drugged sandwiches were delivered to the bus for the children so they would be asleep during the assault. The youths slumped down in their seats, their heads below the windows of the bus. This gave the GIGN officers a clear view of the six terrorists. The GIGN men attacked at 3:47 p.m. in overwhelming heat. After a hard fight, nine gendarmes rescued 29 children, although one girl was killed.

GIGN takes its orders from the French Ministry of Defense, but its members remain policemen, with powers of arrest and rules of engagement that change according to whether they are in action against civilian criminals or terrorists. Most of the 700 or so GIGN actions have been police operations. These include hostage-rescue, jail and riot suppression, and high-risk arrests. About 500 hostages have been rescued, over 1,000 criminals arrested, and five officers killed.

ORGANIZATION

The 87 full-time operators in GIGN are organized into four 15-man groups commanded by an officer, a command and support unit, and a four-man hostage negotiation cell. Two of the teams specialize in water operations. The other two teams specialize in high-altitude, low opening (HALO) and high-altitude, high opening

GIGN snipers

GIGN's firearms training is considered to be the best in the world. Being policemen rather than soldiers, GIGN operators are (perhaps uniquely) concerned with arresting rather than killing armed criminals and terrorists. The patience and control of their snipers is legendary (see Sniping, pp138–139).

FR sniper rifle
This is the French FR sniper rifle, which is used by GIGN snipers during their operations.

▶ **Fast response**
For rapid deployment to any location in France, GIGN officers can call upon the services of the French Air Force. This Puma helicopter has just landed a GIGN team in southern France.

Cross-training

Because of GIGN's practical experience and reputation, other counter-terrorist groups, such as the German GSG-9, the US Federal Bureau of Investigation (FBI), and the US Army's elite Delta Force, come to France for specialized training. GIGN trained the Saudi National Guard in the use of paralyzing gas, demolitions, and room clearing as preparation for their successful assault on the terrorist-held Grand Mosque in Mecca in 1979. GIGN personnel also travel to the Middle East and the United States for cross-training with counter-terrorist agencies.

Working with the FBI
This is a hostage-rescue drill being carried out on the FBI's training ground in the United States. GIGN personnel often cross-train with American and European counter-terrorist units.

(HAHO) parachute techniques that can get GIGN reconnaissance teams rapidly anywhere in the world.

ENTRY REQUIREMENTS

Only the best policemen with five years of exemplary service may apply to join GIGN. Only 10 percent pass the initial week-long selection training. Those who are successful then undertake eight months of continuation training and probationary work. During this period they learn marksmanship, close-quarter combat skills, parachuting, and combat swimming. Another mandatory skill is being able to rappel to the ground from a hovering helicopter.

Once qualified, operatives must maintain their fitness and keep their shooting skills sharp by firing up to 300 rounds each day up to standard.

▲ **Hostage-rescue drill**
A GIGN officer during hostage-rescue training. His submachine gun uses a high-intensity flashlight as a sight, for snap shooting in low light.

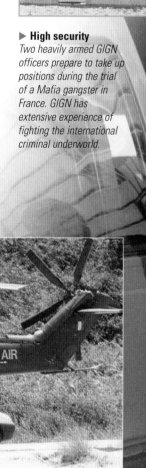

▶ **High security**
Two heavily armed GIGN officers prepare to take up positions during the trial of a Mafia gangster in France. GIGN has extensive experience of fighting the international criminal underworld.

French GIGN: Marseilles, 1994

Terrorist bombing
The aftermath of a GIA bomb in a busy shopping district in Algeria. The GIA has been waging war since 1992.

BACKGROUND

The *Groupe Islamique Armé* (GIA) is Algeria's most violent Islamic terrorist group. It resorted to violence after the victory of the *Front Islamique de Salut* (FIS, or Islamic Salvation Front) in the Algerian legislative elections of December 1991 was declared void by the government. The regime also called off a general election due to be held in 1992. As well as waging war against the government, the GIA regarded France, the former colonial power, as a principal enemy. It blamed the French for backing the increasingly anti-Islamic government of Liamine Zeroual, who came to power in 1994, and for sustaining Algeria's government in the civil war that had erupted in the country in 1992. There was some truth in this, as the French were supplying military equipment for use against the Islamic insurgents. In retaliation, the GIA decided to strike directly at France by hijacking a civil airliner and flying it to Paris, the French capital. The group hoped that this act would attract worldwide publicity for its cause.

In 1994, four well-trained Algerian hijackers landed Air France Flight 8969 at Marseilles airport in southern France. France's elite *Groupe d'Intervention de la Gendarmerie Nationale* (GIGN) was deployed to resolve the highly volatile situation and rescue the hostaged passengers and crew on board. The success of the mission raised the profile of GIGN worldwide.

On December 24, 1994, four terrorists of the Algerian *Groupe Islamique Armé* (GIA, or Armed Islamic Group), who were opposed to Algeria's military government (and its French allies), hijacked an Air France Airbus at Boumediene airport, Algiers. They were disguised as airport security men. With 230 passengers and crew, the aircraft was waiting for take-off when the terrorists produced AK-47 assault rifles and demanded to be flown to Paris, France. To emphasize their seriousness, they shot dead an Algerian policeman and a Vietnamese diplomat on the tarmac in front of the aircraft.

THE GIGN ASSAULT PLAN

The elite French *Groupe d'Intervention de la Gendarmerie Nationale* (GIGN) was hastily recalled and began practicing rescue tactics on an identical Air France Airbus, intending to carry out a rescue in Algeria. However, the Algerian Army's commando force wanted to make a full-frontal assault on the plane, regardless of the safety of the hostages, so the GIGN was denied permission to get involved.

In the meantime the terrorists released 63 hostages, but, angry that they were being prevented from flying to Paris, France, also killed a young French chef. Finally, the Algerian government relented, and at 2:00 a.m. on December 26 the plane left for France, with terrorists and hostages aboard.

By the time the aircraft landed for refueling at Marseilles airport, before continuing on to Paris, the GIGN units were in position. Snipers were placed around and on top of the control tower. Paratroopers from the *Escadron Parachutiste d'Intervention de la Gendarmerie Nationale* (EPIGN) were camouflaged in long grass by the airport's runway. And GIGN's eight-man assault teams, with three mobile-stairway trucks to get them onto the aircraft, were deployed. A police officer in the airport control tower was ready to negotiate.

Flight 8969 was not going to be allowed to fly to Paris. Reports suggested that the terrorists intended to blow it up over the capital. It then emerged that the terrorists had indeed set explosive charges. They also demanded much more fuel than was necessary to reach Paris.

▶ **Aircraft rescue**
GIGN personnel storm the hijacked Air France Airbus at Marseilles airport in December 1994. The firefight was mainly at the front of the plane, around the cockpit. Because of the confined spaces involved and the risks to passengers, such actions are fraught with danger.

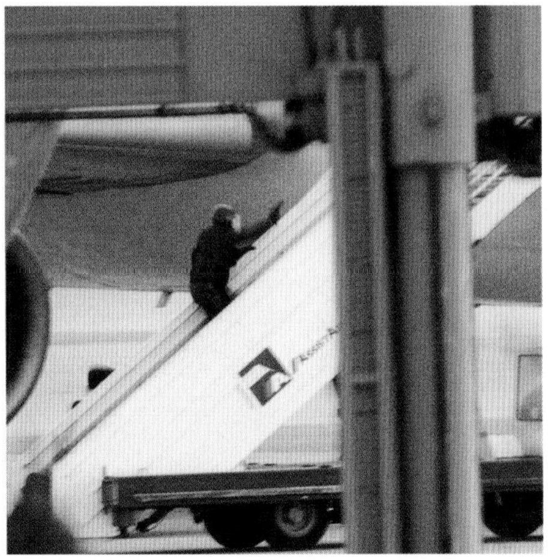

◀ **Stealthy approach**
A GIGN officer, his pistol cocked ready for action, makes his way up the steps to the aircraft. During an aircraft assault speed is essential. The GIGN team had to disarm the terrorists before they could kill the hostages or set off explosives.

Cross-border cooperation

As well as hostage-rescue operations, the French GIGN is heavily involved in the fight against international organized crime. This means working closely with the police forces of neighboring countries, especially Italy and Spain. When major criminals are caught and put on trial, GIGN officers often provide security. This is because wealthy criminals have the resources and contacts to organize rescue attempts. GIGN officers therefore provide sniper cover and armed guards around the court.

Security measures *These GIGN officers formed part of the security apparatus put in place for the trial of a senior Mafia figure, who was arrested in southern France.*

▲ **After the mission** *GIGN officers photographed after the operation on the hijacked plane at Marseilles airport. An undoubted success, the mission left nine GIGN men wounded, but firmly established the unit's ability to fulfil its role.*

A TENSE STAND-OFF

Pressure was growing from the French government for an assault to be made on the aircraft before 10:00 p.m. on December 26 – the terrorists' deadline for their demands for fuel and permission to take off to be met. At 1:00 p.m., the terrorists allowed service crew on board to clean the aircraft and provide food. Disguised GIGN operatives were able to install miniature cameras and listening devices. The GIGN commander continued to resist the pressure to move in, deciding to wait until twilight. Then, at 4:50 p.m., the Airbus's engines started, the plane moved toward the control tower, and gunfire from the cockpit smashed its windows.

INTO ACTION

The assault began with a GIGN sniper on the control tower roof firing heavy, silenced rounds into the cockpit to disorient the hijackers. The assault teams entered the aircraft from the mobile stairways after throwing in stun grenades. One terrorist was killed, but heavy fire from the others in the cockpit wounded six GIGN men. Eight men from GIGN then stormed the smoking plane, firing into the cockpit. At the same time, others moved to the rear of the aircraft and evacuated hostages through the emergency doors, using escape chutes. The navigator jumped from the cockpit window. After 10 minutes of intense gunfire, the remaining terrorists were dead. Remarkably, no passengers were killed and the crew in the cockpit were safe. The action was a high-profile validation of the GIGN's skills.

▶ **End of the drama** *A GIGN members helps a passenger away after her two-day ordeal in the hijacked Airbus. The GIGN had saved the hostages, as well as foiling an attack on Paris.*

Intelligence agencies

Every special forces operation requires accurate intelligence: For planning and executing a mission, and then for evaluating its success. National intelligence agencies gather data from many different sources – some secret, others public (such as the Internet) – which they then collate and interpret. This process turns raw data into usable intelligence material.

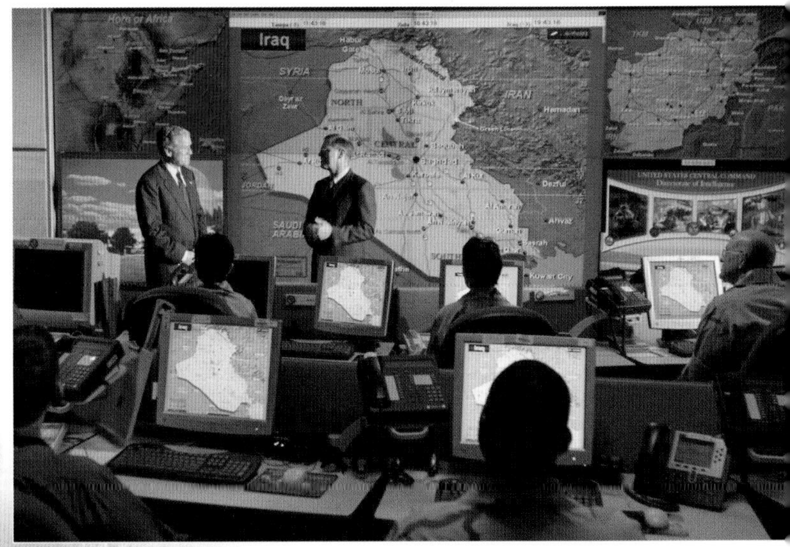

▲ **Intelligence center**
President George W. Bush (back left) at US Central Command Center, McDill Air Force Base, Florida, during the Iraq war in 2003.

The successful planning and execution of special forces operations requires accurate and timely intelligence. The organizations responsible for gathering this information are national intelligence agencies. Some intelligence agencies, such as the United States Central Intelligence Agency (CIA), have their own special forces units, which deploy into regions of potential conflict ahead of military units. They are capable of defending

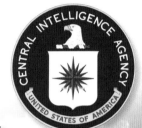

CIA badge

FBI badge

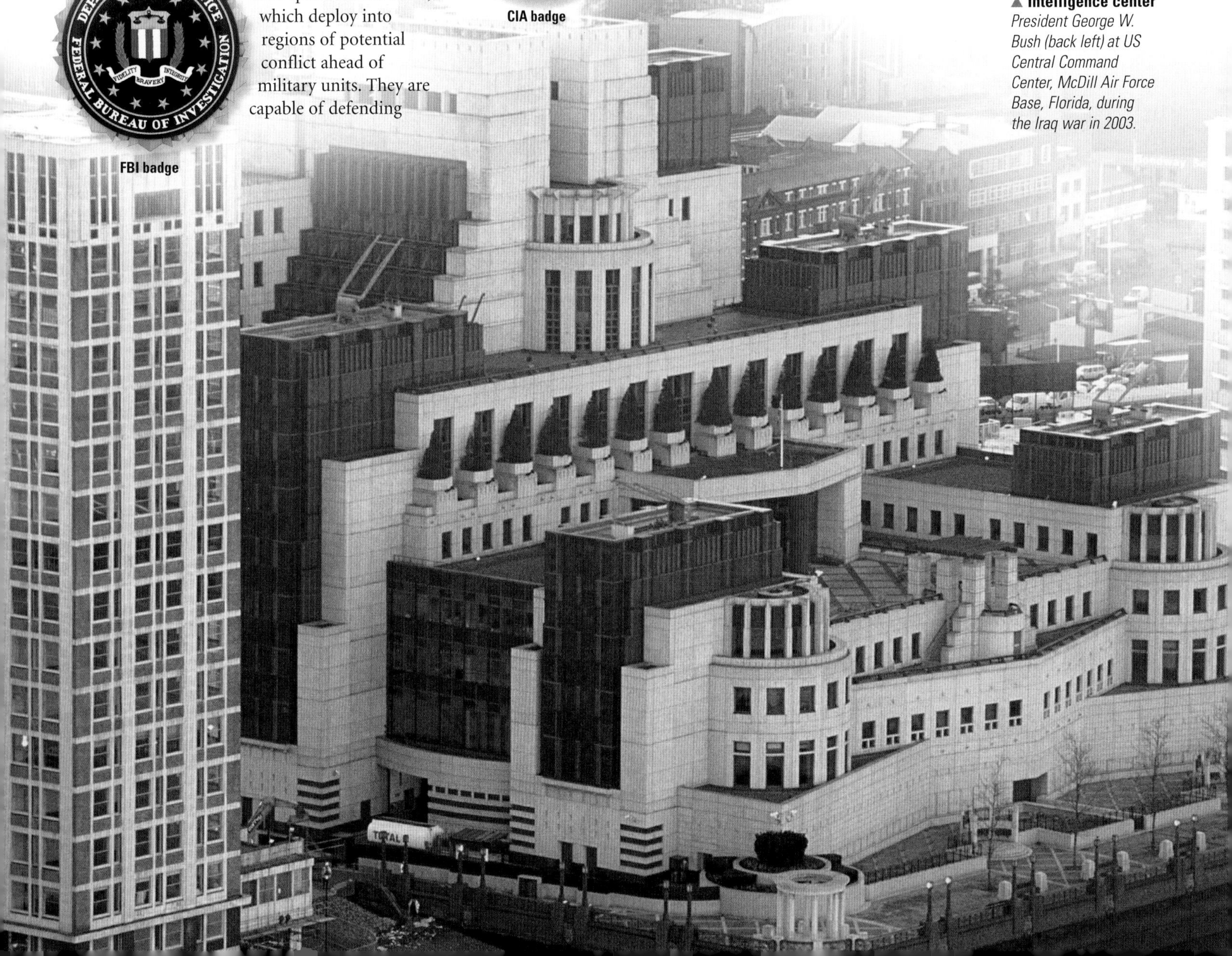

themselves and taking offensive action, as was shown in the Yemen in 2002, when a CIA unit killed a group of terrorists in a car using a missile fired from a pilotless aircraft. National law-enforcement agencies, such as the US Federal Bureau of Investigation (FBI), also maintain special operations teams, which act on intelligence generated by FBI field agents.

Secrecy is the keystone of all intelligence-agency operations. Without human sources inside enemy organizations providing data, there can be no intelligence. Here lies the dilemma facing every intelligence agency: Does it act on information received, and risk revealing and perhaps causing the death of its source? When special forces take immediate offensive action in response to "inside" information, the source runs the risks of discovery. But when sources of intelligence must be preserved, special forces operations are planned to leave no trace of intervention – or at least no trace until the immediate need for secrecy has receded.

NATIONAL AGENCIES

The US Directorate of Intelligence produces information about threats to US interests; the CIA coordinates operations, and supports the President and the National Security Council on issues of national significance. In Britain, MI6 (or the Security Intelligence Service, SIS) deals with foreign intelligence, while MI5 (or the Security Service) works domestically. Both collaborate with GCHQ (the Government Communications Headquarters), which, like the US National Security Agency, monitors all forms of global telecommunications traffic.

SHARING INFORMATION

In order to be useful, intelligence must be timely and shared between relevant organizations. Intelligence agencies are often very reluctant to share information that might jeopardize their sources. However, in the face of the global terrorist threat, very strenuous efforts are being made by Western governments to eliminate such rivalry, and improve communications between all intelligence agencies.

International cooperation

Sharing intelligence can be problematic when the agencies are from different countries. Agreements to share intelligence, as exist between the US and Britain, are based on mutual trust. In multinational operations, such as those involving the UN, highly classified information cannot simply be shared among personnel who might need it, if the various countries involved do not have prior intelligence-sharing agreements.

Interpol HQ, Lyons
Interpol's base in France is the center of international policing.

▶ **Terrorist leader**
Osama bin Laden (b. 1957), leader of the al Qaeda terrorist network, is a prime focus of Western intelligence agencies. He is blamed for the September 11, 2001, attacks on the United States.

▼ **CIA, Langley**
The headquarters of the US Central Intelligence Agency in Langley, Virginia – the largest intelligence agency in the world.

◀ **MI6 headquarters**
Britain's foreign intelligence HQ in London, England, has reinforced glass windows and thickened walls to defend against terrorist attack.

EQUIPMENT AND TECHNIQUES

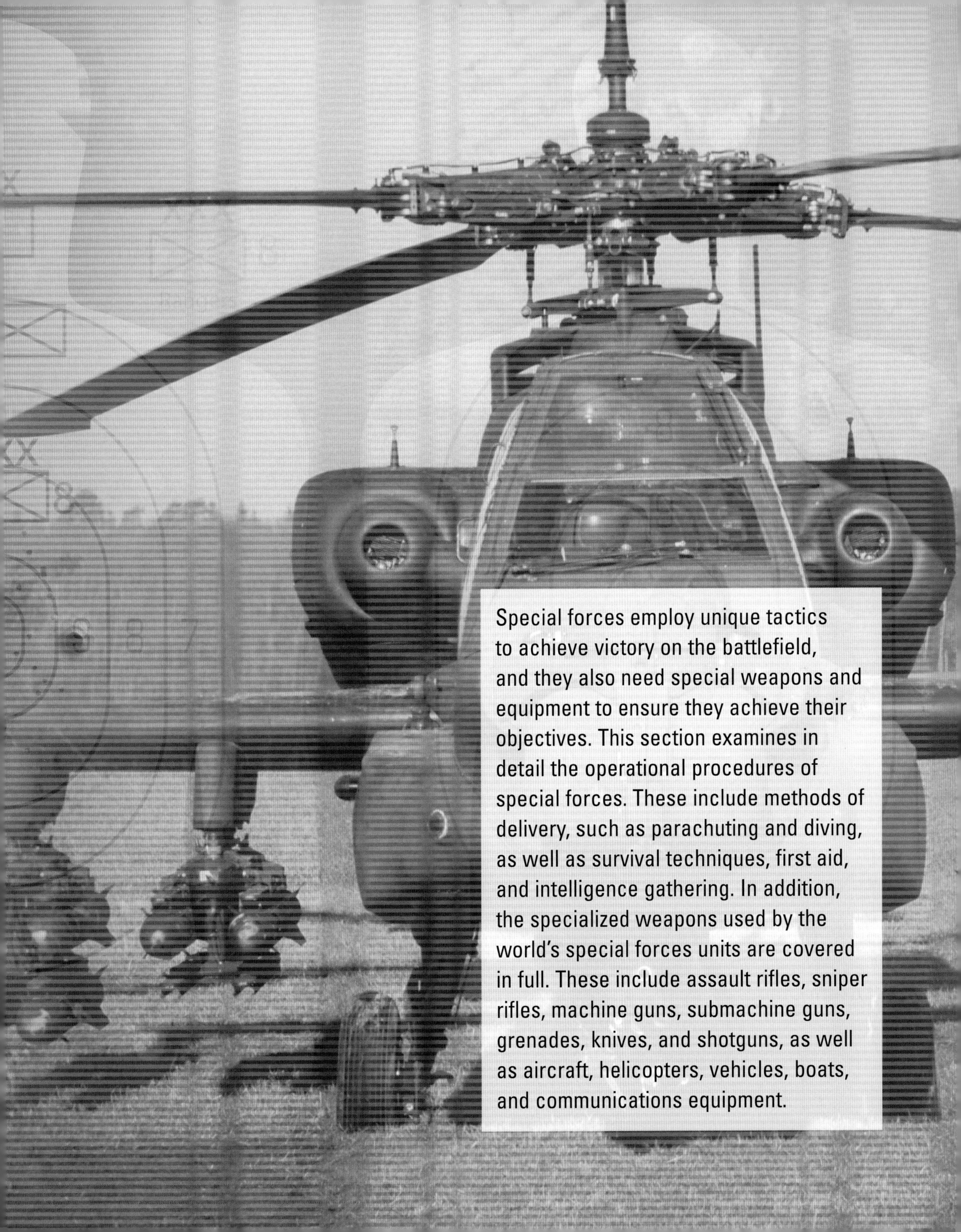

Special forces employ unique tactics to achieve victory on the battlefield, and they also need special weapons and equipment to ensure they achieve their objectives. This section examines in detail the operational procedures of special forces. These include methods of delivery, such as parachuting and diving, as well as survival techniques, first aid, and intelligence gathering. In addition, the specialized weapons used by the world's special forces units are covered in full. These include assault rifles, sniper rifles, machine guns, submachine guns, grenades, knives, and shotguns, as well as aircraft, helicopters, vehicles, boats, and communications equipment.

Methodology

The organization and methods of special forces units in waging war are very different from those of conventional troops. Special forces have to be totally self-reliant for long periods of time, and must often create their own strategies, methods, and equipment lists to achieve success in unpredictable operations. Another essential skill is the ability to take calculated risks under pressure.

▲ **The "buddy system"** *Members of special forces patrols pair up on operations. Each man supports the other and they work together for the duration of the mission.*

Modern special forces work in small teams for ease of concealment, resupply, and movement. The British Special Air Service (SAS) favors four-man teams. There is good reason for this. If one person is wounded, for example, two can carry him, while the fourth leads the party. In addition, within the four-man team there is a so-called "buddy system" in which soldiers form close-knit pairs and get to know each other extremely well, work together, and protect each other.

◄ **Signals expertise** *A member of the British Pathfinders unit uses a radio to transmit intelligence from behind enemy lines to headquarters. The ability to communicate with their home base is essential to all special forces units.*

A TEAM OF MULTI-SKILLED SOLDIERS

Each special forces team usually contains experts in the basic skills of demolitions, radio communication, and first aid. When vehicles are used, there must be at least one mechanic capable of improvising major repairs as well as routine servicing. Each man will have more than one area of expertise to ensure that a mission can continue even if the principal specialist is wounded or killed.

Special forces operations

Special forces can achieve an effect proportionally far greater than their numbers or the resources at their disposal might suggest. This is becoming ever more important as modern technology enables what military strategists call "effects-based warfare" – military operations that use just enough force to create the required political or tactical effect, and which cease as soon as the effect has been achieved. One special forces team working in a large area, liaising with local inhabitants, investigating enemy positions and targets, and directing airstrikes, can achieve more, with greater accuracy and with less risk to local people, than a large military force using conventional battlefield tactics.

M16/M203 *The M16 assault rifle and M203 grenade launcher combination gives special forces soldiers extensive firepower.*

Special forces adopt the best equipment for the task at hand. They are also experienced enough to utilize any unfamiliar equipment they might be given or that they might capture in the field. Within each patrol unit there will be a variety of weapons and calibers to ensure a level of firepower appropriate for the enemy they are likely to encounter, for the goal of the mission, and for the environment in which they are operating. A lightly equipped patrol will typically

► **Weapons mix** *Each special forces patrol, such as this unit of the US Marines, usually has a mix of weapons for maximum firepower.*

◀ **Vehicles**
This heavily laden British Parachute Regiment Land Rover is equipped with fuel, tools, and spares for the vehicle. It also carries extra supplies of food, medicines, water, and ammunition. In this way the vehicle can become a base for operations.

"Chinese parliament"

There is far more equality in special forces units than in their conventional counterparts. When planning a mission, decisions are often taken via a "Chinese parliament," in which each team member's views are considered, irrespective of rank. Special operations require a very wide range of skills and expertise, so each team member must be specialized in at least one area. Experience normally counts above rank in terms of command, so the overall commander may be a sergeant rather than an officer with less experience. The team will be ordered to achieve certain objectives, but will not be instructed how to achieve them: It is up to them to decide. During an operation every team member's life is at risk, so the "Chinese parliament" may also be convened while the mission is in progress.

Rest period
A special forces patrol takes a break while on an exercise. Mission objectives are likely to be discussed.

have rapid-fire 5.56-mm. assault rifles, such as the Colt Commando or AR-15. Disposable anti-tank rockets or M-28 grenade launchers provide heavier firepower; and a 7.62-mm. sniper rifle or semi-automatic rifle enables the patrol to engage the enemy at greater ranges, thus reducing the chance of being captured or killed. Individuals may also carry pistols for self-defense, for close-target reconnaissance, and for moments of intense activity such as prisoner snatches.

STAYING SUPPLIED

Patrols carry food, water, weapons, and ammunition on their vehicles, if the mission is using them, but each man also carries a day's rations and at least 200 rounds of ammunition.

▼ **Webbing**
Patrol members carry essential items in their webbing (a canvas belt with shoulder straps). Included here are survival packs of food and water, as well as ammunition and navigational equipment.

Special forces tactics

Special forces tactics vary according to the role each unit is expected to play. Each unit's tactics must be understood and memorized by every member. Before a mission, the commander will decide exactly what each person is to do under every circumstance. If there is time, the patrol practices these procedures. However, if time is short, each operative has been trained to carry out the unit's tactics without further orders.

Tactics enable the individuals in a special forces unit to work together to complete the various types of operation they have been trained to undertake. Most units keep a large textbook, usually known as Standard Operating Procedures (SOP), describing their tactics, plus standard lists of the minimum equipment each member must carry, how they should communicate, and so on. Special forces operatives are expected to memorize every detail of this book and, unless there are very good operational reasons, carry out their missions in accordance with its rules.

Everything, from the format the commander uses to give orders to the sequence of events in each type of operation, is standardized so each soldier knows what to expect. On an operation there is no room for misunderstanding. When people become tired, or a situation becomes confused, there must be simple, reliable drills to be put into operation. This

Operational techniques

Special forces units mount operations using whatever means gives them the most tactical advantage. Parachuting, helicopters, diving, swimming, and small boats provide an element of surprise, but are affected by bad weather and limit the amount of equipment that can be carried. During the 2003 Iraq War, US airborne units parachuted into the west and north of Iraq, capturing key airfields into which reinforcements were flown.

Helicopters
Helicopters are the most reliable form of covert transport. They are capable of bringing vehicles and large amounts of stores and equipment into small landing areas with relatively little noise.

▼ Head-on contact drills
Special forces practice contact drills constantly, rehearsing exactly what to do if attacked, when speed and aggression make the difference between surviving and dying. If attacked from the front, the troops run forward to adopt the formation shown below. If the assault is a success, troops will then rapidly withdraw to the emergency rendezvous.

▲ Arcs of fire
Survival often depends upon the patrol carefully observing all that is around them, and ensuring that each man's weapon covers specific arcs, which must always overlap (shown in dark green), giving arcs of fire of 360 degrees.

▲ **Master tacticians**
Each member of a special forces patrol is highly trained in small-unit tactics. They are practiced over and over again until they become second nature. On operations, any mistakes can be fatal for the whole team.

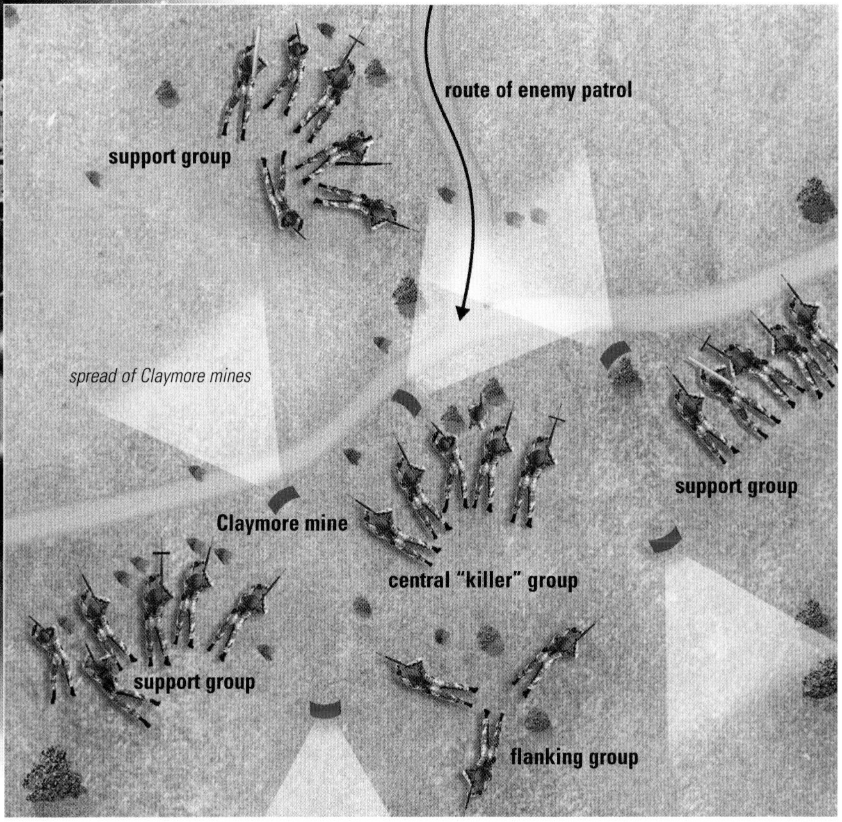

▲ **Special forces ambush position**
Ambush operations are complex, and can often last for days and even weeks. The central "killer group" sets off the ambush, often by detonating Claymore mines. Support groups on either side prevent any enemy escaping, and flanking groups ensure that enemy soldiers are unable to attack from the rear. The unit commander will take great care to ensure that the arcs of fire do not put his men in danger from each other.

prevents mistakes and speeds up the planning. Often there will only be time to learn a few key grid references and to allocate the main operational tasks before going into action.

OPERATIONS

On operations, all daily routines are firmly established. Just before dawn, the patrol will be packed up and ready to move. The unit will watch and wait for 30 minutes in a strong defensive position with their weapons covering the surrounding terrain. This process, known as "stand to," is repeated at dusk, because experience shows that dawn and dusk are the most likely times for an enemy attack. The enemy tends either to creep close in the darkness to attack using the first light of day, or, having located the patrol by daylight, to use the growing cover of darkness to launch an attack. At night troops can be tired and their concentration low.

Special forces team is ambushed

Special forces team charges ambushers

▲ **Anti-ambush drill**
A well-planned ambush usually kills everybody who enters its killing zone. Anti-ambush drills require immediate action with no room for hesitation. The only hope is to escape the first bursts of fire and run forward over the top of the enemy.

On patrol, the team will stop every 30 minutes and go into an "all-round defense" configuration – lying side-by-side in a tight circle facing outward. They listen for signs of being followed, and the commander might move forward to reconnoiter. He will also nominate features on the route as rendezvous points to return to if the unit becomes separated. If a patrol suspects it is being followed, the troops go into an immediate ambush position to one side. In dangerous territory, special forces teams live "hard" – not cooking or even whispering, and resting only in ambush positions, with no more than half the patrol sleeping at any one time.

Standard Operating Procedures are followed at all times. They dictate, for example, how many unit members can clean their weapons at the same time, or when the radio operator can contact base. Adherence to these tactics minimizes the risk of failure.

Survival techniques

Special operations carry much greater risks than conventional military operations and usually take place in enemy territory, often in inhospitable terrain and bad weather. Although operations are carefully prepared, they can still go wrong, and so special forces always assume that the worst will happen. For this reason, every special forces soldier is trained to survive and to find a way to return to base.

The ability to survive disaster and failure is a key requirement of special forces personnel. Military planners are skilled in assessing mission options, and will often decide to run risks knowing that things could go wrong. They assume that every soldier they send out has the knowledge to operate in any sort of environment, and will evade capture by the enemy, if anything goes wrong. Failing that, commanders know that all special forces personnel are trained to resist interrogation.

▶ **Navigation**
British commandos study their map and compass. Navigation skills are important for survival, and mean special forces units can find their way home.

FOOD, WATER, AND CLOTHING

It is not possible to carry rations for more than a 10-day mission, so special forces teams rely on hiding supplies in secret caches, or on resupply from their base. If neither of these options is feasible, then they must supplement their supplies with food and water foraged from the immediate environment. Water must always be purified, because dysentery can put a soldier out of action.

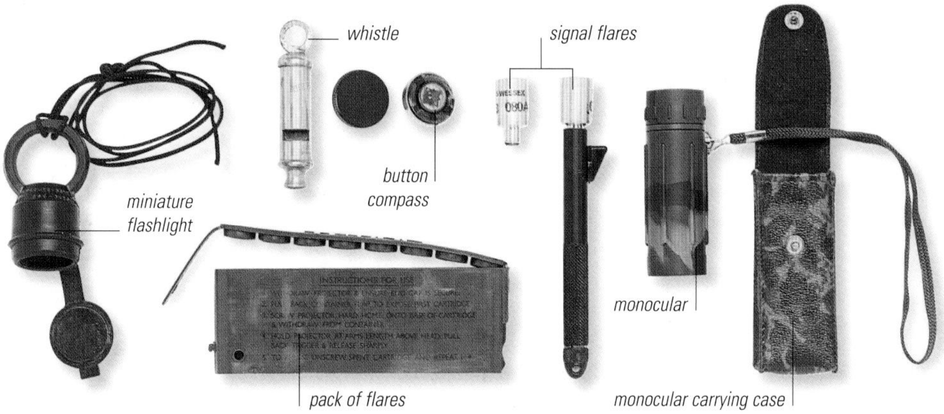

▲ **Survival kit**
A range of survival equipment that might be carried on operations.

Resistance to interrogation

Although proficient in evasion tactics, by their very nature special forces units operate in areas where capture is a constant possibility. For this reason they are trained to withstand enemy interrogation. They learn the various methods used by interrogators, and how best to react. Soldiers also learn how to conduct their own psychological war, generating and channeling aggression to resist. Although such training can never replicate a live situation, it can reduce the extreme shock of capture and help people find ways of coping.

Training exercise
A British paratrooper (right) takes a special forces soldier prisoner prior to a resistance-to-interrogation exercise. This can last for up to 48 hours.

▼ **Shelter**
Royal Marines rest in a tent during training in the Arctic. Shelter is vital in such extreme weather conditions.

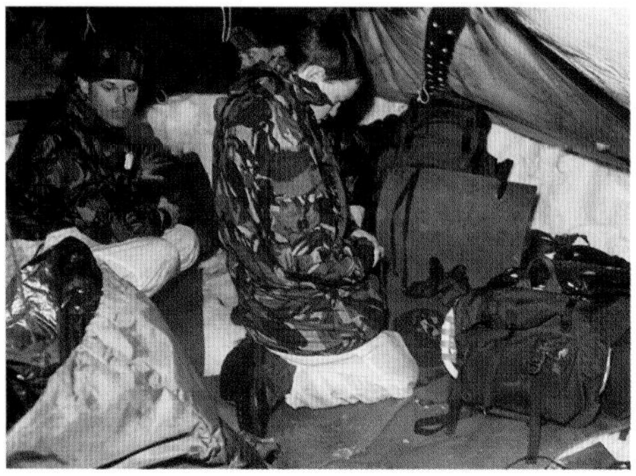

Remaining fit and healthy when living for long periods under hostile conditions demands constant attention to basic hygiene, especially to the cleanliness of the feet, teeth, and any wounds. Even in moderate climates, soldiers often get drenched with perspiration while on the move. Under these circumstances, wet clothing can be dangerous because it drains away body heat. Soldiers learn to conserve dry clothing, and to avoid the disastrous hazard of cold weather exposure. It is also likely that, without shelters, personnel will be freezing cold at night, or when they are stationary for long periods while on observation duty.

Living off the land

By living off the land, special forces can add to their rations to make them last longer, but living solely off the land is a full-time occupation. In a survival situation, knowing what not to eat is often the most important skill. Humans can survive without food for up to 10 days, depending upon the climate and an individual's condition, but a daily supply of fresh water is always vital.

Field craft
A special forces soldier prepares a chicken for cooking.

EXTREME CONDITIONS

Special forces units undertake survival training in a variety of different climatic conditions to prepare for any mission, anywhere in the world. The jungle, with its humid heat, insects, and thick vegetation, is a harsh and potentially unhealthy environment. Soldiers get used to wearing wet, dirty clothing by day, only changing into their dry clothes at night when secure in their camp. When operating behind enemy lines, special forces adopt what is known as "hard routine." This means not cooking, talking, or building shelters, and moving around with great care to avoid unnecessary noise. Every scratch or insect bite must be immediately disinfected to avoid infection, and, because the effort of moving through thick jungle can lead to heat exhaustion, fluid levels must be constantly maintained.

If hot, steamy jungle conditions present a unique set of problems, so too does the opposite extreme: The freezing environment in the Arctic. Cold weather problems such as frostbite and exposure are a constant threat. Dehydration is an equally serious problem, despite the abundance of snow and ice. Cold winds, ultra-dry air, and the heavy perspiration caused by long-distance skiing while carrying a heavy pack mean a high fluid intake is needed. A soldier's pack must also contain enough food to sustain him for the length of the mission. Because Arctic rations are packed in dehydrated form, they require the addition of water before they can be eaten. To melt snow and ice requires large amounts of stove fuel, all of which adds to the weight of a soldier's pack.

Desert conditions also present challenges for special forces teams. Vegetation is sparse, and living off the land is almost impossible. Lack of water is also a real danger to the success of a mission. Searing temperatures can cause heat exhaustion and dehydration in a very short space of time, especially for troops carrying heavy packs and weapons. To combat these threats, each soldier must carry enough water to supply him with as much as 4 gallons (19 liters) per day. Soldiers must also take tablets to replace minerals, such as salt, which are lost through sweat.

Every environment presents its own challenge to special forces units, and it is therefore crucial that all personnel should be expert in the tactics and techniques that offer the best chance of survival.

▼ Essential items
A selection of invaluable tools that might make the difference between life and death for a special forces unit.

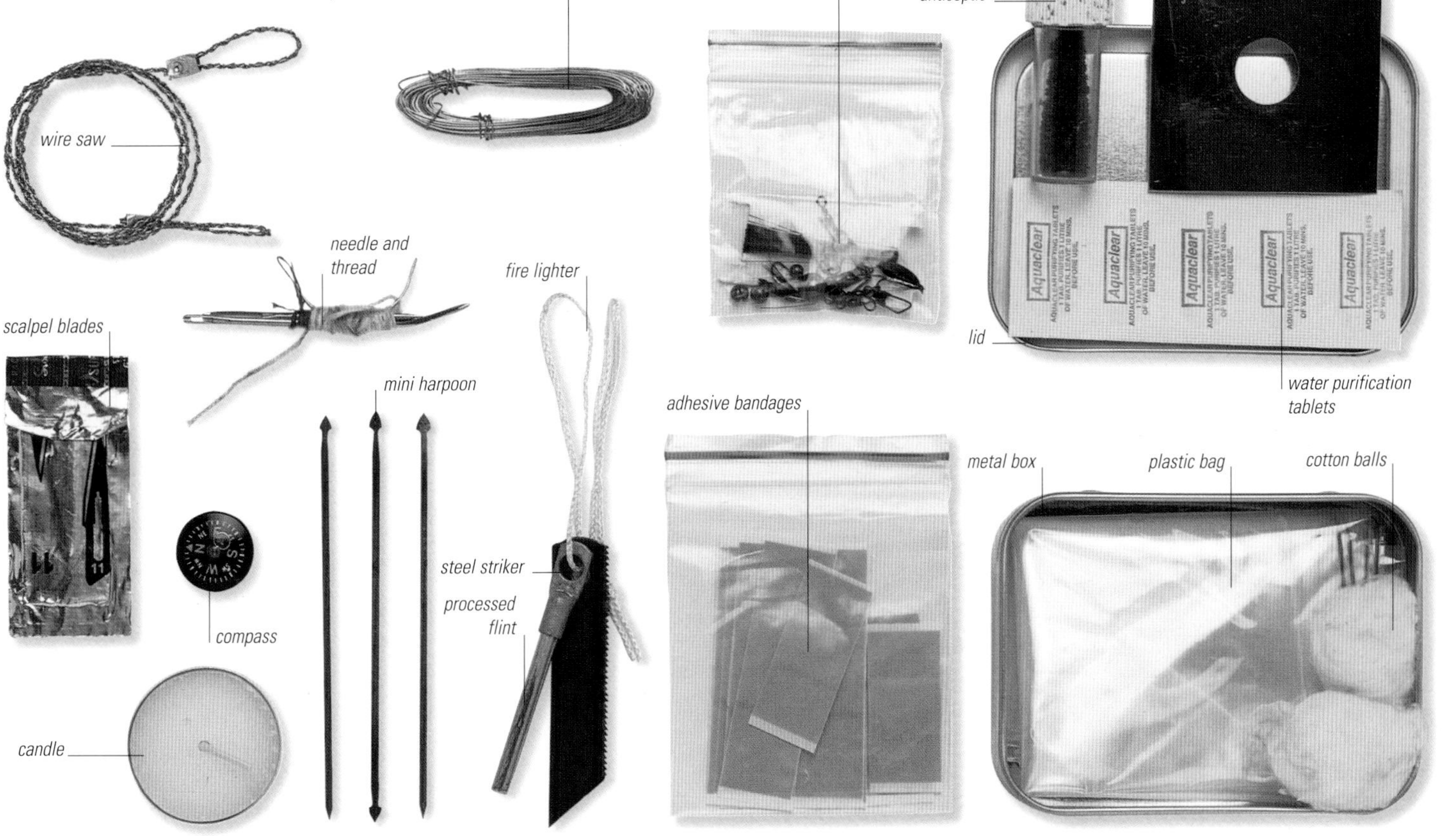

Parachuting

Parachuting is a fundamental special forces skill, but it poses a number of difficulties for a mission, including a high risk of injury on landing, the possibility of an accident in the air, and the need for calm weather. Until recently, parachuting seemed likely to be phased out in favor of helicopter delivery. However, campaigns such as the 2003 US-led invasion of Iraq have re-established parachuting as a reliable and rapid method of getting troops and equipment into enemy territory.

▲ 82nd Airborne Division
Troops of the US 82nd Airborne Division board a C-141 Starlifter transport plane.

Parachuting is used to get lightly equipped units very quickly into areas where surprise and shock action can create a military advantage. Low-flying aircraft can avoid radar detection and then ascend very quickly to parachuting height just before the troops jump. Parachute drops can thus be undetectable, enabling small teams to enter an area in complete secrecy. For example, steerable parachutes allow special forces units to land in isolated forest clearings and quickly disappear into the trees.

Specialized high-altitude parachuting is another method of avoiding detection. The teams use oxygen masks, jump at night, and navigate in the air using compass bearings. Most radar systems cannot detect parachutists, but even if a drop from high altitude was detected, paratroopers are able to freefall or glide very long distances, so it would be impossible for the enemy to guess their eventual landing site.

The limitations of parachuting, even in calm weather, are that only a limited amount of equipment can be taken in with the troops. This restricts the length of the operation, because resupply from the air is likely to give

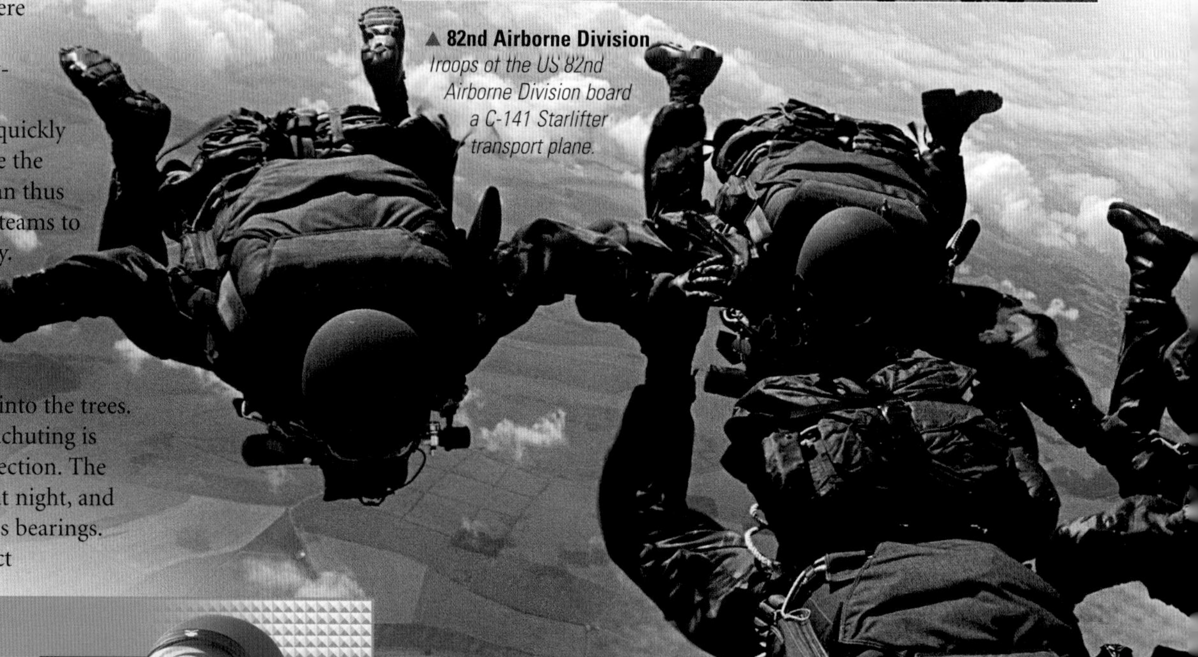

▲ Linked descent
A four-man team from the British Pathfinder Platoon during a HALO descent, having dropped from a C-130 Hercules transport plane. The men link together so that they will all land in the same drop area.

HALO and HAHO

High-altitude parachuting enables special forces teams to jump undetected, and then to travel in the air for considerable distances before landing. HALO (high-altitude, low-opening) parachuting involves a long freefall descent to around 2,000 ft. (600 m.), in which a team can travel laterally many miles from the jump point. Parachutists hold onto each other in the air while the leader navigates with a compass. HAHO (high-altitude, high-opening) jumps are done with steerable parachutes, which give greater landing accuracy.

Breathing equipment
For high-altitude drops, oxygen-breathing equipment is essential.

away the position of patrols on the ground. Special forces units parachuting into Arctic regions take a sledge to carry their equipment. The sledge leaves the aircraft on a pallet under a heavy-drop parachute. The mission team follow the sledge out of the plane, steering their parachutes so that they land close to it. Extracting a special forces team from the zone of

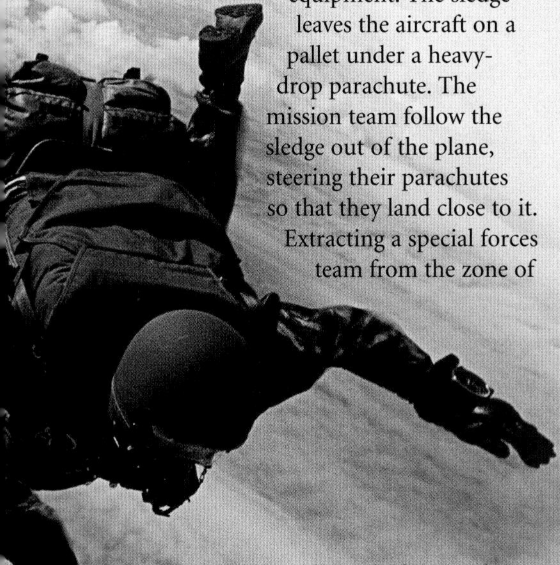

operations at the end of a parachute mission can also be a problem, unless there is a flat area large enough for an emergency landing strip or unless the troops can walk to a suitable helicopter landing site.

MARINE PARACHUTING

When marine special forces jump into the sea, they first drop an inflatable boat loaded with supplies. Once they are in the water, troops cut the boat free of its parachute, and use the craft to make their way to the designated coastal landing site. By parachuting into the sea well away from their target area, units can be reasonably certain that their landing will not be detected. Special forces teams also use this method if they need to make an attack on an enemy surface ship.

LARGE-SCALE DROPS

The use of transport aircraft, capable of carrying several hundred paratroopers and their vehicles, enables a larger assault force with heavier equipment to land in one drop. This greatly increases the speed with which units can become effective on the ground. The US Army Rangers and the 101st Airborne Division are often deployed in this way.

Modern parachutes, such as the Irvin model used by Britain's Parachute Regiment, enable jumps to be made at ultra-low level (300 ft./90 m.). This technique minimizes the time that troops spend in the air, when they are vulnerable to detection and to enemy fire from the ground.

◀ **Kit check**
A French Foreign Legionnaire checks his parachute prior to a training jump.

▶ **Sea deployment**
US Navy SEALs leave their aircraft for a sea landing. They wear flippers to aid their speed in the water.

▲ **Fixed-line drops**
These paratroopers are operating conventional parachutes. The canopy-opening mechanism is attached to a wire in the aircraft. When the paratrooper jumps, the parachute opens automatically. This method is used to deploy large units quickly, and means that all the troops land within the pre-designated drop zone.

Ram air parachute

Ram air parachutes are steerable and act like a flying wing. They enable special forces personnel to glide from the parachute opening point to a specific landing site, which is often small and some distance away. From high altitudes, these parachutes provide greater accuracy than conventional types.

Steerable parachutes
Ram air parachutes are steered by toggles attached to the paratrooper's harness, which open vents on the parachute to rotate it.

Diving and swimming

Special forces water operations are unpredictable and difficult, requiring very highly trained, experienced troops. Sheltered waters, such as rivers, lakes, and estuaries, are relatively stable environments in which to operate. But only the most experienced special forces units can operate and survive in coastal waters or the open ocean, and they need specialized equipment to work at maximum efficiency.

Seas and inland waterways offer many potential routes of undetected entry (infiltration) for special forces. Additionally, the economic value of shipping, oilrigs, and other maritime facilities makes them likely terrorist targets. For these reasons, special forces must be capable of operating underwater, in adverse conditions if necessary, to deal with such terrorist threats. In addition, they must be able to perform underwater approaches to a target during conventional military operations.

▶ **Underwater base**
These two US Navy SEAL divers are shooting a training film on procedures for exiting and entering submerged submarines.

INTELLIGENCE-GATHERING AT SEA

In war, ground forces often use ships and ports to land armor, supplies, and troops. Capturing a port is therefore usually the first objective of any invasion. Landing a large force requires surprise, and is dangerous, time-consuming, and logistically demanding. Special forces are therefore required to provide vital and reliable information about the beaches and any underwater hazards in the landing area. Their survey work (hydrography) must be carried out in secret if the invasion is to be a success. If the survey work is detected by an enemy, it could compromise the main landing in its most vulnerable phase.

Methods of delivery

Divers and swimmers are very limited in the distances they can move from the sea to their targets or landing points. They need to be dropped off as close as possible to their target area. However, because they are vulnerable they must remain undetected. Submarines are therefore often ideal as delivery vehicles. The smaller types of submarine (non-nuclear, diesel boats) allow swimmers and equipment to leave via the escape hatch while still submerged. This is, however, a dangerous and time-consuming operation. Alternatively, small boats can be launched from submarines offshore.

Submarine deployment
British special forces rigid inflatable boats being prepared for launch from a submarine.

▲ **Navigation at sea**
A British Special Boat Service diver using a swimboard, with a luminous compass for underwater navigation.

THE SPECIALISTS

Special forces divers and swimmers do not make long approach swims or dives to their targets in wartime. This is because swimming is often undertaken at night and is slow and extremely tiring. Divers from units such as the British Special Boat Service (SBS), for example, are expected to be able to swim 1,640 ft. (500 m.). But this is considered a maximum distance, and swims will often be much shorter.

Weapons and water

Weapons immersed in water can malfunction. They will fire when wet, but a barrel full of water can affect gas pressure. The gun may explode when the trigger is pulled. Troops often use condoms to cover the gun barrel. Salt water rapidly corrodes the barrel, firing pin, magazine spring, and other working parts. In addition, sand, mud, and grit will soon clog the magazine. Thus, cleaning and lubrication are very important tasks.

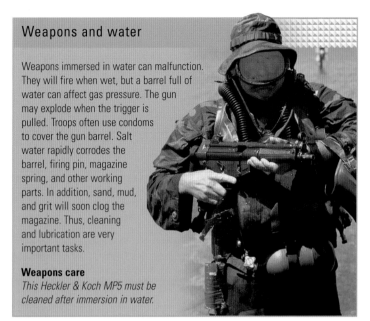

Weapons care
This Heckler & Koch MP5 must be cleaned after immersion in water.

SPECIALIZED EQUIPMENT

Covert underwater missions require the use of closed-circuit, "rebreather" diving gear, which produces no bubbles. Their use, especially at night, requires very high levels of training, and oxygen sets can be lethal if used at depths greater than 33 ft. (10 m.). The US Navy has small submarines designed for delivering the specialized amphibious forces of the Sea, Air, and Land (SEAL) teams. It is also developing underwater living chambers for use in longer reconnaissance missions. Many special forces units use midget submarines and underwater scooter-type vehicles to extend the ranges at which they can operate. In such ways, innovation continues to expand the methods by which special forces are able to operate in waterways and at sea.

▼ **SEAL divers**
Two US SEAL divers come ashore following an underwater approach. On actual operations the journey to the target will be made during the night.

▼ **Evacuation at sea**
A US SEAL swimmer boards a CH-46 Sea Knight twin-rotor helicopter following a mission in the sea.

Sniping

It is only relatively recently that sniping has been accepted as a legitimate part of warfare. Previously, soldiers regarded snipers in much the same way that sailors looked on early submarines: As dishonest and unfair. The ideal sniper is a solitary person, able to kill his target in cold blood after hours of painstaking stalking or lying in wait, and then make an effective escape.

▶ Counter-terrorism
This is a counter-terrorist sniper. His targets often position themselves among civilians for cover.

Special forces snipers use much the same techniques as regular army snipers when carrying out assassination missions. The main difference is that special forces snipers often operate behind enemy lines. This means that, once the mission is completed, the snipers must be able to cover long distances very quickly in order to avoid capture by the enemy.

Although regular snipers often take shots against ordinary enemy soldiers and a wide range of targets that will damage enemy morale, special forces snipers only put themselves at risk for high value targets, such as senior enemy commanders, or targets that are vital to an operation, such as soldiers guarding an installation under attack.

OPERATIONS

Snipers are particularly useful in counter-terrorist operations, where they need to identify specific individuals and kill them without endangering innocent people. The US Navy's Sea, Air and Land teams (SEALs) see

◀ Sniper camouflage
Snipers operate in all types of terrain. This sniper wears white to blend into the snow.

Sniper rifles

Originally, sniper rifles (see pp148–151) were either upgraded versions of existing service rifles or less robust but more accurate sporting weapons. Today, however, most snipers use specially made military sniper rifles. Quality of manufacture and materials is vital, and a third of the rifles are routinely rejected during testing. A rifle with a locking bolt action is stronger and more rigid than a semi-automatic, so most sniper weapons have a single-shot bolt action. The barrel must be far thicker than that of a normal rifle to ensure that it vibrates evenly when fired. Nothing should touch the barrel except at the breach end, and the stock must be adjustable to the individual shooter.

Remington M24
This is the carrying case, accessories, and tools for the M24 sniper rifle produced by Remington.

One shot, one kill

For a sniper to be effective, he must be able to guarantee a kill with just one shot. To try a second shot means running a very high risk of being spotted and attracting enemy artillery and small-arms fire in a position from where it is not possible to withdraw safely. Snipers have their greatest effect on enemy morale. A series of one-shot kills with no effective retaliation makes the enemy feel vulnerable and impotent.

Expert shot
Snipers are trained to kill with their first shot. There is usually no second chance.

sniping as vital to reducing the chances of civilian casualties, for example.

Hostage-release operations often use a ring of snipers, linked by radio, on the roofs of buildings surrounding the hostage location. The snipers keep up a running commentary on any targets they can safely take a shot at, while a controller tries to determine a moment when all targets are in a position to be hit simultaneously. If such a moment occurs, he orders the snipers to fire together. This kind of coordinated response requires enormous concentration and discipline, as well as the accuracy needed by all snipers.

TRAINING

Snipers train extensively, not just in marksmanship with a variety of weapons but also in a wide range of other skills, such as camouflage, concealment, observation, and ground movement. Most sniper courses also include psychological assessment to ensure that candidates are emotionally suitable for the job. Snipers usually work at between 1,970 and 3,280 ft. (600 and 1,000 m.) from their target – over twice the range of conventional weapons – so they undergo extensive training in long-range shooting. They also learn to use heavier weapons like the .50 Barrett gun, which can destroy truck engines and disable armored vehicles at ranges of over 3,280 ft. (1,000 m.).

The British Royal Marines' Commachio Group trains snipers to work in the North Sea on ships and offshore platforms to protect oil rigs and gas wells. During training, sniper teams are also instructed in other activities, such as directing naval gunfire and destroying small enemy vessels at long ranges.

▶ **Sniper suit**
This is a British sniper's woodland camouflage suit.

▼ **Sniper sights**
Sniper rifles are equipped with sophisticated sights to allow long-range shots.

◀ **Sniper and spotter**
Snipers usually operate with a spotter. The spotter indicates targets.

Demolitions

Demolitions are one of the basic special forces skills, which every soldier learns and in which at least one member of each patrol will be an expert. Considerable training and practice is required before a special forces demolitions specialist is ready for operations. He has to know about explosives and their placement, as well as have common sense and a wide-ranging engineering knowledge.

▲ **Destroying bridges**
A British military engineer places a demolition charge on the superstructure of a bridge over a canal. Destroying the bridge's struts will cause it to collapse into the canal.

Special forces missions are planned to create an effect on the enemy far greater than the numbers of people involved or the resources they utilize. One way they can do this is to use explosives to destroy enemy targets. Sabotage objectives are chosen with particular care; the aim is to create maximum damage, confusion, and disruption.

When placing explosives, time-delay fuses and diversionary explosions are used to allow the special forces team to escape. During World War II (1939–45), for example, British Special Air Service (SAS) soldiers used time-delay fuses to destroy aircraft behind enemy lines during the campaign in North Africa. Additional time-delay charges may also be laid to make it dangerous to repair the damage after the first charges have exploded. These booby traps can severely damage the morale of enemy troops.

CHARGES AND TARGETS

Although delayed action fuses may be electronic or radio-initiated, it can be more reliable to use old-fashioned safety fuse. Made with gunpowder inside a plastic-coated cable, a typical fuse burns at the rate of 4 in. (10 cm.) every 12 to 16 seconds, setting off a blasting cap that detonates the explosive.

Special forces demolitions operations are limited by the weight of explosive that can be carried by soldiers on foot, and the time

Sabotage targets

Sabotage targets are the most carefully researched of all potential targets in modern warfare. Moving targets, like trains entering tunnels or on bridges, can only be attacked after considerable time spent observing. It may be necessary to find the target before it can be destroyed, for example, the buried Iraqi fiber-optic communication cable destroyed by the British Special Boat Service (SBS) during the 1991 Persian Gulf War. Disabling facilities like communications centers requires prior surveillance to determine what should be destroyed.

Placing charges
British paratroopers learn how to place explosive charges to destroy a railroad. A small amount of explosives can severely damage enemy supply lines.

▲ **Sabotaging aircraft**
These aircraft were destroyed by British SAS soldiers in Africa in World War II.

available to lay the charges. When the target is known, suitable charges can be prepared at base and the precise location and weight for each charge calculated in advance. Examining architects' plans is useful. Modern structures, for example, especially those made from reinforced concrete, have built-in demolition points, which makes the placement of explosives easy.

MULTIPLE CHARGES

If a target is in an isolated location or guards are absent, a string of smaller charges can be laid at various key points on the structure. These are linked together by detonation cord ("det cord") or coretex. This is reinforced, white plastic cable that contains high-explosive. Several smaller charges, carefully positioned and linked by det cord, can be far more effective than one or two larger charges.

To destroy some structures, especially large bridges, it may be necessary to set off charges in a particular order, thus putting severe strain on already damaged points of the structure. This string of explosions can be controlled using electrical detonators and an electronic control box called an "exploder."

▲ **Claymore anti-personnel mine**
The 700 steel balls are scattered by detonating an explosive charge behind them.

◀ **Explosive force**
As can be seen, the effects when explosives are detonated can be dramatic. However, the skill for special forces soldiers lies in being able to place the charges correctly so the force of the explosion will cause maximum damage.

▲ **Detonating cord**
This white plastic cord is filled with high-explosive. It explodes at about 20,000 ft. (6,100 m.) per second.

The explosives are wired up using det cord, and to ensure the cord does not break as it explodes, the charges are usually linked in a circle and not a straight line. A detonator is taped to each end of the det cord ring main (the circle of explosives) and the detonators connected by wire to the exploder. The exploder sets off the detonator using an electrical pulse.

Special forces units also lay anti-personnel devices such as Claymore mines to disrupt enemy troop movements and for camp perimeter security.

Explosives

Modern plastic explosive like PE4 is very stable. Small pieces can even be set alight using a match, and will burn very fiercely. The explosive can be broken up and worked into different shapes like plasticine. Quantities of PE4 can be linked together using detonation cord to explode simultaneously, as if still in one piece.

Plastic explosives
PE4 plastic explosive (bottom left), detonating cord (top), and detonator (bottom right).

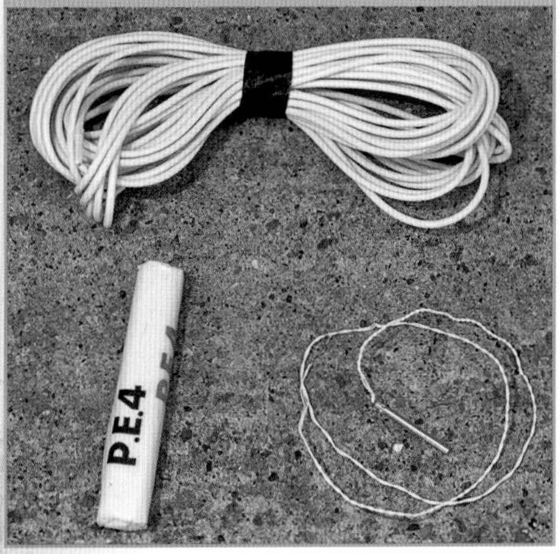

Intelligence gathering

The collection of accurate and timely information is an important part of the work of special forces. Although spy satellites and surveillance aircraft have reduced the need for human intelligence gathering, small special forces teams operating behind enemy lines still have a vital function in modern warfare. In many cases there is still no substitute for specialists on the ground.

Military intelligence relates to information about an enemy or potential conflict, which is gathered for the sake of military advantage. The collection of such intelligence is a crucial aspect of special forces operations. Units such as the British Special Air Service (SAS), Australian SAS, and Russian *Spetsnaz* are trained to gather information about enemy strengths and weaknesses. They do this by operating in small groups behind enemy lines, and staying hidden in observation posts (OPs). Information is gathered by means of observation scopes and rangefinders and is then sent back to headquarters via long-range communications equipment. Information is sent in so-called "burst form," whereby the transmission lasts a fraction of a second, reducing the chance of detection.

▶ **Target designation**
A US soldier uses laser-assisted observation binoculars to determine the position of the enemy.

▼ **Eavesdropping**
This US Air Force Airborne Warning and Control System (AWACS) aircraft can intercept signals and jam communications, as well as receive friendly transmissions.

A RANGE OF TECHNIQUES

There are a number of ways of gathering military intelligence. The oldest form of information is human intelligence, abbreviated in military terms to "humint." This means using special agents or informers, to gather data from captured enemy personnel or by interrogating members of the local population.

▼ **Situation reports**
A US Delta Force team sends its situation report ("sitrep") via radio.

Living with the locals

Special forces are particularly useful in cultivating human intelligence ("humint") from the local population in a region. Developing agents among native peoples has many benefits. Locals know the terrain well, can blend into the environment where foreign troops might stand out, and may already have the kind of information and contacts that the special forces need. These operations are often part of a general "hearts and minds" campaign, aimed at winning over local people. The ways in which this is achieved depend on the circumstances, but generally activities include the provision of medical assistance, food, and supplies, and sometimes military training.

Radio signals
A British SAS signaler in Borneo in the 1960s sets up his radio in a native hut.

This type of information, often retrieved by small teams of special forces, can be very valuable if it is reliable – although this is not always the case. A recent example of the use of "humint" is the targeting of Iraqi dictator Saddam Hussein on two occasions during the US-led war in Iraq in 2003. It is widely believed that agents on the ground called in airstrikes to attempt to kill Saddam.

Another form of intelligence-gathering is "sigint," or signals intelligence – the collection of information through the interception of communications. Modern armed forces have many sophisticated ways of listening in to radio signals, from satellite systems and submarines to the Airborne Warning and Control System (AWACS) aircraft.

The newest form of intelligence-gathering is electronic intelligence, or "elint." This generally involves hacking into computer systems and even telephone calls. Orbiting spy satellites and high-altitude unmanned aerial reconnaissance vehicles are also in widespread use.

SPECIAL FORCES AND TECHNOLOGY

The gathering of "sigint" and "elint" can also be carried out by special forces teams, especially when communications are otherwise very secure. Inside hostile territory, special forces can tap into fiber-optic cables, which satellites and aircraft cannot do: This technique was attempted by the British SAS inside Iraq during the 1991 Gulf War.

To be of use, the collected data must be transmitted quickly and securely back to the central command post. Thus, special forces teams are equipped with state-of-the-art communications equipment to upload their information to either a satellite or a circling AWACS aircraft.

▼ OV-1 Bronco
The US OV-1 Bronco is used as an aerial reconnaissance platform to spot targets for airstrikes and artillery.

◀ Submarines
Submarines carry a range of electronic equipment that can collect signals intelligence.

UAVs

Unmanned aerial vehicles (UAVs) are an increasingly important part of military operations. The United States has two advanced UAVs, the Predator and the Global Hawk. The Predator is operated by a Central Intelligence Agency (CIA) team. Special forces teams, working in conjunction with aerial probes, have proved to be very effective. They were used in the US war against the Taliban in Afghanistan in 2002.

Ceaseless surveillance
The Predator UAV can monitor a target for 24 hours without having to land.

First aid

Special forces teams must be self-sufficient. This includes being able to keep seriously wounded people alive until they can be evacuated, which may mean a wait of hours or even days. All team members are qualified in life-saving first aid techniques, with at least one being up to paramedic standard. Special forces medics can also help to win the "hearts and minds" of a local population by providing life-saving medical care.

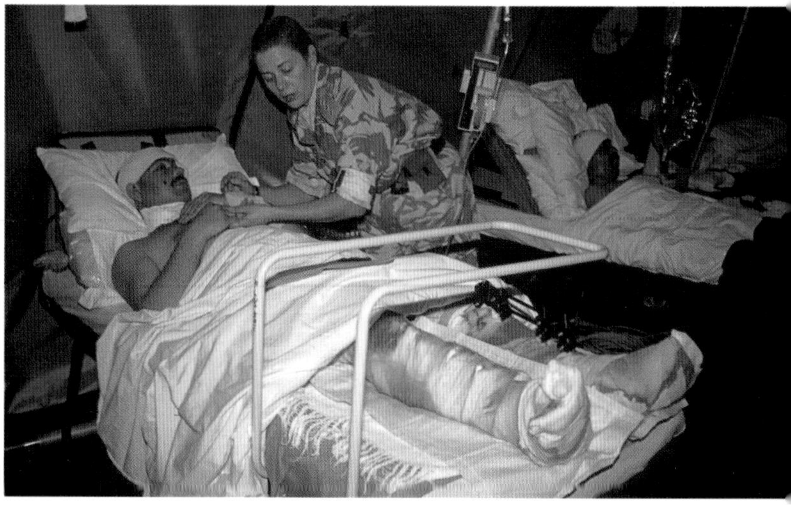

▲ **Field hospital**
Hospitals near the fighting have the equipment and drugs to save the lives of wounded soldiers.

First aid is a vital skill for every member of a special forces team, particularly because there will be times when units will be forced to split up and soldiers will be required to operate on their own. The need for medical care during combat also means that every special forces operative must be able to administer emergency field dressings. For these reasons, each man must carry a comprehensive medical kit at all times, and be able to treat himself if wounded.

Battlefield first aid invariably deals with severe trauma, as the wounds inflicted by the high-velocity rounds and shell splinters of modern weapons are severe. Loss of blood and shock are the main killers. Ultra-fit soldiers, if their condition can be stabilized, will survive for some time. It is sometimes more beneficial to stabilize a badly wounded person before they are evacuated, even if it causes a delay. The vibration, movement, and noise inside a helicopter ambulance makes it difficult to monitor badly injured patients and to perform complex life-saving procedures.

▼ **Water tablets**
Water sterilization tablets are imperative to successful first aid in the field. Wounded soldiers need clean drinking water to aid their recovery.

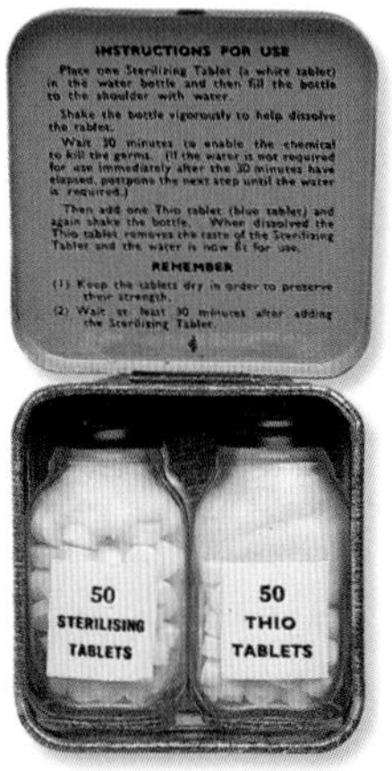

MEDICAL PROCEDURES

The airway and pulse of a wounded soldier must be checked, and external heart massage and mouth-to-mouth resuscitation started immediately if required. With facial wounds that restrict breathing, a plastic airway must first be inserted into the throat. With severe face and neck wounds, it may be necessary to cut into the throat to insert a breathing tube.

Loss of blood must be stopped as quickly as possible, using pressure, field dressings, and improvised padding, such as clothing

▼ **Medical kit**
This British medical kit contains items essential to survival following the infliction of a wound. A simple field dressing, for example, can slow the loss of blood from a bullet wound.

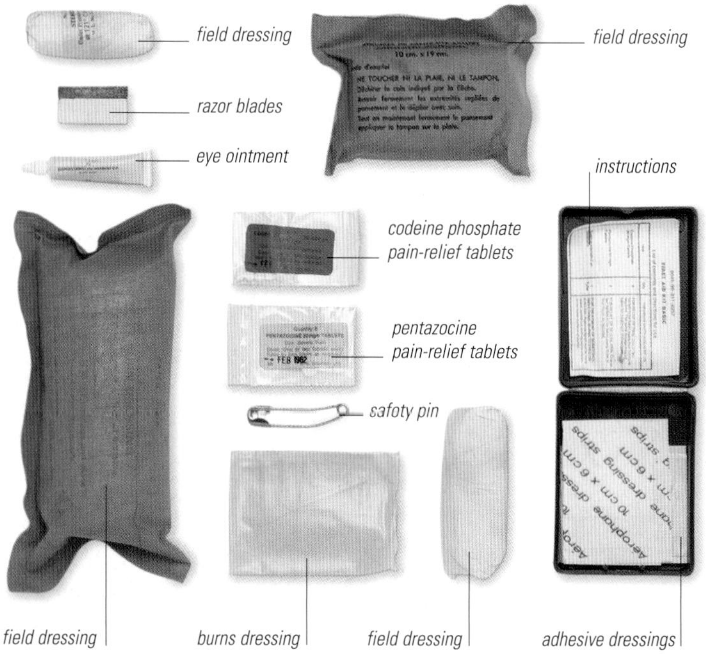

Hygiene

When living for long periods in poor conditions, often continually wet and cold, personal hygiene is crucial. The feet must be regularly washed, dried, and powdered. Dry socks should be worn whenever possible, and blisters must be dressed and protected. Long marches while carrying heavy loads causes chafing, which can become painful and infected. In the jungle, soldiers use antibiotic talcum powders to prevent cuts and insect bites from becoming infected.

Cleanliness
Simple shaving can prevent fungal infections. For elite units operating behind enemy lines, and far away from medical facilities, personal hygiene is crucial.

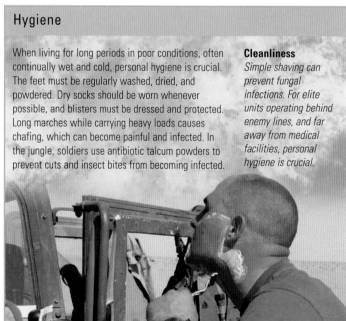

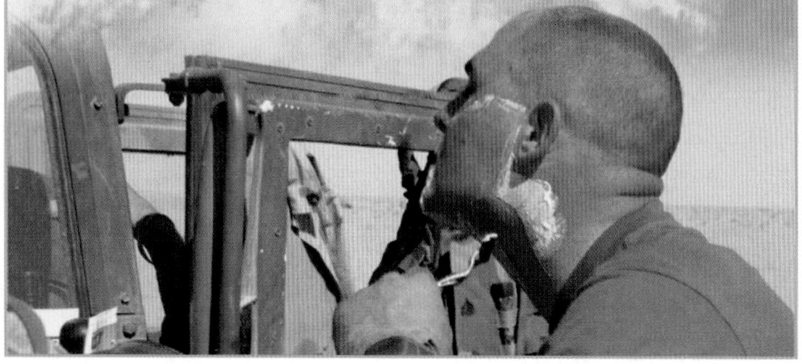

wrapped in plastic bags, kept firmly in place with bandages. It is vital that checks are made on the entry point of each bullet or piece of shrapnel, and on the exit point, which will be very much larger. To maintain blood pressure, intravenous fluids must be introduced as quickly as possible using a large needle inserted into a vein.

Special forces teams use morphine sparingly, as each member must retain the ability to fight even if wounded. Morphine can impair consciousness and depress breathing, so lessening the chances of survival. The impact of modern weapons makes complex bone fractures common. All broken bones must be immobilized.

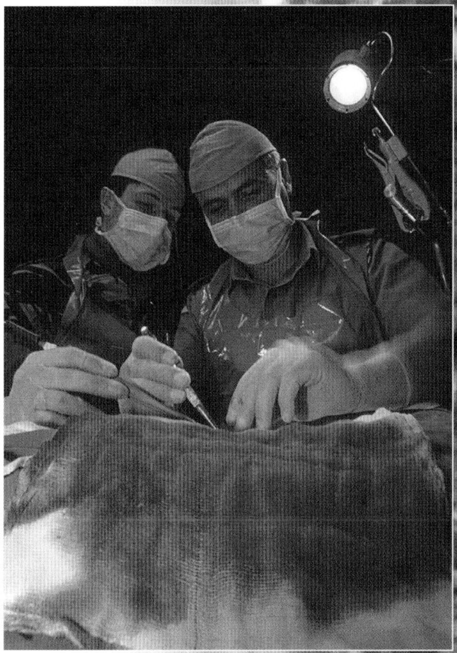

▶ **Surgery**
In the field, special forces soldiers will administer first aid to keep the patient alive. He will then be sent to a hospital for surgery.

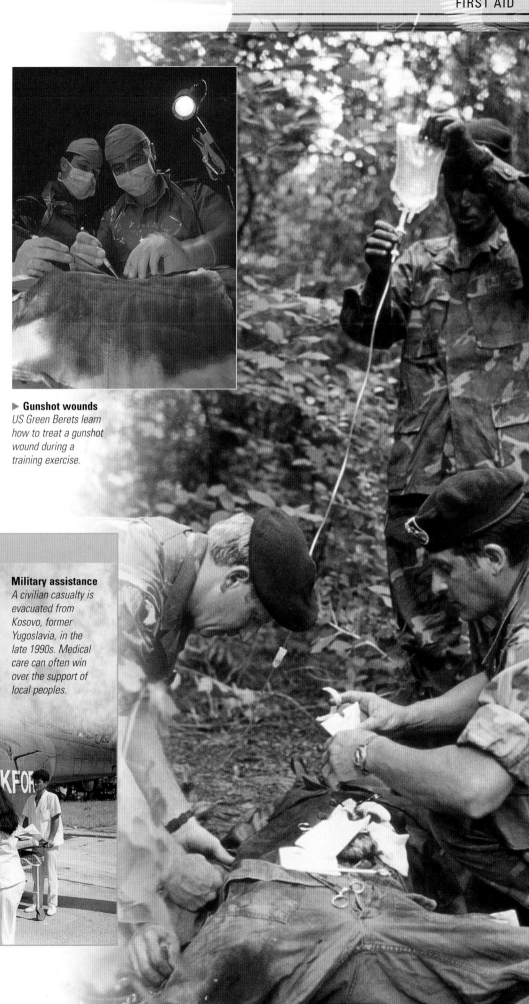

EVACUATION

Carrying a casualty out to where helicopter or fixed-wing evacuation can take place presents serious problems for a four-man special forces team. They can only move slowly, one man acting as scout while the other two carry the casualty on a makeshift stretcher. This is exhausting and dangerous, exposing the whole unit to possible enemy detection.

▶ **Gunshot wounds**
US Green Berets learn how to treat a gunshot wound during a training exercise.

Humanitarian aid

Special forces are invariably the first military units to arrive in a war zone. The provision of medical treatment is a standard method of gaining the confidence of local people. As well as gathering military intelligence, special forces teams are also trained to assess the humanitarian situation and order in specific supplies plus reinforcements once suitable airfields have been secured. US Army A-Team members are trained as civil engineers to build roads, bridges, and landing strips, and to ensure there are ample supplies of fresh water.

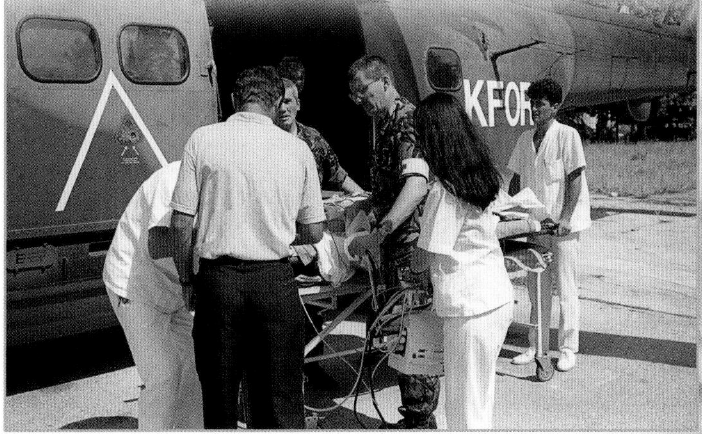

Military assistance
A civilian casualty is evacuated from Kosovo, former Yugoslavia, in the late 1990s. Medical care can often win over the support of local peoples.

Pistols

The pistol is the standard sidearm of all special forces units and is regarded as a back-up weapon only. However, its compact size means it can be easily concealed, making it ideal for undercover missions. All the pistols featured here are semi-automatic, which means that the trigger must be pulled each time a bullet is fired (a full automatic will keep firing until the magazine is empty). Each gun has range of 100 to 130 ft. (30 to 40 m.).

▲ **H&K Mark 23** (1991)
The Mark 23 is manufactured by German firearms company Heckler & Koch. The magazine has a capacity of 10 rounds.

Length	9.6 in. (24.5 cm.)
Weight	2.4 lb. (1.1 kg.)
Rate of fire	40 rpm.
Caliber	.45-in.

▲ **FN Five-seveN** (1996)
The Five-seveN pistol is designed by Belgian manufacturer FN Herstal. The magazine holds 20 rounds of ammunition.

Length	8.1 in. (20.8 cm.)
Weight	1.7 lb. (760 g.)
Rate of fire	40 rpm.
Caliber	5.7-mm.

▲ **H&K P-10** (1994)
A number of German law enforcement agencies use the P-10. The magazine in the handle of the pistol can store 10 rounds.

Length	6.8 in. (17.3 cm.)
Weight	1.4 lb. (645 g.)
Rate of fire	35 rpm.
Caliber	9-mm.

▲ **Smith & Wesson 340 PD** (1952)
The Smith & Wesson 340 PD is a snub-nosed revolver used by the US Navy Sea, Air and Land (SEAL) teams. The magazine cylinder carries five bullets.

Length	6.3 in. (16 cm.)
Weight	12 oz. (340 g.)
Rate of fire	18 rpm.
Caliber	.357-in.

▲ Beretta M92F (1976)
The M92F is the standard sidearm of all the US special forces. It is also used by many other branches of the US armed forces. The magazine stores 15 rounds.

Length 8.6 in. (22.3 cm.)	
Weight 2.1 lb. (954 g.)	
Rate of fire 40 rpm.	
Caliber 9-mm.	

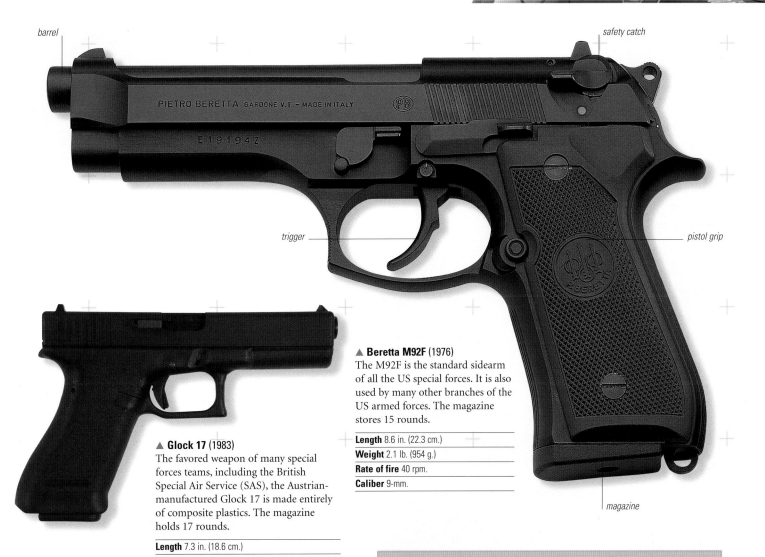

▲ Glock 17 (1983)
The favored weapon of many special forces teams, including the British Special Air Service (SAS), the Austrian-manufactured Glock 17 is made entirely of composite plastics. The magazine holds 17 rounds.

Length 7.3 in. (18.6 cm.)	
Weight 1.5 lb. (703 g.)	
Rate of fire 40 rpm.	
Caliber 9-mm.	

▲ Sig Sauer P-225 Para (1980)
The P-225 Para is a Swiss-made, compact semi-automatic pistol, and is used by Swiss and German police units. Its magazine capacity is eight rounds.

Length 7 in. (18 cm.)	
Weight 1.6 lb. (740 g.)	
Rate of fire 30 rpm.	
Caliber 9-mm.	

Back-up weapons

The pistol is often the last line of defense in any firefight, and is carried as back-up for a soldier's primary weapon – usually an assault rifle. Contrary to the popular Hollywood image, a pistol has an effective range of only 100 to 130 ft. (30 to 40 m.), and is therefore of limited use in battle. However, if a soldier runs out of ammunition for his main weapon, then the pistol becomes his only means of self defense. Therefore, it is essential that the pistols used by special forces teams are highly dependable in all conditions.

Taking aim
Target practice with pistols is a crucial part of special forces training. Personnel on undercover operations, especially, may have to depend on their handgun skills to save their lives.

Military sniper rifles

The sniper rifle is one of the most useful assets in a special forces team. An expert sniper can be deployed to provide deadly covering fire from a great distance, or can sneak undetected into hostile territory to kill an important individual, such as a high-ranking enemy officer. Capable of hitting a target at distances of up to about 6,000 ft. (1,800 m.), the sniper rifle is an awesome weapon.

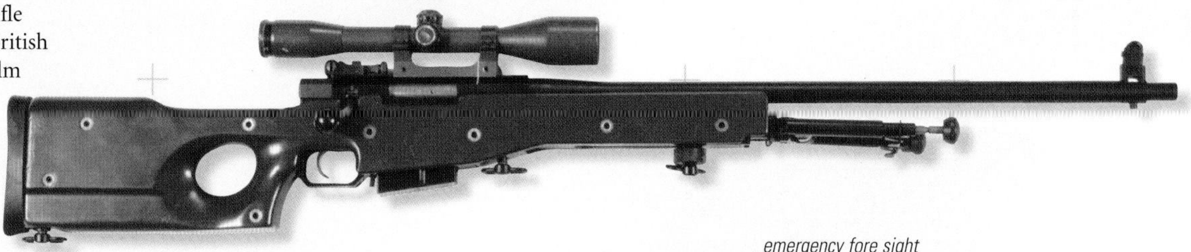

▶ **Accuracy International L96A1** (1985)
The L96A1 is the standard issue sniper rifle of the British Army. It was designed by British Olympic shooting gold-medallist, Malcolm Cooper. It has an effective range of 3,035 ft. (925 m.).

Length 47 in. (119.4 cm.)
Weight 14.3 lb. (6.5 kg.)
Rate of fire 10 rpm.
Caliber 7.62-mm.

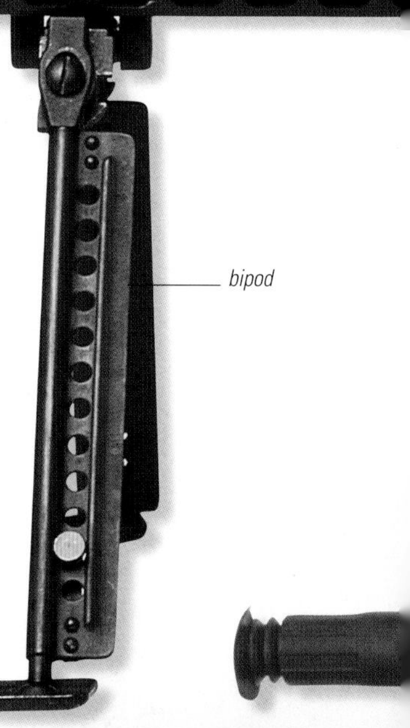

▲ **Barrett M82A1** (1983)
The American-made Barret M82A1 is one of the most powerful sniper rifles in the world, and is favored by many special forces units, such as the United States Marine Corps. Effective to a range of 6,000 ft. (1,830 m.), the M82A1 is capable of bringing down a helicopter with a single shot. The gun's magazine holds 10 rounds of ammunition.

Length 61 in. (154.9 cm.)
Weight 29.5 lb. (13.4 kg.)
Rate of fire 10 rpm.
Caliber 12.7-mm.

Sniping tactics

The distance between the sniper and his target depends largely on the surrounding terrain and the concentration of enemy troops in the area. Most sniping missions (see pp138–139) take place far behind enemy lines, where it is imperative that the sniping team gets close enough to the target to guarantee a high level of accuracy, yet remains far enough away to enable it to leave the area without being discovered once the mission is over. In most cases the target is killed before the shot is even heard, such is the range of modern sniper rifles.

Sniping in pairs
A sniping team consists of two people: The sniper and his spotter. The spotter sights targets and watches for enemy patrols and other threats.

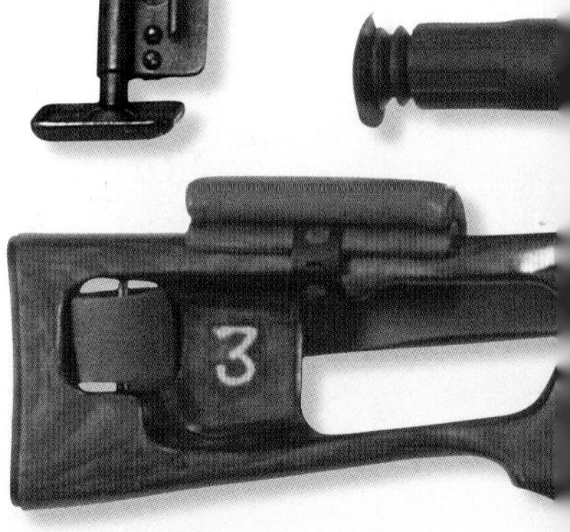

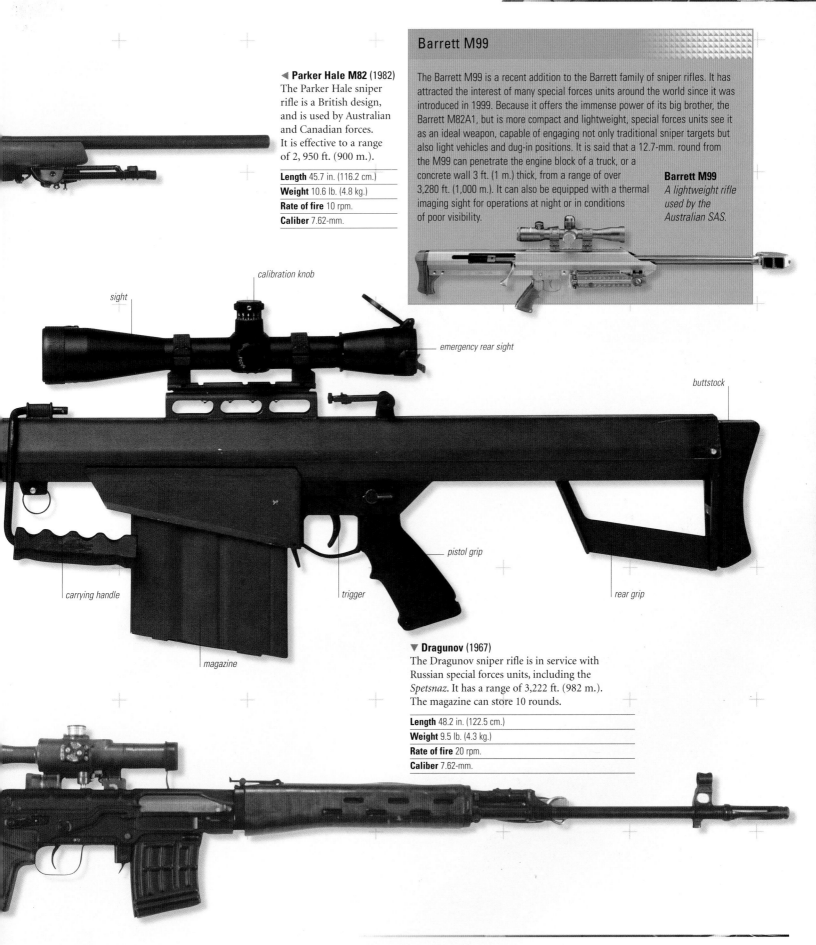

◀ **Parker Hale M82** (1982)
The Parker Hale sniper rifle is a British design, and is used by Australian and Canadian forces. It is effective to a range of 2, 950 ft. (900 m.).

Length 45.7 in. (116.2 cm.)	
Weight 10.6 lb. (4.8 kg.)	
Rate of fire 10 rpm.	
Caliber 7.62-mm.	

Barrett M99

The Barrett M99 is a recent addition to the Barrett family of sniper rifles. It has attracted the interest of many special forces units around the world since it was introduced in 1999. Because it offers the immense power of its big brother, the Barrett M82A1, but is more compact and lightweight, special forces units see it as an ideal weapon, capable of engaging not only traditional sniper targets but also light vehicles and dug-in positions. It is said that a 12.7-mm. round from the M99 can penetrate the engine block of a truck, or a concrete wall 3 ft. (1 m.) thick, from a range of over 3,280 ft. (1,000 m.). It can also be equipped with a thermal imaging sight for operations at night or in conditions of poor visibility.

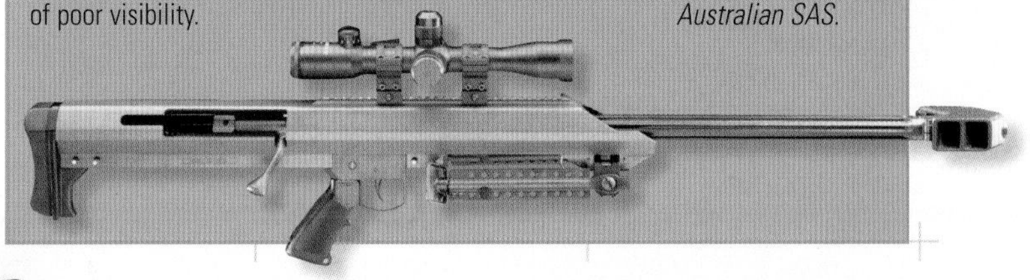

Barrett M99
A lightweight rifle used by the Australian SAS.

▼ **Dragunov** (1967)
The Dragunov sniper rifle is in service with Russian special forces units, including the *Spetsnaz*. It has a range of 3,222 ft. (982 m.). The magazine can store 10 rounds.

Length 48.2 in. (122.5 cm.)	
Weight 9.5 lb. (4.3 kg.)	
Rate of fire 20 rpm.	
Caliber 7.62-mm.	

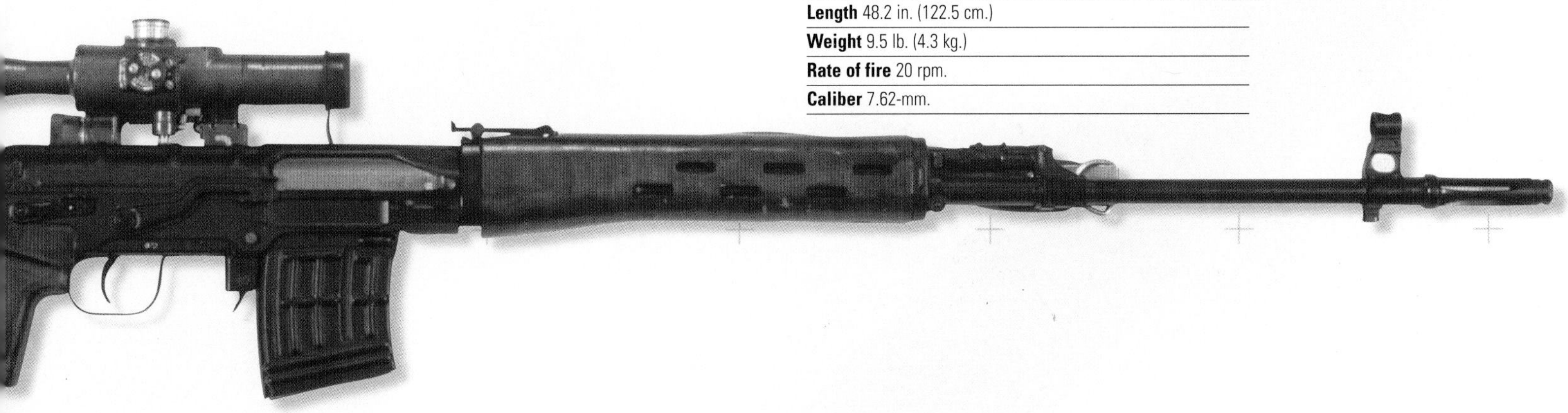

Police sniper rifles

The sniper rifle is not restricted to military use. It is also employed internationally by many law-enforcement agencies. The police sniper rifle is used in hostage-rescue situations and counter-terrorist operations, and in the provision of protection for VIPs. Because they are often deployed at close-range, police sniper rifles do not need as great a maximum effective range as military sniper rifles.

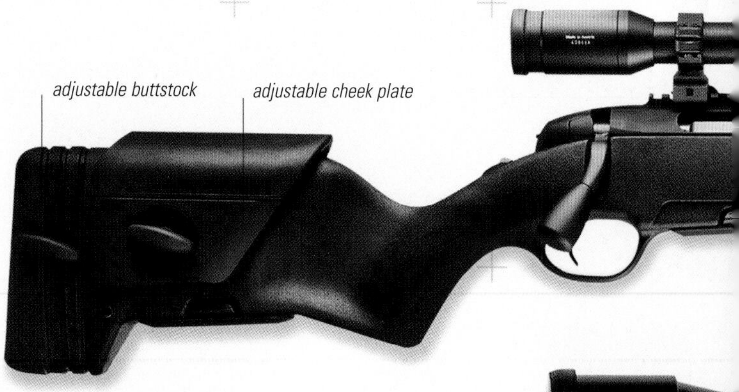

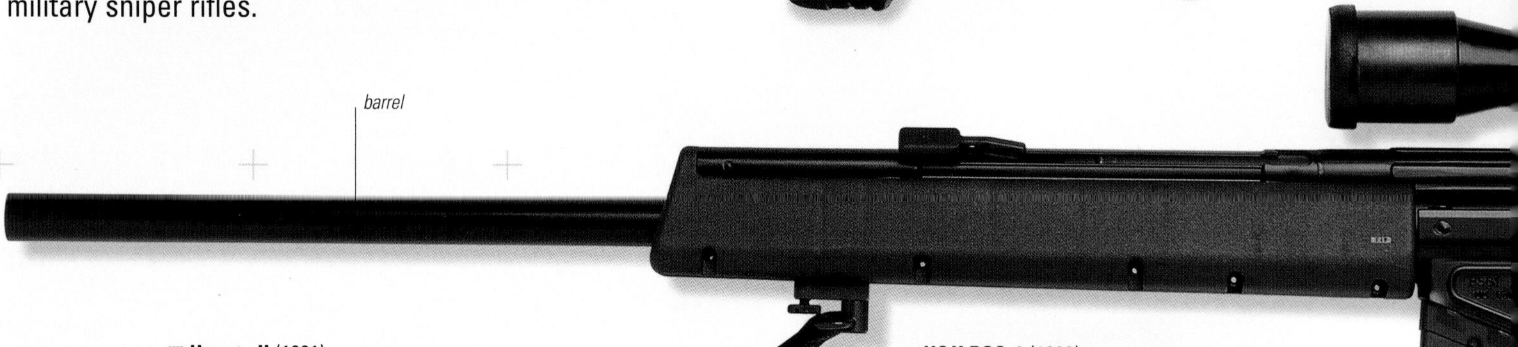

▼ Hecate II (1991)
The Hecate II is manufactured by the Belgian gun producer FN Herstal. It is a 12.7-mm. sniper rifle, and this increased caliber gives it the capability of damaging or destroying vehicles. It has an effective range of over 4,875 ft. (1,500 m.). It can be fitted with a silencer, and has a seven-round magazine.

Length	54.3 in. (138 cm.)
Weight	30.4 lb. (13.8 kg.)
Rate of fire	20 rpm.
Caliber	12.7-mm.

▲ H&K PSG-1 (1986)
The PSG-1 is regarded as the finest police sniper rifle available. It can be fitted with a 5- or 20-round magazine and has an effective range of 3,280 ft. (1,000 m.).

Length	47.6 in. (120.8 cm.)
Weight	14.3 lb. (6.4 kg.)
Rate of fire	20 rpm.
Caliber	7.62-mm.

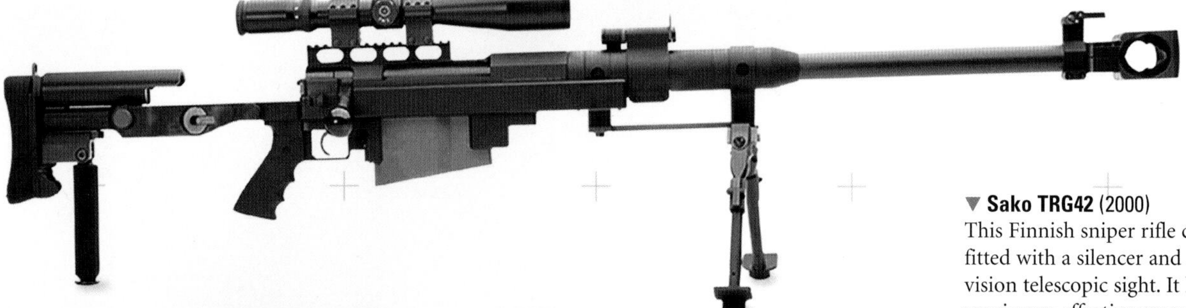

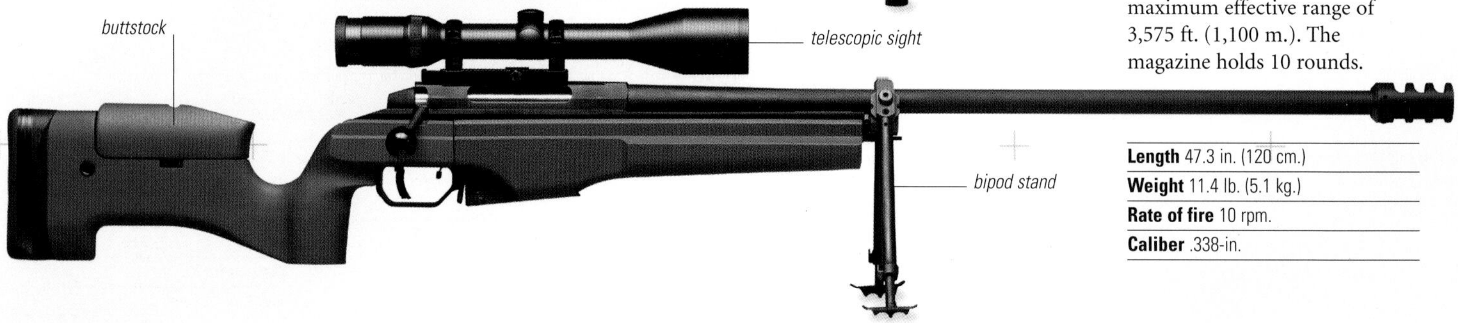

▼ Sako TRG42 (2000)
This Finnish sniper rifle can be fitted with a silencer and a night vision telescopic sight. It has a maximum effective range of 3,575 ft. (1,100 m.). The magazine holds 10 rounds.

Length	47.3 in. (120 cm.)
Weight	11.4 lb. (5.1 kg.)
Rate of fire	10 rpm.
Caliber	.338-in.

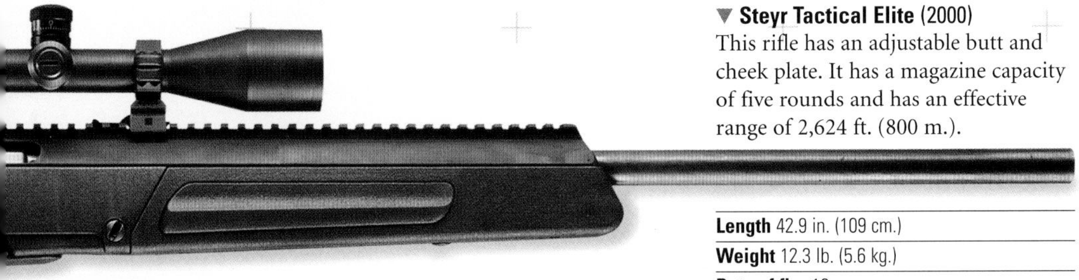

▼ Steyr Tactical Elite (2000)
This rifle has an adjustable butt and cheek plate. It has a magazine capacity of five rounds and has an effective range of 2,624 ft. (800 m.).

Length	42.9 in. (109 cm.)
Weight	12.3 lb. (5.6 kg.)
Rate of fire	10 rpm.
Caliber	.308-in.

Hostage-rescue

Situations in which law-enforcement agencies are likely to use a sniper rifle place great pressure on the police marksman and the weapon. In a hostage situation, the marksman may get only one opportunity to disable the hostage-taker, and that shot must hit the target the first time without causing other casualties. In some circumstances, the sniper may be called upon to incapacitate a target without causing fatal injuries.

Rooftop deployment
A police marksman takes aim from a rooftop firing position. He is in constant radio contact with his commanding officer.

► Remington M24 (1987)
The M24 Sniper Weapon System is used in the United States by police Special Weapons and Tactics (SWAT) teams. Its effective range is 2,600 ft. (800 m.) and it has a five-round magazine.

Length	43 in. (109.2 cm.)
Weight	14.3 lb. (6.5 kg.)
Rate of fire	10 rpm.
Caliber	7.62-mm.

◄ H&K MSG90 (1987)
Made by German manufacturer Heckler & Koch, the MSG90 is the standard police sniper rifle of British anti-terrorist squads. It can be fitted with a 5- or 20-round magazine and has an effective range of 3,280 ft. (1,000 m.).

Length	45.9 in. (116.5 cm.)
Weight	14.1 lb. (6.4 kg.)
Rate of fire	23 rpm.
Caliber	7.62-mm.

Shotguns

When a situation calls for maximum stopping power within a confined space, there is no better weapon than a shotgun. Special forces teams often use shotguns in urban operations, especially where a building needs to be cleared room-by-room. Despite their short range and otherwise limited operational utility, they remain a useful asset in the special forces arsenal. All the weapons shown are pump action models, each capable of fast reloading.

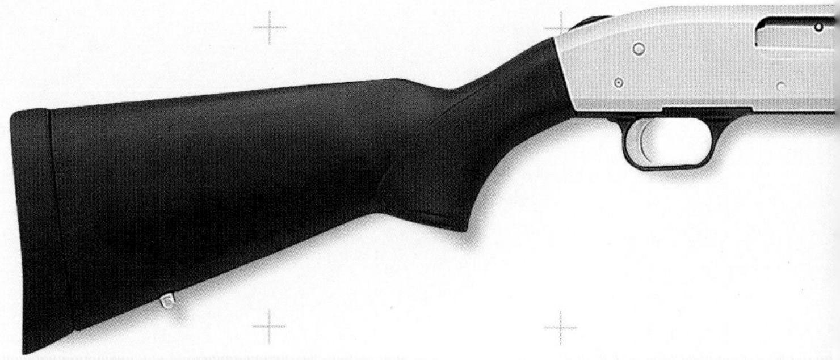

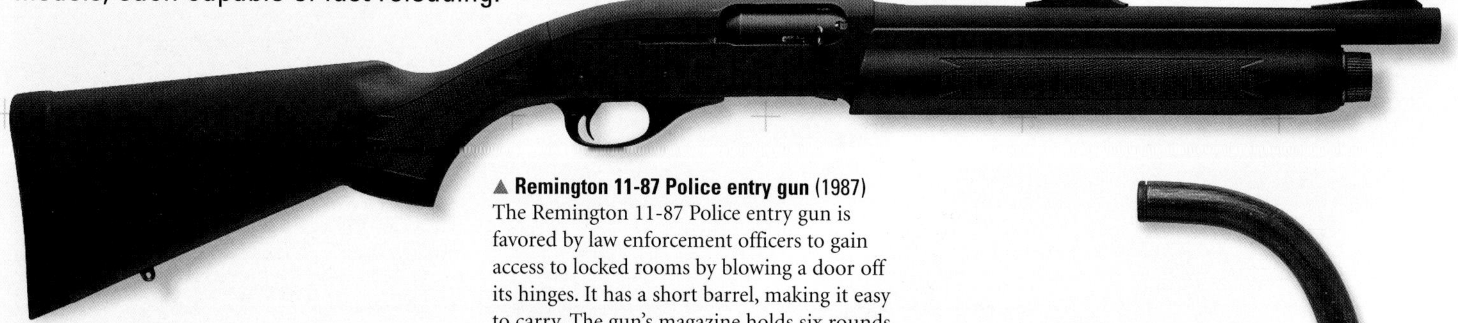

▲ **Remington 11-87 Police entry gun** (1987)
The Remington 11-87 Police entry gun is favored by law enforcement officers to gain access to locked rooms by blowing a door off its hinges. It has a short barrel, making it easy to carry. The gun's magazine holds six rounds.

Length	34 in. (86.3 cm.)
Weight	7.5 lb. (3.4 kg.)
Rate of fire	10 rpm.
Caliber	12-gauge

▲ **Spas 12** (1978)
The Spas 12 is from the Italian manufacturer Franchi. Its name stands for Sporting Purpose Automatic Shotgun. It is in service with Special Weapons and Tactics (SWAT) teams in the United States and other national forces. The Spas 12 has a folding stock, and the magazine holds eight shells.

Length	41in. (104.1 cm.)
Weight	9.7 in. (4.4 kg.)
Rate of fire	10 rpm.
Caliber	12-gauge

Shotgun ammunition

The choice of ammunition for a shotgun is determined by the mission. The two main types in use today are buck shot (shot pellets) and slugs used by civilian shotgun owners. In operations, a slug round is effective for shooting open locked doors, while buck shot spreads out over a large area and can simultaneously wound or kill more than one enemy.

Tried and tested
The Remington brand of ammunition is a popular choice. Shown here are buck shot (right) and slug rounds (far right).

▲ **Mossberg 500 Mariner** (1978)
The Mossberg 500 Mariner has a special corrosion-resistant finish, making it suitable for use in hostile weather conditions and for coastal operations. The Mariner's magazine holds six rounds.

Length 38.5 in. (97.8 cm.)
Weight 7.3 lb. (3.3 kg.)
Rate of fire 10 rpm.
Caliber 12-gauge

Maximum stopping power

In combat operations in general – and house-clearing missions in particular – the shotgun can offer a useful option to special forces teams. Capable of delivering immense firepower at a short range, shotguns can be used to blow open locked doors, and can kill or injure everyone in a room with a single shot. The British SAS even used shotguns in the jungles of Malaya during actions against communist terrorists in the 1950s. However, shotguns do have their limitations. They are impractical for use in hostage rescue situations, where the risk of injuring or killing innocent people is too great.

Hitting hard
A US soldier takes aim with his Remington 870 combat shotgun.

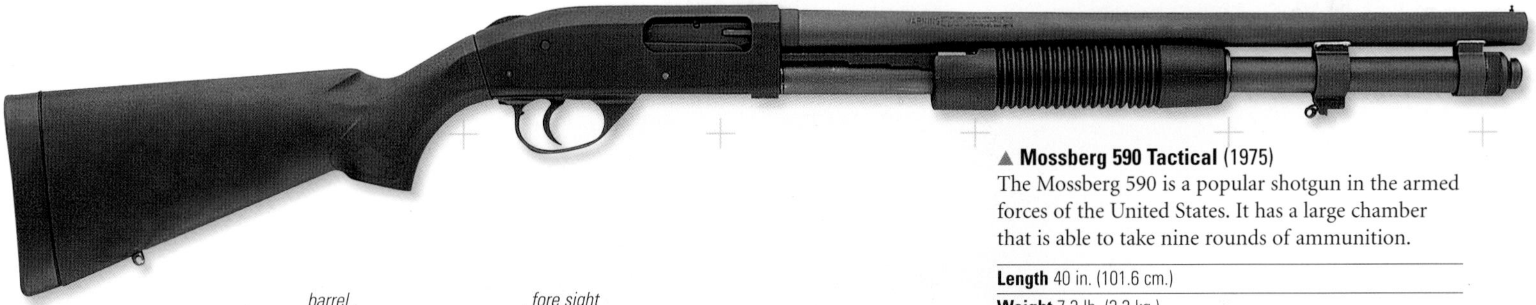

▲ **Mossberg 590 Tactical** (1975)
The Mossberg 590 is a popular shotgun in the armed forces of the United States. It has a large chamber that is able to take nine rounds of ammunition.

Length 40 in. (101.6 cm.)
Weight 7.3 lb. (3.3 kg.)
Rate of fire 10 rpm.
Caliber 12-gauge

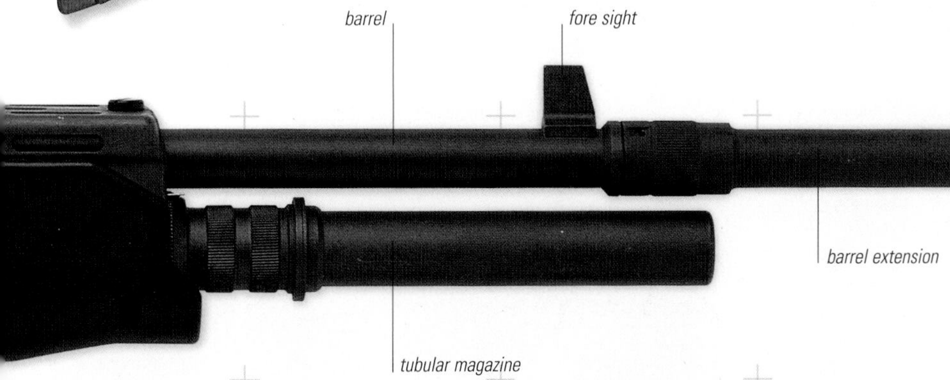

▼ **Remington 11-87 Police** (1987)
This shotgun is popular with a great number of law-enforcement agencies in the United States, including most police departments, hence its name. The gun has a magazine capacity of seven rounds.

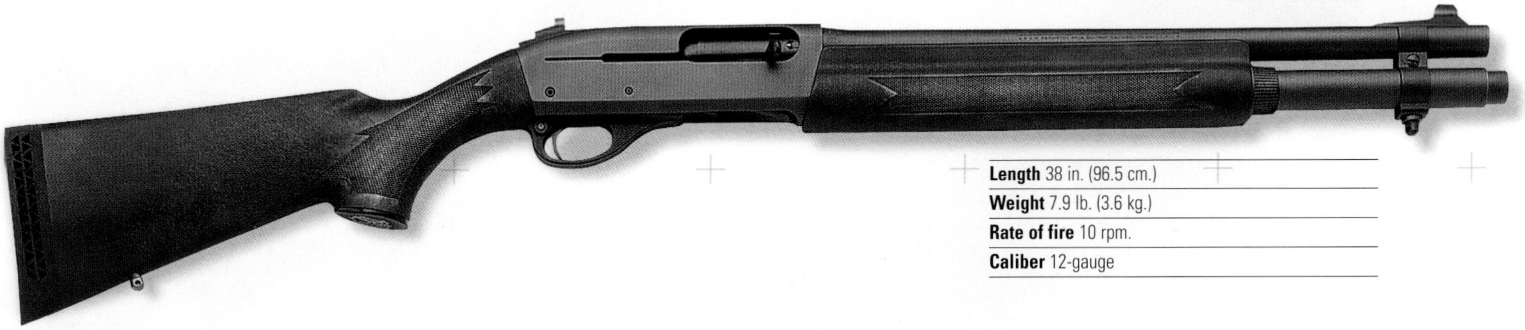

Length 38 in. (96.5 cm.)
Weight 7.9 lb. (3.6 kg.)
Rate of fire 10 rpm.
Caliber 12-gauge

Assault rifles

The assault rifle is the standard weapon of any special forces team. It is lightweight and flexible, yet capable of delivering vast amounts of firepower. The designs used by special forces teams around the world are many and varied, each tailored to fulfill a particular role. From the general purpose AK-74 to the compact Colt Commando, the assault rifle is the most important part of any soldier's field equipment.

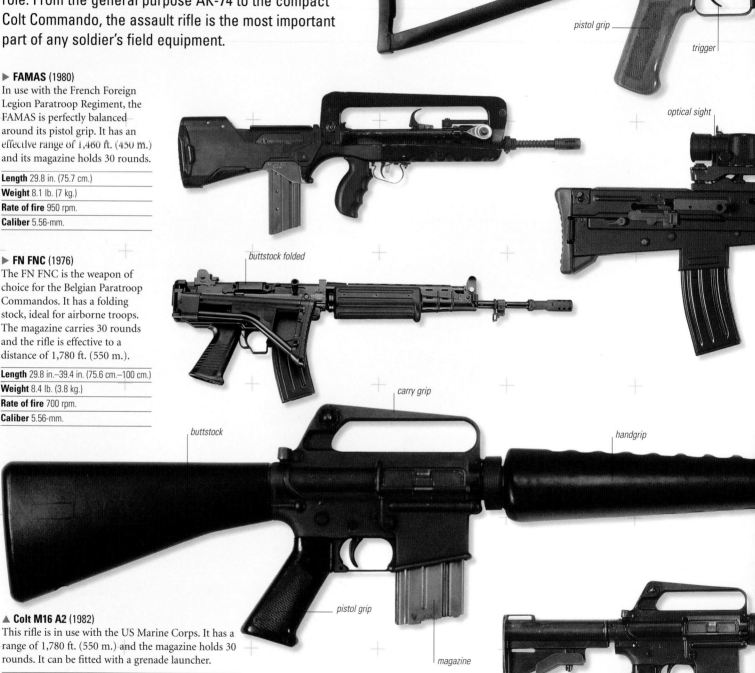

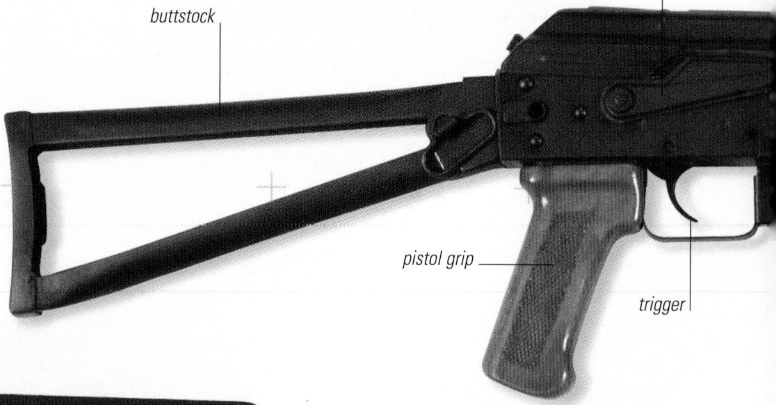

▶ FAMAS (1980)
In use with the French Foreign Legion Paratroop Regiment, the FAMAS is perfectly balanced around its pistol grip. It has an effective range of 1,460 ft. (450 m.) and its magazine holds 30 rounds.

Length 29.8 in. (75.7 cm.)
Weight 8.1 lb. (7 kg.)
Rate of fire 950 rpm.
Caliber 5.56-mm.

▶ FN FNC (1976)
The FN FNC is the weapon of choice for the Belgian Paratroop Commandos. It has a folding stock, ideal for airborne troops. The magazine carries 30 rounds and the rifle is effective to a distance of 1,780 ft. (550 m.).

Length 29.8 in.–39.4 in. (75.6 cm.–100 cm.)
Weight 8.4 lb. (3.8 kg.)
Rate of fire 700 rpm.
Caliber 5.56-mm.

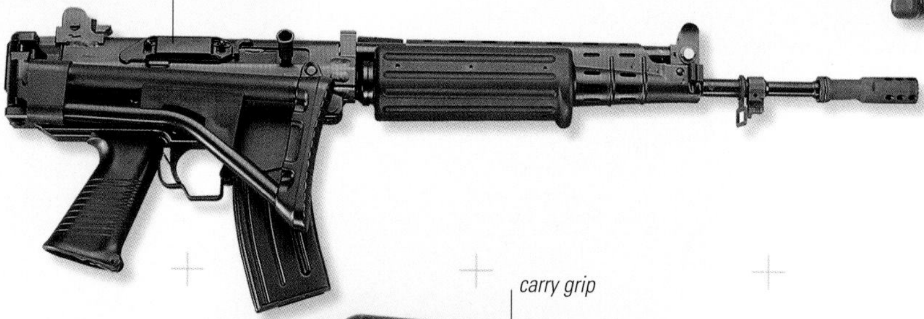

▲ Colt M16 A2 (1982)
This rifle is in use with the US Marine Corps. It has a range of 1,780 ft. (550 m.) and the magazine holds 30 rounds. It can be fitted with a grenade launcher.

Length 39.4 in. (100 cm.)
Weight 7.5 lb. (3.4 kg.)
Rate of fire 800 rpm.
Caliber 5.56-mm.

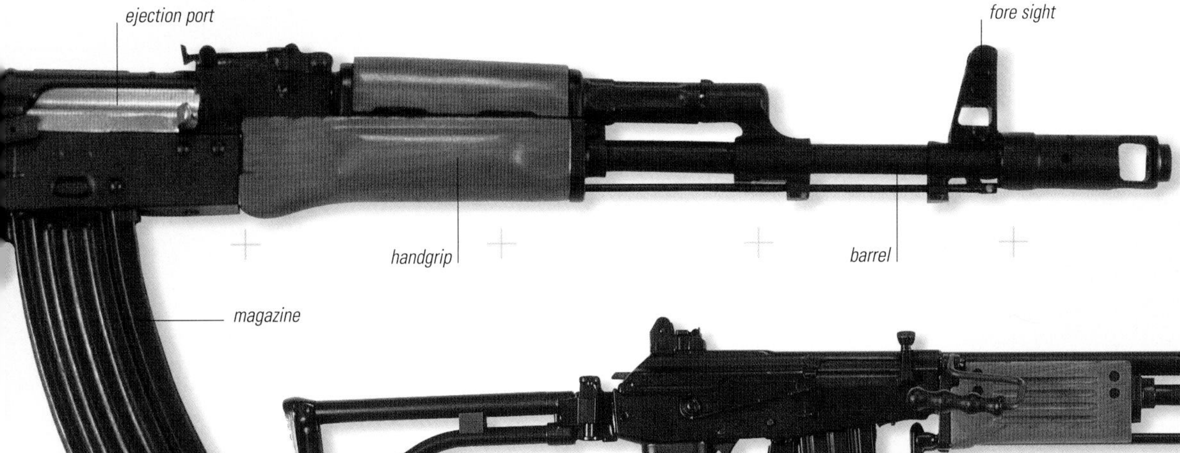

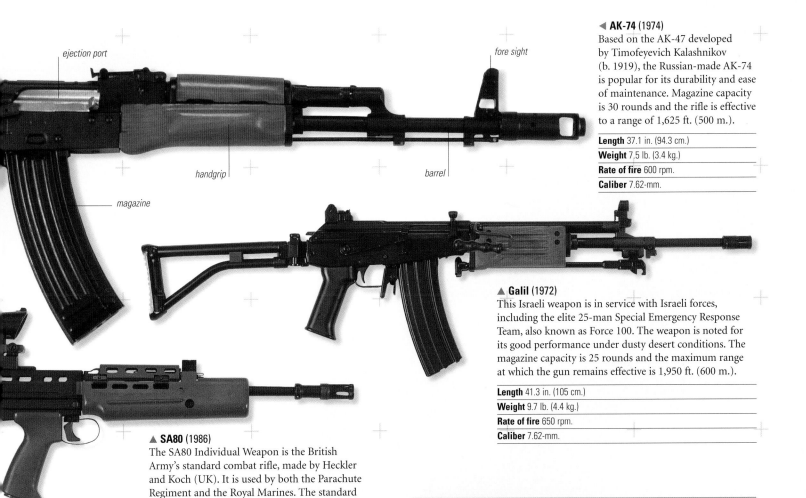

◄ **AK-74** (1974)
Based on the AK-47 developed by Timofeyevich Kalashnikov (b. 1919), the Russian-made AK-74 is popular for its durability and ease of maintenance. Magazine capacity is 30 rounds and the rifle is effective to a range of 1,625 ft. (500 m.).

Length 37.1 in. (94.3 cm.)
Weight 7.5 lb. (3.4 kg.)
Rate of fire 600 rpm.
Caliber 7.62-mm.

▲ **Galil** (1972)
This Israeli weapon is in service with Israeli forces, including the elite 25-man Special Emergency Response Team, also known as Force 100. The weapon is noted for its good performance under dusty desert conditions. The magazine capacity is 25 rounds and the maximum range at which the gun remains effective is 1,950 ft. (600 m.).

Length 41.3 in. (105 cm.)
Weight 9.7 lb. (4.4 kg.)
Rate of fire 650 rpm.
Caliber 7.62-mm.

▲ **SA80** (1986)
The SA80 Individual Weapon is the British Army's standard combat rifle, made by Heckler and Koch (UK). It is used by both the Parachute Regiment and the Royal Marines. The standard optical sight gives a 400 percent magnification of the target, increasing the accuracy of the aim. The magazine can take 30 rounds and the rifle's range is 1,625 ft. (500 m.).

Length 30.9 in. (78.5 cm.)
Weight 8.4 lb. (3.8 kg.)
Rate of fire 650 rpm.
Caliber 5.56-mm.

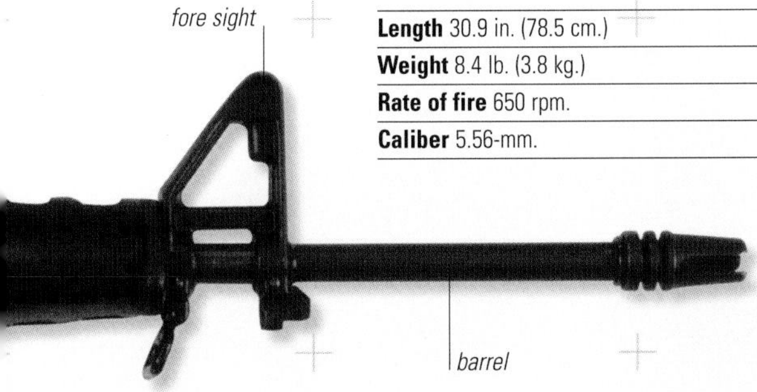

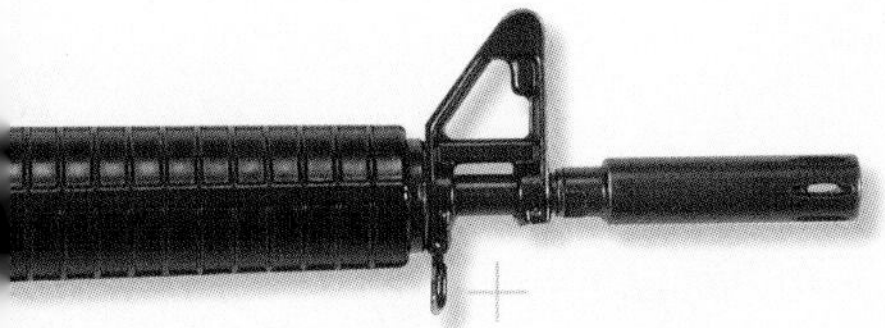

◄ **Colt Commando** (1969)
This assault rifle is in service with US and Israeli special forces units. It can be field-stripped without the need for special tools. The rifle is effective to a range of 1,170 ft. (360 m.), and the magazine can hold 30 rounds.

Length 30 in. (76.2 cm.)
Weight 5.4 lb. (2.4 kg.)
Rate of fire 700 rpm.
Caliber 5.56-mm.

Field stripping

One of the most important considerations in the design of an assault rifle is the ease with which it can be maintained in the field. A soldier's personal weapon is the most important part of his equipment, and he must be able to keep it in serviceable order with the minimum of effort, no matter what the conditions. From the outset of his military career, a soldier is taught to strip and service his rifle to the level where he can carry out the procedure even in complete darkness. A rifle that is not maintained properly is liable to jam or seize up, and could ultimately cost the soldier his life.

AK-47
Shown broken down as if being field stripped.

Submachine guns

The submachine gun has established itself as the most practical special forces weapon. Its immense firepower and compact size lends it to many types of operation, particularly in urban and hostage-rescue situations. The weapons can also be concealed easily, for clandestine missions. Submachine guns are also in service with civilian security and protection teams.

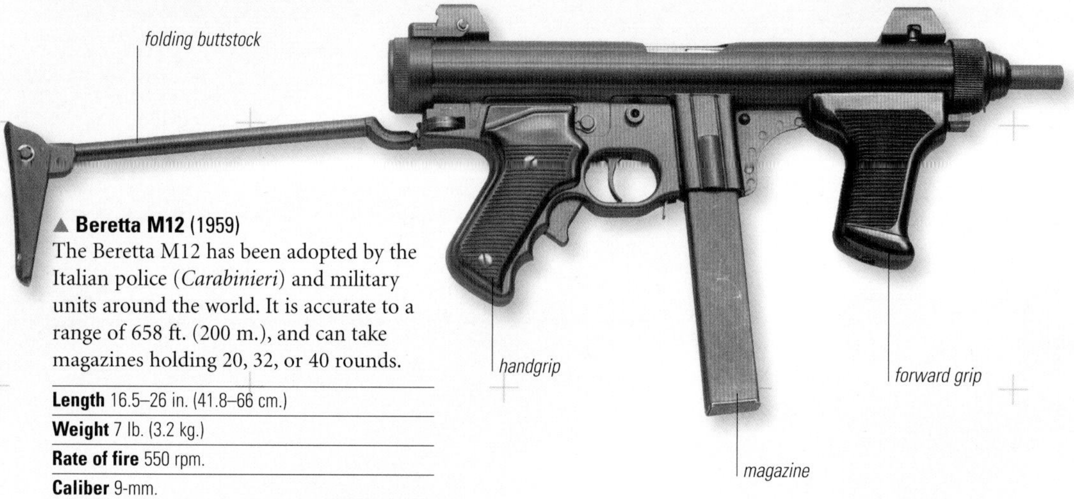

▲ **Beretta M12** (1959)
The Beretta M12 has been adopted by the Italian police (*Carabinieri*) and military units around the world. It is accurate to a range of 658 ft. (200 m.), and can take magazines holding 20, 32, or 40 rounds.

Length	16.5–26 in. (41.8–66 cm.)
Weight	7 lb. (3.2 kg.)
Rate of fire	550 rpm.
Caliber	9-mm.

▲ **AUG PARA** (1986)
This weapon is derived from the AUG family of assault rifles, designed and manufactured by the Austrian company Steyr. Its shortened barrel makes it suitable for airborne troops. Its magazine holds 25 or 32 rounds.

Length	26 in. (66.5 cm.)
Weight	7.3 lb (3.3 kg.)
Rate of fire	700 rpm.
Caliber	9-mm.

▼ **FN P90** (1990)
The P90 is a state-of-the-art design from Belgium's FN (Fabrique Nationale) Herstal. Intended for law enforcement, it has low recoil, an innovative top-loading magazine, and a high rate of fire.

Length	19.7 in. (50 cm.)
Weight	5.5 lb. (2.5 kg.)
Rate of fire	900 rpm.
Caliber	5.7-mm.

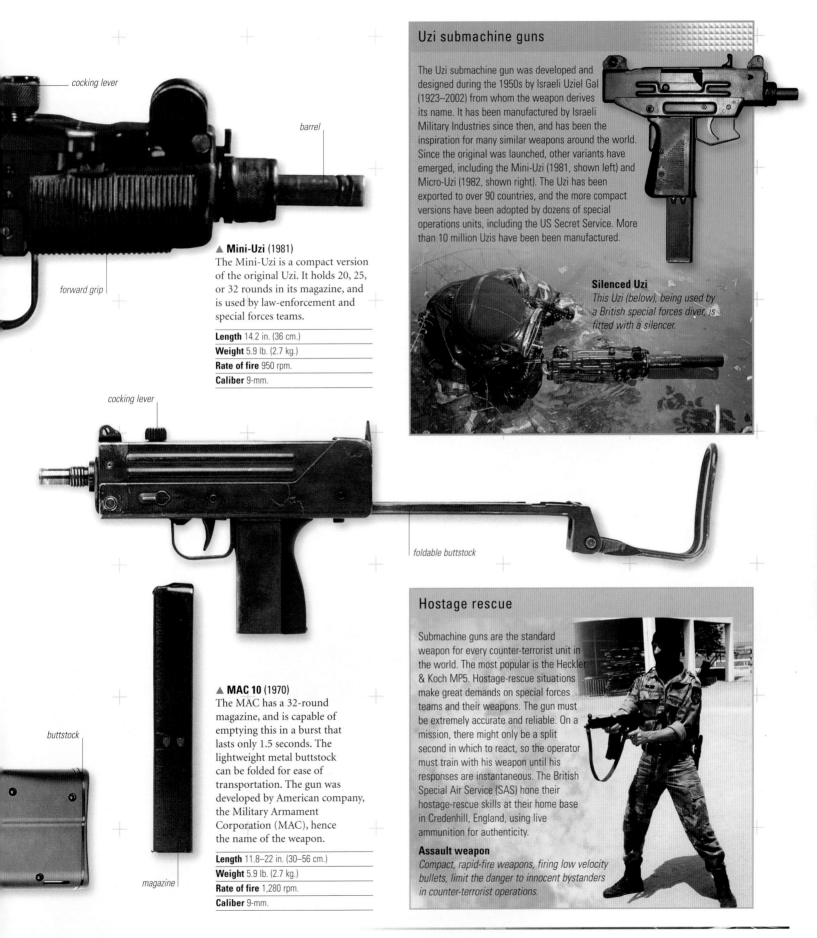

▲ **Mini-Uzi** (1981)
The Mini-Uzi is a compact version of the original Uzi. It holds 20, 25, or 32 rounds in its magazine, and is used by law-enforcement and special forces teams.

Length	14.2 in. (36 cm.)
Weight	5.9 lb. (2.7 kg.)
Rate of fire	950 rpm.
Caliber	9-mm.

Uzi submachine guns

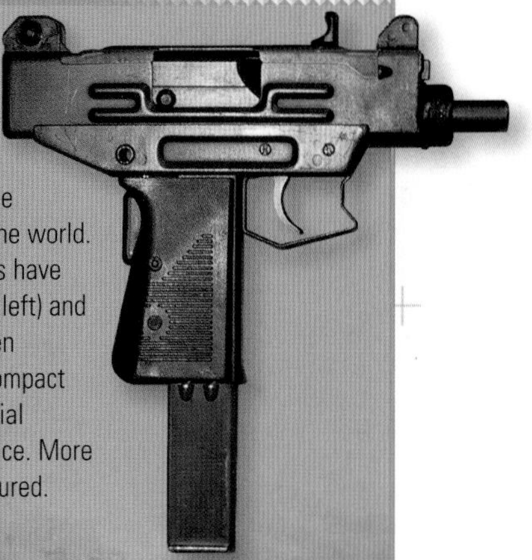

The Uzi submachine gun was developed and designed during the 1950s by Israeli Uziel Gal (1923–2002) from whom the weapon derives its name. It has been manufactured by Israeli Military Industries since then, and has been the inspiration for many similar weapons around the world. Since the original was launched, other variants have emerged, including the Mini-Uzi (1981, shown left) and Micro-Uzi (1982, shown right). The Uzi has been exported to over 90 countries, and the more compact versions have been adopted by dozens of special operations units, including the US Secret Service. More than 10 million Uzis have been been manufactured.

Silenced Uzi
This Uzi (below), being used by a British special forces diver, is fitted with a silencer.

▲ **MAC 10** (1970)
The MAC has a 32-round magazine, and is capable of emptying this in a burst that lasts only 1.5 seconds. The lightweight metal buttstock can be folded for ease of transportation. The gun was developed by American company, the Military Armament Corporation (MAC), hence the name of the weapon.

Length	11.8–22 in. (30–56 cm.)
Weight	5.9 lb. (2.7 kg.)
Rate of fire	1,280 rpm.
Caliber	9-mm.

Hostage rescue

Submachine guns are the standard weapon for every counter-terrorist unit in the world. The most popular is the Heckler & Koch MP5. Hostage-rescue situations make great demands on special forces teams and their weapons. The gun must be extremely accurate and reliable. On a mission, there might only be a split second in which to react, so the operator must train with his weapon until his responses are instantaneous. The British Special Air Service (SAS) hone their hostage-rescue skills at their home base in Credenhill, England, using live ammunition for authenticity.

Assault weapon
Compact, rapid-fire weapons, firing low velocity bullets, limit the danger to innocent bystanders in counter-terrorist operations.

Heckler & Koch MP5

Introduced in 1964, the MP5 9-mm. submachine gun was made by the German armaments company Heckler & Koch and represented a major improvement over other submachine guns of the time. It featured many design innovations, notably a new firing mechanism (see box opposite), and was engineered to a high standard. This resulted in it being adopted by many special forces, most famously the British Special Air Service (SAS).

▶ **MP5SD** (1975)
Designed for specialized applications where sound and flash need to be suppressed, such as in the silent killing of enemy guards. Capable of taking magazines that hold 15 or 30 rounds, it has a range of 328 ft. (100 m.).

Length 21.6 in. (55 cm.)
Weight 6.3 lb. (2.9 kg.)
Rate of fire 800 rpm.
Caliber 9-mm.

▲ **MP5A3** (extended)
With the metal strut stock extended, the A3 can be fired from the shoulder. A mini flashlight has been mounted at the front below the barrel to aid targeting in low-light conditions. All MP5s can be fitted with image intensifiers, optical sights, aiming projectors, and several infrared sights.

The future

Heckler & Koch has been working on a successor to the MP5 range of submachine guns. This development has led to the creation of the UMP 45 (Universal Machine Pistol 45). The entire stock is made from polymer material, giving great strength allied to low weight. The stock itself can be folded onto the right side of the gun, reducing its overall length. In addition, the UMP can be fired one-handed if necessary.

▶ **Covert MP5K** (1976)
For undercover operations, an MP5K can be fitted inside a specially designed briefcase. The case has a trigger on the underside of the carrying handle. (For weapon specifications see MP5K.)

The UMP
The UMP fires the .45 ACP (Automatic Colt Pistol) round instead of the 9-mm. cartridge used in other submachine guns.

Firing mechanism

The MP5 has a special firing mechanism that uses a closed bolt. Most submachine guns fire from an open bolt, which means that when the trigger is pulled the bolt flies forward to chamber a round and then fires it. This results in a shift in the gun's balance, which can result in a shot being off-target. The MP5, however, starts with the bolt closed. All that happens when the trigger is pulled is that the hammer is released, which fires the round.

The MP5
MP5 submachine guns are superbly engineered, with the working parts being made from top-quality steel. They fire even in wet, muddy conditions.

◀ **MP5 NAVY** (1980)
A variant designed especially for the US Navy's Sea, Air, and Land (SEAL) teams. It can take either 15- or 30-round magazines and has a range of 328 ft. (100 m.).

Length	19.2–27.1 in. (49–69 cm.)
Weight	7.7 lb. (3.5 kg.)
Rate of fire	800 rpm.
Caliber	9-mm.

▲ **MP5A3** (1964)
This model has a single metal strut stock that can slide forward to reduce the overall length of the weapon. Magazines can hold either 15 or 30 rounds. It has a range of 328 ft. (100 m.).

Length	19.2–27.1 in. (49–69 cm.)
Weight	5.61 lb. (2.55 kg.)
Rate of fire	800 rpm.
Caliber	9-mm.

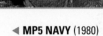

▶ **MP5K** (1976)
Designed for close-quarters use, the K version (from the German *Kurz* meaning short) can be easily concealed and carried. Magazine options are 15 or 30 rounds, and its effective range is 164 ft. (50 m.).

Length	12.5 in. (32 cm.)
Weight	4.4 lb. (2 kg.)
Rate of fire	900 rpm.
Caliber	9-mm.

Machine guns

The machine gun gives a special forces team greater firepower during a firefight. Although they have similar rates of fire as assault rifles, machine guns generally have larger magazines, typically holding up to 100 rounds, and an increased range of more than 3,250 ft. (1,000 m.). They come in a variety of shapes and sizes, from the 5.56-mm. SAW (also called the Minimi) to the devastating M2 Browning. Machine guns can be carried by hand, or mounted on a vehicle or a tripod.

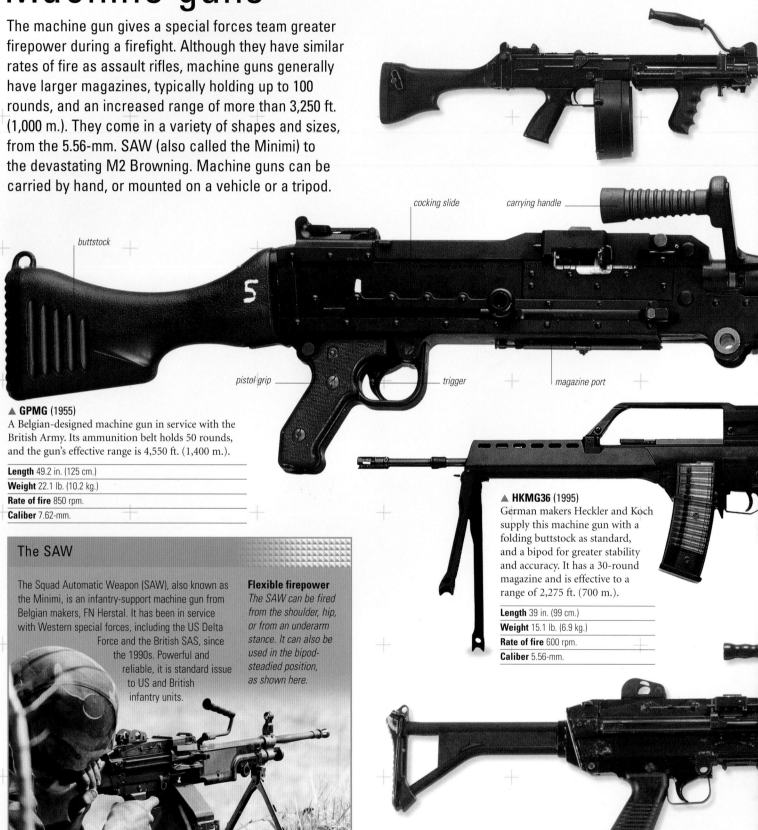

▲ **GPMG** (1955)
A Belgian-designed machine gun in service with the British Army. Its ammunition belt holds 50 rounds, and the gun's effective range is 4,550 ft. (1,400 m.).

Length	49.2 in. (125 cm.)
Weight	22.1 lb. (10.2 kg.)
Rate of fire	850 rpm.
Caliber	7.62-mm.

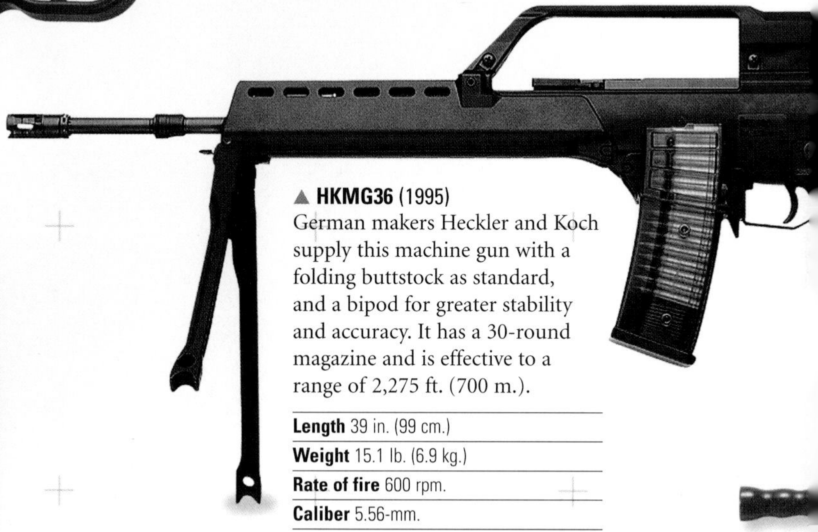

▲ **HKMG36** (1995)
German makers Heckler and Koch supply this machine gun with a folding buttstock as standard, and a bipod for greater stability and accuracy. It has a 30-round magazine and is effective to a range of 2,275 ft. (700 m.).

Length	39 in. (99 cm.)
Weight	15.1 lb. (6.9 kg.)
Rate of fire	600 rpm.
Caliber	5.56-mm.

The SAW

The Squad Automatic Weapon (SAW), also known as the Minimi, is an infantry-support machine gun from Belgian makers, FN Herstal. It has been in service with Western special forces, including the US Delta Force and the British SAS, since the 1990s. Powerful and reliable, it is standard issue to US and British infantry units.

Flexible firepower
The SAW can be fired from the shoulder, hip, or from an underarm stance. It can also be used in the bipod-steadied position, as shown here.

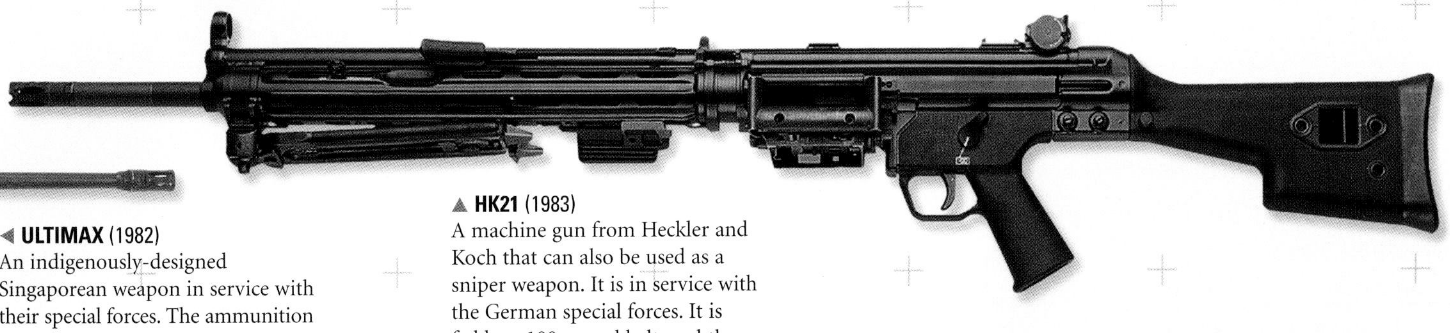

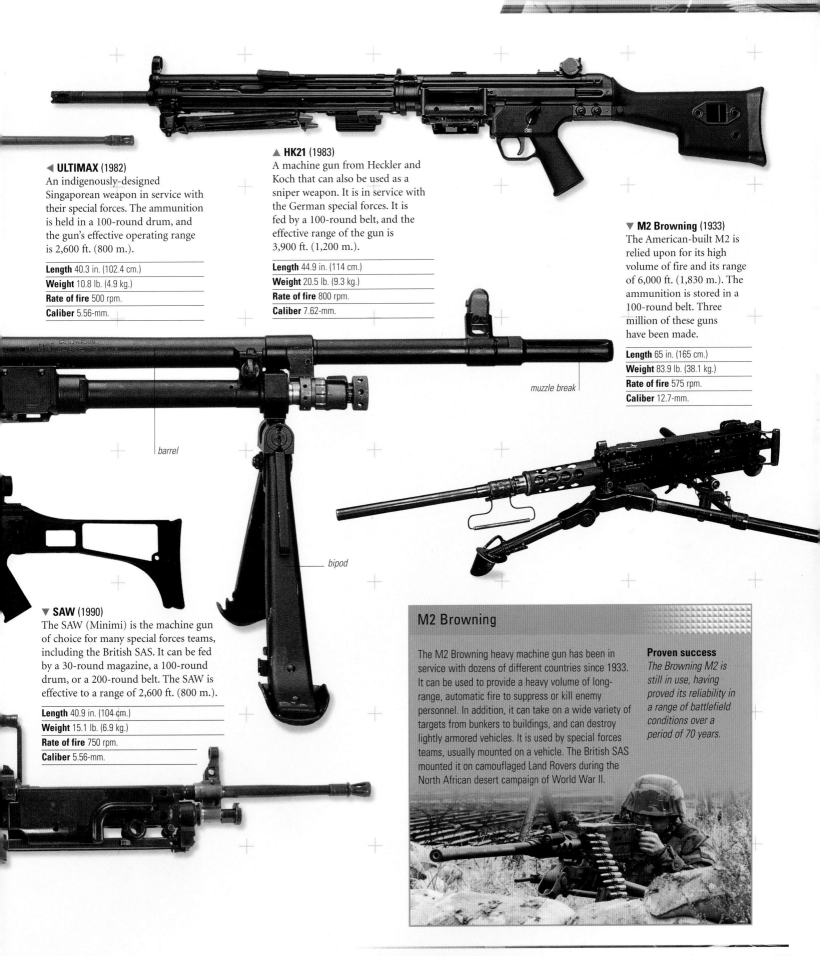

◀ ULTIMAX (1982)
An indigenously-designed Singaporean weapon in service with their special forces. The ammunition is held in a 100-round drum, and the gun's effective operating range is 2,600 ft. (800 m.).

Length 40.3 in. (102.4 cm.)
Weight 10.8 lb. (4.9 kg.)
Rate of fire 500 rpm.
Caliber 5.56-mm.

▲ HK21 (1983)
A machine gun from Heckler and Koch that can also be used as a sniper weapon. It is in service with the German special forces. It is fed by a 100-round belt, and the effective range of the gun is 3,900 ft. (1,200 m.).

Length 44.9 in. (114 cm.)
Weight 20.5 lb. (9.3 kg.)
Rate of fire 800 rpm.
Caliber 7.62-mm.

▼ M2 Browning (1933)
The American-built M2 is relied upon for its high volume of fire and its range of 6,000 ft. (1,830 m.). The ammunition is stored in a 100-round belt. Three million of these guns have been made.

Length 65 in. (165 cm.)
Weight 83.9 lb. (38.1 kg.)
Rate of fire 575 rpm.
Caliber 12.7-mm.

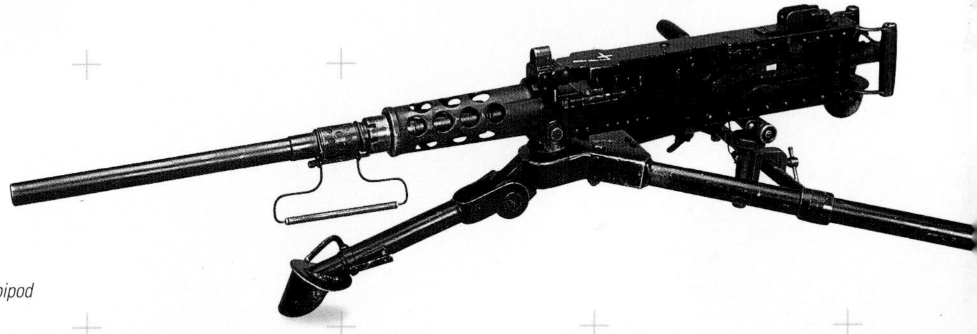

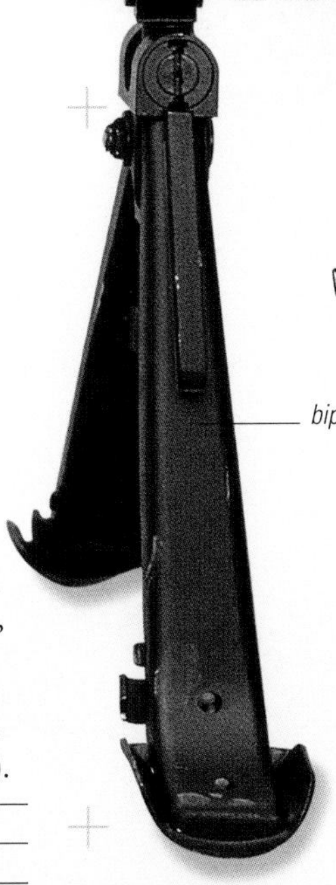

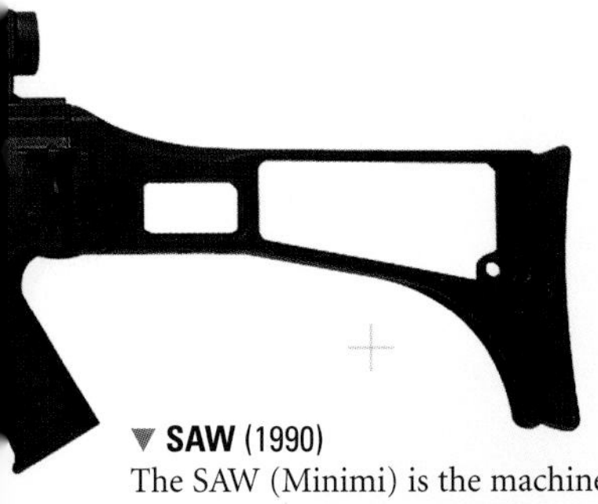

▼ SAW (1990)
The SAW (Minimi) is the machine gun of choice for many special forces teams, including the British SAS. It can be fed by a 30-round magazine, a 100-round drum, or a 200-round belt. The SAW is effective to a range of 2,600 ft. (800 m.).

Length 40.9 in. (104 cm.)
Weight 15.1 lb. (6.9 kg.)
Rate of fire 750 rpm.
Caliber 5.56-mm.

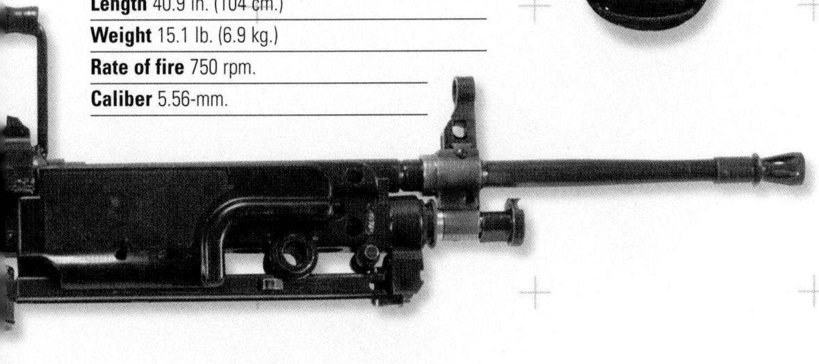

M2 Browning

The M2 Browning heavy machine gun has been in service with dozens of different countries since 1933. It can be used to provide a heavy volume of long-range, automatic fire to suppress or kill enemy personnel. In addition, it can take on a wide variety of targets from bunkers to buildings, and can destroy lightly armored vehicles. It is used by special forces teams, usually mounted on a vehicle. The British SAS mounted it on camouflaged Land Rovers during the North African desert campaign of World War II.

Proven success
The Browning M2 is still in use, having proved its reliability in a range of battlefield conditions over a period of 70 years.

Grenades and grenade launchers

Grenades are thrown in the final few yards of an assault to shock or kill the enemy. When fired at longer ranges, they keep the enemy's heads down so that they cannot fire back, and are particularly effective when thrown through windows. A special forces team takes the most suitable grenade for its mission: Stun grenades are appropriate for a hostage-rescue operation, but for an all-out assault a vehicle-mounted automatic grenade launcher is vital because of its long range and rate of fire.

◀ **Stun grenade** (1970)
The stun grenade, also known as a "flashbang," is used by special forces hostage-rescue teams. The combination of intense light and deafening noise that the grenade produces disorients all those who are exposed to it. Unlike fragmentation grenades, which detonate on a time-delay of five seconds, stun grenades explode only three seconds after the pull ring is removed, allowing less time for them to be intercepted. Stun grenades were used to great effect by the British Special Air Service (SAS) during the Iranian Embassy siege rescue in London in 1980 (see pp50–51).

Length	4.1 in. (10.4 cm.)
Weight	11.4 oz. (320 g.)
Throwing range	148 ft. (45 m.)
Blast radius	33 ft. (10 m.)

Fragmentation grenades

A fragmentation grenade is a modern anti-personnel weapon designed to explode into tiny fragments when detonated to kill or maim anyone in the blast area – usually a radius of 33 ft. (10 m.). The HG 85 (shown) fragments into 2,000 pieces upon detonation. The HG 85 is in use with the British, Dutch, and Swiss armed forces.

HG 85
When the pull ring is removed and the grenade is thrown, the explosive shatters the fragment case into lethal shards.

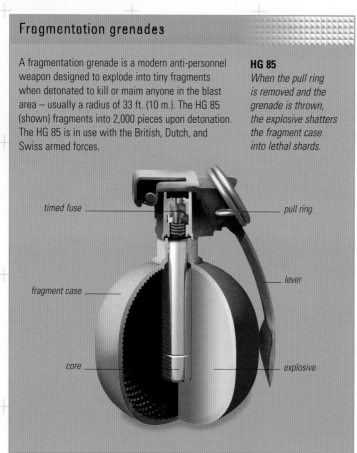

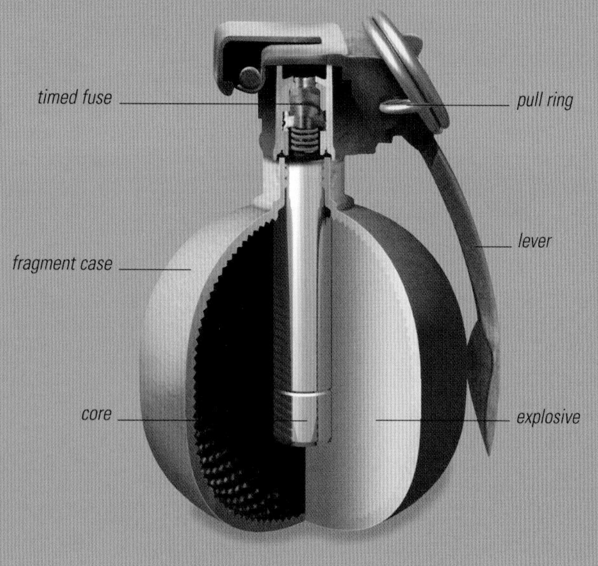

▶ **Heckler & Koch 40-mm Grenade Machine Gun** (1977)
The Grenade Machine Gun can deliver vast amounts of firepower from 1.3 miles (2.2 km.) away. It fires various 40-mm. grenades, including fragmentation and smoke grenades, and has a 32-round magazine. Its weight usually requires it to be vehicle-mounted.

Length	46.5 in. (118 cm.)
Weight	132 lb. (60 kg.)
Rate of fire	350 rpm.
Caliber	40-mm. grenade

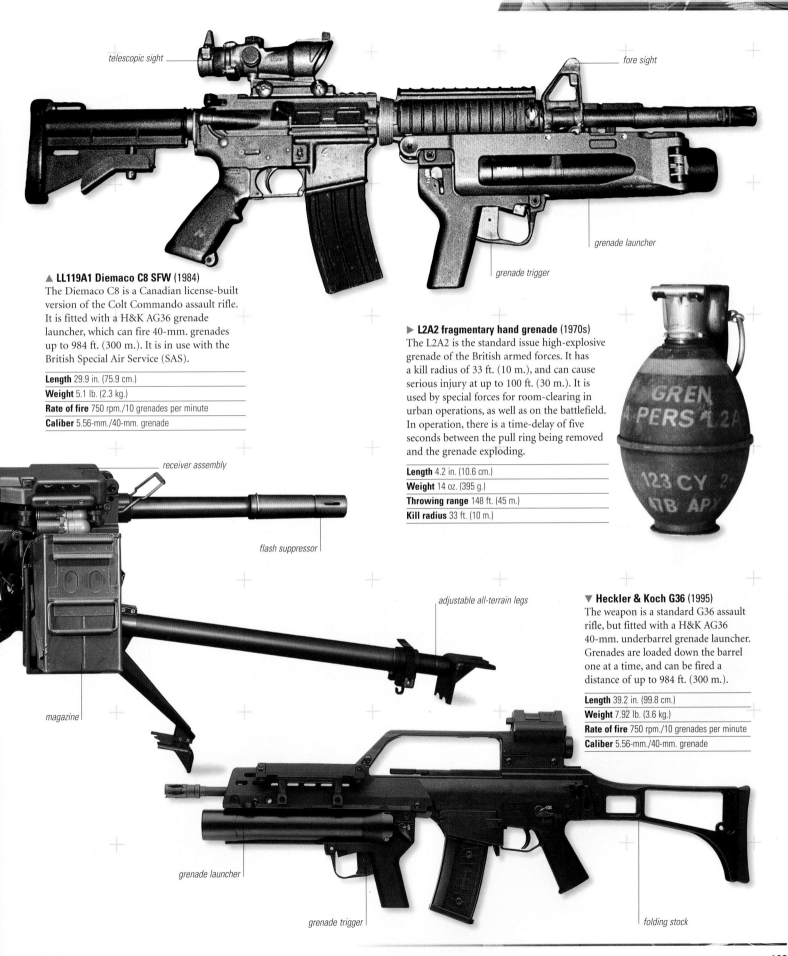

▲ LL119A1 Diemaco C8 SFW (1984)
The Diemaco C8 is a Canadian license-built version of the Colt Commando assault rifle. It is fitted with a H&K AG36 grenade launcher, which can fire 40-mm. grenades up to 984 ft. (300 m.). It is in use with the British Special Air Service (SAS).

Length	29.9 in. (75.9 cm.)
Weight	5.1 lb. (2.3 kg.)
Rate of fire	750 rpm./10 grenades per minute
Caliber	5.56-mm./40-mm. grenade

► L2A2 fragmentary hand grenade (1970s)
The L2A2 is the standard issue high-explosive grenade of the British armed forces. It has a kill radius of 33 ft. (10 m.), and can cause serious injury at up to 100 ft. (30 m.). It is used by special forces for room-clearing in urban operations, as well as on the battlefield. In operation, there is a time-delay of five seconds between the pull ring being removed and the grenade exploding.

Length	4.2 in. (10.6 cm.)
Weight	14 oz. (395 g.)
Throwing range	148 ft. (45 m.)
Kill radius	33 ft. (10 m.)

▼ Heckler & Koch G36 (1995)
The weapon is a standard G36 assault rifle, but fitted with a H&K AG36 40-mm. underbarrel grenade launcher. Grenades are loaded down the barrel one at a time, and can be fired a distance of up to 984 ft. (300 m.).

Length	39.2 in. (99.8 cm.)
Weight	7.92 lb. (3.6 kg.)
Rate of fire	750 rpm./10 grenades per minute
Caliber	5.56-mm./40-mm. grenade

Knives and survival tools

There are many types of knives used by special forces. Often they are the personal property of the individual since many armies do not issue them as standard. Far removed from the movie depiction of a dagger clenched between the teeth, the knife is rarely used in combat. Its use is primarily for survival: To cut a path through dense foliage in the jungle, to prepare traps to catch animals for food, or to build shelters. All the knives shown are made by the US manufacturer, Cold Steel.

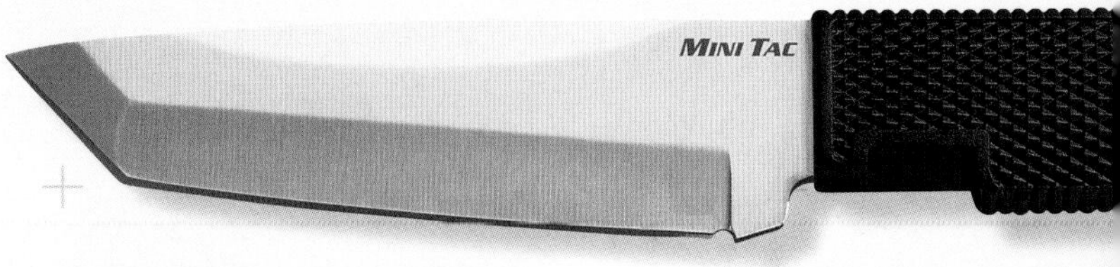

▶ Bolo machete
This large knife is best suited to hacking through dense jungle foliage, and is also good for chopping wood.

Length 16.1 in. (41 cm.)
Weight 17.3 oz. (484 g.)

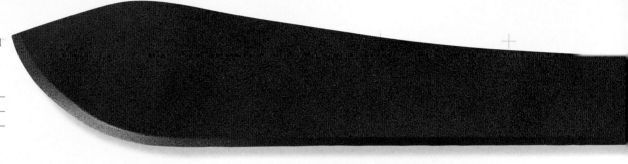

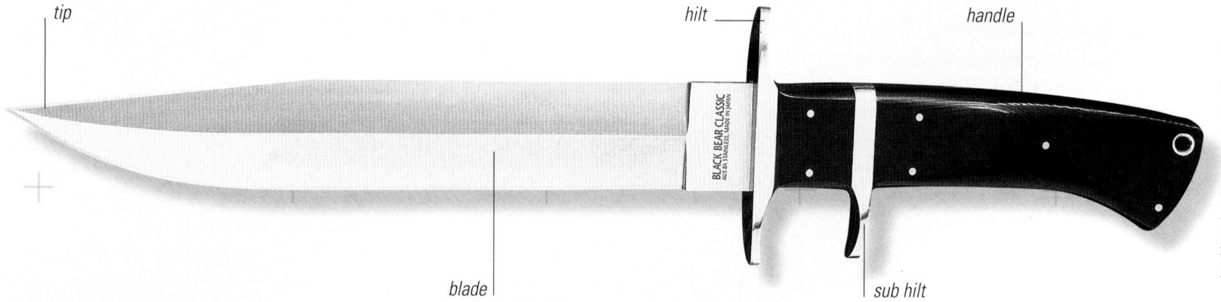

◀ Black Bear Classic
This long combat knife is designed with a sub hilt to eliminate the possibility of the handle becoming lodged, or the hand slipping onto the blade.

Length 13.5 in. (33.7 cm.)
Weight 12.7 oz. (355 g.)

Bayonets

Bayonet training is an important part of any soldier's combat instruction. It teaches a recruit how to summon and control aggression during an assault. The practical use of the bayonet on a modern battlefield is limited, but US and British special forces were involved in hand-to-hand fighting with bayonets fixed during the operation against Taliban and Al Qaeda forces in the Tora Bora region of Afghanistan in 2002.

Training to kill
A US Marine practices his bayonet skills during basic training.

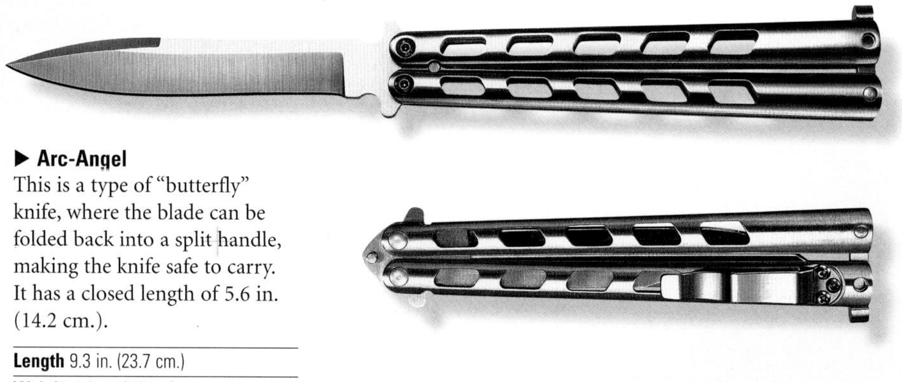

▶ Arc-Angel
This is a type of "butterfly" knife, where the blade can be folded back into a split handle, making the knife safe to carry. It has a closed length of 5.6 in. (14.2 cm.).

Length 9.3 in. (23.7 cm.)
Weight 4.3 oz. (120 g.)

◀ Mini Tac
This blade is a "neck knife" design – a knife worn around the neck on a cord for easy access. Its 4 in. (10.2 cm.) blade is made of extra thin, wide stainless steel for maximum cutting power and control.

Length 7.4 in. (18.7 cm.)
Weight 2.2 oz. (61 g.)

Basic survival

All special forces soldiers carry some sort of knife when they go on deployment. Depending on the mission, the knife may be just a back-up, or it may become vital in case of emergency. For example, a soldier may need to free himself from tangled parachute cord following an aerial descent. In other cases, the knife is an essential survival tool. In jungle environments it is needed to cut paths through thick vegetation, build shelters, and skin animals for food.

Building a shelter
A soldier uses his combat knife to chop branches to construct an A-frame shelter in the jungle.

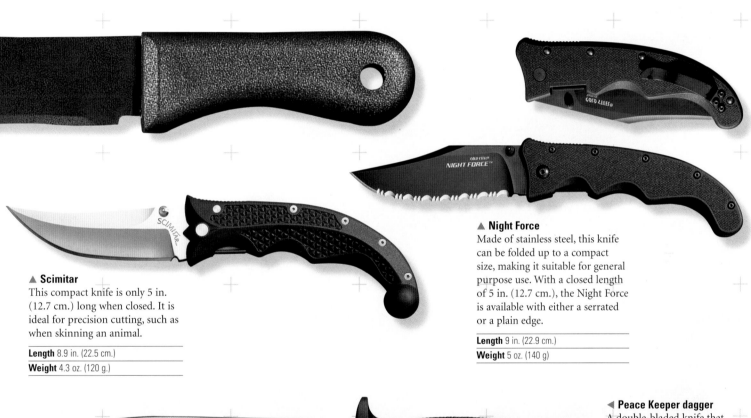

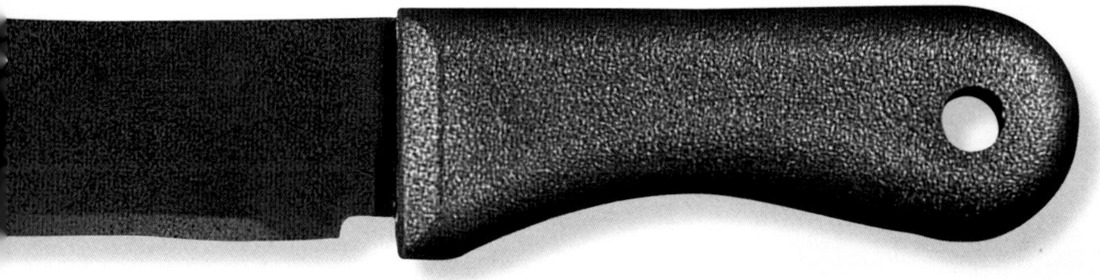

▲ Night Force
Made of stainless steel, this knife can be folded up to a compact size, making it suitable for general purpose use. With a closed length of 5 in. (12.7 cm.), the Night Force is available with either a serrated or a plain edge.

Length 9 in. (22.9 cm.)
Weight 5 oz. (140 g)

▲ Scimitar
This compact knife is only 5 in. (12.7 cm.) long when closed. It is ideal for precision cutting, such as when skinning an animal.

Length 8.9 in. (22.5 cm.)
Weight 4.3 oz. (120 g.)

◀ Peace Keeper dagger
A double-bladed knife that can be used for survival purposes, or in hand-to-hand combat if necessary.

Length 12 in. (30.5 cm.)
Weight 7.9 oz. (221 g.)

▶ Survival rescue knife
The blade has a black powder coating that protects the carbon steel, making this a knife that is suitable for the harshest environments. It has a non-slip rubber handle.

Length 10.3 in. (26.2 cm.)
Weight 8 oz. (224 g.)

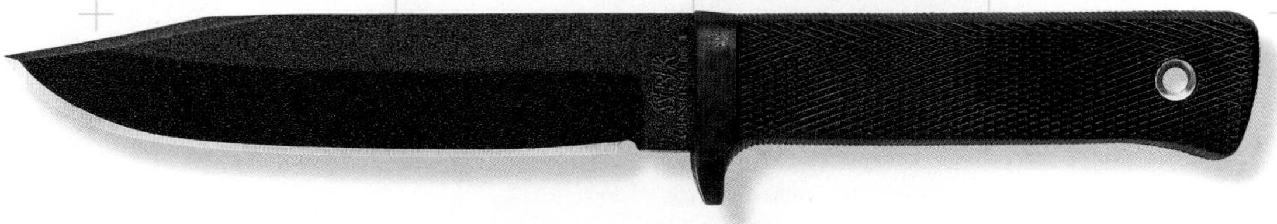

Missiles and missile launchers

Missiles are used by special forces teams as a means of attacking enemy armor, aircraft, and fortified positions. Due to their size and weight, most types are transported on vehicles, although some are man-portable. A primary role of special forces units is to laser-designate targets for aircraft-launched missiles.

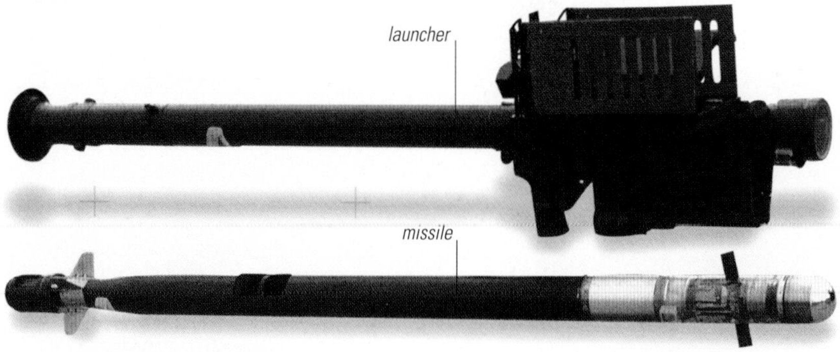

▲ Stinger (ATAS) (1996)
The Air-to-Air Stinger (ATAS) is an improved version of previous air-launched Stinger missiles. It is fitted to the fire-support aircraft of the US Airborne Divisions, such as Apache attack helicopters.

Length (launcher) 59 in. (150 cm.)
Weight (launcher) 12.5 lb. (5.68 kg.)
Range (missile) 5 miles (8 km.)
Speed (missile) 1,575 mph. (2,520 kph.)

▼ M136 AT4 (1980)
The M136 AT4 is the US Army's primary light anti-tank weapon. It is simple to use and easy to carry, and is deployed with all US special forces teams on assault operations.

Length (launcher) 40 in. (102 cm.)
Weight (launcher and missile) 14.8 lb. (6.7 kg.)
Range (missile) 985 ft. (300 m.)
Speed (missile) 562.5 mph. (900 kph.)

Anti-tank missiles

Folding fin rockets
Armor-piercing rockets, such as these on a Russian Ka-52 Black Shark helicopter, can devastate an armored column. The rockets have folding fins that deploy once they are launched.

The advance in anti-tank missile technology has given special forces teams the ability to engage armored targets in battle. Lightweight anti-tank weapons are not powerful enough to destroy a tank, but can disable the vehicle by knocking its tracks off or damaging the engine. Missiles mounted on vehicles, however, are very effective at destroying armor. Attack helicopters armed with high-explosive missiles are capable of destroying most armored vehicles at ranges of up to 5 miles (8 km.).

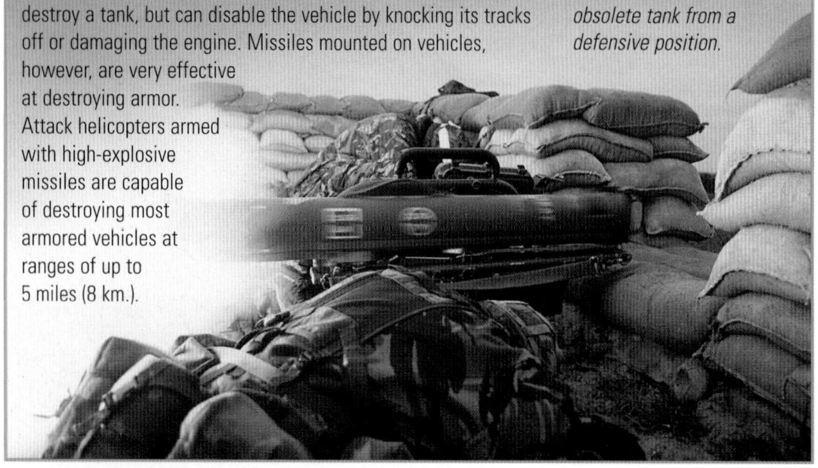

Effective defence
British troops practice-fire a Milan missile at an obsolete tank from a defensive position.

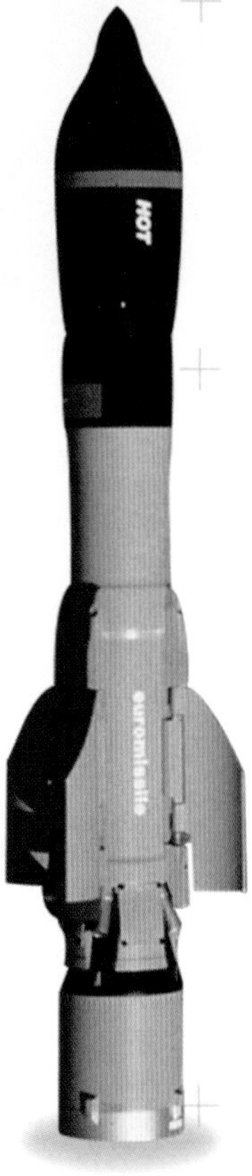

▲ Hot (1974)
The Franco-German Hot is vehicle- and helicopter-mounted.

▲ Trigat (2004)
The Trigat is the newest pan-European missile.

▲ Milan (1975)
An anti-tank missile used by 41 countries around the world.

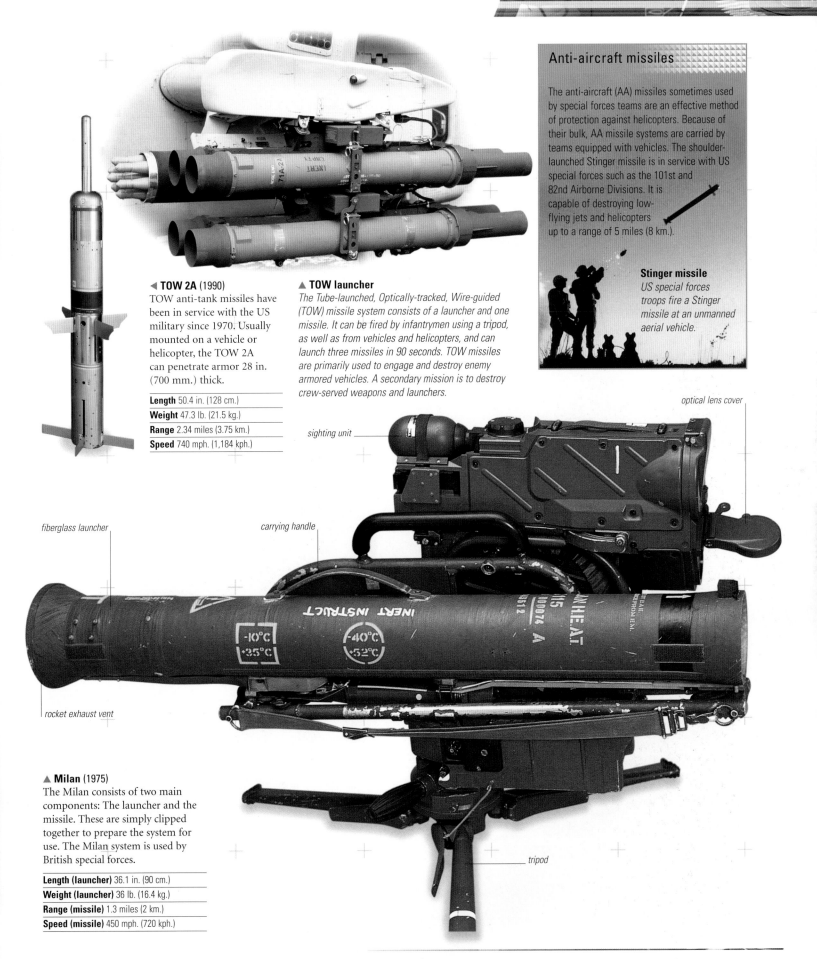

◄ **TOW 2A** (1990)
TOW anti-tank missiles have been in service with the US military since 1970. Usually mounted on a vehicle or helicopter, the TOW 2A can penetrate armor 28 in. (700 mm.) thick.

Length	50.4 in. (128 cm.)
Weight	47.3 lb. (21.5 kg.)
Range	2.34 miles (3.75 km.)
Speed	740 mph. (1,184 kph.)

▲ **TOW launcher**
The Tube-launched, Optically-tracked, Wire-guided (TOW) missile system consists of a launcher and one missile. It can be fired by infantrymen using a tripod, as well as from vehicles and helicopters, and can launch three missiles in 90 seconds. TOW missiles are primarily used to engage and destroy enemy armored vehicles. A secondary mission is to destroy crew-served weapons and launchers.

Anti-aircraft missiles

The anti-aircraft (AA) missiles sometimes used by special forces teams are an effective method of protection against helicopters. Because of their bulk, AA missile systems are carried by teams equipped with vehicles. The shoulder-launched Stinger missile is in service with US special forces such as the 101st and 82nd Airborne Divisions. It is capable of destroying low-flying jets and helicopters up to a range of 5 miles (8 km.).

Stinger missile
US special forces troops fire a Stinger missile at an unmanned aerial vehicle.

▲ **Milan** (1975)
The Milan consists of two main components: The launcher and the missile. These are simply clipped together to prepare the system for use. The Milan system is used by British special forces.

Length (launcher)	36.1 in. (90 cm.)
Weight (launcher)	36 lb. (16.4 kg.)
Range (missile)	1.3 miles (2 km.)
Speed (missile)	450 mph. (720 kph.)

Vehicles

Vehicles play a key part in most special forces missions. From the Light Armored Vehicle (LAV) used by the US Marine Corps, to the famous "Pink Panther" Land Rover used by the British Special Air Service (SAS) Mobility Troop during the 1991 Persian Gulf War, vehicles allow special forces to travel rapidly and to penetrate behind enemy lines. Often lightweight and deployable by parachute, vehicles provide a platform for weaponry, such as machine guns. They are also a means of transporting communications gear and other equipment.

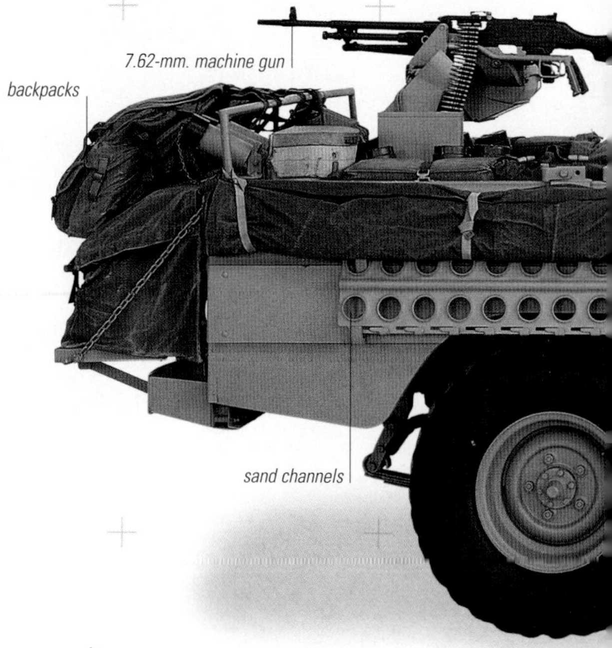

Light Armored Vehicle (LAV)

A Light Armored Vehicle (LAV) is an all-terrain, all-weather vehicle. It can be equipped for many roles, including anti-tank, air-defense, and communications. The LAV provides the US Marine Corps (USMC) with the tactical mobility to reach and engage potential threats and the weaponry (principally a 152-mm. cannon) to defeat a wide range of targets. It is popular with the USMC because it can be transported easily and can be deployed via a variety of aircraft, including the C-130 Hercules and CH-53E Stallion helicopter. The LAV has been so successful that many other nations have developed their own versions.

Amphibious LAV
The LAV can be set up for amphibious operations with only three minutes of preparation.

Air defense LAV
The anti-aircraft version of the LAV bristles with surface-to-air missiles, cannon, and powerful radars to detect incoming planes. It is a highly effective mobile anti-air defense platform.

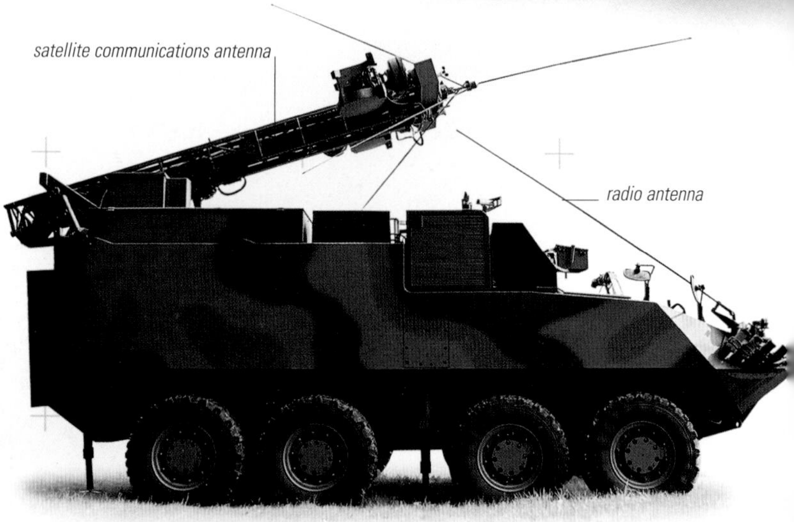

▲ **Piranha Comms** (1985)
This version of the versatile Light Armored Vehicle (LAV) is equipped as a communications center. It is fitted with sophisticated satellite equipment to transmit and receive long-range signals.

Length	23 ft. (7 m.)
Weight	23,980 lb. (10,900 kg.)
Range	410 miles (56 km.)
Crew	4
Armament	None

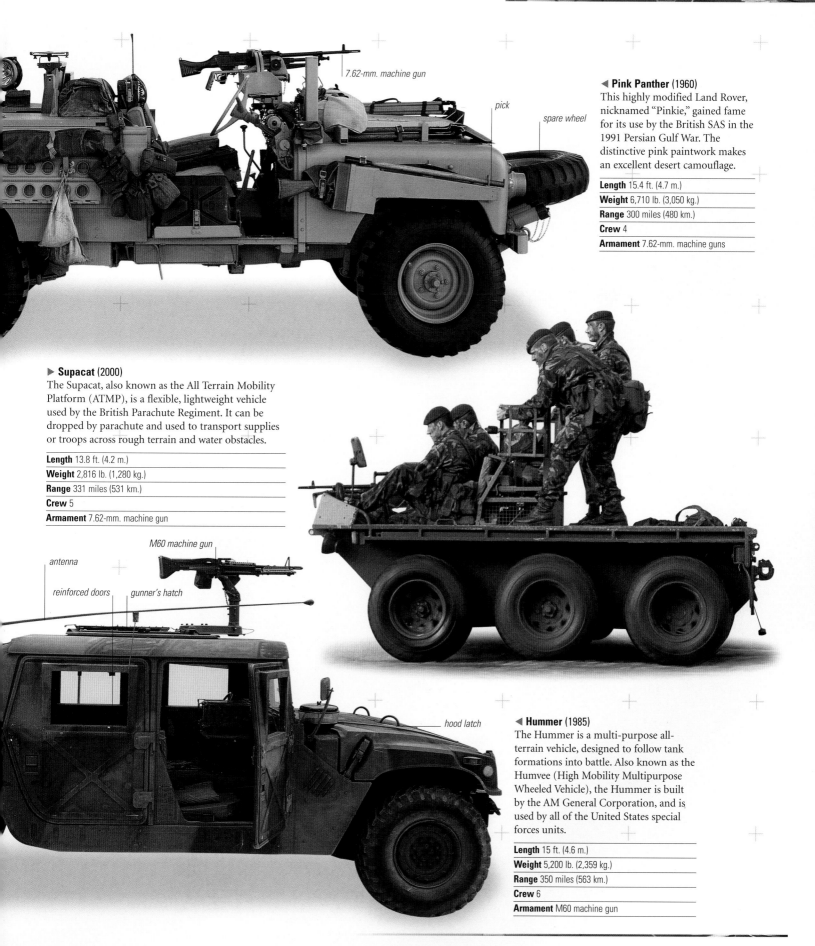

◀ **Pink Panther** (1960)
This highly modified Land Rover, nicknamed "Pinkie," gained fame for its use by the British SAS in the 1991 Persian Gulf War. The distinctive pink paintwork makes an excellent desert camouflage.

Length	15.4 ft. (4.7 m.)
Weight	6,710 lb. (3,050 kg.)
Range	300 miles (480 km.)
Crew	4
Armament	7.62-mm. machine guns

▶ **Supacat** (2000)
The Supacat, also known as the All Terrain Mobility Platform (ATMP), is a flexible, lightweight vehicle used by the British Parachute Regiment. It can be dropped by parachute and used to transport supplies or troops across rough terrain and water obstacles.

Length	13.8 ft. (4.2 m.)
Weight	2,816 lb. (1,280 kg.)
Range	331 miles (531 km.)
Crew	5
Armament	7.62-mm. machine gun

◀ **Hummer** (1985)
The Hummer is a multi-purpose all-terrain vehicle, designed to follow tank formations into battle. Also known as the Humvee (High Mobility Multipurpose Wheeled Vehicle), the Hummer is built by the AM General Corporation, and is used by all of the United States special forces units.

Length	15 ft. (4.6 m.)
Weight	5,200 lb. (2,359 kg.)
Range	350 miles (563 km.)
Crew	6
Armament	M60 machine gun

Submersibles

Submersibles (small underwater vessels) have long been used as a means of delivering and recovering special forces troops and secret agents. They have been involved in some of the most daring actions undertaken by special forces because the difficulty of detecting them makes them ideal for clandestine operations. Modern technology has created ever more sophisticated miniature vessels.

▶ **Swimmer Delivery Vehicle** (1983)
The US-built Swimmer Delivery Vehicle (SDV) can take combat swimmers into enemy waters or along a coastline. It is being replaced by the Advanced SEAL Delivery System (see below).

Length	22 ft. (6.7 m.)
Weight	39,600 lb. (18,000 kg.)
Diving depth	325 ft. (100 m.)
Speed	6 knots
Crew	1

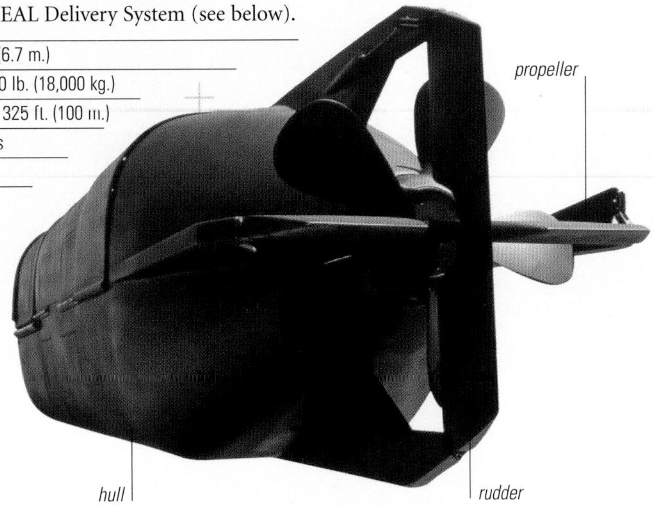

◀ **Advanced SEAL Delivery System** (2003)
The Advanced SEAL Delivery System (ASDS) is the US Navy's latest mini-submarine. It is designed to covertly deliver and recover up to 16 US Navy Sea, Air, and Land troops (SEALs) from a zone of operations.

▼ **The URF** (1976)
The URF submersible is operated by the Royal Swedish Navy. It is designed for submarine rescue up to a depth of 1,495 ft. (460 m.), and is carried aboard the Swedish Navy ship *Belos*.

Length	45 ft. (13.9 m.)
Weight	114,400 lb. (52,000 kg.)
Diving depth	1,495 ft. (460 m.)
Speed	3 knots
Crew	4

Submersible technology

The idea of delivering a small team of highly trained saboteurs into enemy territory by submarine is not new, but modern materials and electronics mean that today's submersibles are far more capable than their predecessors. Miniaturization of technology means mini-subs can be be fitted with sophisticated sonar, electronics, and propulsion systems. Modern mini-subs are also able to dock with larger vessels, allowing them to be transported much farther than they could travel on their own.

Mini-submarines
The British were pioneers of submersible technology. Special forces like the Special Boat Service (SBS) use mini-subs for covert operations.

▶ **Mini-submersible**
The Advanced SEAL Delivery System (ASDS) mini-submersible is carried on the back of a nuclear-powered submarine. When the destination is in range, the SDV is released and travels on under its own power. It is in service with the US Navy.

The Sea Dagger submersible (2002)

The Sea Dagger series of submarines are special operations vehicles developed by Swedish submarine designers, Kockums. The Autonomous Swimmer Delivery Vehicle (ASDV) variant of the Sea Dagger (below) carries, delivers, and retrieves up to six special forces combat swimmers. Its role is to secretly deliver the operational team close to the enemy shoreline, then withdraw while the team carries out its mission. It is not armed with any weapons, relying instead on its small size and stealth to avoid detection. Typical missions for the swimmers include the sabotage of enemy ships and docks, reconnaissance, emplacement of special marker beacons to lead in an amphibious attack, and assault operations. The Sea Dagger submersible returns to pick up the swimmers at a designated rendezvous point once they have completed their mission.

Stealth technology
The Sea Dagger uses stealth technology to obscure itself. By absorbing or reflecting away enemy radar waves, it can remain undetected.

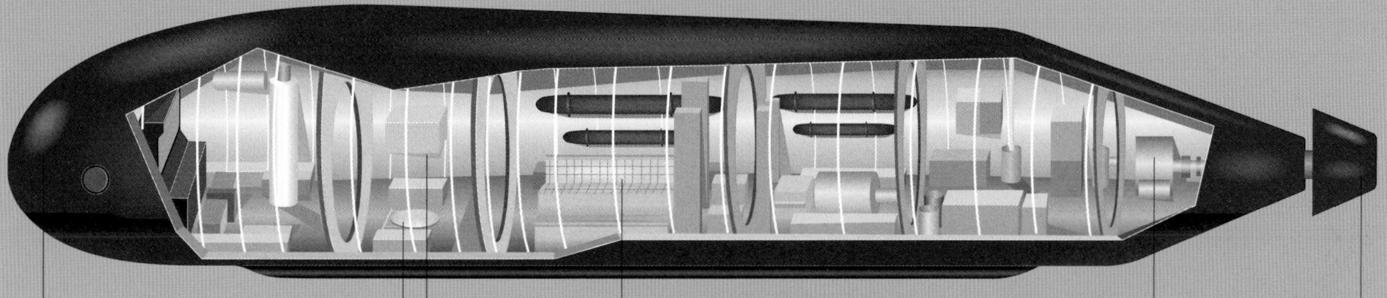

▶ **The Viking Project**
The pan-Scandinavian Viking Class has been developed as a next generation diesel-electric submarine. It is designed for attack patrol missions, as well as covert surveillance.

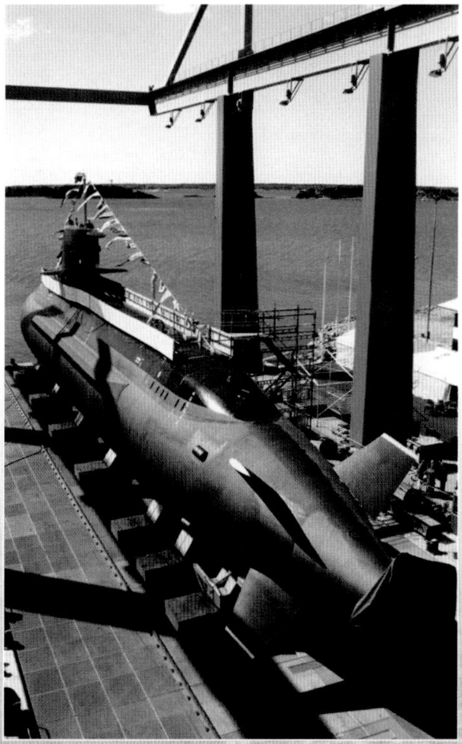

Virginia Class submarines (2004)

The Virginia Class is a new generation of attack submarine. It is an advanced stealth multi-mission nuclear-powered submarine for anti-submarine warfare and special forces operations. It has been designed to replace the aging Los Angeles Class attack submarines, but has also been developed to incorporate the needs of special forces teams. From an integrated ocean interface – essentially a large opening in the hull – the Virginia Class can launch the Advanced SEAL Delivery System mini-submarine (see opposite).

The next generation
The Virginia Class is a marked leap forward in terms of submarine technology and multi-mission capability.

Communications equipment

Effective and secure communications are vital to any special forces mission. Modern technology allows a unit to use global positioning system (GPS) technology, orbiting satellites, and digital radios to call for airstrikes, to keep in contact with their superiors and each other, and to send back intelligence. In addition, laser target designators are an integral link between ground forces and attack aircraft, permitting accurate targeting of bombs.

▶ Motorola AN/PRC-112 (1990)
This personal radio is carried by US special forces teams on combat search-and-rescue missions or forward observation actions, for calling in airstrikes and artillery bombardments.

Length	6 in. (15.24 cm.)
Weight	28 oz. (784 g.)
Frequency	121 Mhz., 225–299.975 Mhz.
Range	20 miles (32 km.)

▲ PRC 319 (1981)
The PRC 319 is a radio designed for British special forces teams as well as long-range reconnaissance units.

Length	11.8 in. (30 cm.)
Weight	18.7 lb. (8.5 kg.)
Frequency	1.5–40 Mhz.
Range	93.7 miles (150 km.)

Tactical radios

The use of personal communications is a key element of special forces tactics. The basic infantry team of about eight men keeps in contact with other squads around them, as well as the mission commanders. Secure radio communications are vital for coordinating the movement of all units on the ground, and for giving and receiving instructions and information. Modern digital radio communications equipment allows each man to be equipped with his own system. This provision is unique to special forces operations. Standard infantry units are usually provided with only one radio, because of the danger of too much radio traffic confusing battlefield communications.

Digital future
The latest digital radios seen in use with British special forces. The radios are lightweight and each man has a mouthpiece, leaving his hands free to carry out his duties.

▶ PRC 320 (1981)
The PRC 320 is a portable, high-frequency radio in service with British special forces units. It was first used in the Falklands War in 1982, when British troops defeated an Argentinian invasion force.

Length	11.8 in. (30 cm.)
Weight	24.2 lb. (11 kg.)
Frequency	2–29.9 Mhz.
Range	18.7 miles (30 km.)

◀ **Trimble Scout M+ GPS** (1991)
Global Positioning System (GPS) sets are an integral part of special forces equipment. The device uses signals from orbiting satellites to allow troops to pinpoint their own location on the ground. It is accurate to within 18 ft. (5 m.).

Length 6.8 in. (17.3 cm.)
Weight 14.2 oz. (0.4 kg.)
Accuracy 18 ft. (5 m.)

Hostage-rescue communications

Special forces units involved in hostage-rescue missions are equipped with the most sophisticated and reliable radio systems. Teams such as the British Special Air Service (SAS) and the US Delta Force have strict communications procedures to coordinate each operation. Specific codewords are agreed for particular actions, and adherence to them is vital for mission success.

Radio contact
A special forces soldier in combat gear holds a radio unit in his left hand. The timing of each move in an assault is coordinated through the communications system.

◀ **Ground Laser Target Designator II** (2001)
The Ground Laser Target Designator II is a compact, lightweight laser target designator and rangefinder. It is designed by Northrop Grumman and is in service with US Navy Sea, Land, and Air (SEAL) teams.

Length 11.4 in. (29 cm.)
Weight 12.6 lb. (5.7 kg.)
Magnification x10
Range 3.1–12.5 miles (5–20 km.)

Target designation

Special forces teams are regularly inserted secretly into enemy territory to identify targets such as missile launch sites for air or artillery attack. US and British planners now use special forces in this role as a part of their overall bombing strategy. Paramount to the success of these missions is the ability of the unit to relay back to its commanders what targets it finds and where they are. Using secure communications equipment, the team can give map coordinates for each target position, or use laser "markers" to guide in "smart" missiles and bombs that lock-on to the laser signals.

Laser guidance systems
A tank explodes having been targeted by laser designation equipment. Once a target has been "painted" by laser, computer-guided missiles are deployed to destroy it.

Diving equipment

Combat diving has been performed by special forces teams for over 60 years. The modern equipment is at the cutting edge of diving technology, enabling the combat diver to survive the extremes of underwater environments while still being able to perform missions. It includes special navigation and communications equipment and a breathing system that allows the diver to swim undetected at depths of 300 ft. (80 m.).

▶ Diving knife
Diving knives are used to cut through ropes or plants that might snare the diver. They can also be used as a tool when laying explosives and for other underwater operations. This is a Divex diving knife. It is 7 in. (18 cm.) long and has a combination serrated/plain cutting edge.

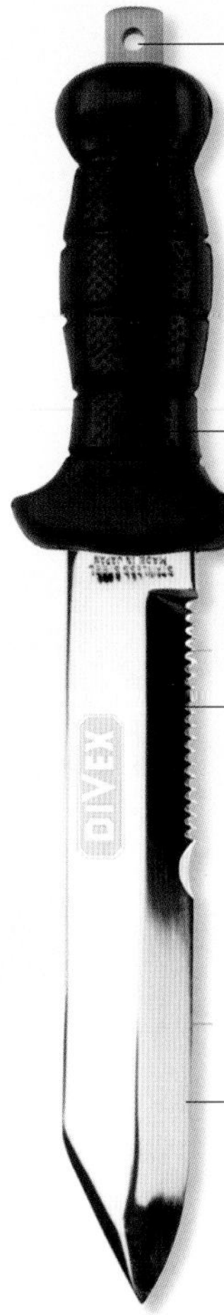

▼ Combat diving equipment
Combat divers rely on many pieces of equipment to complete their mission. These include the breathing apparatus worn on the chest, a navigational swimboard containing a compass, as well as protective camouflage clothing. The diver also has easy access to the equipment kept in his waist pouches.

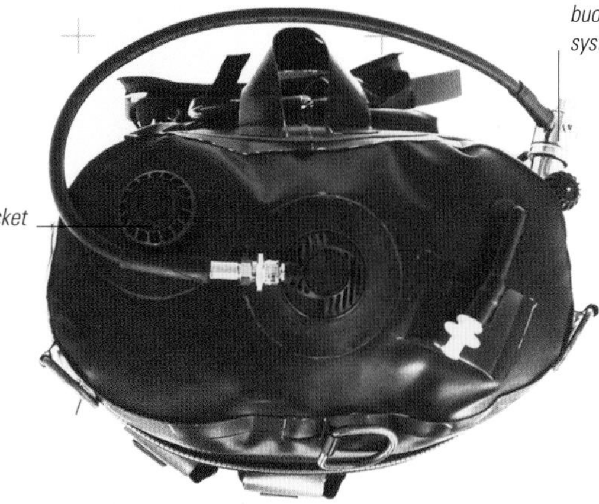

top view

back view

Covert infiltration

Combat diving is the preferred method of infiltration into enemy waters. Electronic detectors placed on the seabed cannot pick up small special forces groups, and divers cannot be seen from the surface because their special breathing equipment does not produce air bubbles. Combat divers can place limpet mines onto enemy naval vessels, or explosives and mines onto dock facilities.

Weapons
Combat swimmers are equipped with specially adapted weapons that can be carried underwater without ruining the mechanisms.

◀ **Waterproof bag**
Non-water resistant equipment, such as weapons, explosives, and communication systems, needs to be protected from the water. An air-tight bag such as this one (left) is ideal for waterproof storage. The bag incorporates a buoyancy tank (shown above), which can be regulated according to need. Air can be pumped in to make the diver rise to the surface, or it can be released to make him descend deeper underwater.

▼ **Mine-clearance diving equipment**
The type of helmet shown below is perfectly suited to operations where communications are key, such as mine-clearance. Known as a closed-circuit reclaim helmet, it limits the amount of noise made during inhalation and exhalation. The large visor gives the diver an excellent view, and no air bubbles escape to obscure his view when used in conjunction with a rebreather system (shown on his back).

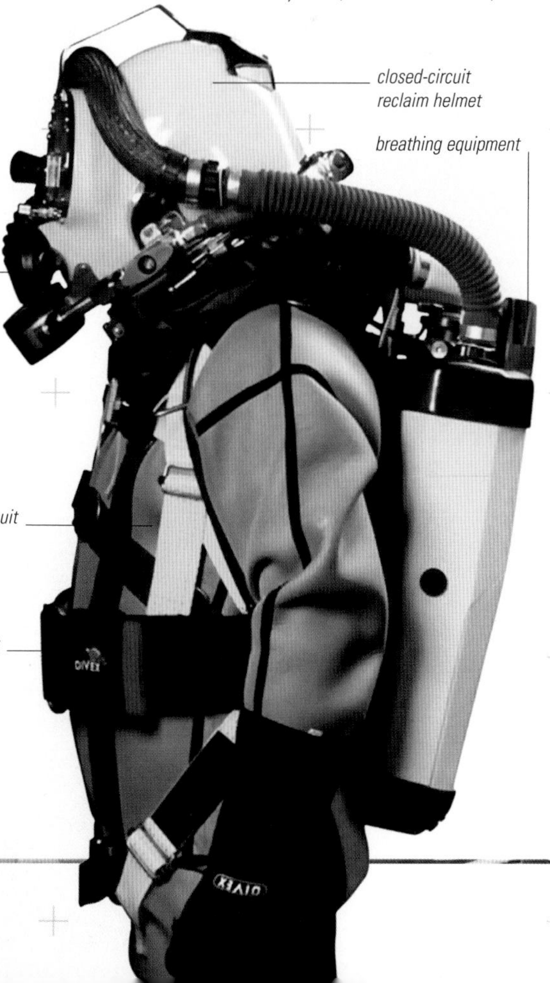

Hostile environments

Underwater operations often take place in the most inhospitable environments, and thus it is imperative that combat swimmers are suitably equipped, not only to perform the mission, but also simply to survive. Even in moderate climates, the temperature of the sea means that hi-tech materials and diving suits must be used to protect against the cold. To trap warm air, divers wear many layers of clothing, such as fleece "woolly bear" suits, in addition to a specially designed rubber drysuit.

Ice diving
A combat swimmer emerges from an ice-hole while training to operate in freezing Arctic waters. Divers are taught to navigate beneath thick sheets of ice.

Small boats

Modern special forces units have always made use of small water-borne craft for their operations, and even though helicopters have largely replaced boats as the primary means of troop delivery, small boats still play a vital role. Patrol vessels are used to guard against terrorist attacks, and high-speed powerboats are deployed to chase down drug smugglers. Small vessels such as the Rigid Raider are still used by special forces units during amphibious assaults.

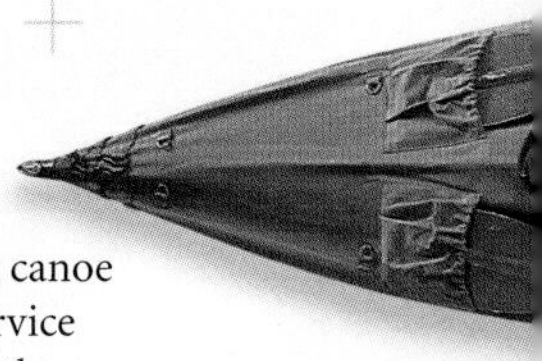

▶ **Klepper folding canoe** (1931)
The design of the two-man folding canoe used by the British Special Boat Service (SBS) has been in service for more than 70 years. Split into two sections, the canoe can be carried by special forces operatives. It is ideal for covert beach landings.

Length 9.75 ft. (3 m.)
Weight 120 lb. (54 kg.)
Range n/a
Speed 3 knots

▶ **SEALs High Speed Boat** (1993)
High Speed Boats (HSBs) are used by US Navy Sea, Air, and Land (SEAL) teams to conduct short-range, all-weather special operations, and can also perform limited coastal patrol and anti-narcotics interception missions.

Length 40 ft. (12.3 m.)
Weight 13,500 lb. (6,136 kg.)
Range 250 miles (400 km.)
Speed 50 knots

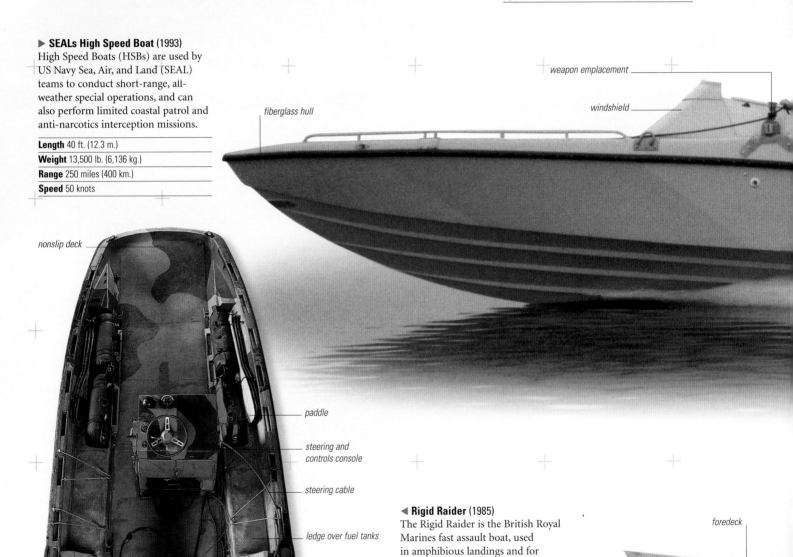

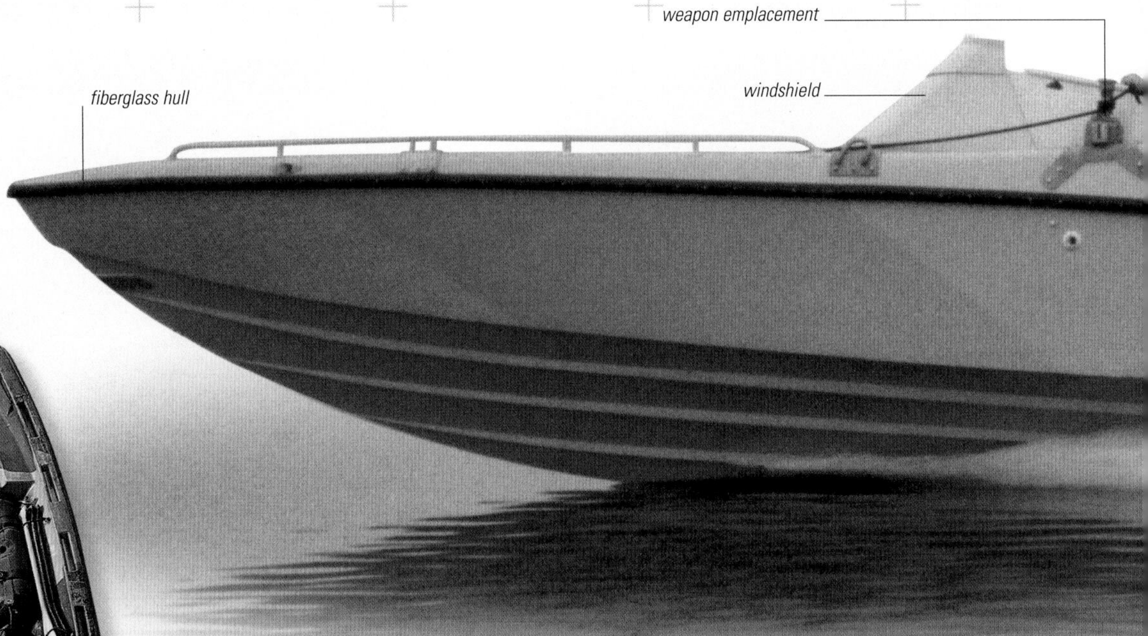

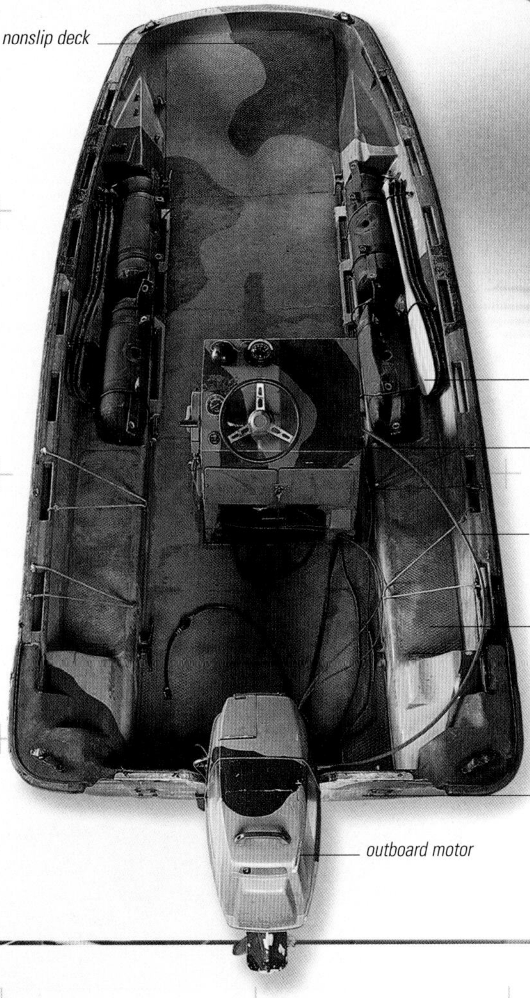

◀ **Rigid Raider** (1985)
The Rigid Raider is the British Royal Marines fast assault boat, used in amphibious landings and for river patrols. Powered by a 250-horsepower engine, it is capable of high speeds, and can carry eight fully armed Royal Marines.

Length 16.9 ft. (5.2 m.)
Weight 2,937 lb. (1,335 kg.)
Range 230 miles (370 km.)
Speed 30 knots

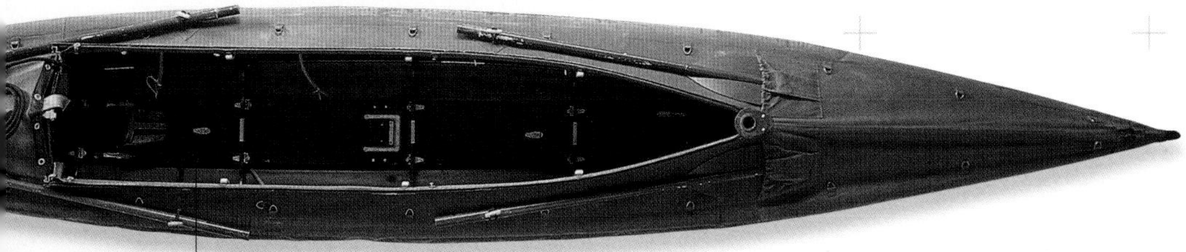

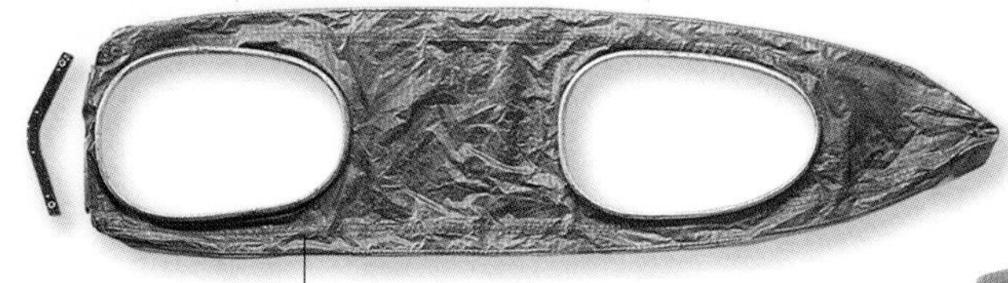

Offshore patrol boats

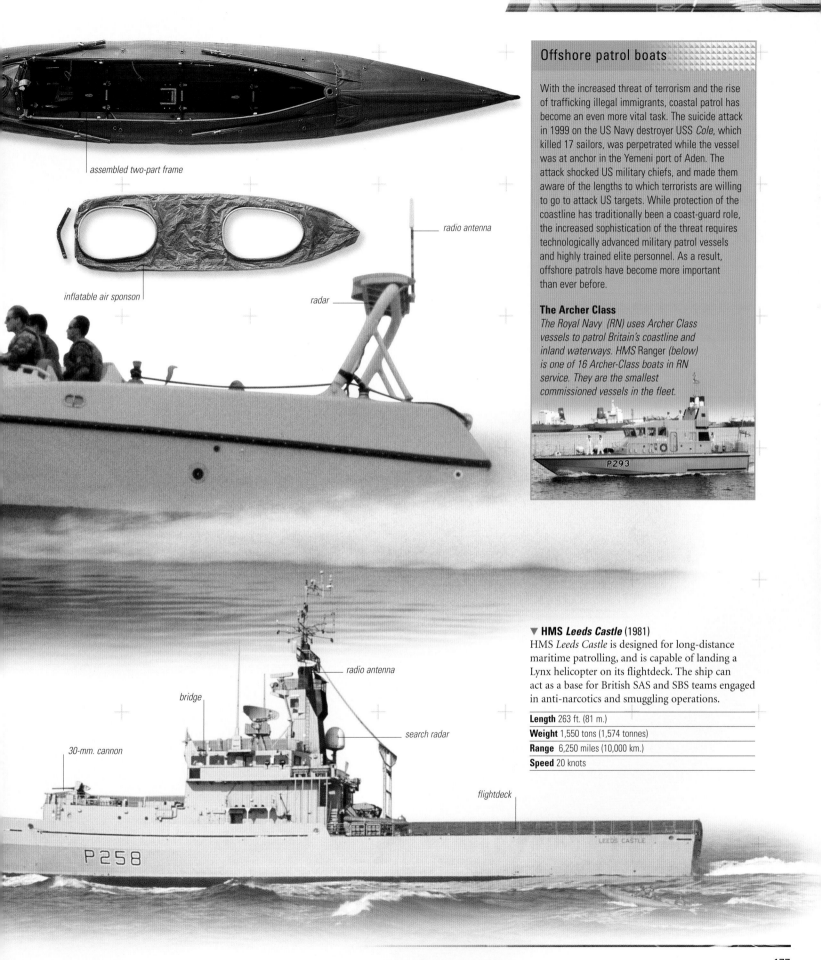

With the increased threat of terrorism and the rise of trafficking illegal immigrants, coastal patrol has become an even more vital task. The suicide attack in 1999 on the US Navy destroyer USS *Cole*, which killed 17 sailors, was perpetrated while the vessel was at anchor in the Yemeni port of Aden. The attack shocked US military chiefs, and made them aware of the lengths to which terrorists are willing to go to attack US targets. While protection of the coastline has traditionally been a coast-guard role, the increased sophistication of the threat requires technologically advanced military patrol vessels and highly trained elite personnel. As a result, offshore patrols have become more important than ever before.

The Archer Class

The Royal Navy (RN) uses Archer Class vessels to patrol Britain's coastline and inland waterways. HMS Ranger *(below) is one of 16 Archer-Class boats in RN service. They are the smallest commissioned vessels in the fleet.*

▼ **HMS *Leeds Castle*** (1981)

HMS *Leeds Castle* is designed for long-distance maritime patrolling, and is capable of landing a Lynx helicopter on its flightdeck. The ship can act as a base for British SAS and SBS teams engaged in anti-narcotics and smuggling operations.

Length	263 ft. (81 m.)
Weight	1,550 tons (1,574 tonnes)
Range	6,250 miles (10,000 km.)
Speed	20 knots

Support and attack aircraft

Special forces teams on the ground are often supported by fixed-wing aircraft. This support includes electronic countermeasures to confuse enemy weapon systems and jam hostile radar systems. In addition, fixed-wing aircraft can also be used to deliver aerial firepower against ground targets. Advanced targeting systems enable aircraft to hit ground targets precisely with bombs, cannons, and rockets.

▶ **Harrier GR7** (1990)
The Harrier GR7 in service with the British Royal Air Force is a VSTOL (Vertical or Short Take-Off and Landing) multi-role attack aircraft. Typical missions include ground-attack in support of infantry, the interception of enemy aircraft, and laser-guided bombing missions.

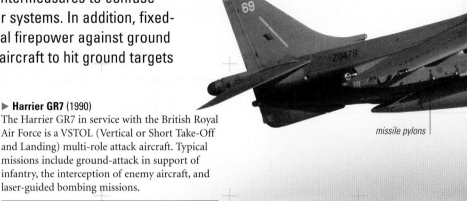

Engine	1 x Rolls Royce Pegasus 11-61
Wingspan	30 ft. (9.2 m.)
Length	47.5 ft. (14.4 m.)
Cruising speed	531 mph. (850 kph.)
Crew	1

Gunships

The AC-130 Spectre Gunship is armed with a formidable array of weapons, with machine guns and mini-cannon capable of delivering heavy firepower in support of special forces on the ground. The plane is also fitted with sophisticated electronic detection sensors to allow it to target enemy tank, artillery, and troop positions from an altitude of 9,750 ft. (3,000 m.). Its predecessor, the AC-130 Spooky Gunship, entered US service during the Vietnam War (1965–75), where it carried out hundreds of missions to disrupt the supply routes of the enemy North Vietnamese Army. The successor AC-130 is still in service, and was used in Afghanistan against Taliban and al Qaeda forces in 2002, and against Saddam Hussein's forces in the Iraq War of 2003.

Flying fortress
The AC-130 Spectre is equipped with a 105-mm. howitzer cannon for destroying fortified positions.

▲ **MC-130 Combat Talon** (1991)
The Combat Talon is used for the deployment of US special forces paratroopers and their equipment. It is capable of flying as low as 250 ft. (75 m.) to avoid detection by enemy radar, and is fitted with an electronic countermeasure system in the nose cone to confuse enemy weapon systems.

Engine	4 x Allison T56-A-15
Wingspan	132.6 ft. (40.4 m.)
Length	97.7 ft. (29.8 m.)
Cruising speed	300 mph. (480 kph.)
Crew	9

▶ **HC-130 Combat Shadow** (1964)
Used on US special forces operations, this plane's primary task is the in-flight refueling of helicopters, but it is also used for troop rescue-and-recovery missions.

Engine	4 x Allison T56-A-15
Wingspan	132.6 ft. (40.4 m.)
Length	97.7 ft. (29.8 m.)
Cruising speed	300 mph. (480 kph.)
Crew	8

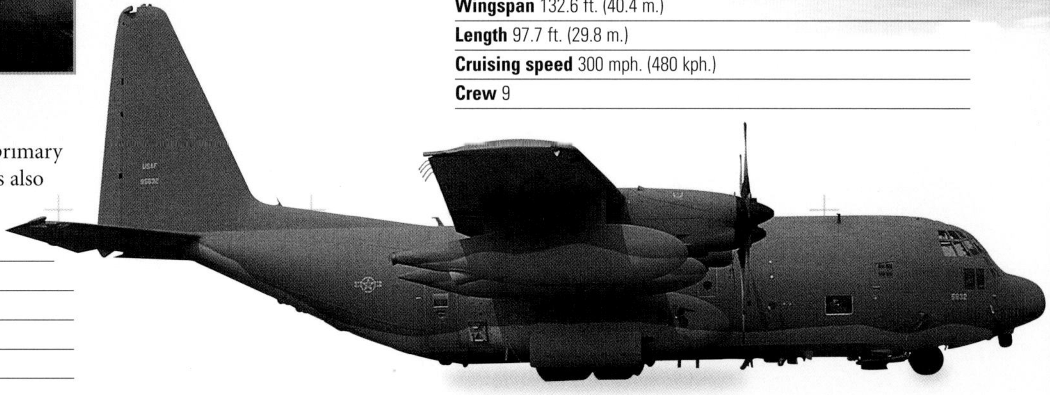

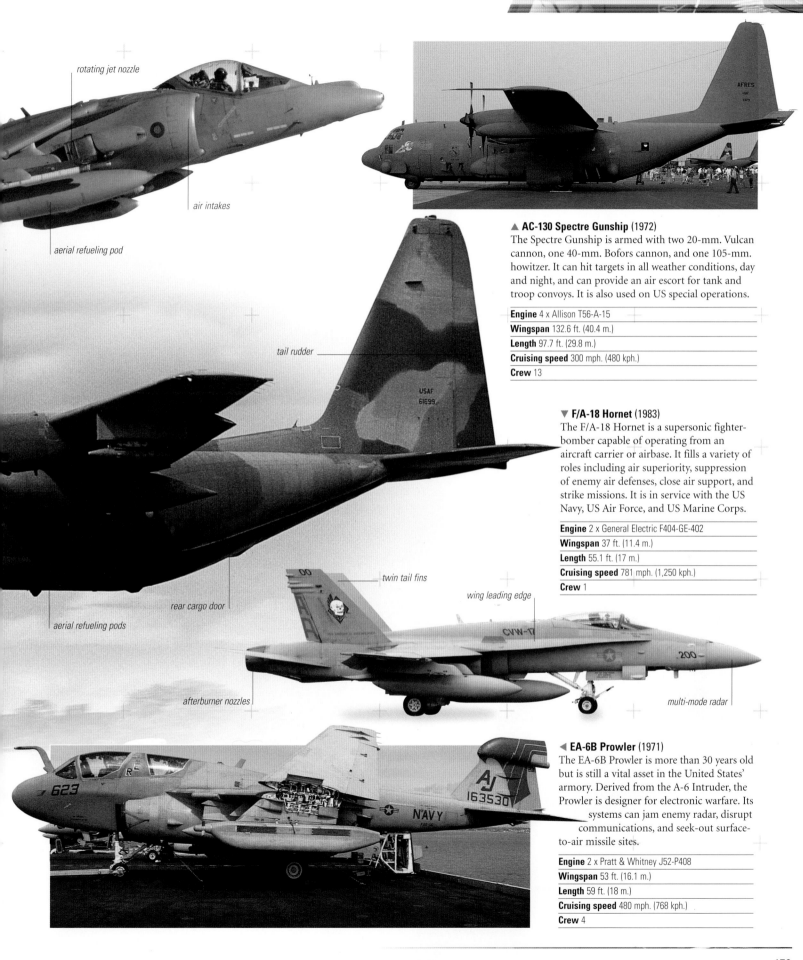

▲ AC-130 Spectre Gunship (1972)
The Spectre Gunship is armed with two 20-mm. Vulcan cannon, one 40-mm. Bofors cannon, and one 105-mm. howitzer. It can hit targets in all weather conditions, day and night, and can provide an air escort for tank and troop convoys. It is also used on US special operations.

Engine 4 x Allison T56-A-15
Wingspan 132.6 ft. (40.4 m.)
Length 97.7 ft. (29.8 m.)
Cruising speed 300 mph. (480 kph.)
Crew 13

▼ F/A-18 Hornet (1983)
The F/A-18 Hornet is a supersonic fighter-bomber capable of operating from an aircraft carrier or airbase. It fills a variety of roles including air superiority, suppression of enemy air defenses, close air support, and strike missions. It is in service with the US Navy, US Air Force, and US Marine Corps.

Engine 2 x General Electric F404-GE-402
Wingspan 37 ft. (11.4 m.)
Length 55.1 ft. (17 m.)
Cruising speed 781 mph. (1,250 kph.)
Crew 1

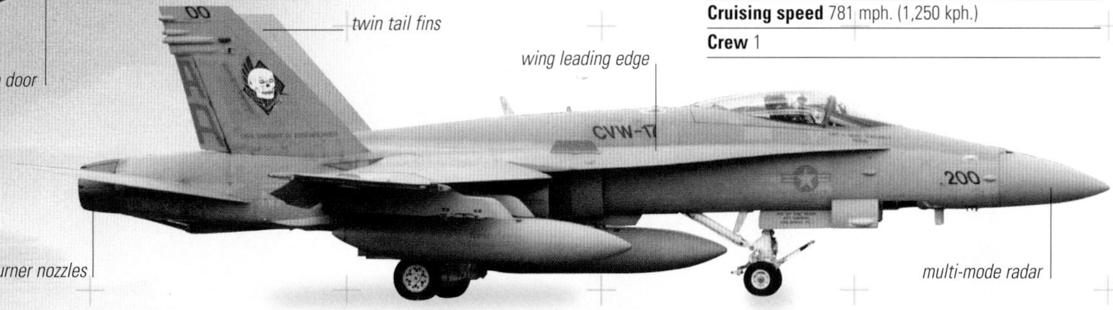

◀ EA-6B Prowler (1971)
The EA-6B Prowler is more than 30 years old but is still a vital asset in the United States' armory. Derived from the A-6 Intruder, the Prowler is designer for electronic warfare. Its systems can jam enemy radar, disrupt communications, and seek-out surface-to-air missile sites.

Engine 2 x Pratt & Whitney J52-P408
Wingspan 53 ft. (16.1 m.)
Length 59 ft. (18 m.)
Cruising speed 480 mph. (768 kph.)
Crew 4

Transport aircraft

Special forces operations require a vast supply chain to keep them in the field. Specialized aircraft transport all the necessary cargo, which could include many types of vehicles, ammunition, and other equipment needed to support teams on the ground. Transport aircraft are also used as a means of delivering special forces units behind enemy lines by parachute, and as a way of resupplying them as the mission progresses.

▼ IL-76 Candid (1974)
The IL-76 Candid medium-range transport aircraft is produced by the Russian aircraft manufacturer Ilyushin. More than 500 aircraft have been produced since it entered service in 1974. It can transport cargo of all types up to a weight of 105,600 lb. (48,000 kg.). It is used by Russian *Spetsnaz* forces for parachute drops and for delivering supplies.

Engine	4 x D-30KP
Wingspan	165.5 ft. (50.6 m.)
Length	152.8 ft. (46.6 m.)
Cruising speed	475 mph. (760 kph.)
Crew	6

Airlift capacity

The giant aircraft used to transport the massive quantities of supplies needed for military operations are a vital link in the logistical chain. Planes such as the US C-5 Galaxy and the C-17 Globemaster are capable of delivering large loads, including vehicles and even other aircraft, over long distances. For special missions, the planes transport all the necessary equipment to the zone of operations. In addition, specially trained transport pilots can fly fast and low over enemy territory in order to resupply special forces units already on the ground, or to deliver a new team by parachute.

Supply planes
C-5 Galaxy and C-17 Globemaster aircraft of the United States Air Force provide an airlift capability second to none.

▼ C-160 Transall (1963)
The C-160 Transall is primarily in service with the French and German air forces. It can be used to drop supplies, or to transport up to 68 fully equipped paratroopers. The C-160 can carry 35,200 lb. (16,000 kg.) of cargo, including tanks and other armored vehicles.

Engine	2 x Rolls Royce Tyne 22
Wingspan	131.2 ft. (40 m.)
Length	106.2 ft. (32.4 m.)
Cruising speed	293 mph. (470 kph.)
Crew	5

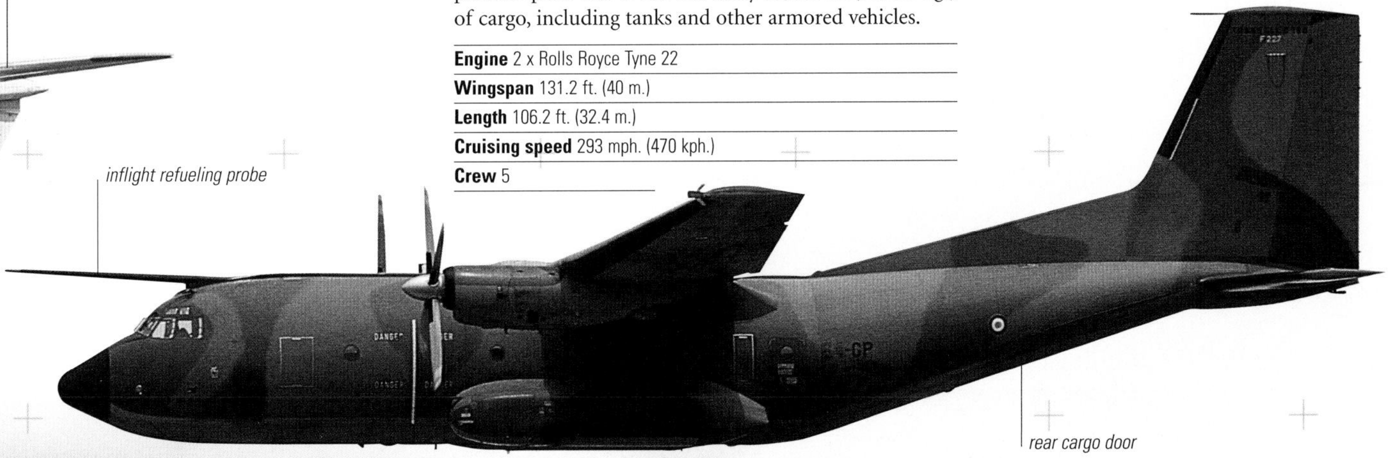

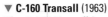

◀ CN-235 Transall (1983)
The CN-235 Transall has take-off and landing capabilities on runways as short as 1,050 ft. (320 m.). Built by the Spanish manufacturer CASA, it can carry 57 fully equipped troops, or 7,810 lb. (3,550 kg.) of cargo. It is used by Spanish special forces.

Engine	2 x General Electric CT7-9C3
Wingspan	84.6 ft. (25.8 m.)
Length	70.1 ft. (21.4 m.)
Cruising speed	283 mph. (455 kph.)
Crew	4

◀ C-141B Starlifter (1979)
The Lockheed C-141B Starlifter, operated by the US Air Mobility Command, is a long-range troop- and cargo-carrying aircraft. It is capable of transporting 155 fully equipped troops or a 66,000 lb. (30,000 kg.) load. There were 241 Starlifters in service in 2003.

Engine	4 x Pratt & Whitney TF33-P-7
Wingspan	160 ft. (48.5 m.)
Length	168.3 ft. (51 m.)
Cruising speed	400 mph. (640 kph.)
Crew	6

Tiltrotor technology

Special forces are always interested in innovative developments in technology. The Boeing V-22 Osprey troop and cargo transport plane uses the tiltrotor design and entered service with the US Marine Corps in 2001. The tiltrotor principle is simple. An engine situated at the end of each wing swings through 90 degrees from vertical to horizontal. This facilitates a vertical take-off or landing like that of a helicopter but, once in the air, allows the plane to reach the speed of a conventional fixed-wing aircraft (320 mph./510 kph.). The technology does have its critics, but the potential for special forces operations is great. The craft enables special forces teams of up to 24 troops to be deployed farther and at twice the speed than by helicopter, but still has the ability to land anywhere, even where there is no conventional runway.

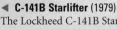

Flexible deployment
The V-22 Osprey being readied for flight aboard an aircraft carrier. The plane can be folded in six minutes for easy transportation aboard a ship or a transport plane, such as the gigantic C-5 Galaxy.

Helicopters

The introduction of helicopters into military service has dramatically changed the way in which special forces operate. In modern conflicts, specially configured helicopters frequently transport teams deep into enemy territory, and extract them once a mission is over. Teams also rely on helicopters to provide fire-support, and to rescue them if fighting becomes too intense.

▶ **OH-58 Kiowa Warrior** (1983)
The Kiowa Warrior is an armed reconnaissance helicopter. It can also provide light fire-support. The mast-mounted sight is a camera that can focus on enemy targets. The Kiowa Warrior is also equipped with a thermal imaging sensor and a laser rangefinder/designator. The helicopter is used by US and Israeli forces.

Engine	1 x Rolls-Royce Allison C30R/3
Rotor span	35 ft. (10.7 m.)
Length	41.2 ft. (12.6 m.)
Cruising speed	103 mph. (165 kph.)
Crew	2

Helicopter armament

The versatility of helicopters means that they can be fitted with a wide range of armaments and equipment to suit any particular mission. Attack helicopters can be equipped with a powerful array of tank-destroying missiles and armor-piercing rockets, whereas reconnaissance helicopters can sneak into enemy territory and designate targets by laser for fighter-bombers to destroy.

Aerial firepower
A British Royal Air Force Chinook, armed with an automatic Gatling gun to provide fire-support for ground forces.

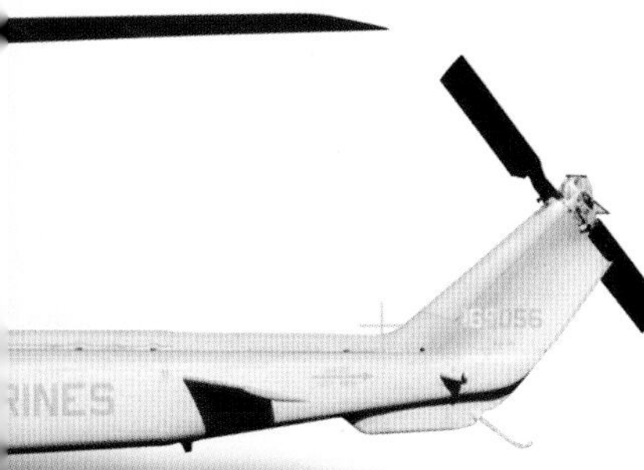

◀ **AH-1W Super Cobra** (1966)
This is an all-weather attack helicopter in service with the US Marines. It is armed with an M197 three-barrel 20-mm. gun. It can also fire Tube-launched, Optically tracked, Wire-guided (TOW), Hellfire, and Stinger missiles.

Engine	2 x General Electric T700-GE-401
Rotor span	47.5 ft. (14.5 m.)
Length	45.2 ft. (13.9 m.)
Cruising speed	173 mph. (276 kph.)
Crew	2

▼ **AH-64A Apache** (1986)
The AH-64 Apache is the primary attack helicopter of the United States military. It can be used for anti-armor search-and-destroy missions, or can provide aerial fire-support for advancing units. It is armed with Hellfire missiles and a 30-mm. gun.

Engine	2 x General Electric T700-GE-701C
Rotor span	47.5 ft. (14.5 m.)
Length	58.2 ft. (17.7 m.)
Cruising speed	171 mph. (274 kph.)
Crew	2

Black Hawk helicopters

The UH-60 Black Hawk has been the workhorse of the US Army's helicopter fleet since it entered service in 1978. Since then, the basic S70 airframe designed by the Sikorsky Corporation has been adapted to produce many different variants. For example, the SH-60 Sea Hawk is used by the US Navy to hunt enemy submarines, and the MH-60 Pave Hawk is a technologically advanced special forces variant, as flown by the US 160th Special Operations Aviation Regiment (SOAR).

The Pave Hawk
An MH-60 Pave Hawk, as used by US special forces. Its protruding nozzle allows it to refuel in mid-air, and thus travel much greater distances.

▼ **CH-53D Sea Stallion** (1981)
The CH-53D Sea Stallion is designed for the transportation of equipment, supplies, and personnel during amphibious operations. It can carry 55 passengers or 14,000 lb. (6,363 kg.) of supplies. It is in service with the US Marine Corps.

Engine	3 x General Electric T64-GE-416/416A
Rotor span	24.1 m. (79 ft.)
Length	99 ft. (30.2 m.)
Cruising speed	103 mph. (165 kph.)
Crew	6

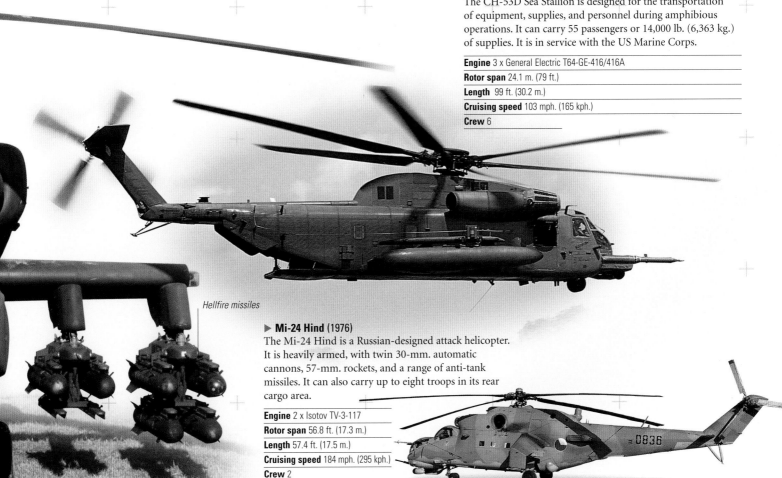

Hellfire missiles

▶ **Mi-24 Hind** (1976)
The Mi-24 Hind is a Russian-designed attack helicopter. It is heavily armed, with twin 30-mm. automatic cannons, 57-mm. rockets, and a range of anti-tank missiles. It can also carry up to eight troops in its rear cargo area.

Engine	2 x Isotov TV-3-117
Rotor span	56.8 ft. (17.3 m.)
Length	57.4 ft. (17.5 m.)
Cruising speed	184 mph. (295 kph.)
Crew	2

Special forces units

This is a list of the world's premier special forces units, arranged alphabetically by name of unit. Names in double quote marks denote units that are named for individuals or geographic regions. Unit titles in native languages are in italics, with English translations in square brackets immediately following.

16 Air Assault Brigade

1st Commando Regiment
Country: Australia
Strength: Classified
Role: Behind enemy lines assault, first aid

1st Special Forces Operational Detachment – Delta (Delta Force)
Country: United States
Strength: 360
Role: Counter-terrorism, hostage-rescue, sabotage, behind enemy lines assault, reconnaissance, foreign unit training

4/73 (Sphinx) Special Observation Post Battery
Country: Britain
Strength: 30
Role: Long-range reconnaissance, forward observation, forward air control

5th Airborne Brigade Pathfinder Platoon (Pathfinders)
Country: Britain
Strength: 40
Role: Medium-range reconnaissance, drop zone organization

10th Mountain Division
Country: United States
Strength: 11,000
Role: Rapid reaction, high-altitude operations, reconnaissance

16 Air Assault Brigade
Country: Britain
Strength: 6,000
Role: Airborne assault, rapid reaction

75th Ranger Regiment (Rangers)
Country: United States
Strength: 2,200
Role: Long-range reconnaissance, airborne assault

82nd Airborne Division
Country: United States
Strength: 14,500
Role: Airborne assault

101st Airborne Division
Country: United States
Strength: 16,000
Role: Airborne assault

148 (Meiktila) Commando Forward Observation Battery
Country: Britain
Strength: 35
Role: Reconnaisance, forward observation, forward air control, naval gunfire support, advanced force operations

160th Special Operations Aviation Regiment (160th SOAR)
Country: United States
Strength: 1,400
Role: Special operations aviation support

707th Special Missions Unit
Country: South Korea
Strength: 200
Role: Counter-terrorism

Airborne Regiment (CAR)
Country: Canada
Strength: 750 troops
Role: Airborne assault, rapid reaction

***Aktionsstyrken* [Action Force]**
Country: Denmark
Strength: 70
Role: Hostage-rescue, countering organized crime

Alfa Brigade
Country: Russia
Strength: Classified
Role: Counter-terrorism, hostage-rescue

1st Special Forces Operational Detachment – Delta Force

Brigada Especial Operativa Halcon
[Falcon Special Operations Brigade]
Country: Argentina
Strength: 75
Role: Counter-terrorism, VIP protection

***Commando Especial Anti-Terrorista* (CEAT)**
[Special Anti-Terrorist Command]
Country: El Salvador
Strength: 50
Role: Counter-terrorism

Commando "Hubert"
Country: France
Strength: 80
Role: Maritime assault, reconnaissance, combat diving

***Comando Raggruppamento Subacquei e Incursori* (COMSUBIN)**
[Divers and Raiders Command]
Country: Italy
Strength: 250
Role: Maritime assault, hostage-rescue

***Escadron Parachutiste d'Intervention de la Gendarmerie Nationale* (EPIGN)**
[National Gendarmerie Intervention Parachute Squadron]
Country: France
Strength: 140
Role: Counter-terrorism, hostage-rescue, VIP protection, intelligence gathering

"Folgore" Parachute Brigade
Country: Italy
Strength: 6,000
Role: Airborne assault

Groupe d'Intervention Gendarmerie Nationale *(GIGN)*

***FroemandsKorpset* [Frogman Corps]**
Country: Denmark
Strength: 50
Role: Maritime counter-terrorism

***Fuerzas Especiales Anti-Terroristas Urbanas* (AFEAU) [Urban Counter-Terrorist Special Forces]**
Country: Colombia
Strength: 100
Role: Counter-terrorism, hostage-rescue

"Givaty" Infantry Brigade
Country: Israel
Strength: 5,000
Role: Long-range reconnaissance, rapid reaction, amphibious assault

"Golany" Infantry Brigade
Country: Israel
Strength: 5,000
Role: Long-range reconnaissance, rapid reaction

***Grenzschutzgruppe-9* (GSG-9)**
[Border Guard Group 9]
Country: Germany
Strength: 250
Role: Counter-terrorism, hostage-rescue

***Groupe d'Intervention Gendarmerie Nationale* (GIGN) [National Gendarmerie Intervention Group]**
Country: France
Strength: 90
Role: Counter-terrorism, hostage-rescue, behind enemy lines operations

***Grupa Reagowania Operacyjno Mobilnego* (GROM) [Operational Maneuver Reconnaissance Group]**
Country: Poland
Strength: 300
Role: Counter-terrorism, hostage-rescue, VIP protection

***Grupo Especiale de Operaciones* (GEO)**
[Operations Special Group]
Country: Spain
Strength: 70
Role: Counter-terrorism, hostage-rescue

***Gruppo Intervento Speciale* (GIS)**
[Special Intervention Group]
Country: Italy
Strength: 100
Role: Counter-terrorism, hostage-rescue

***Hærens Jegerkommando* (HJK)**
[Army Ranger Command]
Country: Norway
Strength: Classified
Role: Airborne assault, counter-terrorism, reconnaissance, sabotage

Immediate Action Unit
Country: China
Strength: Classified
Role: Counter-terrorism, hostage-rescue

***JaegerKorpset* [Ranger Corps]**
Country: Denmark
Strength: 70
Role: Counter-terrorism

Joint Task Force 2 (JTF 2)
Country: Canada
Strength: 300
Role: Behind enemy lines assault, counter-terrorism, hostage-rescue

***Kommando Spezialkraefte* (KSK) [Special Operations Command]**
Country: Germany
Strength: 1,000
Role: Hostage-rescue, long-range reconnaissance, combat rescue

***Korps Commando Troepen* (KCT) [Army Commando Corps]**
Country: Netherlands
Strength: 800
Role: Long-range reconnaissance, covert assault, intelligence gathering

***Légion Étrangère De Français 2éme Régiment Étranger de Parachutistes* [French Foreign Legion 2nd REP]**
Country: France
Strength: 1,300
Role: Rapid reaction, airborne assault

***Le Groupe de Combat en Milieu Clos* (GCMC) [Close Quarters Combat Group]**
Country: France
Strength: 16
Role: Maritime counter-terrorism, nautical sabotage

Navy SEALs

British Special Air Service (SAS)

Marine Commando Force
Country: India
Strength: 1,000
Role: Maritime operations, counter-terrorism

***Ministerstvo vnutrennykh del* (MVD) [Ministry of Internal Affairs]**
Country: Russia
Strength: 200,000
Role: Civil order, law enforcement

Mobile Communications Team (MCT)
Country: United States
Strength: Classified
Role: Special operations communications support

***Mobiles Einsatz Kommando* (MEK) [Mobile SWAT Team]**
Country: Austria
Strength: Classified
Role: Counter-terrorism, hostage-rescue

"Nahal" Infantry Brigade
Country: Israel
Strength: 5,000
Role: Airborne assault, border patrol

National Security Guards
Country: India
Strength: 7,500
Role: Counter-terrorism, VIP protection, bomb disposal

Navy SEALs
Country: United States
Strength: 2,500
Role: Maritime assault, counter-terrorism, reconnaissance, combat diving

Navy Special Boat Units
Country: United States
Strength: 600
Role: Maritime assault, special operations support

Naval Special Warfare Development Group (Dev Group/SEAL Team Six)
Country: United States
Strength: 200
Role: Maritime counter-terrorism, hostage-rescue

No 7 Squadron SF Flight Royal Air Force
Country: Britain
Strength: Classified
Role: Special operations aviation support

No 8 Flight Army Air Corps
Country: Britain
Strength: Classified
Role: Special forces aviation support

***Nucleo Operativo Centrale di Sicurezza* (NOCS) [Central Operational Security Nucleus]**
Country: Italy
Strength: 100
Role: Counter-terrorism, hostage-rescue, VIP protection

Parachute Brigade
Country: Israel
Strength: 5,000
Role: Airborne assault

Parachute Regiment
Country: Britain
Strength: 2,500
Role: airborne assault

Royal Marines

Reaction, Assistance, Intervention, Dissauder (RAID) [Reaction, Assistance, Intervention, Dissuasion]
Country: France
Strength: 60
Role: Counter-terrorism, hostage-rescue, VIP protection

Royal Marines
Country: Britain
Strength: 5,000
Role: Amphibious assault

S'13
Country: Israel
Strength: Classified
Role: Maritime operations, combat diving

"San Marco" Battalion
Country: Italy
Strength: 1,500
Role: Amphibious assault

Spetsnaz *[Troops of Special Purpose]*

Special Air Service (SAS)
Country: Australia
Strength: Classified
Role: Counter-terrorism, hostage-rescue, sabotage, hearts and minds operations, behind enemy lines assault, reconnaissance

Special Air Service (SAS)
Country: Britain
Strength: Classified
Role: Counter-terrorism, hostage-rescue, behind enemy lines assault, reconnaissance, VIP protection, foreign unit training

Special Air Service (SAS)
Country: New Zealand
Strength: Classified
Role: Counter-terrorism, hostage-rescue, reconnaissance, behind enemy lines assault

Special Boat Service (SBS)
Country: Britain
Strength: Classified
Role: Maritime assault, counter-terrorism, hostage-rescue, maritime reconnaissance

Special Forces Brigade
Country: Jordan
Strength: 5,000
Role: Airborne assault

Special Forces Brigade
Country: South Africa
Strength: Classified
Role: Airborne assault, reconnaissance

Special Forces (Green Berets)
Country: United States
Strength: 6,000
Role: Behind enemy lines assault, humanitarian and civic operations, reconnaissance, counter-terrorism, foreign unit training

Special Operations State Militia
Country: Russia
Strength: 2,000
Role: Counter-terrorism, anti-narcotics, internal security

Special Protection Group
Country: India
Strength: 3,000
Role: VIP protection, combat search and rescue, internal security, hostage-rescue

Spetsnaz [Troops of Special Purpose]
Country: Russia
Strength: 8,000
Role: Counter-terrorism, behind enemy lines assault, VIP protection, reconnaissance

Unit 217
Country: Israel
Strength: Classified
Role: Counter-terrorism, undercover operations, behind enemy lines assault

Unit 262
Country: Israel
Strength: Classified
Role: Counter-terrorism, hostage-rescue, behind enemy lines assault

United States Air Force Special Tactics Teams (SSTs)
Country: United States
Strength: Classified
Role: First aid, forward air control, combat search and rescue

United States Marine Corps Fleet Anti-Terrorism Security Team (USMC FAST)
Country: United States
Strength: 500
Role: Maritime security, installation security, counter-terrorism

United States Marine Corps Force Recon (USMC Force Recon)
Country: United States
Strength: Classified
Role: Long-range reconnaissance, behind enemy lines assault

Very Shallow Water Mine Countermeasures Detachment (US VSWMCM)
Country: United States
Strength: 18 troops + 4 bottlenose dolphins
Role: Mine clearance, explosive ordnance disposal, reconnaissance

Index

Page numbers in bold type denote the main reference to a spread title. Page numbers in *italic* type indicate an illustration or its caption.

Acknowledgments

There is a cohort of people without whose stalwart efforts in the face of adversity this book could never have been completed. Adopting the SAS motto, "Who Dares Wins," in true special forces style my publisher Mary Thompson calmly said "Yes" to all manner of demands from me as the author, and from her DK marketing colleagues regarding the content, style, and production schedule of this book. All were impossible by the usual "standards," but she kept the faith.

Editor Peter Darman at the Brown Reference Group was our harassed Mission Ops Officer, pulling photos, design, and text together, keeping calm as we ran out of time.

The production team at Dorling Kindersley applied firm and much appreciated quality control: Marianne Markham, the managing art editor, Martyn Page, the senior managing editor, and Bryn Walls, the art director, aided and abetted by Ian Spick (on design), Julian Dams (on DTP), and Louise Daly (on production). Thanks are also due to Neal Cobourne and Francis Wong (jacket designers), Caroline Reed (jacket editor), Kathryn Wilkinson (editorial assistance), and Jennifer Williams (US editor).

A book like this requires a vast amount of highly coordinated effort from many people. At the Brown Reference Group were art director Dave Goodman, senior designer Stefan Morris, and designers Thor Fairchild, Matthew Greenfield, Dan Newman, Joe Conneally, and Colin Tilley-Loughrey. The digital artworks were by Mark Walker. On the editorial side were Lindsey Lowe, Tim Cooke, Dennis Cove, Mark Hawkins-Dady, and Felicity Crowe. For finding photographs of secretive people, my thanks to picture manager Susannah Jayes. For additional text, I am particularly grateful to James Murphy and John Davison. And, of course, to Ashley Brown: cricketer and sax-playing percussionist.

For advice, I am grateful to William F. Owen, ex-soldier, fellow author, and weapons and intelligence expert; former Parachute Regiment officer Godfrey McFall; and former special forces medic Bob Leitch. Thanks also to Helen Arthur, the wife of my late friend and comrade Dick; Major KeWee Petterson of Norway's FIST-H; Ian Tandy; and Sergeant-Major Butler at HQ SOCOM. And my grateful thanks, as on many other occasions, to the Operations Officer at HQ HUGHFOR: my literary agent Barbara Levy.

PICTURE CREDITS
(b=bottom, c=center, l=left, r=right, t=top)

AFP: 92bl, 120br; **AKG:** 25bl, 33br; **Art Archive:** 24bc & br, 41cr; **Associated Press:** 56bc, 86c, 120b, 123tl; **Australian War Memorial:** 29bl; **Aviation Photographs International:** 27cr, 30tc, 32cr & cl, 35c, 39cl, 85t, 146cr, 147cl & bl, 148tc, 148-149t & b, 154, 155, 157cl, 160tr, 160-161b, 163cr, 166cl, tr & br, 167tc, 170bl, 172bl, 177cr & b, 178bl & br, 178-179t & c, 179 bl & br; 182-183t & b, 183; **Aviation Picture Library:** 34tr, 179tr, 180, 181t, 182tc; **Bae:** 20bl & br; **Barrett:** 149tr; **Beretta:** 147tr, 156cl; **Brown Reference Group:** 12-13b, 19cl, 34tc, 35c, 53b, 54c, 55tr, 60br, 60-61, 61tl, 62tl & tr, 62-63, 66, 66-67, 67br, 70tr, 71tr, 82tr, 86bl, 87br, 94bl, 94-95, 95tr, 96tl & bc, 97tl & tr, 98cr, 99tr & cr, 100, 101, 108, 109, 134tr, 136-137, 137br, 139br, 142cl, 143b & c, 147br, 151tr, 153tr, 156-157t, 166c, 171cr, 178bl, 181br; **Cold Steel:** 164, 165; **Colt:** 25tr; **Corbis:** 12tr, 18tr, 25bc, 35tr, 54-55, 58tl & bc, 68tr & br, 69, 71cl & b, 76cr, 84tl, 92cr, 96cr, 96-97, 102br, 104tc, tr, c & br, 105tl, 106c & br, 107tr, 122tl, 125tr, 170tr, 171cl, 173c; **Divex:** 174, 175tl, tr, cl & br, 176-177; **DK Images:** 28cl, tc & tr, 30bl & br, 36bc & tr, 40cl, 43tc, 47bl, 67tr, 78c, 90tc, 98tc, 132cr, 133b, 139tr, 144c & br, 148-149c, 152-153b, 168-169t & b, 169, 172-173b, 176bl, 177tl; **FN Herstal:** 146cl, 150bc, 156br, 160bl; **Getty Images:** 61tr; **Heckler & Koch:** 146tr, 150-151c, 151bc, 158, 159tl, c & br, 160-161c, 161t, 162-163, 163b; **Kockums:** 170cr; **Magnum:** 93l; **Hugh McManners:** 50bc, 112, 113, 136bl, 175bl; **Military Picture Library:** 12tc, 16bl & br, 21cr, 46br, 46-47, 47br, 48, 49, 53tl, 54tr, 60tr, 61bc, 68bc, 70br, 72bc, 73br, 78bl & tr, 79, 86br, 88br, 91tl, 94tc, 98bl, 98-99, 107l, 110c & bl, 110-111, 111, 121tr, 128bl, c & br, 129, 130, 130-131, 132bl & br, 133tl, 134bl, 135c & br, 137tl & tr, 138cl & tr, 138-139, 139tl, 140bl & tr, 140-141, 141, 142br, 143cr, 144tr, 145, 148bl, 159tr, 160-161cl, 161cr & br, 162tr, 163t, 164bl, 165tr, 166bl, 167b, 172cl, 172-173t, 173br, 182bl; **Mossberg:** 152-153t, 153c; **Mowag:** 168cl, bl & cr; **Newspix:** 64bl; **Northrup Grumman:** 170cl, 170-171; **Popperfoto:** 21tl, 119br; **Press Association:** 64-65, 65tl, 72tl, 73tl & tr, 78bc, 80tl, cr &bc, 102bl & tr, 103cl & b, 114tl, 117br, 118tl, 123tr & br; **Raytheon:** 167tl; **Remington:** 138bl, 151cr, 152tl, 153bl; **Rex:** 13c, 14bl, 16tr, 18bl, 20tr, 21b, 52tl & br, 53tr, 55cl, 60cl & bl, 62bc, 63cr & br, 65cr, 72tr & br, 74tr, 75tr, 80-81, 81tr, 83br & tl, 84bc, 85bl, 87l, 88bl & tr, 89tr, 90cr, 92tl & tr, 93br, 95br, 99cl, 102tl, 103tr, 104bl, 106tr, 107br, 110tr, 114tr, cr, & bl, 115l & br, 118bl & tr, 116br, 118-119, 122bc, 122-123, 124b, cl & c, 125, 135tr, 142tr, 144bl, 157tr, 172bl; **RHL:** 24bl, 24-25t, 25cl, 26bl & br, 26-27, 27tl, tr & bc, 29tl & br, 30-31, 30c, 32bl, 32-33, 33tl, tr & c, 34bl & br, 36tl & bl, 36-37, 37tl & tr, 38tl & tr, 38-39, 39tr & c, 40tr, 40-41, 42bl & tr, 43tr, 56tl, cr & br, 57, 70tl & cl, 82bl, 90bl, 91tl , 140br; **Tim Ripley:** 52cr; **Sako:** 150bl; **Smith & Wesson:** 146bl; **Steyr:** 65br, 150-151t, 156cl; **Topham:** 30tr, 34-35, 42br, 59t & bl, 70bl, 88tl, 89tl & b, 120tr; **TRH:** 12bl, 13tr & br, 14, 15 16tc, 17, 18-19b, 28b, 29cl & cr, 30tl, 35br, 37br, 39br, 40tl & bl, 41tr, 43cl & br, 54bl, 47tr & cl, 50, 51, 55br, 58cr, 58br, 62br, 64tr, 68c, 74bl & br, 75tl & b, 76, 76-77, 83tr, 84tr, 85cr, 86tr, 87tr, 90tr, 91b, 94tr & br, 96br, 105cr & b, 106br, 115tr, 116bl & tr, 117t & cl, 120bl, 121tl, 128tr, 132tr, 134-135, 135tl, 136tr, 142bc, 157br, 167tr, 173tr.